Certificate of The Justice of The Peace

I do herby certify that Lucian H Raines, Henry
Wyche, Jackson, B, Mash, William H Reynolds, were
duly sworne — to performe Their duty as appraisers of The Estate of Richard Mitchell, deceased,
as directed in The foregoing warrant This 13th
day of May. 1856   John C Browning, o
                                                        B

Inventory and Appraisment of The perishable property
of Richard Mitchell deceased This May 17th 1856

No.			$	cts
1	Bill	a man	1000	00
2	Sambo	"	400	00
3	Sam	"	1200	00
4	Lemon	"	1100	00
5	Jerry	"	1000	00
6	Billy	"	1000	00
7	George	"	1200	00
8	Sam	"	1100	00
9	Mats	"	12.000	00
10	Edmond	"	1,000	00
11	Albert	a boy	800	00
12	Yellow Bill	a man	1150	00
13	Chance	, a, boy	650	00
14	John	" "	600	00
15	Anthony	" "	600	00
16	Ishmeal	, a , man	800	00
17	Phillip	a Boy	800	00
18	Rhubin	" "	800	00
19	Doctor	" "	1000	00
20	Old Anthony		700	00
21	" Ben		600	00

The end papers of this volume are reproductions from documents pertaining to the settlement of a Georgia estate. Such legal action was a daily occurrence in the slave country. Sometimes everything was sold at auction and the proceeds were divided among heirs. Sometimes, as here, a board of appraisers established the value of every item in each category, such as tools, mules, horses, slaves, wagons, and household goods, and then divided everything in each category into equal lots to the number of heirs. The value of each category in each lot (and the total value of each lot) being approximately equal to every other, drawings for lot numbers were then made and each heir took possession of his or her property. Slaves here were valued as low as five dollars. Sometimes estates had to pay someone to take certain ones. In every case, by auction or by division, the probability of separation of families was very great. In every case, also, the value of many slaves tore to shreds the argument that all slaves were well cared for because they were valuable property.

A Bibliography of Antislavery in America

A BIBLIOGRAPHY OF ANTISLAVERY IN AMERICA

BY DWIGHT LOWELL DUMOND

Ann Arbor: *The University of Michigan Press*

Publication of this book was made possible by a grant from the
Horace H. Rackham School of Graduate Studies, The University of Michigan.

A BIBLIOGRAPHY OF PRINTED ANTISLAVERY LITERATURE

This is the literature written and circulated by those active in the antislavery movement and used by the author. It is believed that no item of major importance has been overlooked. British literature widely circulated in this country is included. Only those congressional speeches given by prominent men and circulated through antislavery channels are listed.

[Abbott, Jacob]. New England and Her Institutions. By One of Her Sons. Hartford, S. Andrus & Son, 1847. 271 p.

Abolition Intelligencer and Missionary Magazine. Monthly. Shelbyville, Kentucky. May, 1822–April, 1823. Edited by John Finley Crow. [Sometimes spelled Crowe.]

ABOLITION SOCIETIES OF THE UNITED STATES

To the Abolition and Manumission Societies in the United States. [Philadelphia, 1817.] 3 p.

Address of a Convention of Delegates from the Abolition Society to the Citizens of the United States. New York, Press of W. Durell, 1794. 7 p.

Address of the American Convention for Promoting the Abolition of Slavery and Improving the Condition of the African Race, Assembled at Philadelphia, in January, 1804, to the People of the United States. Philadelphia, S. W. Conrad, 1804. 8 p.

An Address to the Free People of Colour and Descendants of the African Race, in the United States, by the American Convention for Promoting the Abolition of Slavery, and Improving the Condition of the African Race. Philadelphia, Printed for the Convention, by Hall & Atkinson, 1819. 6 p.

The Committee to Whom Was Referred the Several Petitions of the Quakers of New England, of the Providence Society for the Abolition of the Slave-trade, and the Petition from the Delegates of the Several Societies for the Same Purpose, in Convention Assembled in Philadelphia, in January, 1794. Report as Followeth: [Philadelphia, Printed by Zachariah Poulson, Jun., 1794]. Broadside, 20 × 33 cm.

Minutes of the Proceedings of a Convention of Delegates from the Abolition Societies Established in Different Parts of the United States, Assembled at Philadelphia, on the First Day of January, One Thousand Seven Hundred and Ninety-four, and Continued by Adjournment, until the Seventh Day of the Same Month Inclusive. Philadelphia, Printed by Zachariah Poulson, Jun[ior], 1794. 30 p.

Minutes of the Proceedings of the Second Convention of Delegates from the Abolition Societies Established in Different Parts of the United States, Assembled at Philadelphia on the Seventh Day of January, One Thousand Seven Hundred and Ninety-five, and Continued, by Adjournments, until the Fourteenth Day of the Same Month, Inclusive. Philadelphia, Printed by Zachariah Poulson, Jun[ior], 1795. 32 p.

Minutes of the Proceedings of the Third Convention of Delegates from the Abolition Societies Established in Different Parts of the United States, Assembled at Philadelphia on the First Day of January, One Thousand Seven Hundred and Ninety-six, and Continued, by Adjournments, until the Seventh Day of the Same Month, Inclusive. Philadelphia, Printed by Zachariah Poulson, Junior, 1796. 32 p.

Minutes of the Proceedings of the Fourth Convention of Delegates from the Abolition Societies Established in Different Parts of the United States, Assembled at Philadelphia, on the Third Day of May, One Thousand Seven Hundred and Ninety-Seven, and Continued, by Adjournments, until the Ninth Day of the Same Month, Inclusive. Philadelphia, Printed by Zachariah Poulson, Junior, 1797. 59 p.

Minutes of the Proceedings of the Fifth Convention of Delegates from the Abolition Societies Established in Different Parts of the United States, Assembled at Philadelphia, on the First Day of June, One Thousand Seven Hundred and Ninety-Eight, and Continued, by Adjournments, until the Sixth Day of the Same Month, Inclusive. Philadelphia, Printed by Zachariah Poulson, Junior, 1798. 20 p.

Minutes of the Proceedings of the Sixth Convention of Delegates from the Abolition Societies Established in Different Parts of the United States, Assembled at Philadelphia, on the Fourth Day of June, One Thousand Eight Hundred, and Continued by Adjournments, until the Sixth Day of the Same Month, Inclusive. Philadelphia, Printed by Zachariah Poulson, Junior, 1800. 35 p.

Minutes of the Proceedings of the Seventh Conventions of Delegates from the Abolition Societies Established in Different Parts of the United States, Assembled at Philadelphia, on the Third Day of June, One Thousand Eight Hundred and One, and Continued by Adjournments until the Sixth Day of the Same Month, Inclusive. Philadelphia, Printed by Zachariah Poulson, Junior, 1801. 55 p.

Minutes of the Proceedings of the Eighth Convention of Delegates from the Abolition Societies Established in Different Parts of the United States, Assembled at Philadelphia, on the Tenth Day of January, One Thousand Eight Hundred and Three, and Continued by Adjournment until the Fourteenth Day of the Same Month, Inclusive. Philadelphia, Printed by Zachariah Poulson, Junior, 1803. 50 p.

Minutes of the Proceedings of the Ninth American Convention for Promoting the Abolition of Slavery and Improving the Condition of the African Race: Assembled at Philadelphia, on the Ninth Day of January, One Thousand Eight Hundred and Four, and Continued by Adjournments until the Thirteenth Day of the Same Month, Inclusive. Philadelphia, Printed by Solomon W. Conrad, 1804. 50 p.

Minutes of the Proceedings of the Tenth American Convention for Promoting the Abolition of Slavery and Improving the Condition of the African Race: Assembled at Philadelphia, on the Fourteenth Day of January, One Thousand Eight Hundred and Five, and Continued by Adjournments until the Seventh Day of the Same Month, Inclusive. Philadelphia, Printed by Kimber, Conrad, & Co., 1805. 47 p.

Minutes of the Proceedings of the Eleventh American Convention for Promoting the Abolition of Slavery and Improving the Condition of the African Race: Assembled at Philadelphia, on the Thirteenth Day of January, One Thousand Eight Hundred and Six, and Continued by Adjournments until the Fifteenth Day of the Same Month, Inclusive. Philadelphia, Printed by Kimber, Conrad, and Co., 1806. 42 p.

Minutes of the Proceedings of the Twelfth American Convention for Promoting the Abolition of Slavery and Improving the Condition of the African Race: Assembled at Philadelphia, on the Ninth Day of January, One Thousand Eight Hundred and Nine, and Continued by Adjournments until the Twelfth Day of the Same Month, Inclusive. Philadelphia, Printed by J. Bouvier, 1809. 33 p.

Minutes of the Proceedings of the Thirteenth American Convention for Promoting the Abolition of Slavery, and Improving the Condition of the African Race: Assembled at Philadelphia, on the Thirteenth Day of January, One Thousand Eight Hundred and Twelve, and Continued by Adjournments until the Sixteenth Day of the Same Month, Inclusive. Hamilton-ville, Printed by John Bouvier, 1812. 48 p.

Minutes of the Proceedings of the Fourteenth American Convention for Promoting the Abolition of Slavery, and Improving the Condition of the African Race: Assembled at Philadelphia, on the Ninth Day of January, 1815—On the Eighth Day of January, 1816—and by Adjournments until the Twelfth of the Same Month, Inclusive. Philadelphia, Printed by W. Brown, 1816. 40 p.

Minutes of the Proceedings of the Fifteenth American Convention for Promoting the Abolition of Slavery, and Improving the Condition of the African Race, Assembled at Philadelphia, on the Fifth Day of August, 1817, and Continued by Adjournments until the Eighth of the Same Month, Inclusive. Philadelphia, Printed for the Convention, Merritt, Printer, 1817. 38 p.

Minutes of a Special Meeting of the Fifteenth American Convention for Promoting the Abolition of Slavery, and Improving the Condition of the African Race, Assembled at Philadelphia, on the Tenth Day of December, 1818, and Continued by Adjournments until the Fifteenth Day of the Same Month, Inclusive. Philadelphia, Printed for the Convention by Hall & Atkinson, 1818. 68 p.

Minutes of the Sixteenth American Convention for Promoting the Abolition of Slavery and Improving the Condition of the African Race, Held at Philadelphia, on the Fifth of October, and the Tenth of November, 1819. Philadelphia, Printed by Order of the Convention, William Fry, Printer, 1819. 65 p.

Minutes of the Seventeenth Session of the American Convention for Promoting the Abolition of Slavery, and Improving the Condition of the African Race, Convened at Philadelphia, on the Third Day of October, 1821. Philadelphia, Atkinson & Alexander, Printers, 1821. 58 p.

Minutes of the Eighteenth Session of the American Convention for Promoting the Abolition of Slavery, and Improving the Condition of the African Race. Convened at Philadelphia, on the Seventh Day of October, 1823. Philadelphia, Printed by Daniel Neall, 1823. 65 p.

Minutes of the Nineteenth Session of the American Convention for Promoting the Abolition of Slavery, and Improving the Condition of the African Race, Convened at Philadelphia on the Fourth Day of October, 1825. Philadelphia, Atkinson & Alexander, Printers, 1825. 35 p.

Minutes of the Adjourned Session of the American Convention for Promoting the Abolition of Slavery, and Improving the Condition of the African Race, Convened at Baltimore, on the Twenty-Fifth of October, 1826. Baltimore, Benjamin Lundy, Printer, 1826. 49 p.

Minutes of the Twentieth Session of the American Convention for Promoting the Abolition of Slavery, and Improving the Condition of the African Race, Convened at Philadelphia, on the Second of October, 1827. Baltimore, Benjamin Lundy, Printer, 1827. 60 p.

Minutes of the Adjourned Session of the Twentieth Biennial American Convention for Promoting the Abolition of Slavery, and Improving the Condition of the African Race, Held at Baltimore, Nov. 1828. Philadelphia, Samuel Parker, Printer, 1828. 68 p.

Minutes of the Twenty-First Biennial American Convention for Promoting the Abolition of Slavery, and Improving the Condition of the African Race, Convened at the City of Washington, December 8, A.D. 1829. And an Appendix Containing the Addresses from Various Societies, Together with the Constitution and By-Laws of the Convention. Philadelphia, Thomas B. Town, Pr., 1829. 72 p.

Minutes of the Twenty-Second Session of the American Convention for Promoting the Abolition of Slavery and Improving the Condition of the African Race, Convened at the City of Washington, Jan. 9th, 1832, and Continued by Adjournment in the City of Philadelphia. Also, of a Special Session Held in the City of Philadelphia, November 21, 1837. Philadelphia, Merrihew and Thompson, 1839. 28 p.

Memorials Presented to the Congress of the United States of America, by the Different Societies Instituted for Promoting the Abolition of Slavery in the States of Rhode Island, Connecticut, New York, Pennsylvania, Maryland, and Virginia. Philadelphia, Francis Bailey, 1792. 31 p.

———

Abolition Society of New York City and Vicinity. The Constitutional Duty of the Federal Government to Abolish American Slavery; An Exposé of the Position of the Abolition Society of New York City and Vicinity. New York, Abolition Society of New York City and Vicinity, 1855. 16 p.

The *Abolitionist*. Weekly. Cazenovia, N. Y. February, 1840–1842. Edited by James C. Jackson.

The *Abolitionist*; or Record of the New England Anti-Slavery Society. Monthly. Boston, Mass. January–December, 1833. Edited by a Committee; William Lloyd Garrison, principal editor. [Organ of the New England Anti-Slavery Society.]

Abstract of the Evidence, Contained in the Report of the Lords of the Committee of Council, Relative to the Slave Trade, and the Treatment of the Slaves in the Sugar Islands: Also, an Abridgement of Such of the Colonial Laws, as Relate to the Treatment of the Slaves. [London] 1790. 83 p.

An *Abstract* of the Evidence Delivered Before a Select Committee of the House of Commons, in the Years 1790 and 1791, on the Part of the Petitioners for the Abolition of the Slave Trade. London, 1791. 135 p.
Same. Cincinnati, Reform Tract and Book Society, 1855. 117 p.

An *Account* of the Late Intended Insurrection among a Portion of the Blacks of This City. Published by Authority of the Corporation of Charleston. Charleston, A. E. Miller, 1822. 46 p.

Adams, Charles Francis. An Oration Delivered Before the Municipal Authorities of the City of Fall River, July 4, 1860. Fall River, Almy & Milne, 1860. 20 p.

Adams, Charles Francis. The Republican Party a Necessity. Speech of Charles Francis Adams, of Massachusetts. Delivered in the House of Representatives, May 31, 1860. [Washington, 1860.] 7 p.

Adams, Charles Francis. What Makes Slavery a Question of National Concern? A Lecture, Delivered by Invitation, at New York, January 30, at Syracuse, February 1, 1855. Boston, Little, Brown, and Co., 1855. 46 p.

Adams, Francis C[olburn]. Uncle Tom at Home; A Review of the Reviewers and Repudiators of "Uncle Tom's Cabin," by Mrs. Stowe. Philadelphia, Willis P. Hazard, 1853. 142 p.

Adams, Henry Gardner. God's Image in Ebony; Being a Series of Biographical Sketches, Facts, Anecdotes, Etc., Demonstrative of the Mental Powers and Intellectual Capacities of the Negro Race. With a Brief Sketch of the Anti-Slavery Movement in America, by F. W. Chesson; and a Concluding Chapter of Additional Evidence, Communicated by Wilson Armistead. London, Partridge and Oakey, 1854. 168 p.

Adams, John Quincy. Address of John Quincy Adams to His Constituents of the Twelfth Congressional District, at Braintree, September 17th, 1842. Boston, J. H. Eastburn, 1842. 63 p.

Adams, John Quincy. Argument of John Quincy

Adams, Before the Supreme Court of the United States, in the Case of the United States, Appellants, vs. Cinque and Others, Africans, Captured in the Schooner Amistad, by Lieut. Gedney, Delivered on the 24th of February and the 1st of March, 1841; with a Review of the Case of the Antelope, Reported in the 10th, 11th, and 12th Volumes of Wheaton's Reports. New York, S. W. Benedict, 1841. 135 p.

Adams, John Quincy. The Jubilee of the Constitution. A Discourse Delivered at the Request of the New York Historical Society, in the City of New York, on Tuesday, the 30th of April, 1839; Being the Fiftieth Anniversary of the Inauguration of George Washington as President of the United States, on Thursday, the 30th of April, 1789. New York, Samuel Colman, 1839. 136 p.

Adams, John Quincy. Letters from John Quincy Adams to His Constituents of the Twelfth Congressional District in Massachusetts. To Which Is Added His Speech in Congress, Delivered February 9, 1837. Boston, Isaac Knapp, 1837. 72 p. [Appended: Verses by John G. Whittier.]

Adams, John Quincy. An Oration Delivered Before the Inhabitants of the Town of Newburyport, At Their Request, on the 61st Anniversary of the Declaration of Independence, July 4, 1837. Newburyport, Charles Whipple, 1837. 68 p.

Adams, John Quincy. Speech of the Hon. John Quincy Adams in the House of Representatives, on the State of the Nation, Delivered May 25, 1836. New York, H. R. Piercy, 1836. 18 p.

Adams, John Quincy. Speech of John Quincy Adams, of Massachusetts, upon the Right of the People, Men and Women, to Petition; on the Freedom of Speech and of Debate in the House of Representatives of the United States; on the Resolutions of Seven State Legislatures and the Petitions of More than One Hundred Thousand Petitioners Relating to the Annexation of Texas to This Union. Delivered in the House of Representatives of the United States, in Fragments of the Morning Hours, from the 16th of June to the 7th of July, 1838, Inclusive. Washington, Gales & Seaton, 1838. 131 p.

Adams, Nehemiah (Pastor of Essex Street Church, Boston). Sermon Preached to the Congregation at the Essex Street Church, October 31, 1852, the Sabbath After the Interment of Hon. Daniel Webster. Second Edition. Boston, Geo. C. Rand, 1852. 23 p.

Adams, Nehemiah. A South-Side View of Slavery; or, Three Months at the South in 1854. Boston, T. R. Marvin and B. B. Mussey & Co., 1854. 214 p.
Third Edition. Boston, T. R. Marvin and B. B. Mussey & Co., 1855. 222 p.

Fourth Edition. Boston, Ticknor and Fields, 1860. 224 p.

Adams, William. The Law and Custom of Slavery in British India, in a Series of Letters to Thomas Fowell Buxton, Esq. Boston, Weeks, Jordan, & Company, 1840. 279 p.

Adams, Reverend William [Pastor of the Central Presbyterian Church, N. Y.]. Christianity and Civil Government. A Discourse Delivered on Sabbath Evening, Nov. 10, 1850. New York, Charles Scribner, 1851. 48 p.

An *Address* to the People of Great Britain, on the Propriety of Abstaining from West India Sugar and Rum. The Tenth Edition, with Additions. London, printed; Philadelphia, Re-printed by Daniel Lawrence, 1792. 16 p.

Address to the People of the United States. The Liberties of the People Subverted; Comprising Section I of the Law of 1793; With a Brief History of the Celebrated Case, Prigg vs. Pennsylvania; and Extracts from the Opinion of the Court. To Which Is Added Art. 4, Sec. 2, Clause 3 of the United States Constitution. All Interspersed with Appropriate Comments. 14 p.

Advocate of Freedom. Semi-Monthly, Weekly. March 8, 1838–April 18, 1839—Brunswick, Maine. April 25, 1839–April 11, 1840—Augusta, Maine. April 11, 1840–June 12, 1841—Hallowell, Maine. Edited by Professor William Smith of Bowdoin. Organ of Maine Anti-Slavery Society.

An *Affectionate* Expostulation with Christians in the United States of America, Because of the Continuance of Negro Slavery Throughout Many Districts of Their Country, Addressed by the Minister, Deacons, and Members of the Congregational Church, Joined by the Congregation, Assembling in Mill Street Chapel, Perth. Glasgow, George Gallie [n.d.]. 8 p.

African Education Society of the United States. Report of the Proceedings at the Formation of the African Education Society: Instituted at Washington, December 28, 1829. With an Address to the Public, by the Board of Managers. Washington, Printed by J. C. Dunn, Georgetown, D. C., 1830. 16 p.

THE AFRICAN INSTITUTION

Report of the Committee of the African Institution, Read to the General Meeting on the 15th of July, 1807. Together with the Rules and Regulations Adopted for the Government of the Society. London, Ellerton and Henderson, 1811. 50 p. [Society established 14 April 1807.]

Second Report of the African Institution, Read at the Annual General Meeting, on the 25th of

March, 1808. London, W. Phillips, 1808. 43 p.

Third Report of the Directors of the African Institution, Read at the Annual General Meeting on the 25th of March, 1809. London, J. Hatchard, 1809. 64 p.

Fourth Report of the Directors of the African Institution, Read at the Annual General Meeting on the 28th of March, 1810. Second Edition. London, J. Hatchard, 1814. 94 p.

Fifth Report of the Directors of the African Institution, Read at the Annual General Meeting on the 27th of March, 1811.

[Reports thereafter did not vary in title. All were published in London; printed by J. Hatchard; and are in first editions at Cornell University.]

Sixth Report . . . 25th March, 1812. 183 p.

Seventh Report . . . 24th March, 1813. 103 p.

Eighth Report . . . 23d of March, 1814. 90 p.

Ninth Report . . . 12th of April, 1815. 140 p.

Special Report . . . 12th of April, 1815, Respecting the Allegations Contained in a Pamphlet Entitled "A Letter to William Wilberforce, Esq.," by R. Thorpe. 157 p.

Tenth Report . . . 27th Day of March, 1816. 80 p.

Eleventh Report . . . 26th Day of March, 1817. 152 p.

Twelfth Report . . . 9th Day of April, 1818. 180 p.

Thirteenth Report . . . 24th Day of March, 1819. 108 p.

Fourteenth Report . . . 17th Day of May, 1820. 146 p.

Fifteenth Report . . . 28th Day of March, 1821. 108 p.

Sixteenth Report . . . 10th Day of May, 1822. 396 p.

Seventeenth Report . . . 16th Day of May, 1823. 103 p.

Eighteenth Report . . . 11th Day of May, 1824. 269 p.

Nineteenth Report . . . 13th Day of May, 1825. 333 p.

Twentieth Report . . . 19th Day of May, 1826. 230 p.

Twenty-first Report . . . 16th Day of June, 1827. 115 p.

Extracts from the Eighteenth and Nineteenth Reports of the Directors of the African Institution, Read at Their Annual General Meetings, Held in London on the 11th Day of May, 1824, and on the 13th Day of May, 1825. Philadelphia, J. R. A. Skerrett, 1826. 40 p.

———

The African Observer. A Monthly Journal Containing Essays and Documents Illustrative of the General Character, and Moral and Legal Effects of Negro Slavery. Philadelphia, Pennsylvania. April, 1827–March, 1828. [Edited by Enoch Lewis, a consistent contributor to the *Genius of Universal Emancipation*.]

African Repository and Colonial Journal. Washington, D. C. March, 1825–January, 1892. Edited by Ralph Randolph Gurley. Published by American Colonization Society. Published as *Liberia*, November, 1892–February, 1909.

African Servitude; When, Why, and By Whom Instituted. By Whom and How Long Shall It Be Maintained? Read and Consider. New York, Davies & Kent, 1860. 54 p.

The *Agitation* of Slavery. Who Commenced and Who Can End It? Buchanan and Fillmore Compared from the Record. Washington, Printed at the Union Office, 1856. 29 p.

Agricola, [pseud.] An Impartial View of the Real State of the Black Population of the United States, and the Advantages Pointed Out to the Free Blacks, of Embracing the Generous Offer of the Colonization Societies. Philadelphia, 1824. 26 p.

Agutter, William. The Abolition of the Slave-Trade Considered in a Religious Point of View. A Sermon Preached Before the Corporation of the City of Oxford, at St. Martin's Church, on Sunday, February 3, 1788. By William Agutter, M.A. of St. Mary Magdalen College. London, J. F. and C. Rivington, 1788. 29 p.

Albany Patriot. Weekly. Albany, N. Y. October 15, 1843–1848. Edited by James C. Jackson until 1846 then by William L. Chaplin. [Jackson, a physician, was a former agent of the Massachusetts Anti-Slavery Society; after 1840, corresponding secretary of the American Anti-Slavery Society.]

Alexander, Ann Tuke. An Address to the Inhabitants of Charleston, South Carolina. Philadelphia, Kimber, Conrad, & Co., 1805. 7 p.

Alexander, Archibald. A History of Colonization on the Western Coast of Africa. Philadelphia, W. S. Martien, 1846. 603 p.

Alger, William Rounseville. The Genius and Posture of America. An Oration Delivered Before the Citizens of Boston, July 4, 1857. Boston, Office Daily Bee, 1857. 60 p.

Alger, William Rounseville. The Historic Purchase of Freedom. An Oration Delivered Before the Fraternity, in the Music Hall, Boston, Dec. 22, 1859, the Two Hundred and Thirty-Ninth Anniversary of the Landing of the Pilgrims at Plymouth. Boston, Walker, Wise and Company, 1859. 44 p.

[Alger was a Unitarian minister of Boston; a noted lecturer and author. The 1859 address was so strongly antislavery that the city refused to publish it.]

Allen, George. Mr. Allen's Report of a Declaration of Sentiments on Slavery, December 5, 1837 [to a Committee of the Convention of Ministers of Worcester County]. Worcester, Henry J. Howland, 1838. 12 p.

Allen, George. Mr. Allen's Speech on Ministers Leaving a Moral Kingdom to Bear Testimony Against Sin; Liberty in Danger, from the Publication of Its Principles; the Constitution a Shield for Slavery; and the Union Better than Freedom and Righteousness. Boston, I. Knapp, 1838. 46 p.

Allen, George. The Complaint of Mexico and Conspiracy Against Liberty. Boston, J. W. Alden, 1843. 32 p.

Allen, George. Resistance to Slavery Every Man's Duty. A Report on American Slavery, Read to the Worcester Central Association, March 2, 1847. Boston, Wm. Crosby & H. P. Nichols, 1847. 40 p. [Allen was one of the "seventy," and an active Free Soiler. His pastorate was at Shrewsbury, Massachusetts.]

Allen, Henry Watkins (Defendant). The Trial of Henry W. Allen, U. S. Deputy Marshal, for Kidnapping, With Arguments of Counsel & Charge of Justice Marvin, on the Constitutionality of the Fugitive Slave Law in the Supreme Court of New York. Syracuse, Daily Journal, 1852. 122 p.

Allen, Isaac. Is Slavery Sanctioned by the Bible? A Premium Tract of the American Tract Society. Boston, American Tract Society [1860]. 24 p.

[Allen, John]. An Essay on the Policy of Appropriations Being Made by the Government of the United States, for Purchasing, Liberating and Colonizing Without the Territory of the Said States, the Slaves Thereof; in Numbers, Some of Which Have Been Published in the Baltimore American, and the Whole of Them in the Genius of Universal Emancipation. By a Citizen of Maryland. Baltimore, B. Lundy, 1826. 40 p.

[Allen, Joseph Henry]. The Great Controversy of States and People. Boston, W. Crosby and H. P. Nichols, 1851. 45 p.

Allen, Joseph Henry. A Reign of Terror. A Sermon Preached in Union Street Church, Bangor, on Sunday Evening, June 1, 1856. Bangor, S. S. Smith, 1856. 16 p. [Allen was a Unitarian clergyman. He was not a member of any antislavery society, but spoke strongly against the institution.]

Allen, William. The Duty of Abstaining from the Use of West India Produce. A Speech Delivered at Coach-Maker's Hall, Jan. 12, 1792. London, T. W. Hawkins, 1792. 24 p.

Allen, William G. The American Prejudice Against Color: An Authentic Narrative, Showing How Easily the Nation Got into an Uproar. By William G. Allen, a Refugee from American Despotism. London, W. & F. G. Cash, 1853. 107 p.

Allen, William G. A Short Personal Narrative by William G. Allen (Colored American) Formerly Professor of the Greek Language and Literature in New York Central College. Resident for the Last Four Years in Dublin. Dublin, Sold by the Author, 1860. 34 p.

Allen, William G. Wheatley, Banneker, and Horton; with Selections from the Poetical Works of Wheatley and Horton and the Letter of Washington to Wheatley, and of Jefferson to Banneker. Boston, Daniel Laing, 1849. 48 p. [Allen was a victim of mob violence before going to England. Mrs. Allen was a white woman.]

Alley, John B. Speech of Hon. John B. Alley, of Mass., on the Principles and Purposes of the Republican Party. Delivered in the House of Representatives of the United States, Monday, April 30, 1860. [Washington, D. C.], Republican Executive Congressional Committee, 1860. 8 p.

Alley, John B. The North Forbearing. The South Aggressive. Speech of Hon. J. B. Alley, of Mass., Delivered in the House of Representatives, January 26, 1861. Washington, D. C., McGill & Withrow, 1861. 8 p.

Allo, Don Lorenzo. Domestic Slavery in Its Relations with Wealth; an Oration Pronounced in the Cuban Democratic Athenaeum of New York, on the Evening of the 1st of January, 1854. New York, W. B. Tinson, 1855. 16 p.

Alton Observer. Weekly. Alton, Ill. September 8, 1836–April 19, 1838. Suspended, August 17–December 28, 1837. Published in Cincinnati, December, 1837–April, 1838 by Elisha W. Chester. [Founded and edited by Elijah P. Lovejoy after his St. Louis Observer was destroyed by a mob.]

An American. A Letter to Lord Brougham on the Subject of American Slavery. London, James Dinnis, 1836. 44 p.

An American. An Inquiry into the Conditions and Prospects of the African Race in the United States; and the Means of Bettering Its Fortunes. Philadelphia, Haswell, Barrington and Haswell, 1839. 214 p.

An American. America's Misfortune; or, A Practical View of Slavery. By an American. Buffalo, Thomas & Lathrop, 1856. 91 p.

American Abolition Society. The Constitutional Duty of the Federal Government to Abolish American Slavery: An Exposé of the Position of the American Abolition Society. New York, American Abolition Society, 1856. 16 p.

American Abolition Society. Abolition Document No. 2.

The Constitution Against Slavery. Speech of Hon. Amos P. Granger, of New York, in the House of Representatives, April 4, 1856. Constitution of the American Abolition Society—Principles and Measures. Declaration of the Convention of "Radical Political Abolitionists," at Syracuse, June 26th, 27th, and 28th, 1855. [New York, 1856.] 6 p.

American Abolition Society. A Review of the Official Apologies of the American Tract Society for Its Silence on the Subject of Slavery, from the New York Daily Tribune. New York, American Abolition Society, 1856. 16 p.

American Abolition Society. Slavery-limitation Abandoned in Theory and Practice, by the Defenders of the Crittenden-Lecompton Compromise. Annual Report of the American Abolition Society, September, 1858. New York, American Abolition Society, 1858. 31 p.

AMERICAN AND FOREIGN ANTI-SLAVERY SOCIETY

An Address to the Anti-Slavery Christians of the United States. [Includes constitution of the society.] New York, John A. Gray, 1852. 16 p.

Address to the Friends of Liberty, by the Executive Committee of the Amer. and For. Anti-Slavery Society. [New York, 1848.] 12 p.

Address to the Inhabitants of New Mexico and California on the Omission by Congress to Provide Them with Territorial Governments and on the Social and Political Evils of Slavery. New York, The American and Foreign Anti-Slavery Society, 1849. 56 p.

Address to the Non-Slaveholders of the South, on the Social and Political Evils of Slavery. New York, American & Foreign Anti-Slavery Society, 1843. 26 p.

Second Edition. New York, American and Foreign Anti-Slavery Society, 1849. 58 p.

American and Foreign Anti-Slavery Reporter. Monthly—Irregular. New York, N. Y. June, 1840–September, 1846.

The [Seventh] Annual Report of the American and Foreign Anti-Slavery Society, Presented at the General Meeting, Held in Broadway Tabernacle, May 11, 1847, with the Addresses, Resolutions, and Treasurer's Reports. New York, William Harned, 1847. 32 p. [Almost, if not quite, without exception, the reports were written by Lewis Tappan.]

The [Eighth] Annual Report of the American and Foreign Anti-Slavery Society Presented at New York, May 9, 1848. With the Resolutions and Addresses. New York, A. & F. Anti-Slavery Society, 1848. 48 p.

The [Ninth] Annual Report of the American and Foreign Anti-Slavery Society, Represented at New York, May 8, 1849, with the Resolutions and Addresses. New York, William Harned, 1849. 96 p.

The [Tenth] Annual Report of the American and Foreign Anti-Slavery Society, Presented at New York, May 7, 1850, with the Addresses and Resolutions. New York, American & Foreign Anti-Slavery Society, 1850. 156 p.

The [Eleventh] Annual Report of the American and Foreign Anti-Slavery Society, Presented at New York, May 0, 1851, with the Addresses and Resolutions. New York, American & Foreign Anti-Slavery Society, 1851. 118 p.

The [Twelfth] Annual Report of the American and Foreign Anti-Slavery Society, Presented at New York, May 11, 1852; with the Addresses and Resolutions. New York, American & Foreign Anti-Slavery Society, 1852. 216 p.

The Thirteenth Annual Report of the American and Foreign Anti-Slavery Society, Presented at New York, May 11, 1853; with the Addresses and Resolutions. New York, Lewis J. Bates, 1853. 216 p.

Appeal to Establish a German Newspaper at Washington. May, 1853.

Letters Respecting a Book "Dropped from the Catalogue" of the American Sunday School Union in Compliance with the Dictation of the Slave Power. New York, American and Foreign Anti-Slavery Society, 1848. 36 p.

Liberty Almanacs.

The Liberty Almanac, No. 1. 1844. Syracuse, Tucker & Kinney, 1844. 36 p.

The Liberty Almanac. No. 2. 1845. Syracuse, Tucker & Kinney, 1845. 36 p.

The Liberty Almanac. No. 3. 1846. Hartford, W. H. Burleigh, 1846. 48 p.

The Liberty Almanac, for 1847. New York, William Harned, 1847. 48 p.

The Liberty Almanac for 1848. New York, William Harned, 1848. 48 p.

The Liberty Almanac for 1850. New York, William Harned, 1850. 48 p.

The Liberty Almanac for 1852. New York, William Harned, 1852. 48 p.

Liberty Tracts. [There are several series of Liberty Tracts, and they are very confused in the catalogues of all libraries, without exception.]

No. 1. Slavery and the Slave Trade at the Nation's Capital. New York, Wm. Harned [1846]. 24 p.

No. 2. Facts for the People of the Free States. New York, Wm. Harned [1846]. 24 p.

Protest and Remonstrance. To the Christian Abolitionists of Great Britain and Ireland Who Met at

Freemasons' Hall, London, August 19, 1846, to Form an Evangelical Alliance. [New York, American and Foreign Anti-Slavery Society, 1847.] 16 p.

Remonstrance Against the Course Pursued by the Evangelical Alliance, on the Subject of American Slavery. New York, W. Harned, 1847. 16 p.

———

AMERICAN ANTI-SLAVERY SOCIETY

Almanacs.

The American Anti-Slavery Almanac for 1836. Volume 1, No. 1. Boston, Webster & Southard, 1836. 48 p.

The American Anti-Slavery Almanac for 1837. Volume 1, No. 2. Boston, N. Southard & D. H. Hitchcock, 1837. 48 p.

The American Anti-Slavery Almanac for 1838. Volume 1, No. 3. Boston, Isaac Knapp, 1838. 48 p. Same. Boston, D. H. Hitchcock. 48 p.

The American Anti-Slavery Almanac for 1839. Volume 1, No. 4. New York, S. W. Benedict, 1839. 48 p. 13 woodcuts.

The American Anti-Slavery Almanac for 1840. New York, S. W. Benedict; Boston, Isaac Knapp, 1840. 48 p.

The American Anti-Slavery Almanac for 1841. Volume 1, No. 6. New York, S. W. Benedict, 1841. 36 p. Same. Published at Cincinnati for the Ohio Anti-Slavery Society.

The American Anti-Slavery Almanac for 1842. Volume II, No. 1. New York, S. W. Benedict. 36 p.

The American Anti-Slavery Almanac for 1843. Volume II. No. 2. Compiled by L. M. Child. New York, American Anti-Slavery Society. 36 p.

The American Anti-Slavery Almanac for 1844. Compiled by D. L. Child, New York, American Anti-Slavery Society. 36 p.

Annual Reports. [Authorship of the first three reports is uncertain. Numbers 4, 5, and 6 were written by Elizur Wright. Number 7, very brief, is by Joshua Leavitt. The address of the New Executive Committee was probably written by Joseph C. Jackson. No reports were printed in pamphlet form for some years thereafter. The American and Foreign Anti-Slavery Society began, with Number 7, its own Annual Reports. The annual reports of the Massachusetts Anti-Slavery Society took the place of the former American Anti-Slavery Society Series. But after January, 1853, the Massachusetts Anti-Slavery Society discontinued publication in its own name, and the responsibility of an annual report once again fell to the American Anti-Slavery Society. The reports for 1854 and 1855 were pre- sented as one, in May, 1855, and were written by Sydney H. Gay. The report for May, 1856, was written by Sydney H. Gay. The reports for 1857 and 1858 were combined in one. The first 38 pages of the 1857 report were written by Sydney H. Gay. The remainder and the 1858 report were by Charles C. Burleigh. The report of 1859 was by Charles C. Burleigh, as was the report for 1860, also called the Anti-Slavery History of the John Brown Year. The report for 1861, by Burleigh, was the last report printed. Burleigh had the next in preparation, but it was never completed. He was one of the most conscientious and accurate workers in the movement.]

First Annual Report of the American Anti-Slavery Society; with the Speeches Delivered at the Anniversary Meeting, Held in Chatham-Street Chapel, in the City of New York, on the Sixth of May, 1834, and by Adjournment on the Eighth, in the Rev. Dr. Lansing's Church; and the Minutes of the Meetings of the Society for Business. New York, Dorr & Butterfield, 1834. 64 p.

Second Annual Report of the American Anti-Slavery Society; with the Speeches Delivered at the Anniversary Meeting, Held in the City of New York, on the 12th May, 1835, and the Minutes of the Meetings of the Society for Business. New York, William S. Dorr, 1835. 87 p.

Third Annual Report of the American Anti-Slavery Society; with the Speeches Delivered at the Anniversary Meeting Held in the City of New York, on the 10th May, 1836, and the Minutes of the Meetings of the Society for Business. New York, William S. Dorr, 1836. 99 p.

Fourth Annual Report of the American Anti-Slavery Society; with the Speeches Delivered at the Anniversary Meeting Held in the City of New York, on the 9th May, 1837, and the Minutes of the Meetings of the Society for Business. New York, William S. Dorr, 1837. 140 p.

Fifth Annual Report of the Executive Committee of the American Anti-Slavery Society, with the Minutes of the Meetings of the Society for Business, and the Speeches Delivered at the Anniversary Meeting on the 8th May, 1838. New York, William S. Dorr, 1838. 152 p.

Sixth Annual Report of the Executive Committee of the American Anti-Slavery Society, with the Speeches Delivered at the Anniversary Meeting Held in the City of New York, on the 7th of May, 1839, and the Minutes of the Meetings of the Society for Business, Held on the Evening and the Three Following Days. New York, William S. Dorr, 1839. 115 p.

Seventh Annual Report of the Executive Committee

of the American Anti-Slavery Society, with the Proceedings at the Anniversary Meeting Held in the City of New York, on the 12th of May, 1840, and the Minutes of the Meetings of the Society for Business, Held on the Evening and the Three Following Days. New York, William S. Dorr, 1840. 88 p.

Annual Report, Presented to the American Anti-Slavery Society, by the Executive Committee, at the Annual Meeting, Held in New York, May 9, 1855. With an Appendix. New York, American Anti-Slavery Society, 1855. 152 p.

Annual Report, Presented to the American Anti-Slavery Society, by the Executive Committee, at the Annual Meeting, Held in New York, May 7, 1856. With an Appendix. New York, American Anti-Slavery Society, 1856. 74 p.

Annual Reports of the American Anti-Slavery Society, by the Executive Committee for the Years Ending May 1, 1857, and May 1, 1858. New York, American Anti-Slavery Society, 1859. 203 p.

Annual Report of the American Anti-Slavery Society, by the Executive Committee, for the Year Ending May 1, 1859. New York, American Anti-Slavery Society, 1860. 144 p.

The Anti-Slavery History of the John Brown Year; being the Twenty-Seventh Annual Report of the American Anti-Slavery Society. New York, American Anti-Slavery Society, 1861. 337 p.

Twenty-Eighth Annual Report of the American Anti-Slavery Society, by the Executive Committee, for the Year Ending May 1, 1861. New York, American Anti-Slavery Society, 1861. 243 p.

Address to the People of Color, in the City of New York, by Members of the Executive Committee of the American Anti-Slavery Society. New York, S. W. Benedict, 1834. 8 p.

A *Collection* of Valuable Documents, Being Birney's Vindication of Abolitionists—Protest of the American A. S. Society—To the People of the United States, or, To Such Americans as Value Their Rights—Letter from the Executive Committee of the N. Y. A. S. Society, to the Exec. Com. of the Ohio State A. S. S. at Cincinnati—Outrage upon Southern Rights. Boston, Isaac Knapp, 1836. 80 p.

The Constitution of the American Anti-Slavery Society: With the Declaration of the National Anti-Slavery Convention at Philadelphia, December, 1833, and the Address to the Public, Issued by the Executive Committee of the Society, in September, 1835. New York, American Anti-Slavery Society, 1838. 12 p.

The *Declaration* of Sentiments and Constitution of the American Anti-Slavery Society, Together with All Those Parts of the Constitution of the United States Which Have Relation to Slavery. New York, American Anti-Slavery Society, 1835. 17 p.

Declaration of Sentiments of the American Anti-Slavery Society. Adopted at the Formation of Said Society, in Philadelphia, on the 4th Day of December, 1833. New York, American Anti-Slavery Society, Penny Tracts, 1833. 4 p. No. 1.

Examination of Mr. Thomas C. Brown, a Free Colored Citizen of S. Carolina, As to the Actual State of Things in Liberia in 1833 and 1834, May 9th & 10th, 1834. New York, American Anti-Slavery Society, 1834. 40 p.

The *Anti-Slavery Examiner*. [The *Examiner* started as a periodical, but became a series of separate monographs after publication of two numbers. There was exceedingly great carelessness in the numbering of the separate titles. The following have been identified:]

Vol. 1. No. 1. Executive Committee of the American Anti-Slavery Society To the People of the United States; or, to Such Americans as Value Their Rights, and Dare to Maintain Them. New York, August, 1836. 8 p.

Vol. 1. No. 2. Grimké, Angelina E. Appeal to the Christian Women of the South. Third Edition. [New York, 1836.] 36 p.

Vol. 1. No. 3. Smith, Gerrit. Letter of Gerrit Smith to Rev. James Smylie of the State of Mississippi. [New York, 1837]. 66 p.

No. 4. Weld, Theodore Dwight. The Bible Against Slavery. An Inquiry into the Patriarchal and Mosaic Systems on the Subject of Human Rights. New York, 1836. 74 p.

Second Edition. New York, 1837. 74 p.

No. 5. [Weld, Theodore Dwight]. The Power of Congress over the District of Columbia. New York, 1838. 57 p. [Originally published in New York *Evening Post*, in 1837, under signature "Wythe." There were at least four editions.]

Fourth Edition. New York, 1838. 56 p.

Also No. 5. Weld, Theodore Dwight. The Bible Against Slavery. An Inquiry into the Patriarchal and Mosaic Systems on the Subject of Human Rights. Third Edition. New York, 1838. 74 p.

No. 6. [Weld, Theodore Dwight]. The Bible Against Slavery. An Inquiry into the Patriarchal and Mosaic Systems on the Subject of Human Rights. Fourth Edition. New York, 1838. 98 p. [After passing through four editions this was out of print for twenty years. It was republished by the Presbyterian Board of Publications in 1864, following Lincoln's Emancipation Proclamation.]

Also No. 6. Narrative of James Williams, an American Slave. [A Prospectus]. New York, 1838. 8 p.

No. 7. Thome, James A., & Kimball, J. Horace.

Emancipation in the West Indies. A Six Months Tour in Antigua, Barbadoes and Jamaica, in the Year 1837. New York, 1838. 128 p.

Another Edition: Anti-Slavery Examiner-Extra. New York, 1838. 32 p.

No. 7a. [Green, Beriah]. The Chattel Principle the Abhorrence of Jesus Christ and the Apostles; or No Refuge for American Slavery in the New Testament. New York, 1839. 71 p.

No. 8. [Birney, James G.]. Correspondence between the Hon. F. H. Elmore, One of the South Carolina Delegation in Congress, and James G. Birney, One of the Secretaries of the American Anti-Slavery Society. New York, 1838. 68 p.

No. 9. Smith, Gerrit. Letter of Gerrit Smith to Hon. Henry Clay. New York, 1839. 54 p.

No. 10. [Weld, Theodore D.]. American Slavery As It Is: Testimony of A Thousand Witnesses. New York, 1839. 224 p. [Some issues of this bear the number 6.]

Also No. 10. Speech of Hon. Thomas Morris of Ohio in Reply to the Speech of Hon. Henry Clay in Senate, February 9, 1839. New York, 1839. 40 p.

No. 11. [Phillips, Wendell]. The Constitution a Pro-Slavery Compact; or Selections from the Madison Papers, etc. New York, 1845. 131 p.

No. 12. Disunion. Address of the American Anti-Slavery Society; and F. Jackson's Letter on the Pro-Slavery Character of the Constitution. New York, 1845. 32 p.

Also No. 12. Green, Beriah. The Chattel Principle the Abhorrence of Jesus Christ and the Apostles; or, No Refuge for American Slavery in the New Testament. New York, 1839. 67 p.

No. 13. [Phillips, Wendell]. Can Abolitionists Vote or Take Office under the United States Constitution? New York, 1845. 39 p.

Also No. 13. On the Condition of the Free People of Color in the United States. New York, 1839. 23 p.

No. 14. Executive Committee. Address to the Friends of Constitutional Liberty, on the Violation by the United States House of Representatives of the Right of Petition. New York, 1840. 12 p.

Anti-Slavery Tracts. New York, 1855–1856

No. 1. [Bowditch, W. I.] The United States Constitution, 12 p.

No. 2. [Bowditch, W. I.] White Slavery in the United States. 8 p.

No. 3. Frothingham, D. B. Colonization. 8 p.

No. 4. Higginson, T. W. Does Slavery Christianize the Negro? 8 p.

No. 5. Palfrey, John G. The Inter-State Slave Trade. 8 p.

No. 6. Hildreth, Richard. The "Ruin" of Jamaica. 12 p.

No. 7. [Foster, S. S.] Revolution the Only Remedy for Slavery. 20 p.

No. 8. Follen, Mrs. Eliza L. To Mothers in the Free States. 4 p.

No. 9. [Barker, Mrs. L. J.] Influence of Slavery upon the White Population, by a Former Resident in the Slave States. 12 p.

No. 10. Burleigh, Charles C. Slavery and the North. 12 p.

No. 11. Hodges, Charles E. Disunion Our Wisdom and Our Duty. 12 p.

No. 12. [Follen, Mrs. E. L.] Where Is Thy Brother? [and Other Poems]. 8 p.

No. 13. Stowe, Mrs. Harriet Beecher. Two Altars; or, Two Pictures in One. New York, 1852. 12 p.

No. 14. Chapman, Maria Weston. "How Can I Help to Abolish Slavery?" or, Counsels to the Newly Converted. 12 p.

No. 15. Cabot, Susan C. What Have We, as Individuals, to Do With Slavery? 7 p.

No. 16. [Patten, W. W.] The Unanimous Remonstrance of the Fourth Congregational Church of Hartford, Connecticut, Against the Policy of the American Tract Society on the Subject of Slavery. 36 p.

No. 17. Beecher, Charles. The God of the Bible Against Slavery. 11 p.

No. 18. [May, Samuel J.] The Fugitive Slave Law and Its Victims. 48 p.

No. 19. Whipple, C. K. Relations of Anti-Slavery to Religion. New York, 1856. 20 p.

No. 20. Higginson, Thomas Wentworth. A Ride Through Kansas. 24 p.

Anti-Slavery Tracts, New Series. [This list follows Samuel J. May. The list in *Anti-Slavery Standard*, May 10, 1862, says No. 18, is O. P. Anderson: A Voice from Harper's Ferry; and No. 20 is The Loyalty and Devotion of Colored Americans. Many are not numbered and so do not have American Anti-Slavery Society imprint.]

No. 1. Child, Mrs. Lydia Maria *Francis*. Correspondence between Lydia Maria Child, and Governor Wise and Mrs. Mason, of Virginia. New York, American Anti-Slavery Society, 1860. 28 p.

No. 2. [Garrison, William Lloyd. Compiler]. Letters on American Slavery from Victor Hugo, De-Tocqueville, Emile de Girardin, Carnot, Passy, Mazzini, Humboldt, O. Lafayette, etc. [New York, American Anti-Slavery Society, 1860.] 24 p.

No. 3. Coffin, Joshua. An Account of Some of the Principal Slave Insurrections, and Others, Which Have Occurred, or Been Attempted, in the United States and Elsewhere, during the Last Two Centuries. With Remarks. Collected from Various

Sources by Joshua Coffin. New York, The American Anti-Slavery Society, 1860. 36 p.

No. 4. [Garrison, William Lloyd]. The New "Reign of Terror" in the Slaveholding States, for 1859–60. New York, American Anti-Slavery Society, 1860. 144 p.

No. 5. [O'Connell, D.] Daniel O'Connell Upon American Slavery; with Other Irish Testimonies. 48 p.

No. 6. Child, Mrs. Lydia Maria *Francis*. The Right Way the Safe Way Proved by Emancipation in the British West Indies, and Elsewhere. New York, American Anti-Slavery Society, 1860. 95 p.

No. 7. [Brown, John]. Testimonies of Capt. John Brown, at Harper's Ferry, with His Address to the Court. New York, American Anti-Slavery Society, 1860. 16 p.

No. 8. Phillips, Wendell. The Philosophy of the Abolition Movement. [New York, American Anti-Slavery Society, 1860]. 48 p.

No. 9. Child, Lydia Maria. The Duty of Disobedience to the Fugitive Slave Act: An Appeal to the Legislators of Massachusetts. [New York, American Anti-Slavery Society, 1860.] 36 p.

No. 10. Garrison, William Lloyd. The "Infidelity of Abolitionism." [New York, American Anti-Slavery Society, 1860.] 12 p.

No. 11. [Hossack, John]. Speech of John Hossack, Convicted of the Violation of the Fugitive Slave Law, Before Judge Drummond, of the United States District Court, Chicago, Illinois. [New York, American Anti-Slavery Society, 1860]. 12 p.

No. 12. Child, Lydia Maria. The Patriarchal Institution as Described by Members of Its Own Family. New York, American Anti-Slavery Society, 1860. 55 p.

No. 13. [Phillips, Wendell]. No Slave-Hunting in the Old Bay State. 1860. 23 p.

No. 14. [Garrison, William Lloyd]. A Fresh Catalogue of Southern Outrages, 1860. 72 p.

No. 15. [May, Samuel J.] The Fugitive Slave Law and Its Victims. 168 p.

No. 16. [Channing, W. E.] Tribute of William Ellery Channing to the American Abolitionists for Their Vindication of Freedom of Speech. 24 p.

No. 17. Phillips, Wendell. Argument of Wendell Phillips, Esq., Against the Repeal of the Personal Liberty Law, Before the Committee of the Legislature, Tuesday, January 29, 1861. Boston, R. F. Wallcut, 1861. 24 p.

No. 18. [Garrison, William Lloyd]. The Loyalty and Devotion of Colored Americans. Boston, R. F. Wallcut, 1861. 24 p.

No. 19. Garrison, William Lloyd. The Abolition of Slavery: The Right of the Constitution under the War Powers. Boston, R. F. Wallcut, 1861. 24 p.

No. 20. [Plumb, D.] The War and Slavery: or, Victory only Through Emancipation. Boston, R. F. Wallcut, 1861. 8 p.

No. 21. [Garrison, William Lloyd]. In Memoriam. Testimonials to the Life and Character of the Late Francis Jackson. Boston, R. F. Wallcut, 1861. 36 p.

No. [22]. [Garrison, William Lloyd]. The Spirit of the South Toward Northern Freemen and Soldiers Defending the American Flag Against Traitors of the Deepest Dye. Boston, R. F. Wallcut, 1861. 24 p.

No. [23]. [Garrison, William Lloyd]. Southern Hatred of American Government, the People of the North and Free Institutions. Boston, R. F. Wallcut, 1862. 48 p.

No. 24. Stephens, A. H. Extract from a Speech by Alexander H. Stephens, Vice-President of the Confederate States, Delivered in the Secession Convention of Georgia, January, 1861. 4 p.

No. 25. Pierce, E. L. The Negroes at Port Royal. Report of Edward Lillie Pierce, Government Agent to the Hon. Salmon P. Chase, Secretary of the Treasury. Boston, R. F. Wallcut, 1862. 36 p.

[*Miniature Anti-Slavery Tracts.* New York, R. G. Williams, 1837–1839.]

No. 1. St. Domingo. 24 p.

No. 2. Caste. 24 p.

No. 3. Colonization. 24 p.

No. 4. Moral Condition of Slaves. 24 p.

No. 5. What Is Abolition? 16 p.

No. 6. The Ten Commandments. 16 p.

No. 7. Danger and Safety. 24 p.

No. 8. Pro-Slavery Bible. 8 p.

No. 9. Prejudice Against Color. 16 p.

No. 10. Northern Dealers in Slaves. 16 p.

No. 11. Slavery and Missions. 24 p.

No. 12. Dr. Nelson's Lecture on Slavery. 16 p.

Debate at the Lane Seminary, Cincinnati. Speech of James A. Thome, of Kentucky, Delivered at the Annual Meeting of the American Anti-Slavery Society, May 6, 1834. Letter of the Rev. Samuel H. Cox, Against the American Colonization Society. Boston, Garrison & Knapp, 1834. 16 p.

Executive Committee to the Abolitionists of Massachusetts; Protest of Massachusetts Board; Reply of the Executive Committee of the American Anti-Slavery Society; Statement of the Rev. A. A. Phelps and Others. Christian Journal—Extra. New York, Wednesday, March 20, 1839. [Probably written by Joseph C. Jackson.]

The *Legion* of Liberty and Force of Truth, Containing the Thoughts, Words, and Deeds, of Some Prominent Apostles, Champions, and Martyrs. New York, American Anti-Slavery Society, 1844. 140 p. [This went through ten editions within three years]. *See* Julius R. Ames.

A *Letter* to Louis Kossuth, Concerning Freedom and Slavery in the United States. In Behalf of the American Anti-Slavery Society. [Signed]: Wm. Lloyd Garrison, President. Sydney Howard Gay, Wendell Phillips, Secretaries. Boston, R. F. Wallcut, 1852. 112 p.

The '*Manifest* Destiny' of the American Union. New York, American Anti-Slavery Society, 1857.

Platform of the American Anti-Slavery Society and Its Auxiliaries. New York, 1853. 35 p.
Same. New York, 1855. 35 p.
Same. New York, 1860. 35 p.

Proceedings of the Anti-Slavery Convention, Assembled at Philadelphia, Dec. 4, 5, 6, 1833. New York, Dorr and Butterfield, 1833. 28 p.

Proceedings of the American Anti-Slavery Society, at Its Second Decade, Held in the City of Philadelphia, Dec. 3d, 4th and 5th, 1853. New York, American Anti-Slavery Society, 1854. 176 p.

Proceedings of the American Anti-Slavery Society at Its Third Decade, Held in the City of Philadelphia, Dec. 3d & 4th, 1863, with an Appendix, and a Catalogue of Anti-Slavery Publications in America 1750–1863. New York, American Anti-Slavery Society, 1864. 175 p.

———

American Baptist Free Mission Society. Anti-Slavery Missions. A Brief View of the Origin, Principles, and Operations of the American Baptist Free Mission Society. [Bristol, 1851.] 4 p.

American Baptist Free Mission Society. Anti-Slavery Missions. Review of the Operations of the American Baptist Free Mission Society for the Past Year. Bristol, Mathews Brothers [1851]. 12 p.

American Board of Commissioners for Foreign Missions. On Receiving Donations from Holders of Slaves. Boston, Perkins & Marvin, [1840]. 20 p.

American Board of Commissioners for Foreign Missions. Report of the Committee on Anti-Slavery Memorials, September, 1845. With A Historical Statement of Previous Proceedings. Boston, T. R. Marvin, 1845. 32 p.

An American Citizen. An Inquiry into the Causes and Origin of Slavery in the United States, No. 4. By an American Citizen, to Which is Prefixed a Letter from a Member of Congress, to the Author. Philadelphia, William S. Young, 1845. 8 p.

An American Citizen. The Ethics of American Slavery; Being a Vindication of the Word of God and a Pure Christianity in All Ages, from Complicity with Involuntary Servitude; and a Demonstration That American Slavery Is a Crime in Substance and Concomitants; by an American Citizen. New York, Ross & Tousey, 1861. 146 p.

An American Citizen. Letter Addressed to the President of the United States [Franklin Pierce] on Slavery, Considered in Relation to the Constitutional Principles of Government in Great Britain and in the United States. By an American Citizen, Boston, Redding & Co., 1855. 91 p.

AMERICAN COLONIZATION SOCIETY

Address of the Board of Managers of the American Colonization Society to the Auxiliary Societies and the People of the United States. Washington, D. C., Davis & Force, 1820. 32 p.

Address of the Board of Managers of the American Colonization Society to Its Auxiliary Societies. Washington [D. C.], Gales and Seaton, 1831. 11 p.

Address of the Managers of the American Colonization Society, to the People of the United States. Adopted at Their Meeting, June 19, 1832. Washington [D. C.], James C. Dunn, 1832. 16 p.

Annual Reports, 1818–1910

The First Annual Report of the American Society for Colonizing the Free People of Colour of the United States. With an Appendix. Washington, Davis and Force, 1818. 28 p.
Same. 49 p.

The Second Annual Report of the American Society for Colonizing the Free People of Colour of the United States. With an Appendix. Washington, Davis and Force, 1819. 131 p.

The Fifth Annual Report of the American Society for Colonizing the Free People of Colour of the United States. Washington City, Davis & Force, 1822. 119 p.

The Sixth Annual Report of the American Society for Colonizing the Free People of Colour of the United States. With an Appendix. Washington City, Davis and Force, 1823. 71 p.

The Seventh Annual Report of the American Society for Colonizing the Free People of Colour of the United States. With an Appendix. Washington, Davis and Force, 1824. 173 p.

The Eighth Annual Report of the American Society for Colonizing the Free People of Colour of the United States. Washington City, James C. Dunn, 1825. 68 p.

The Ninth Annual Report of the American Society for Colonizing the Free People of Colour of the United States. With an Appendix. Washington City, Way & Gideon, 1826. 66 p.

The Tenth Annual Report of the American Society for Colonizing the Free People of Colour of the United States. Washington, Way & Gideon, 1827. 101 p.

The Eleventh Annual Report of the American Society for Colonizing the Free People of Colour of the United States. With an Appendix. Washington, James C. Dunn, 1829. 80 p.

The Twelfth Annual Report of the American Society for Colonizing the Free People of Colour of the United States. With an Appendix. Washington, James C. Dunn, 1829. 80 p.

The Thirteenth Annual Report of the American Society for Colonizing the Free People of Colour of the United States. With an Appendix. Second Edition, Washington, James C. Dunn, 1830. 55 p.

The Fourteenth Annual Report of the American Society for Colonizing the Free People of Colour of the United States. With an Appendix. Washington, James C. Dunn, 1831. 34 p.

The Fifteenth Annual Report of the American Society for Colonizing the Free People of Colour of the United States. With an Appendix. Washington, James C. Dunn, 1832. 56 p.

The Sixteenth Annual Report of the American Society for Colonizing the Free People of Colour of the United States. With an Appendix. Washington, James C. Dunn, 1833. 44 p.

The Seventeenth Annual Report of the American Society for Colonizing the Free People of Colour of the United States. Washington, James C. Dunn, 1834. 45 p.

The Eighteenth Annual Report of the American Society for Colonizing the Free People of Color of the United States, with the Proceedings of the Annual Meeting, January 19, 1835; with a General Index to the Annual Reports, and Proceedings at the Annual Meetings of the Society, from the First to the Eighteenth, Both Inclusive. Washington, 1835. 32 p.

The Twenty-Fourth Annual Report of the American Colonization Society, with the Abridged Proceedings of the Annual Meeting, and of the Board of Directors; at Washington, January 19, 1841, to Which is Added the Late Despatches from Liberia. Second Edition. Washington, Joseph Etter, 1841. 48 p.

The Twenty-Fifth Annual Report of the American Colonization Society, with the Abridged Proceedings of the Annual Meeting, and of the Board of Directors, at Washington, January 18, 1842. Washington, J. & S. Gideon, 1842. 24 p.

Twenty-Sixth Annual Report of the American Society for Colonizing the Free People of Color of the United States. With an Appendix. Washington, Alexander & Barnard, 1843. 38 + 18 p.

Twenty-Eighth Annual Report of the American Colonization Society with the Proceedings of the Board of Directors, and of the Society at Its Annual Meeting, January 21, 1845. Washington, C. Alexander, 1845. 32 p.

Twenty-Ninth Annual Report of the American Colonization Society, with the Proceedings of the Board of Directors, and of the Society at Its An-nual Meeting, January 20, 1846. Washington, C. Alexander, 1846. 43 p.

Thirtieth Annual Report of the American Colonization Society, with the Proceedings of the Board of Directors, and of the Society at Its Annual Meeting, January 19, 1847. Washington, C. Alexander, 1847. 43 p.

Thirty-First Annual Report of the American Colonization Society with the Proceedings of the Board of Directors, and of the Society at Its Annual Meeting, January 18, 1848. Washington, C. Alexander, 1848. 60 p.

Thirty-Second Annual Report of the American Colonization Society, with the Proceedings of the Board of Directors, and of the Society at Its Annual Meeting, January 16, 1849. Washington, C. Alexander, 1849. 59 p.

Thirty-Third Annual Report of the American Colonization Society, with the Proceedings of the Board of Directors, and of the Society at Its Annual Meeting, January 15, 1850. Washington, C. Alexander, 1850. 46 p.

Thirty-Fourth Annual Report of the American Colonization Society, with the Proceedings of the Board of Directors and of the Society; and the Addresses Delivered at the Annual Meeting, January 21, 1851. To Which Is Added an Appendix, Containing Sentiments of the Press; Memorials to Congress in Favor of Steamships to Africa; Commerce of Africa; a Table Exhibiting the Cost of Colonization and a Table of Emigrants. Washington, C. Alexander, 1851. 84 p.

Thirty-Fifth Annual Report of the American Colonization Society, with the Proceedings of the Board of Directors and of the Society; and the Addresses Delivered at the Annual Meeting, January 20, 1852. To Which Is Added an Appendix, Containing Information about Going to Liberia; Things Which Every Emigrant Ought to Know, Messrs. Fuller and Janifer's Report; and a Table of Emigrants. Washington, C. Alexander, 1852. 52 p.

Thirty-Sixth Annual Report of the American Colonization Society, with the Proceedings of the Board of Directors and of the Society; and the Addresses Delivered at the Annual Meeting, January 18, 1853. Washington, C. Alexander, 1853. 36 p.

Thirty-Seventh Annual Report of the American Colonization Society, with the Proceedings of the Board of Directors and of the Society; and the Addresses Delivered at the Annual Meeting, January 17, 1854. Washington, C. Alexander, 1854. 43 p.

Thirty-Eighth Annual Report of the American Colonization Society, with the Proceedings of the Board of Directors and of the Society; and the

Addresses Delivered at the Annual Meeting, January 16, 1855. Washington, C. Alexander, 1855. 56 p.

Thirty-Ninth Annual Report of the American Colonization Society, with the Proceedings of the Board of Directors and of the Society, January 15, 1856. Washington, C. Alexander, 1856. 40 p.

Fortieth Annual Report of the American Colonization Society, with the Proceedings of the Board of Directors and of the Society, January 20, 1857. Washington, C. Alexander, 1857. 50 p.

Forty-First Annual Report of the American Colonization Society, with the Proceedings of the Board of Directors and of the Society, January 19, 1858. Washington, C. Alexander, 1858. 60 p.

Forty-Second Annual Report of the American Colonization Society, with the Proceedings of the Board of Directors and of the Society, January 18, 1859. Washington, C. Alexander, 1859, 56 p.

Forty-Third Annual Report of the American Colonization Society, with the Proceedings of the Board of Directors and of the Society, January 17, 1860. Washington, C. Alexander, 1860. 70 p.

Forty-Fourth Annual Report of the American Colonization Society, with the Proceedings of the Board of Directors and of the Society, January 15, 1861. Washington, C. Alexander, 1861. 567 p.

Condition of the American Colored Population, and of the Colony at Liberia. Boston, Pierce & Parker, 1833. 24 p.

Constitution, Government and Digest of the Laws of Liberia, as Confirmed and Established by the Board of Managers of the American Colonization Society, May 23, 1825. Washington City, Way & Gideon, 1825. 11 p.

Correspondence Relative to the Emigration to Hayti of the Free People of Colour in the United States, Together with the Instructions to the Agent Sent Out by President Boyer. New York, Mahlon Day, 1824. 32 p.

A Few Facts Respecting the American Colonization Society and the Colony of Liberia. Washington, Way and Gideon, 1830. 16 p.

Information About Going to Liberia, with Things Which Every Emigrant Ought to Know; Report of Messrs. Fuller and Janifer; Sketch of the History of Liberia; and the Constitution of the Republic of Liberia. Washington, American Colonization Society, 1832. 24 p.

Memorial of the Semi-Centennial Anniversary of the American Colonization Society, Celebrated at Washington, January 15, 1867. With Documents Concerning Liberia. Washington, The Society, 1867. 191 p.

The Memorial of the American Colonization So-

ciety. Washington City, Way & Gideon, 1826. 8 p.

To the Public. Address of the Board of Managers of the American Colonization Society. [Washington, Columbian Star Office, 1822.] 16 p.

———

A View of Exertions Lately Made for the Purpose of Colonizing the Free People of Colour, in the United States, in Africa, or Elsewhere. City of Washington, Jonathan Elliot, Pennsylvania Avenue, 1817. 23 p.

The American Intelligencer. Philadelphia, Pa.
Vol. 1. Nos. 1–3. May, September, 1841; and September, 1844.
Vol. 1. No. 1. J. J. Gurney: Familiar Letters on the West Indies.
Vol. 1. No. 2. W. E. Channing: Review of Gurney's Letters.
Vol. 1. No. 3. C. D. Cleveland: Address of the Liberty Party of Pennsylvania to the People of the State.

The American Jubilee. Monthly. New York, N. Y. March, 1854–April, 1855. Continued as Radical Abolitionist, August, 1855–December, 1858. Edited by William Goodell.

American Missionary Association. Missionary Boards in Relation to Slavery, Caste, and Polygamy. New York, American Missionary Association, 1854. 32 p.

American Missionary Association. The Persecutions of Missionaries of the American Missionary Association: Their Expulsion and That of Other Anti-Slavery Christians from the States of Kentucky and North Carolina; and the Imprisonment of the Rev. Daniel Worth. From the Fourteenth Annual Report of the American Missionary Association, October 10, 1860. 16 p.

The American Pioneer: With a New and Useful Plan to Establish Free Labor, in the United States; by an American. Boston, Allen & Co., 1854. 24 p.

AMERICAN REFORM TRACT AND BOOK SOCIETY

An Abstract of the Evidence Delivered Before a Select Committee of the House of Commons, in the Years 1790 and 1791, on the Part of the Petitioners for the Abolition of the Slave Trade. Cincinnati, American Reform Tract & Book Society, 1855. 117 p.
Same. Cincinnati, American Reform Tract and Book Society, 1859. 117 p.

Occasional Tracts. Cincinnati [1860].
No. 1. Separation from Sin and Sinners. 24 p.
No. 3. Catechism for Free Working Men, by the Son of a Blacksmith. 4 p.

No. 5. Slavery in Rebellion, An Outlaw, How to Deal with It. 12 p.

No. 8. Stone, A. L. Emancipation. 12 p.

No. 13. Sunderland, Byron. God's Judgments for National Sins. 12 p.

To All Evangelical Christians. The Suppressed Tract! and the Rejected Tract! Given Word for Word as Submitted to the Publishing Committee of the American Tract Society. Read and Judge. Shall the Society or the Committee Rule? New York, American Reform Tract and Book Society, 1858. 24 p. [Copy of original title page:] Scriptural Duties of Masters. Comprising a Pastoral Address of the Rt. Rev. William Meade, D.D., of Virginia: A Sermon of the Rev. John C. Young, D.D., of Kentucky; and Brief Selections from Publications of the Rev. Drs. John B. Adger, C. C. Jones, James W. Alexander, and Rev. A. T. Holmes, and a Notice from Rev. Dr. Thomas Smyth.

Tracts.

No. 1. The Law and the Testimony Concerning Slavery. 24 p.

No. 2. Hebrew Servitude and American Slavery. Cincinnati. 8 p.

No. 3. On Slavery. Cincinnati. 24 p.

No. 4. Agitation—The Doom of Slavery. 16 p.

No. 5. Slavery and the Bible. 12 p.

No. 6. The Bible Gives No Sanction to Slavery. By a Tennesseean. Cincinnati. 32 p.

No. 7. A Tract for Sabbath Schools. [Slave Auction in Washington.] 4 p.

No. 10. Duty of Voting for Righteous Men for Office. 8 p.

No. 14. Fee, John G., Pastor of the Church at Berea, Madison Co., Ky. Colonization. The Present Scheme of Colonization Wrong, Delusive, and Retards Emancipation. 48 p.

No. 15. Fellowship with Slavery. Report Republished from the Minister of the Evangelical Association, Rhode Island. 32 p.

No. 19. Thompson, George, Mendi Mission, West Africa. Pleas for Slavery Answered. 24 p.

No. 20. A Tract for the Free States. Let Every One Read and Consider before He Condemns.— A Safe and Generous Proposition for Abolishing Slavery. Cincinnati, American Reform Tract & Book Society, 1856. 12 p.

No. 37. The Family and Slavery. By a Native of the Southwest. 24 p.

No. 60. Aydelott, B. P. Prejudice Against Colored People. 21 p.

No. 67. Rev. Wm. Knibb, Missionary to the Island of Jamaica; Compiled from an Address by Rev. S. Williams. 8 p.

No. 68. Old Moses: or, The Praying Negro; and "Does the Lord Jesus Love Colored People?" 8 p. [Wolcott, Samuel T.] Fellowship with Slavery. 32 p.

American Reform Tract and Book Society. The Child's Book on Slavery; or, Slavery Made Plain. Cincinnati, American Reform Tract and Book Society, [1857]. 143 p.

———

American Slavery. Demonstrations in Favor of Dr. Cheever, in Scotland. Letter of Sympathy from Distinguished Clergymen and Other Gentlemen. Speeches at Meetings in Edinburgh and Glasgow, by Drs. Candlish, Guthrie, Alexander, Buchanan, and Smyth. And a Statement of Dr. Cheever's Case, by Rev. H. Batchelor. Letter of Dr. Guthrie to the Presbyterian. New York, J. A. Gray, Printer, 1860. 77 p.

American Slavery. A Protest Against American Slavery, by One Hundred and Seventy-Three Unitarian Ministers. Boston, B. H. Greene, 1845. 20 p. Approved and Published by the Rhode Island and Massachusetts Christian Conference in New Bedford.

American Slavery. Report of a Meeting of Members of the Unitarian Body, Held at the Freemasons' Tavern, June 13th, 1851, to Deliberate on the Duty of English Unitarians in Reference to Slavery in the United States. Rev. Dr. Hutton in the Chair. [London] E. T. Whitfield, 1851. 23 p.

American Tract Society. The Tract Society and Slavery. Speeches of Chief Justice Williams, Judge Parsons, and Ex-Governor Ellsworth: Delivered in the Center Church, Hartford, Conn. at the Anniversary of the Hartford Branch of the American Tract Society, January 9th, 1859. Second Edition. Hartford, E. Geer, 1859. 26 p.

American Tract Society. The Enormity of the Slave Trade; and the Duty of Seeking the Moral and Spiritual Elevation of the Colored Race. Speeches of Wilberforce, and Other Documents and Records. New York, American Tract Society [1846]. 144 p.

American Tract Society. Minute Adopted on the 18th March, 1858, by the Publishing Committee, Explanatory of Their Position in Relation to the Report and Resolutions, of the Committee of Fifteen, as Sanctioned at the Anniversary of 1857, and the Act of the Executive Committee Adopting Such Minute. [New York, 1858]. 20 p.

American Tract Society. Responsibilities of the Publishing Committee under the Constitution [of the American Tract Society]. New York, Tract House, 1858. 16 p.

American Tract Society, New York Branch. Testimony of Five of the Society's Founders. Historical Facts Limiting Its Issues to Publications in Which Evangelical Christians Agree. [n.p., n.d.] 16 p.

American Union for the Relief and Improvement of the Colored Race. Expositions of the Objects and Plans of the American Union for the Relief and Improvement of the Colored Race. Boston, Light & Horton, 1835. 23 p.

American Union for the Relief and Improvement of the Colored Race. Report of the Executive Committee of the American Union, At the Annual Meeting of the Society, May 25, 1836. Boston, Perkins and Marvin, 1836. 39 p.

[Ames, Julius Rubens]. "Liberty." The Image and Superscription on Every Coin Issued by the United States. Extracts on Slavery. [New York, American Anti-Slavery Society] 1837. 231 p. Continued as the Legion of Liberty. *See* American Anti-Slavery Society.

Ames, Julius R. Sentiments Expressed by the Southerners Themselves on the Subject of Slavery. Boston, Charles Whipple [n.d.]. 19 p.

Amherstburg, Ontario, Convention. Minutes and Proceedings of the General Convention, for the Improvement of the Colored Inhabitants of Canada, Held by Adjournments in Amherstburg, C. W., June 16th & 17th, 1853. Windsor, C. W., Bibb & Holly, 1853. 23 p.

Amistad Case. The African Captives. Trial of the Prisoners of the Amistad on the Writ of Habeas Corpus, Before the Circuit Court of the United States for the District of Connecticut, at Hartford; Judges Thompson and Judson, September Term, 1839. New York, American Anti-Slavery Society, 1839. 47 p.

Amistad Case. Africans Taken in the Amistad. Congressional Documents, Containing the Correspondence, etc., in Relation to the Captured Africans. New York, Anti-Slavery Depository, 1840. 48 p. [Reprint of House Executive Document, No. 185, 26 Cong., 1 Sess.]

An Analysis of the Imperial Act for the Abolition of Slavery, Passed August 28th, 1833; And of the Acts of the Jamaica Legislature for Carrying the Same into Effect. London, J. Rider, [1833]. 48 p.

Anderson, Osborne Perry. A Voice from Harper's Ferry. A Narrative of Events at Harper's Ferry; with Incidents Prior and Subsequent to Its Capture by Captain Brown and His Men. By Osborne Perry Anderson, One of the Number. Boston, Printed for the Author, 1861. 72 p.

Anderson, James. Observations on Slavery; Particularly with a View to Its Effects on the British Colonies, in the West Indies. Manchester, J. Harrop, 1799. 38 p.

Anderson, William [slave]. Life and Narrative of William Anderson, or the Dark Deeds of American Slavery Revealed, Containing Scriptural Views of the Origin of the Black Man and White Man. Also, A Simple and Easy Plan to Abolish Slavery in the U[nited] States, Together with Some Account of the Services of Colored Men, in the Revolutionary War—Day and Date, and Interesting Facts. Written by Himself. Chicago, Daily Tribune Book and Job Office, 1857. 59 p.

Anderson, William Wemyss. Jamaica and the Americans. New York, Stanford and Swords, 1851. 30 p.

Andover Theological Seminary, Anti-Slavery Society. Apology for Anti-Slavery, August 22, 1833. [Signed]; D. T. Kimball, President. L. F. Laine, Sec. 4 p.

Andrews, Charles C. The History of the New York African Free Schools, from Their Establishment in 1787, to the Present Time. Also a Brief Account of the Successful Labors, of the New York Manumission Society. New York, M. Day, 1830. 145 p.

Andrews, E[than] A[llen]. Slavery and the Domestic Slave Trade in the United States. In a Series of Letters Addressed to the Executive Committee of the American Union for the Relief and Improvement of the Colored Race. Boston, Light and Steam, 1836. 201 p. [Andrews was a lawyer, and classical scholar; professor of ancient languages at the University of North Carolina, 1822–1828. He went to New England and was very active in antislavery work.]

Andrews, John Albion. Speeches by John A. Andrews at Hingham and Boston, Together with His Testimony Before the Harper's Ferry Committee of the Senate, in Relation to John Brown. Also, the Republican Platform, and Other Matters. Boston, Republican State Committee, 1860. 16 p. [John A. Andrews was bitterly opposed to slavery from the days of his youth. He was a lawyer, a Unitarian, and an active political-action, antislavery man.]

Anti-Colonization Meeting, London, 1833. Speeches Delivered at the Anti-Colonization Meeting in Exeter Hall, London, July 13, 1833, by James Cropper, Esq., William Lloyd Garrison, Rev. Nathaniel Paul, Daniel O'Connell, Esq., M.P., Mr. Buckingham, M.P., Mr. Hunt, Rev. Mr. Abrahams, George Thompson, Esq., etc. Boston, Garrison & Knapp, 1833. 40 p.

The Anti-Slavery Alphabet. Philadelphia, Printed for the Anti-Slavery Fair, Merrihew & Thompson, 1847.

Anti-Slavery Bazaar. Report of the Twenty-First National Anti-Slavery Bazaar. Boston, J. B. Yerrington & Son, Printers, 1855. 36 p.

Anti-Slavery Bugle. Weekly. New Lisbon, Ohio. June 30, 1845–1861. [Founded and published by B. S. Jones and his wife, Elizabeth H. Jones, until 1849. Then edited by Marius Robinson. Organ of Ohio Anti-Slavery Society.]

Anti-Slavery Conference, Manchester, Eng. Report of the Proceedings of the Anti-Slavery Conference and Public Meeting, Held at Manchester, on the 1st August, 1854, in Commemoration of West India Emancipation. London, William Tweedie, 1854. 40 p.

Anti-Slavery Convention of American Women. An Address to Free Colored Americans, Issued by an Anti-Slavery Convention of American Women, Held in the City of New York, by Adjournment from the 9th to the 12th of May, 1837. New York, William S. Dorr, 1837. 32 p.

Anti-Slavery Convention of American Women, Philadelphia, 1838. Address to the Free Colored People of the United States. Philadelphia, Merrihew and Gunn, 1838. 12 p.

[Anti-Slavery Convention of American Women. Philadelphia, 1838]. Address to Anti-Slavery Societies. Philadelphia, Merrihew and Gunn, 1838. 14 p.

[Anti-Slavery Convention of American Women. Philadelphia, 1838]. Address to the Senators and Representatives of the Free States, in the Congress of the United States. Philadelphia, Merrihew and Gunn, 1838. 11 p.

Anti-Slavery Convention of American Women. Philadelphia, 1839. An Address from the Convention of American Women, to the Society of Friends, on the Subject of Slavery. Philadelphia, Printed; Bristol [Eng.], Reprinted, J. Wright, 1840. 8 p.

Anti-Slavery Convention of American Women. [Weld, Angelina E. *Grimké*] An Appeal to the Women of the Nominally Free States, Issued by an Anti-Slavery Convention of American Women, Held by Adjournment from the 9th to the 12th of May, 1837. New York, W. S. Dorr, 1837. 68 p. Same. Second Edition. Boston, I. Knapp, 1838. 70 p.

Anti-Slavery Convention of American Women. Proceedings of the Anti-Slavery Convention of American Women Held in the City of New York, May 9th, 10th, 11th, and 12th, 1837. New York, William S. Dorr, 1837. 23 p.

Anti-Slavery Convention of American Women. Proceedings of the Anti-Slavery Convention of American Women Held in Philadelphia, May 15th, 16th, 17th and 18th, 1838. Philadelphia, Merrihew & Gunn, 1838. 18 p.

Anti-Slavery Convention of American Women. Proceedings of the Third Anti-Slavery Convention of American Women, Held in Philadelphia, May 1st,

2d and 3d, 1839. Philadelphia, Printed by Merrihew and Thompson, 1839. 28 p.

Anti-Slavery Convention, London, 1843. Proceedings of the General Anti-Slavery Convention Called by the Committee of the British and Foreign Anti-Slavery Society and Held in London, from Tuesday, June 13th, to Tuesday, June 20th, 1843. London, John Snow, 1843. 360 p.

Anti-Slavery Hymns, Designed to Aid the Cause of Human Rights, Containing Original Hymns Written by Abby H. Price, and Others of Hopedale Community, with a Choice Selection from Other Authors. Hopedale, Mass., Community Press, 1844. 36 p.

The Anti-Slavery Intelligencer, and Coloured Man's Advocate. Weekly. Cadiz, Ohio. Volume 1, No. 1. Fourth Month 25, 1835. Edited by Lydia Lewis. William Lewis, Proprietor. Probably only one issue.

The Anti-Slavery Record. Monthly. New York, N. Y. January, 1835–December, 1837. Published by R. G. Williams for the American Anti-Slavery Society.

Anti-Slavery Reporter. Monthly. New York, N. Y. Volume 1. Nos. 1–6. June 1833–November 1833. Published by the American Anti-Slavery Society. Vol. 1. No. 1. A Letter to Thomas Clarkson, by James Cropper; and Prejudice Vincible, by Charles Stuart. June, 1833.
Vol. 1. No. 2. Three Months in Jamaica; Correspondence on the Colonization Society; [etc.]. July, 1833.
Vol. 1. No. 3. Extracts from Clarkson's Thoughts on the Practicability; the Safety, and the Advantages to All Parties Concerned of the Emancipation of the Slaves. August, 1833.
Vol. 1. No. 4. Justice and Expediency; or, Slavery Considered with a View to Its Rightful and Effectual Remedy, Abolition, by John G. Whittier. September, 1833.
Vol. 1. No. 5. Address of the New York City Anti-Slavery Society. October, 1833. [Continued as American Anti-Slavery Reporter].

American Anti-Slavery Reporter. Monthly. New York, N. Y.
Volume 1. Nos. 1–8. January, 1834–August, 1834. Published by the American Anti-Slavery Society.
Vol. 1. No. 1. Review of the Speeches and Proceedings of the Recent Annual Meeting of the American Colonization Society. January, 1834. 1–16 p.
Vol. 1. No. 2. The Moral Character of Slave-holding; Letters from the Southwest to Mr. Tappan; Review of the Colonization Society Concluded. February, 1834. 17–23 p.
Vol. 1. No. 3. Narrative of the Life of Thomas

Cooper, by Isaac T. Hooper; Letter from the Southwest. March, 1834.

Vol. 1. No. 4. The Debt of the American Colonization Society. Anti-Slavery in the Great Valley [Lane Seminary]. Two Letters from the Southwest. April, 1834.

Vol. 1. No. 5. Review of a Colonization Article in "The Literary and Theological Review" [signed: A.L.C.]; Lane Seminary. May, 1834.

Vol. 1. No. 6. Anniversary of the American Anti-Slavery Society. June, 1834.

Vol. 1. No. 7. The Domestic Slave Trade, by David Lee Child. July, 1834.

Vol. 1. No. 8. To the Members of the Society of Friends; St. Domingo, Results of Emancipation. August, 1834.

The Anti-Slavery Reporter. Monthly. London, England. June, 1825–July, 1836. Superseded by the British Emancipation. Published by the London Society for the Mitigation and Abolition of Slavery Throughout the British Dominions.

ANTI-SLAVERY WAFERS

Designed to Further the Cause of Emancipation, by Continually Exposing the Sin of Slavery. [Mottoes, of the size of a large postage stamp, and prepared for pasting on letters, etc., after the fashion of modern Red Cross Seals.]

A man may sell himself to work for another, but he cannot sell himself to be a slave—*Blackstone*.

Those are man-stealers who abduct, keep, sell, or buy slaves. *Grotius, 1650.*

Slaveholding is injustice which no considerations of policy can extenuate. *Bishop Horsley, 1785.*

Man-stealers! The worst of thieves; in comparison of whom, highway robbers and housebreakers are innocent. *Rev. J. Wesley, 1777.*

The children of men are by nature free, and cannot without injustice be either reduced to or held in slavery. *Judge Jay, 1786.*

The Almighty God has no attribute that can take sides with slave-holders. *Thomas Jefferson.*

Anti-Slavery. Be not partakers of other men's sins.

Anti-Slavery. Where the spirit of the Lord is, there is liberty. *2 Cor. iii. 17.*

Anti-Slavery. Woe unto him that buildeth his house by unrighteousness. *Bible.*

There are seven millions of slaves in the world, held by professedly Christian nations.

No Union with Slaveholders.

While men despise *fraud,* and loathe *rapine,* and abhor *blood,* they shall reject with indignation the wild and guilty phantasy, that man can hold property in man. *Brougham.*

All men are created free and equal, and have an inalienable right to liberty. *Fundamental principle of American Government.*

I thought it my duty to expose the monstrous impiety and cruelty, not only of the slave trade, but of slave-holding itself, in whatever form it is found. *Gran. Sharpe, 1787.*

Liberty is the right of every human creature as soon as he breathes the vital air; and no human law can deprive him of that right. *Rev. J. Wesley, 1777.*

The owners of slaves are licensed robbers, and not just proprietors of what they claim. *Mr. Rice, Kentucky, 1780.*

To hold a man in Slavery is to be every day guilty of robbing him of his liberty, or of man-stealing. *Jonathan Edwards, 1791.*

Anti-Slavery. Remember them that are in bonds as bound with them.

Proclaim liberty to the captive, and the opening of the prison doors to them that are bound. *Isaiah, LX, 1.*

Every slaveholder is guilty of reducing human beings to the condition of brutes and things.

Anti-Slavery. In Christian America there is no marriage for the slave.

Is not this the fact that I have chosen, to loose the hands of wickedness, to undo the heavy burdens, and to let the oppressed go free, and that ye break every yoke.

My God what wish can prosper, or what prayer, For those who deal in Cargoes of despair; Or drive a loathsome traffic, gauge and span, And buy the muscles and the bones of man. *Cowper.*

He that holds another man as property, is more detestable than the *robber* and the *assassin* combined. *Thomas Day, 1776.*

Slaves are liable, as chattels, to be sold by the master at his pleasure, and may be taken in execution for debt. *Kentucky law of Descent.*

Time has proved that slavery and education are incompatible. *Cassius M. Clay, 1845.*

All meetings of slaves, at any meeting-house or school, for learning to read or write, shall be deemed unlawful. *Virginia Code, 1819.*

The Christian religion classes manstealers with murderers of fathers and mothers. *Bishop Porteous.*

He that stealeth a man, and selleth him, or if he be found in his hand, he shall surely be put to death. *Exodus, xxi. 16.*

Anti-Slavery. Love worketh no ill to his neighbor, therefore Love is the fulfilling of the Law. *Rom. xiii. 10.*

Pure religion, and undefiled before God and the Father is this, to visit the fatherless and the widows in their affliction, and to keep himself unspotted from the world.

All who fellowship with slaveholders are abettors and promoters of theft, robbery, and concubinage.

In America Slaves are joined to Churches, as members, to enhance their price on the auction-block. Is every Free Church to Have a SLAVE STONE in It?—*Rev. Dr. Duncan of the Free Church.*

Are we then fanatics? Are we Enthusiasts? Because we say to all slaveholders, Do not rob, Do not murder. *Charles James Fox.*

The Negroes are destitute of the Gospel, and ever will be, under the present state of things. *Synod of South Carolina and Georgia, 1834.*

To be a slave, is to be denied the privilege of reading the Gospel of the Son of God. *Elijah P. Lovejoy, 1837.*

To be a slave, is to be shut out from all enjoyment in this world, and all hope in the next. *Elijah P. Lovejoy, 1837.*

Negroes are not free agents, have no personal liberty, no faculty of acquiring property, but are themselves property, at the will of their masters. *Patterson, in Convent, 1787.*

Why ought Slavery to be Abolished? Because it is incurable injustice. *William Pitt.*

Let sorrow bathe each blushing cheek,
Bend piteous o'er the tortured slave,
Whose wrongs compassion cannot speak,
Whose only refuge is the grave. *Mrs. Morton.*

Anti-Slavery. God hath made of one blood all nations. *Acts. xvii. 26.*

Anti-Slavery. Whatsoever ye would that men should do unto you, do ye even so to them. *Matt. vii. 12.*

There is no respect of persons with God. *Rom. ii 11.* In the churches of the U. S. separate pews are generally provided for the Negroes.

Thou shalt love thy neighbor as thyself. *Matthew, xxii. 29.*

Slaves shall be deemed, held, taken, reputed, and judged in law to be chattels personal. *South Carolina Code.*

Have we separated ourselves from our moderate brethren to form an alliance with manstealers. *Rev. H. Grey, Moderator of the Free Church General Assembly for 1846.*

Anti-Slavery. The righteous considereth the cause of the poor; but the wicked regardeth not to know it. *Prov. xxix. 7.*

Shall the throne of iniquity have fellowship with thee, which frameth mischief by a law. *Psalm, xciv. 20.*

Anti-Slavery. Who will stand up for me against the evil-doers, or who will stand up for me against the workers of iniquity. *Psalm, xciv. 16.*

Anti-Slavery. Woe unto him that useth his neighbour's service without wages, and giveth him not for his work. *Jer. xxii. 13.*

Anti-Slavery. Thou shalt not steal. *Ex. xx. 15.*

There are three millions of slaves in the United States *of Christian* (?) America.

Is not every slave a brother or a sister, ought we not then to seek for immediate, universal, and unconditional *emancipation.*

Oppression is the forerunner of revolution, are not Slaveholders then tampering with the internal peace of America.

The slave can do nothing, possess nothing, nor acquire anything but what must belong to his master. *Louisiana Civil Code.*

In America 30,000 slaves are members of the Presbyterian Church, and these men and women have no legal marriage.

Every slave in America is a stolen man or woman —every slaveholder is a man-stealer.

Slaves regard all instruction, addressed especially to themselves, as a device of their masters, to make them more obedient and profitable to them. Such are the workings of slavery.

———

An *Appeal* and Caution to the British Nation; with Proposals for the Immediate or Gradual Emancipation of the Slaves. Indemnity Must Precede Emancipation. By a Member of the Dominican Legislature. London, John Richardson, 1824. 82 p.

Appeal of the Independent Democrats in Congress to the People of the United States: Shall Slavery be Permitted in Nebraska? [Signed by:] S. P. Chase, Chas. Sumner, J. R. Giddings, E. Wade, G. Smith, A. DeWitt. [Washington, 1844.] 8 p.

An *Appeal* on the Subject of Slavery; Addressed to the Members of the New England and New Hampshire Conferences of the Methodist Episcopal Church. Together with a Defence of Said Appeal, in Which Is Shown the Sin of Holding Property in Man. Boston, D. H. Ela, 1835. 48 p. [Signed:] S. W. Wilson, A. D. Merril, LeR. Sunderland, G. Storrs, J. Perkins.

Appeal to the Hearts and Consciences of British Women [on the Subject of Slavery]. Leicester, A. Cockshaw, 1828. 16 p.

The *Appendix:* or, Some Observations on the Expediency of the Petition of the Africans, Living in Boston, &, Lately Presented to the General Assembly of This Province. To Which Is Annexed, the Petition Referred to. Likewise, Thoughts on Slavery. With a Useful Extract from the Massachusetts Spy of January 28, 1773, by Way of an Address to the Members of the Assembly. By a Lover of Constitutional Liberty. Boston, N. E. Printed and Sold by E. Russell [1773]. 15 p.

Appleton, Nathan. Letter to the Hon. Wm. C. Rives, of Virginia, on Slavery and the Union, by Nathan Appleton of Boston, Mass. Boston, J. H. Eastburn, 1860. 17 p.

Appleton, Nathan, and Palfrey, John G. Correspondence Between Nathan Appleton and John G. Palfrey, Intended as a Supplement to Mr. Palfrey's Pamphlet on the Slave Power. Boston, Eastburn's Press, 1846. 20 p. [Palfrey was a Unitarian minister, a historian, professor of sacred literature at Harvard, and owner and editor of the *North American Review*. He was actively opposed to slavery, having freed the slaves in Louisiana which he inherited from his father.]

Appleton, Nathaniel. Considerations on Slavery. In a Letter to a Friend. Boston, Edes and Gill, 1767. 16 p.

Archer, Armstrong. A Compendium of Slavery, as It Exists in the Present Day in the United States of America. To Which Is Prefixed, a Brief View of the Author's Descent from an African King on One Side, and from the Celebrated Indian Chief Powhattan on the Other; in Which He Refers to the Principal Transactions and Negotiations Between This Notable Chief and the English Colony under the Famous Captain Smith, on the Coast of Virginia, in the Year 1608, as Well as to His Still More Illustrious Daughter, the Princess Pocahontas, Who Excited So Much Interest in England. By Armstrong Archer. London, The Author, 1844. 68 p.

Arguments in Support of the Proposed Bill for the Registration of Slaves in the West Indian Colonies; Being a Reply to the Work of Mr. Chalmers, Entitled Proofs and Demonstrations How Much the Projected Registry of Colonial Negroes Is Unfounded and Uncalled For. Extracted from the Philanthropist for Jan., 1817. London, Bensley and Son, 1817. 44 p.

Armistead, Wilson, ed. Anthony Benezet. From the Original Memoir: Revised, with Additions. London, A. W. Bennett, 1859. 144 p.

[Armistead, Wilson, 1819?–1868]. Calumny Refuted by Facts from Liberia; with Extracts from the Inaugural Address of the Coloured President Roberts; an Eloquent Speech of Hilary Teague, a Coloured Senator; and Extracts from a Discourse by H. H. Garnett, a Fugitive Slave, on the Past and Present Condition, and Destiny of the Coloured Race. Presented to the Boston Anti-Slavery Bazaar, of the Coloured Race. Presented to the Boston Anti-Slavery Bazaar, U. S., by the Author of "A Tribute for the Negro." London, C. Gilpin; New York, W. Harned, Anti-Slavery Office; [etc., etc.] 1848. 46 p.

Armistead, Wilson. A Cloud of Witnesses Against Slavery and Oppression. Containing the Acts, Opinions, and Sentiments of Individuals and Societies in All Ages. London, William Tweedie, 1853. 154 p.

Armistead, Wilson. Further Testimonies in Favor of Freedom; a Supplement to "A Cloud of Witnesses" Against Slavery and Oppression, Containing Additional Sentiments and Opinions from All Sources. London, William Tweedie, 1858. 212 p.

[Armistead, Wilson]. The Garland of Freedom; a Collection of Poems, Chiefly Anti-Slavery. Selected from Various Authors by a Friend of the Negro. 3 Vols. London, W. and F. G. Cash, 1853–1854.

Armistead, Wilson. Memoir of Paul Cuffe[e], a Man of Colour. Compiled from Authentic Sources. London, Edmund Fry, 1840. 64 p.

Armistead, Wilson. A Tribute for the Negro; Being a Vindication of the Moral, Intellectual and Religious Capabilities of the Coloured Portion of Mankind with Particular Reference to the African Race. Illustrated by Numerous Biographical Sketches, Facts, Anecdotes, Etc., and Many Superior Portraits and Engravings. Manchester [Eng.], William Irwin, 1848. 564 p.

[Armistead, Wilson]. Five Hundred Thousand Strokes for Freedom. A Series of Anti-Slavery Tracts, of Which Half a Million Are Now First Issued by the Friends of the Negro. London, W. & F. Cash, 1853. 352 p. [This volume consists of the series of 82 tracts published by the Leeds Anti-Slavery Society, for distribution at home and in the United States, as follows:]

No. 1. Brief Definition of Negro Slavery. 4 p.

No. 2. Slavery Described by a Member of Congress. 1 p.

No. 3. Startling Facts Relative to Slavery at the Present Time. 1 p.

No. 4. The Slave-Trade, Its Extent and Horrors. 8 p.

No. 5. Statistics of the Coloured Race. 2 p.

No. 6. Workings of American Slavery as Regards Caste and Prejudice. 4 p.

No. 7. Slavery a System of Inherent Cruelty. 12 p.

No. 8. Slavery Considered in Its Various Relations and Consequences. 28 p.

No. 9. Sales by Auction of Men, Women, and Children. 4 p.

No. 10. The Farewell of a Virginia Slave-Mother to Her Daughter, Sold into Southern Bondage. 4 p.

No. 11. Traffic in Human Affections, with Reflections Thereon. 4 p.

No. 12. Alleged Exaggerations of Slavery Considered. 2 p.

No. 13. The Negro Our Brother Man. 1 p.

No. 14. The Death of the Slave, by Maria Lowell [poem]. 1 p.

No. 15. Auctioneering Advertisements. 1 p.

No. 16. A Slave Auction in a Southern City. 1 p.
No. 17. Sale of Aged Negroes. 1 p.
No. 18. Business Letter from a Slave-Trader. 1 p.
No. 19. Unfavorable Influence of the American Churches on the Progress of Emancipation. 8 p.
No. 20. Expurgated American Literature. Mutilation and Suppression of Works Containing Anti-Slavery Literature. 4 p.
No. 21. Clerical Oppressors. 4 p.
No. 22. Reproof of the American Church, by the Bishop of Oxford. 12 p.
No. 23. Slave-Branding. 4 p.
No. 24. Secrets of the Prison-House. 2 p.
No. 25. Negro Boy Sold for a Watch. 2 p.
No. 26. The Blind Slave Boy. 2 p.
No. 27. Scene on Board a Steam-Boat at Wilmington. 2 p.
No. 28. Kidnapping a Man Out of Slavery into Freedom. 2 p.
No. 29. Man-Stealing and Religion. 2 p.
No. 30. Paradise of Negro Slaves—A Dream, by Dr. Rush. 4 p.
No. 31. Slaveholding Weighted in the Balance of Truth, and Its Comparative Guilt Illustrated. 24 p.
No. 32. The Fugitive Slave Bill, and Its Effects. 24 p.
No. 33. Opinions of American Ministers, on Slavery and the Fugitive Slave Bill. 4 p.
No. 34. Fugitive Slaves: Douglass, Pennington, Wells Brown, Garnett, Bibb, and Others. 12 p.
No. 35. Singular Escapes from Slavery. 8 p.
No. 36. Fugitive Settlements in Canada. 4 p.
No. 37. Prayer for the Negro. 1 p.
No. 38. A Voice from Old England. 1 p.
No. 39. Murderous Treatment of a Slave Girl. 1 p.
No. 40. Plantation Scenes. 1 p.
No. 41. Sale and Separation of a Family. 1 p.
No. 42. Murder of an Infant. 1 p.
No. 43. The Slave-Ship. 4 p.
No. 44. The Englishman's Duty to the Free and the Enslaved American. 18 p.
No. 45. Slavery Hostile to Religion, Teaches Blasphemy, and Is a School for Atheism. 2 p.
No. 46. Appalling Features of Slavery. 2 p.
No. 47. Think of the Slave. 2 p.
No. 48. The Gentlemen Farmers of Virginia Attending Their Cattle Market. 2 p.
No. 49. A Slave Auction in Virginia. 2 p.
No. 50. The Quadroon Girl. 2 p.
No. 51. An Auction Sale of a Young Woman. 4 p.
No. 52. The Christian Slave. 4 p.
No. 53. Tender Mercies of the Domestic Institution. 1 p.
No. 54. Conversation on Slavery between a Lady in Scotland, and a Relative of Hers, Who Had Lately Returned from Baltimore. 1 p.
No. 55. The Bible against Slavery. 1 p.

No. 56. The Order of the Family Required It. 1 p.
No. 57. Song of Humanity. 1 p.
No. 58. The American Slave-Ship. 1 p.
No. 59. Hunting Slaves with Blood-Hounds. 4 p.
No. 60. Tender Mercies of Slavery. 2 p.
No. 61. Slavery Always Diabolical. 2 p.
No. 62. Scene in the Jail at Washington. 2 p.
No. 63. Slaves Happy! 2 p.
No. 64. Sale of Slaves in Virginia. 2 p.
No. 65. The Virginia Slave Crop. 4 p.
No. 66. Voices from Slavery. 4 p.
No. 67. Slaveholding Piety. 1 p.
No. 68. Blasting Influence of Slavery on the Social Circle. 1 p.
No. 69. Dreadful Effects of Irresponsible Power. 1 p.
No. 70. The Slave Trade in Columbia. 1 p.
No. 71. Opinions of Eminent Persons in Various Ages Respecting Slavery and the Slave Trade. 8 p.
No. 72. Confessions of Slaveholders; or of Those Living in the Midst of Slavery. 4 p.
No. 73. A Few Words on Abstinence from Slave Produce. 2 p.
No. 74. Parting of a Slave Mother and Her Son. 2 p.
No. 75. A Contrast. 2 p.
No. 76. Slaveholding Inconsistencies. 2 p.
No. 77. Phoebe Morel. 1 p.
No. 78. The Witnesses. 1 p.
No. 79. Intellect and Capabilities of the Negro Race. 12 p.
No. 80. Results of Immediate Emancipation. 8 p.
No. 81. Who Are Responsible for Slavery? 2 p.
No. 82. To the Friends of Emancipation; an Appeal to Christians of All Denominations. 8 p.

Armitage, Jacob. The State of Ohio vs. Forbes and Armitage, Arrested upon the Requisition of the Government of Ohio, on Charge of Kidnapping Jerry Phinney and Tried Before the Franklin Circuit Court of Kentucky, April 10, 1846. 41 p.

Armstrong, George Dodd. A Discussion on Slaveholding. Three Letters to a Conservative, by George D. Armstrong, D.D., of Virginia. And Three Conservative Replies by C. Van Rensselaer, D.D., of New Jersey. I. On the Scriptural Doctrine of Slaveholding. II. On Emancipation and the Church. III. On the Historical Argument for Slaveholding. Together with Two Rejoiners, on Slaveholding, Schemes of Emancipation, Colonization, etc. Philadelphia, J. M. Wilson, 1858. 137 p.

Arnot, William. The Race for Riches, and Some Pits into Which the Runners Fall; Six Lectures, Applying the Word of God to the Traffic of Men. American Edition. With Preface and Notes by Stephen Colwell. Philadelphia, Lippincott, Grambo & Co., 1853. 181 p.

The Arrest, Trial, and Release of Daniel Webster, a

Fugitive Slave. Correspondence of the Anti-Slavery Standard. Philadelphia, Pennsylvania Anti-Slavery Society, 1859. 31 p.

Arvine, K. Our Duty to the Fugitive Slave; a Discourse Delivered on Sunday, Oct. 6, in West Boylston, Ms., and in Worcester, Dec. 15. Boston, John P. Jewett & Co., 1850. 31 p.

Asher, Jeremiah. Incidents in the Life of Rev. J. Asher, Pastor of Shiloh (Coloured) Baptist Church, Philadelphia, U. S. With an Introduction by Wilson Armistead. London, C. Gilpin, 1850. 80 p.

Ashley, James Monroe. Success of the Calhoun Revolution: The Constitution Changed and Slavery Nationalized by Usurpations of the Supreme Court. Speech of Hon. James M. Ashley, of Ohio. Delivered in the U. S. House of Representatives, May 29, 1860. Washington, D. C., Buell & Blanchard, Printers, 1860. 30 p. [Ashley was prominent in emancipation and reconstruction measures in the House of Representatives.]

Ashley, James Monroe. The Rebellion—Its Causes and Consequences. A Speech Delivered by Hon. J. M. Ashley, at College Hall in the City of Toledo, Tuesday Evening, Nov. 26, 1861. Toledo, Pelton and Waggoner, 1861. 21 p.

Ashley, James Monroe. Speech of Hon. J. M. Ashley, of Ohio, in the House of Representatives, April 11, 1862, on the Bill for the Release of Certain Persons Held to Service or Labor in the District of Columbia. Washington, D. C., Scammell & Co., Printers, 1862. 8 p.

Ashmun, George. Speech of Mr. Geo. Ashmun, of Mass., on the Mexican War. Delivered in the House of Representatives of the U. S., Feb. 4, 1847. Washington, J. & G. S. Gideon, 1847. 16 p.

Ashmun, Jehudi. History of the American Colony in Liberia from December 1821 to 1823. Washington, Way & Gideon, 1826. 42 p.

Association of Friends for Promoting the Abolition of Slavery, and Improving the Condition of the Free People of Color. An Address to the Citizens of the United States on the Subject of Slavery. Philadelphia, Merrihew and Thompson, 1838. 24 p.

Association of Friends for Promoting the Abolition of Slavery, and Improving the Condition of the Free People of Color. An Address to the Society of Friends, on the Subject of American Slavery, by "The Association of Friends for Promoting the Abolition of Slavery," &c. Philadelphia, Merrihew and Thompson, 1842. 8 p.

Association of Friends for Promoting the Abolition of Slavery, and Improving the Condition of the Free People of Color. An Address to the Members of the Society of Friends, by the Association of Friends for Promoting the Abolition of Slavery,

and Improving the Condition of the Free People of Color. Philadelphia, Merrihew and Thompson, 1843. 12 p.

[Association of Liverpool]. Negro Slavery; or, A View of Some of the More Prominent Features of That State of Society, as It Exists in the United States of America and in the Colonies of the West Indies, Especially in Jamaica. London, Richard Taylor, 1823. 92 p.

Atkins, Smith Dykins. Democracy and Dred Scott. Speech Delivered by Smith D. Atkins, Before the Freeport Wide Awakes, at Plymouth Hall, Monday Evening, Aug. 14, 1860. Published by Order of the Joint-Executive Committee of the Freeport Wide Awakes, and the Republican Club. [Freeport, Ill., 1860.] 24 p.

Atkins, Thomas. American Slavery. Just Published: A Reply to the Letter of Bishop Hopkins, of Vermont, on This Important Subject. New York, W. G. Green [n.d.]. 13 p.

[Atkinson, Edward]. Cheap Cotton by Free Labor; by a Cotton Manufacturer. Boston, A. Williams & Co., 1861. 52 p.

Atlee, Edwin Pitt. An Address, Delivered Before the Female Anti-Slavery Society of Philadelphia, in the Session Room of the Second Presbyterian Church . . . in the First Month (January) 1834. By E. P. Atlee, M.D. To Which Is Added an Appendix. Philadelphia, Printed by T. K. Collins & Co., 1834. 27 p. [Atlee, a Philadelphia physician, was a close friend of both Garrison and Lundy.]

Atlee, Edwin Pitt. An Address to the Citizens of Philadelphia, on the Subject of Slavery. Delivered on the 4th of 7th Month (July), A. D. 1833. By Edwin P. Atlee . . . Philadelphia, Pub. by Particular Request; W. P. Gibbons, Printer, 1833. 15 p.

An Attempt to Demonstrate the Practicability of Emancipating the Slaves of the United States of North America, and of Removing Them from the Country, Without Impairing the Right of Private Property, or Subjecting the Nation to a Tax. By a New-England Man. New York, G. & C. Carvil, 1825. 75 p.

Atwater, Horace Cowles. Incidents of a Southern Tour; or, The South, as Seen with Northern Eyes. Boston, Magee, 1857. 120 p.

Atwood, John. The Blessings of Freedom Illustrated, and the Horrors of Slavery Delineated. Boston, Printed for the Author, 1824. 36 p.

Aunt Sally; or, The Cross the Way to Freedom. A Narrative of the Slave-life and Purchase of the Mother of Rev. Isaac Williams, of Detroit, Michigan . . . Cincinnati, American Reform Tract and Book Society, 1862. 216 p.

Authentic and Impartial Narrative of the Tragical

Scene Which Was Witnessed in Southampton County (Virginia) on the 22d of August Last, When Forty-five of Its Inhabitants (Mostly Women and Children) Were Inhumanely Massacred by the Blacks. [Southampton Va.], Warner & West, 1831. 38 p.

An Authentic Report of the Debate in the House of Commons, June the 23rd, 1825, on Mr. Buxton's Motion Relative to the Demolition of the Methodist Chapel and Mission House in Barbadoes, and the Expulsion of Mr. Shrewsbury, a Wesleyan Missionary, from That Island. London, J. Hatchard and Son, 1825. 119 p.

Auxiliary Society of Frederick County, Va. for Colonizing the Free People of Colour in the United States. The Annual Report of the Auxiliary Society of Frederick County, Va., for Colonizing the Free People of Colour in the United States. With an Appendix. Winchester [Va.], The Auxiliary Society, 1820. 40 p.

Aves [Thomas]. Case of the Slave-Child, Med. Report of the Arguments of Counsel, and of the Opinion of the Court, in the Case of Commonwealth vs. Aves: Tried and Determined in the Supreme Judicial Court of Massachusetts. Boston, I. Knapp, 1836. 40 p.

Aydelott, Benjamin Parham. Our Country's Evils and Their Remedy. Cincinnati, George L. Weed, 1843. 60 p. [Aydelott was pastor of Christ Church, Cincinnati, and active in separation movement from slaveholding churches.]

Babington, Churchill. The Influence of Christianity in Promoting the Abolition of Slavery in Europe. A Dissertation Which Obtained the Hulsean Prize for the Year 1845. Cambridge, J. & J. J. Deighton, 1846. 199 p.

Backus, Isaac. Godliness Excludes Slavery. Boston, Printed by Benjamin Edes [1785]. 14 p. [Backus was a noted Baptist champion of religious liberty.]

Bacon, Ephraim. Abstract of a Journal Kept by E. Bacon, Assistant Agent of the United States, to Africa: with an Appendix, Containing Extracts from the North American Review, on the Subject of Africa. Containing Cuts, Showing a Contrast between Two Native Towns. Third Edition. Philadelphia, Clark & Raser, Printers, 1824. 48 p.

Bacon, Ephraim. Abstract of a Journal of E. Bacon, Assistant Agent of the United States, to Africa: with an Appendix, Containing Extracts from Proceedings of the Church Missionary Society in England, for the Years 1819–20. To Which Is Prefixed, an Abstract of the Journal of the Rev. J. B. Cates . . . In an Overland Journey, Performed in Company with Several Natives, in the Months of February, March, and April, 1819. The Whole Showing the Successful Exertions of the British and American Governments, in Repressing the Slave Trade. Philadelphia, S. Potter, & Co., 1821. 06 p.

Bacon, Leonard. A Discourse Preached in the Center Church, in New Haven, August 27, 1828, at the Funeral of Jehudi Ashmun; Colonial Agent of the American Colony of Liberia. With the Address at the Grave by R. R. Gurley. New Haven, Hezekiah Howe, 1828. 36 p. [Bacon was a strong colonizationist and bitter opponent of immediate emancipation. He was equally opposed to slavery and to organized antislavery effort.]

[Bacon, Leonard]. Review of Pamphlets on Slavery and Colonization. First Published in the Quarterly Christian Spectator; for March, 1833. Second Edition. New-Haven, A. H. Maltby; Boston, Pierce and Parker, 1833. 24 p.

Bacon, Leonard. Slavery Discussed in Occasional Essays, from 1833 to 1846. By Leonard Bacon, Pastor of the First Church of New Haven. New York, Baker and Scribner, 1846. 247 p.

Bacon, Thomas. Four Sermons, Preached at the Parish Church of St. Peter, in Talbot County, in the Province of Maryland, by the Rev. Thomas Bacon. Viz. Two Sermons to Black Slaves, and Two Sermons for the Benefit of a Charity Working-School, in the Above Parish, for the Maintenance and Education of Orphans and Poor Children, and Negroes. London, Printed by J. Oliver, 1753. Reprinted at Bath, by R. Cruttwell, 1783. 192 p.

Bacon, Thomas. Four Sermons, upon the Great and Indispensible Duty of All Christian Masters and Mistresses to Bring Up Their Negro Slaves in the Knowledge and Fear of God. Preached at the Parish Church of St. Peter in Talbot County, in the Province of Maryland. By the Rev. Thomas Bacon, Rector of the Said Parish. London, J. Oliver, 1750. 142 p.

Bailey, Nathaniel P. Our Duty as Taught by the Aggressive Nature of Slavery; A Discourse Preached in the Baptist Church, Akron, O., on Thanksgiving Day, Nov. 22, 1855. Akron, Ohio, Teesdale, Elkins & Co., 1855. 24 p.

Bailey, Rufus William. The Issue, Presented in a Series of Letters on Slavery. New York, 1837. 110 p.

[Baird, Robert]. A Letter to Lord Brougham, on the Subject of American Slavery. By an American. London, J. Dinnis, 1835. 44 p.

Baird, Robert. The Progress and Prospects of Christianity in the United States of America; with Remarks on the Subject of Slavery in America, and on the Intercourse Between British and American

Churches. London, Partridge and Oakey, 1851. 78 p.

Baker, James Loring. Slavery. Philadelphia, J. A. Norton, 1860. 19 p.

Baldwin, Ebenezer. Observations on the Physical, Intellectual, and Moral Qualities of Our Colored Population: With Remarks on the Subject of Emancipation and Colonization. By Ebenezer Baldwin. New Haven, L. H. Young, 1834. 52 p.

Baldwin, Roger Sherman. Argument of Roger S. Baldwin, of New Haven, before the Supreme Court of the United States, in the Case of the United States, Appellants, vs. Cinque, and Others, Africans of the Amistad. New York, S. W. Benedict, 1841. 32 p.

Baldwin, Roger Sherman. Speech of Hon. R. S. Baldwin, of Connecticut, in Favor of the Admission of California into the Union, and on the Territorial Bills, and the Bill in Relation to Fugitive Slaves, in Connection with Mr. Bell's Compromise Resolutions. Delivered in Senate of the United States, March 27 and April 3, 1850. Washington [D. C.], Congressional Globe Office, 1850. 20 p.

Baldwin, Roger Sherman. Speech of Hon. R. S. Baldwin, of Connecticut, on the Bill to Establish a Territorial Government in Oregon. Delivered in the Senate of the United States, June 5, 1848. Washington, Congressional Globe Office, 1848. 8 p.

Ball, Charles. Slavery in the United States: A Narrative of the Life and Adventures of Charles Ball, a Black Man, Who Lived Forty Years in Maryland, South Carolina, and Georgia, as a Slave, under Various Masters, and Was One Year in the Navy with Commodore Barney During the Late War. Containing an Account of the Manners and Usages of the Planters and Slaveholders of the South; a Description of the Condition and Treatment of the Slaves; with Observations upon the State of Morals Amongst the Cotton Planters, and the Perils and Sufferings of a Fugitive Slave, Who Twice Escaped from the Cotton Country. New York, John S. Taylor, 1837. 517 p.
Same. Pittsburgh, J. T. Shyrock, 1853. 446 p.

Ballou, Adin. A Discourse on the Subject of American Slavery, Delivered in the First Congregational Meeting House in Mendon, Mass., July 4, 1837. Boston, I. Knapp, 1837. 88 p.

Ballou, Adin. The Voice of Duty. An Address Delivered at the Anti-Slavery Picnic at Westminster, Mass., July 4, 1843. By Adin Ballou. Milford, Mass., Community Press, 1843. 12 p. [Ballou was founder of Hopedale Community, first of the Utopian settlements. He was a close follower of Woolman's philosophy, though not a Quaker.]

Bandinal, James. Some Account of the Trade in Slaves from Africa as Connected with Europe and America; from the Introduction of the Trade into Modern Europe, Down to the Present Time, Especially with Reference to the Efforts Made by the British Government for Its Extinction. London, Longman, Brown, and Co., 1842. 323 p.

Banneker, Benjamin. Copy of a Letter from Benjamin Banneker, to the Secretary of State, with His Answer. Philadelphia, Daniel Lawrence, 1792. 15 p.

Barber, Edward Downing. An Oration, Delivered before the Addison County Anti-Slavery Society, on the Fourth of July, 1836. Middlebury [Vt.], Knapp & Jewett, 1836. 16 p. [Barber, active in antislavery politics, was editor of the Anti-Masonic Republican of Middlebury, Vermont.]

Barber, John Warner. A History of the Amistad Captives, Being a Circumstantial Account of the Capture of the Spanish Schooner Amistad, by the Africans on Board; Their Voyage, and Capture near Long Island, New York; with Biographical Sketches of Each of the Surviving Africans; Also an Account of the Trials Had on Their Case, Before the District and Circuit Courts of the United States, for the District of Connecticut. New Haven, Ct., E. L. & J. W. Barber, 1840. 32 p.

Barham, Joseph Facter. Considerations on the Abolition of Negro Slavery, and the Means of Practically Effecting It. London, James Ridgway, 1823. 85 p.
Third Edition. London, James Ridgway, 1824. 85 p.

Barker, Joseph, Compiler. Interesting Memoirs and Documents Relating to American Slavery, and the Struggle Now Making for Complete Emancipation. London, 1846. 286 p.

Barker, Joseph. Slavery and Civil War; or, The Harper's Ferry Insurrection, with a Review of Discourses on the Subject by Rev. W. H. Furness, J. R. Giddings, and Wendell Phillips. [Philadelphia, 1860.] 24 p.

Barnes, Albert. The Church and Slavery. Philadelphia, Parry & McMillan, 1857. 196 p. [Barnes was a Presbyterian minister of Morristown, New Jersey, and Philadelphia.]

Barnes, Albert. An Inquiry into the Scriptural Views of Slavery. Philadelphia, Perkins & Purves, 1846. 384 p.
Same. Philadelphia, Parry & McMillan, 1855. 384 p.

Barnes, Albert. Our Position. A Sermon Preached Before the General Assembly of the Presbyterian Church in the United States, in the Fourth Presbyterian Church in the City of Washington, May 20, 1852. New York, Newman & Ivison, 1852. 39 p.

Barnes, William. American Slavery. A Sermon, Preached at Hampton, Conn., April 14th, 1843, The Day of the Annual Public Fast. Hartford, Elihu Geer, 1843. 23 p.

Barnett, James. Personal Liberty for All Men. Speech of Hon. James Barnett, of Madison, on the Personal Liberty Bill, in [N. Y.] Assembly, March 14, 1860. Albany, Weed, Parsons and Company, 1860. 7 p.

Barrow, David. Involuntary, Unmerited, Perpetual, Absolute, Hereditary Slavery Examined, on the Principles of Nature, Reason, Justice, Policy, and Scripture. Lexington, D. & C. Bradford, 1808. 50 p.

Barrows, Elijah Porter, Jr. A View of the American Slavery Question. By E. P. Barrows, Jr., Pastor of the First Free Presbyterian Church, New York. New York, John S. Taylor, 1836. 114 p.

Barrows, L. D. The Substance of an Anti-Slavery Address, Delivered on the Annual Fast of 1844, Before the Congregation of the M. E. Church of Nashua and Nashville. Nashua, Murray & Kimball, 1844. 16 p.

Barstow, A. C. Speeches of Hon. A. C. Barstow, Rev. Geo. T. Day, Rev. A. Woodbury, Hon. Thomas Davis, and Resolutions Adopted, at a Meeting of Citizens Held in Providence, R. I., December 2d, 1859, on the Occasion of the Execution of John Brown. Providence, Amsbury & Co., 1860. 32 p.

Bartley, Thomas W. Speech on the Subject of the Law to Organize the Territories of Kansas and Nebraska, Delivered Before a Convention of the People, Held at Mansfield [Ohio], on the 20th of July, 1854. Mansfield, J. Y. Glessner, 1854. 35 p.

Bascom, Henry Bidleman. Methodism and Slavery: with Other Matters in Controversy Between the North and the South; Being a Review of the Manifesto of the Majority, in Reply to the Protest of the Minority, of the Late General Conference of the Methodist E. Church, in the Case of Bishop Andrew. By H. B. Bascom. Frankfort, Ky., Hodges, Todd & Pruett, 1845. 165 p. [This was the Southern protest against exclusion of Bishop Andrew from office because his wife was a slaveholder.]

Bassett, Geo. W. Slavery Examined by the Light of Nature. Sermon Preached by Rev. Geo. W. Bassett, at the Congregational Church, Washington, D. C., Sunday, February 28, 1858. [Washington, D. C., 1858.] 8 p.

Bassett, William. Letter to a Member of the Society of Friends, in Reply to Objections Against Joining Anti-Slavery Societies. Boston, I. Knapp, 1837. 41 p.

Bassett, William. Society of Friends in the United States: Their Views of the Anti-Slavery Question, and Treatment of the People of Colour. Compiled from Original Correspondence. Darlington, J. Wilson, 1840. 26 p.

Bassett, William. Proceedings of the Society of Friends in the Case of William Bassett. Worcester, Mass., Joseph S. Wall, 1840. 24 p.

[Batchelder, Samuel]. The Responsibility of the North in Relation to Slavery. Cambridge, Allen & Farnham, 1856. 15 p.

Bates, Barnabas. Remarks on the Character and Exertions of Elias Hicks, in the Abolition of Slavery, Being an Address Delivered Before the African Benevolent Societies, in Zion's Chapel, New York, March 15, 1830. New York, Mitchell and Davis, 1830. 20 p.

Baxter, Richard. Baxter's Directions to the Slaveholders, Revived. First Printed in London in 1673. To Which is Subjoined a Letter from the Worthy Anthony Benezet, Late of This City, Deceased, to the Celebrated Abbe Reynal, with His Answer, Which Were First Published in the Brussels Gazette, March 7, 1782. Philadelphia, Francis Bailey, 1775. 16 p.

Bayard, James Asheton. Abolition, and the Relation of Races. Speech of Hon. James A. Bayard, of Delaware. Delivered in the Senate of the United States, April 8, 1862. [Washington, D. C., L. Towers & Co., 1862.] 15 p.

Bayly, Thomas Henry. Speech of Mr. Bayly of Accomack, on the Bill to Prevent Citizens of New York from Carrying Slaves Out of This Commonwealth, and to Prevent the Escape of Persons Charged with the Commission of Any Crime, and in Reply to Mr. Scott of Fauquier, Delivered in the House of Delegates of Virginia, on the 25th and 26th of February 1841. Published by Members of the Senate and House of Delegates. Richmond, Printed by Shepherd and Colin, 1841. 38 p.

Beardsley, Rev. W., and Others. Narrative of Facts Respecting Alanson Work, Jas. E. Burr, and Geo. Thompson, Prisoners in the Missouri Penitentiary for the Alleged Crime of Negro Stealing. Prepared by a Committee. Quincy, Quincy Whig Office, 1842. 37 p.

Beecher, Catharine Esther. An Essay on Slavery and Abolitionism, with Reference to the Duty of American Females. By Catherine E. Beecher. Philadelphia, H. Perkins; Boston, Perkins & Marvin, 1837. 152 p.

Beecher, Charles. The Duty of Disobedience to Wicked Laws. A Sermon on the Fugitive Slave Law. New York [etc.], John A. Gray, 1851. 22 p.

Beecher, Edward (President of Illinois College). Narrative of Riots at Alton; in Connection with the Death of Rev. Elijah P. Lovejoy. Alton, George Holton, 1838. 159 p.

Beecher, Henry Ward. A Discourse Delivered at the

Plymouth Church, Brooklyn, N. Y., upon Thanksgiving Day, November 25th, 1847. New York, Cady & Burgess, 1848. 27 p.

Beecher, Henry Ward. Freedom and War. Discourses on Topics Suggested by the Times. Boston, Ticknor and Fields, 1863. 445 p.

Beecher, Henry Ward. Great Speech, Delivered in New York City, on the Conflict of Northern and Southern Theories of Man and Society, Jan. 14, 1855. Rochester, A. Strong & Co., 1855. 16 p.

Beecher, Lyman. The Ballot Box a Remedy for National Crimes. A Sermon Entitled, "The Remedy for Dueling by Rev. Lyman Beecher, D.D., Applied to the Crime of Slaveholding." By One of His Former Parishioners. Boston, I. Knapp, 1838. 36 p.

Belfast, Anti-Slavery Society. To the Christian Churches of the United States. The Address of the Belfast Anti-Slavery Society. Belfast, H. M'Kendrick, 1841. 12 p.

Belsham, William. An Essay on the African Slave Trade. Philadelphia, D. Humphreys, 1790. 15 p. [A strong argument against inferiority of Negroes, by an English historian.]

Beman, Nathan Sidney Smith. Antagonisms in the Moral & Political World: A Discourse Delivered in the First Presbyterian Church, Troy, New York, on Thanksgiving Day, Nov. 18th, 1858. By N. S. S. Beman. Troy, N. Y., A. W. Scribner & Co., 1858. 36 p.

Benedict, George Wyllys. An Oration, Delivered at Burlington, Vt., on the Fourth of July, 1826. Being the Fiftieth Anniversary of American Independence. By George W. Benedict, A.M. Burlington, E. & T. Mills, 1826. 26 p.

[Benezet, Anthony]. Brief Considerations on Slavery, and the Expediency of Its Abolition. With Some Hints on the Means Whereby It May Be Gradually Effected. Recommended to the Serious Attention of All, and Especially to Those Entrusted with the Powers of Legislation. Burlington, Isaac Collins, 1773. 16 p.

Benezet, Anthony. A *Caution* and Warning to Great Britain, and Her Colonies, in a Short Representation of the Calamitous State of the Enslaved Negroes in the British Dominions. Collected from Various Authors, and Submitted to the Serious Consideration of All, More Especially of Those in Power. To Which Is Added, an Extract of a Sermon, Preached by the Bishop of Gloucester, Before the Society for the Propagation of the Gospel. By Anthony Benezet. Philadelphia, Henry W. Miller, 1766. 35 p.
Same. Philadelphia, D. Hall and W. Sellers, 1767. 52 p.
Same. Second Edition. Philadelphia, Printed; London, Reprinted and Sold by James Phillips, 1784. 46 p.

Benezet, Anthony. A Mite Cast into the Treasury; Or, Observations on Slave Keeping. Philadelphia, Printed 1772. 24 p.

[Benezet, Anthony]. Notes on the Slave Trade. [Philadelphia, 1780.] 8 p.

[Benezet, Anthony]. Observations on the Enslaving, Importing, and Purchasing of Negroes; with Some Advice Thereon, Extracted from the Epistle of the Yearly Meeting of the People Called Quakers, Held in London in the Year 1748.
Second Edition, Germantown, Christopher Sower, 1760. 16 p.

[Benezet, Anthony]. The Potent Enemies of America Laid Open: Being Some Account of the Baneful Effects Attending the Use of Distilled Spirituous Liquors and the Slavery of the Negroes. [Signed:] A Lover of Mankind. Philadelphia, Joseph Crukshank, 1774. 48 p.

[Benezet, Anthony]. Serious Reflections Affectionately Recommended to the Well-Disposed of Every Religious Denomination, Particularly Those Who Mourn and Lament on Account of the Calamities Which Attend Us; and the Insensibility That So Generally Prevails. [Philadelphia, 1780?] 4 p.

[Benezet, Anthony]. Serious Considerations on Several Important Subjects; Viz. on War and Its Inconsistency with the Gospel: Observations on Slavery. And Remarks on the Nature and Bad Effects of Spirituous Liquors. Philadelphia, Printed by J. Crukshank, 1778. 48 p.

[Benezet, Anthony]. A Short Account of That Part of Africa, Inhabited by the Negroes; with Respect to the Fertility of the Country; the Good Disposition of Many of the Natives, and the Manner by Which the Slave Trade is Carried On. Extracted from Several Authors, in Order to Shew the Iniquity of that Trade, and the Falsity of the Arguments Usually Advanced in Its Vindication. With a Quotation from George Wallis's System of the Laws, &c. and a Large Extract from a Pamphlet, Lately Published in London, on the Subject of the Slave Trade. Philadelphia, W. Dunlap, 1762. 56 p.

[Benezet, Anthony]. A Short Account of That Part of Africa, Inhabited by the Negroes. With Respect to the Fertility of the Country; the Good Disposition of Many of the Natives, and the Manner by Which the Slave Trade Is Carried On. Extracted from Divers Authors, in Order to Shew the Iniquity of That Trade, and the Falsity of the Arguments Usually Advanced in Its Vindication. With Quotations from the Writings of Several Persons of Note, Viz. George Wallis, Francis Hutcheson, and James Foster, and a Large Extract from a Pamphlet, Lately Published in London, on the Subject of the Slave Trade.
Second Edition, with Large Additions and Amend-

ments. Philadelphia, Printed by W. Dunlap, 1762. 80 p.

Third Edition. Printed by W. Dunlap, Philadelphia, in the Year 1762; London, Reprinted by W. Baker and J. W. Galabin, 1768. 80 p.

[Benezet, Anthony]. Short Observations on Slavery, Introductory to Some Extracts from the Writing of Abbé Raynal, on That Important Subject. [Philadelphia, Enoch Story, 1785.] 12 p.

Benezet, Anthony. Some Historical Account of Guinea, Its Situation, Produce, and the General Disposition of Its Inhabitants. With an Inquiry into the Rise and Progress of the Slave-Trade, Its Nature, and Lamentable Effects. Also a Republication of the Sentiments of Several Authors of Note, on This Interesting Subject; Particularly an Extract of a Treatise by Granville Sharp. Philadelphia, J. Crukshank, 1771. 144 + 53 p.

Benezet, Anthony. Views of American Slavery, Taken a Century Ago. Anthony Benezet, John Wesley. Philadelphia, Published by the Association of Friends for the Diffusion of Religious and Useful Knowledge, 1858. 138 p.

Bennett, Henry. Kansas Must Be Free! The Political Effects of Slavery. Speech of Hon. Henry Bennett, of New York, on the Bill for the Admission of Kansas as a Free State. Delivered in the House of Representatives, June 30, 1856. Philadelphia, Morning Times, 1856. 16 p.

Same. Washington, D. C., Buell and Blanchard, 1856. 13 p.

Betker, John P. The M. E. Church and Slavery, as Described by Revs. H. Mattison, W. Hosmer, E. Bowen, D.D., D. DeVinne, and J. D. Long, with a Bible View of the Whole Subject. By Rev. John P. Betker. Syracuse, N. Y., S. Lee, 1859. 32 p.

Bevan, William. The Moral Influence of Slavery. The Substance of a Paper Presented to the Anti-Slavery Convention, Held in London, June, 1840. London, Thomas Ward and Co., 1840. 31 p.

Bibb, Henry. Narrative of the Life and Adventures of Henry Bibb, an American Slave, Written by Himself, with an Introduction by Lucius C. Matlack. New York, the Author, 1849. 264 p.

Bidlake, John. Slave Trade. A Sermon, Preached at Stonehouse Chapel, on Sunday, December 28, 1788. By John Bidlake, A.B. of Christ Church, Oxford. Second Edition. Plymouth, M. Haydon and Son, 1789. 32 p.

Bigelow, John. Jamaica in 1850; or, the Effects of 16 Years of Freedom on a Slave Colony. New York, George P. Putnam, 1851. 214 p.

Bingham, John Armor. The Assault upon Senator Sumner, a Crime Against the People. Speech of Hon. John A. Bingham, of Ohio, in the House of Representatives, July 9, 1856. Washington, D. C., Buell & Blanchard, 1856. 8 p.

Bingham, John Armor. Bill and Report of John A. Bingham, and Vote on Its Passage, Repealing the Territorial New Mexican Laws Establishing Slavery and Authorizing Employers to Whip "White Persons" and Others in Their Employment, and Denying Them Redress in the Courts. [Washington, D. C., 1858.] 7 p.

Bingham, John A. Kansas Contested Election. Speech of Hon. J. A. Bingham, of Ohio, in the House of Representatives, March 6, 1856. Washington, [D. C.], Buell & Blanchard, 1856. 12 p.

Bingham, John Armor. The Lecompton Conspiracy. Speech of Hon. John A. Bingham, of Ohio. Delivered in the House of Representatives, January 25, 1858. Washington, D. C., Buell & Blanchard, 1858. 8 p.

Bingham, John Armor. Speech of the Hon. John A. Bingham, of Ohio, in Reply to Hon. John J. Crittenden, of Kentucky, in the House of Representatives, April 11, 1862, on the Bill to Emancipate Slaves, and to Prohibit Slavery and Perpetuate Liberty Forever in the National Capital. [Washington, D. C.] Scammell & Co., Printers, 1862. 8 p.

Bingham, Kinsley Scott. Speech of Mr. Bingham, of Michigan, on the Admission of California. Delivered in the House of Representatives, June 4, 1850. Washington [D. C.], Congressional Globe Office, 1850. 22 p.

Birbeck, Morris. An Appeal to the People of Illinois, on the Question of a Convention. Shawneetown, C. Jones, 1823. 25 p.

Birney, James G. Address to the Ladies of Ohio. [Cincinnati, 1835.] 16 p.

Birney, James Gillespie. The American Churches the Bulwarks of American Slavery. By an American. London, Ward & Co., 1840. 40 p.

Same. Second Edition. Newburyport, Charles Whipple, 1842. 44 p.

Same. Third (Second) American Edition, Enlarged by an Appendix by Another Hand. Newburyport, Charles Whipple, 1842. 48 p.

Same. Enlarged by a Supplement [by William Goodell]. Boston, 1843. 48 p.

Same. Concord, N. H., Parker Pillsbury, 1885. 48 p.

Birney, James Gillespie. Correspondence between James G. Birney, of Kentucky, and Several Individuals of the Society of Friends. Haverhill, Essex Gazette Office, 1835. 8 p.

Birney, James Gillespie. Correspondence, between the Hon. F. H. Elmore, One of the South Carolina Delegation in Congress, and James G. Birney, One of the Secretaries of the American Anti-Slavery Society. New York, American Anti-Slavery Society, 1838. 68 p. [The Anti-Slavery Examiner, No. 8.]

Birney, James Gillespie. Examination of the Decision of the Supreme Court of the United States, in the Case of Strader, Gorman and Armstrong vs. Christopher Graham, Delivered at Its December Term, 1850: Concluding with an Address to the Free Colored People, Advising Them to Move to Liberia. Cincinnati, Truman & Spofford, Publishers, 1852. 46 p.

[Birney, James Gillespie]. Headlands in the Life of Henry Clay. No. 1 from 1797 to 1827. Boston, Leavitt & Alden [1844]. 8 p. [From the Emancipator, September 17, 1844. This was a *Liberty Tract*. Remainder of the *Headlands,* etc., may be found in *Emancipator*.]

Birney, James Gillespie. Letter on Colonization, Addressed to the Rev. Thornton J. Mills, Corresponding Secretary of the Kentucky Colonization Society. New York, Office of the Anti-Slavery Reporter, 1834. 46 p. [First published in *Emancipator-Extra*, August 26, 1834.]
Same. Boston, Garrison & Knapp, 1834. 46 p.
Same. New York, American Anti-Slavery Society, 1838. 46 p.

Birney, James Gillespie. A Letter on the Political Obligations of Abolitionists, by James G. Birney: With a Reply by William Lloyd Garrison. [First published in *Emancipator*.] Boston, Dow & Jackson, Printers, 1839. 36 p.

Birney, James G. Letters to Ministers and Elders on the Sin of Holding Slaves, and the Duty of Immediate Emancipation. By James G. Birney. [New York, S. W. Benedict & Co., 1834.] 18 p.
Same. [Published as:] Mr. Birney's Second Letter. To the Ministers and Elders of the Presbyterian Church in Kentucky. [n.p., 1834.] 16 p.

[Birney, James G.]. Liberian Colonization; or, Reasons Why the Free Colored People Should Remove to Liberia; by an Abolitionist and Colonizationist. New York, John A. Gray, 1857. 36 p.

Birney, James Gillespie. Sinfulness of Slaveholding in All Circumstances; Tested by Reason and Scripture. Detroit, Charles Willcox, 1846. 60 p.

Bishop, Joel Prentiss. Secession and Slavery: or, The Effect of Secession on the Relation of the United States to the Seceded States and to Slavery Therein; Considered as a Question of Constitutional Law, Chiefly under Authority of Decisions of the Supreme Court. By Joel Prentiss Bishop. Boston, 1863. 108 p.

Bissell, William Henry. The Slave Question. Speech of Mr. William H. Bissell, of Illinois, in the House of Representatives, Thursday, February 21, 1850, in Committee of the Whole on the State of the Union, [etc.]. [Washington, D. C.] Buell & Blanchard [1850]. 8 p.

Bittinger, Joseph Baugher. A Plea for Humanity. A Sermon Preached in the Euclid Street Presbyterian Church, Cleveland, Ohio. Cleveland, Medall, Cowles & Co., 1854. 28 p.

Blackstone Massachusetts Chronicle. Weekly. Blackstone, Mass. February 26–September 2, 1848. Edited by Oliver Johnson.

Blagden, G. W. Remarks, and a Discourse on Slavery. Boston, Ticknor, Reed & Fields, 1854. 30 p.

Blake, Harrison Gray. Slavery in the District. Speech of Hon. H. G. Blake, of Ohio, Delivered in the House of Representatives, April 11, 1862, on the Bill for the Release of Certain Persons Held to Service or Labor in the District of Columbia. [Washington, D. C., Scammell & Co., 1862.] 8, 4 p.

Blanchard, Jonathan. A Debate on Slavery: Held in the City of Cincinnati, on the First, Second, Third, and Sixth Days of October, 1845, upon the Question: Is Slavery in Itself Sinful, and the Relation between Master and Slave, a Sinful Relation? Affirmative: Rev. J. Blanchard. Negative: N. L. Rice. Cincinnati, W. H. Moore & Co.; New York, M. H. Newman, 1846. 482 p.

Blanchard, Jonathan. Sermon on Slave-Holding: Preached by Appointment, before the Synod of Cincinnati, at Their Late Stated Meeting at Mount Pleasant, Ohio, October 20th, 1841. By Rev. J. Blanchard, Cincinnati, 1842. 8 p.

Blanchard, Joshua Pollard. Principles of the Revolution: Showing the Perversion of Them and the Consequent Failure of Their Accomplishment. Boston, Damrell & Moore, 1855. 24 p.

Bleby, Henry. Speech of Rev. Henry Bleby, Missionary from Barbadoes, on the Results of Emancipation in the British W. I. Colonies. Delivered at the Celebration of the Massachusetts Anti-Slavery Society, Held at Island Grove, Abington, July 31st, 1858. Boston, R. F. Wallcut, 1858. 36 p.

Bliss, Philemon. Citizenship: State Citizens, General Citizens. Speech of Hon. Philemon Bliss, of Ohio. Delivered in the House of Representatives, January 7, 1858. Washington, D. C., Buell & Blanchard, 1858. 8 p.

Bliss, Philemon. Complaints of the Extensionists— Their Falsity. Speech of Hon. Philemon Bliss, of Ohio, in the House of Representatives, May 21, 1856. [n.p., 1856.] 16 p.

Bliss, Philemon. Congress Must Govern Its Territory —Man Not Property. Speech of Hon. Philemon Bliss, of Ohio. In the House of Representatives, January 15, 1857. Washington, D. C., Buell & Blanchard [1857]. 8 p.

Bliss, Philemon. The Federal Judiciary. Speech of Hon. Philemon Bliss, of Ohio, in the United States House of Representatives, February 7, 1859. [n.p., n.d.] 8 p.

Bliss, Philemon. Success of the Absolutists. Their Idealism; What and Whence Is It? Speech of Hon.

Philemon Bliss, of Ohio, in the House of Representatives, May 24, 1859. Washington, D. C., Buell & Blanchard, 1858. 15 p.

[Blunt, Joseph]. An Examination of the Expediency and Constitutionality of Prohibiting Slavery in the State of Missouri. By Marcus [pseud.] New York, C. Wiley & Co., 1819. 22 p.

Boardman, Henry A. The American Union: A Discourse Delivered on Thursday, December 12, 1850, the Day of the Annual Thanksgiving in Pennsylvania, and Reported on Thursday, December 19, in the Tenth Presbyterian Church, Philadelphia. Philadelphia, Lippincott, Grambo & Co., 1851. 56 p.

Booth, Abraham. Commerce in the Human Species, and the Enslaving of Innocent Persons, Inimical to the Laws of Moses, and the Gospel of Christ. A Sermon, Preached in Little Prescot Street, Goodman's Fields, London, Jan. 29, 1792. By Abraham Booth, A.M. Pastor of a Baptist Church. London, Printed; Philadelphia, Re-Printed and Sold by Daniel Lawrence, 1792. 40 p.
Same. Third Edition. London, L. Wayland, 1792. 24 p.

Booth, Sherman M. Unconstitutionality of the Fugitive Act. Argument of Byron Paine, Esq. and Opinion of Hon. A. D. Smith, Associate Justice of the Supreme Court of the State of Wisconsin. Habeas Corpus Trial. Before Justice Smith. In the Matter of the Petition of Sherman M. Booth for a Writ of Habeas Corpus, and to Be Discharged from Imprisonment. [Milwaukee ? 1854 ?] 35 p.

Boreas, pseud. *See* George Cabot.

Boston Citizens. Address of the Committee Appointed by a Public Meeting, Held at Faneuil Hall, September 24, 1846, for the Purpose of Considering the Recent Case of Kidnapping from Our Soil, and of Taking Measures to Prevent the Recurrence of Similar Outrages. With an Appendix. Boston, White & Potter, Printers, 1846. 42 p.

Boston Citizens. A Memorial to the Congress of the United States, on the Subject of Restraining the Increase of Slavery in New States to Be Admitted into the Union. Prepared in Pursuance of a Vote of the Inhabitants of Boston and Its Vicinity, Assembled at the State House, on the Third of December, A.D. 1819. Boston, Sewell Phelps, 1819. 22 p. [Submitted Dec. 15, 1819, by a committee consisting of Daniel Webster, George Blake, Josiah Quincy, James T. Austin, and John Gallison.]

Boston Constitutional Meeting, 1850. Proceedings of the Constitutional Meeting at Faneuil Hall, November 26, 1850. Boston, Beals & Greene, 1850. 46 p.

Boston. Convention of Delegates on Proposed Annexation of Texas, 1845. Proceedings of a Convention of Delegates, Chosen by the People of Massachusetts, without Distinction of Party, and Assembled at Faneuil Hall, in the City of Boston, on Wednesday, the 29th Day of January, A.D. 1845, to Take into Consideration the Proposed Annexation of Texas to the United States. Pub. by Order of the Convention. Boston, Eastburn's Press, 1845. 18 p.

Boston Female Anti-Slavery Society. Right and Wrong in Boston. Report of the Boston Female Anti-Slavery Society; with a Concise Statement of Events Previous and Subsequent to the Annual Meeting of 1835. Boston, Boston Female Anti-Slavery Society, 1836. 108 p.

Boston Female Anti-Slavery Society. Right and Wrong in Boston, in 1836. Annual Report of the Boston Female Anti-Slavery Society; Being a Concise History of the Cases of the Slave Child, Med, and of the Women Demanded as Slaves of the Supreme Judicial Court of Massachusetts, with All the Other Proceedings of the Society. Boston, Isaac Knapp, 1836. 90 p.

Boston Female Anti-Slavery Society. Right and Wrong in Boston. Annual Report of the Boston Female Anti-Slavery Society, with a Sketch of the Obstacles Thrown in the Way of Emancipation by Certain Clerical Abolitionists and Advocates for the Subjection of Woman, in 1837. Boston, Isaac Knapp, 1837. 120 p.

Boston Female Anti-Slavery Society. Right and Wrong in the Anti-Slavery Societies. Seventh Annual Report of the Boston Female Anti-Slavery Society. Presented October 14, 1840. Boston, Isaac Knapp, 1840. 36 p.

Boston Female Anti-Slavery Society. Eighth Annual Report of the Boston Female Anti-Slavery Society. Presented October 13, 1841. Boston, Published by the Society, 1841. 24 p.

Boston Female Anti-Slavery Society. Ten Years of Experience. Ninth Annual Report of the Boston Female Anti-Slavery Society. Presented Oct. 12, 1842. Boston, Oliver Johnson, 1842. 47 p.

Boston Female Anti-Slavery Society. Eleventh Annual Report of the Boston Female Anti-Slavery Society. Adopted October 9, 1844. New York, Office of the American Anti-Slavery Society, W. S. Dorr, Printer [1844]. 48 p.

Boston. Garrison Meeting, 1846. Proceedings of a Crowded Meeting of the Colored Population of Boston, Assembled the 15th July, 1846, for the Purpose of Bidding Farewell to William Lloyd Garrison, on His Departure for England: With His Speech on the Occasion. Dublin, Webb and Chapman, 1846. 16 p.

Boston. School Board Committee. Report of a Special Committee of the Grammar School Board, Presented August 29, 1849, on the Petition of Sundry Colored Persons, Praying for the Abolition of the Smith School; with an Appendix. Boston, J. H. Eastburn, 1849. 71 p.

Boston. School Board Committee. Report to the Primary School Committee, June 15, 1846, on the Petition of Sundry Colored Persons, for the Abolition of the Schools for Colored Children. With the City Solicitor's Opinion. Boston, J. H. Eastburn, 1846. 38 p.

Boston. School Board Committee. Report of the Minority of the Committee of the Primary School Board, on the Caste Schools of the City of Boston; with Some Remarks on the City Solicitor's Opinion. Boston, A. J. Wright, 1846. 36 p.

Boston Memorial to Congress. A Memorial to the Congress of the United States on the Subject of Restraining the Increase of Slavery in the New States to Be Admitted to the Union, Prepared in Pursuance of a Vote of the Inhabitants of Boston and Its Vicinity, Assembled at the State House, on the Third of December, A.D. 1819. Boston, Sewell Phelps, 1819. 22 p.

The Boston Mob of "Gentlemen of Property and Standing." Proceedings of the Anti-Slavery Meeting Held in Stacy Hall, Boston, on the Twentieth Anniversary of the Mob of October 21, 1835. Boston, R. F. Wallcut, 1855. 76 p.

The *Boston* Slave Riot and Trial of Anthony Burns. Containing the Report of the Faneuil Hall Meeting; the Murder of Batchelder; Theodore Parker's Lesson for the Day; Speeches of Counsel on Both Sides, Corrected by Themselves; a Verbatim Report of Judge Loring's Decision; and Detailed Account of the Embarkation. Boston, Fetridge and Company, 1854. 86 p.

[Boston Vigilance Committee]. Address of the Committee Appointed by a Public Meeting, Held at Faneuil Hall, September 24, 1846, for the Purpose of Considering the Recent Case of Kidnapping from Our Soil, and of Taking Measures to Prevent the Recurrence of Similar Outrages. Boston, White & Potter, 1846. 42 p.

Boston Young Men's Anti-Slavery Association for the Diffusion of Truth. Constitution of the Boston Young Men's Anti-Slavery Association for the Diffusion of Truth. Together with a List of Its Officers and Members. Boston, Garrison and Knapp, 1833. 12 p.

[Bourne, George]. Presbyter. An Address to the Presbyterian Church Enforcing the Duty of Excluding All Slaveholders from the "Communion of Saints," New York, April 16, 1832. New York, 1833. 16 p.

Bourne, George. The Book and Slavery Irreconcilable. With Animadversions upon Dr. Smith's Philosophy. By George Bourne. Philadelphia, J. M. Sanderson & Co., 1816. 141 p.

[Bourne, George]. A Condensed Anti-Slavery Bible Argument; By a Citizen of Virginia. New York, Printed by S. W. Benedict, 1845. 91 p.

Bourne, George. Man-Stealing and Slavery Denounced by the Presbyterian and Methodist Churches. Together with an Address to All the Churches. By Rev. George Bourne. Boston, Garrison & Knapp, 1834. 19 p.

Bourne, George. Picture of Slavery in the United States of America. Middletown, Conn., Edwin Hunt, 1834. 227 p.
Same. Boston, Isaac Knapp, 1838. 227 p.

[Bourne, George]. Slavery Illustrated in Its Effects upon Woman and Domestic Society. Boston, I. Knapp, 1837. 127 p. [Sometimes attributed, but wrongly, to Angelina E. Grimké.]

Bouton, Nathaniel. The Good Land in Which We Live: A Discourse Preached at Concord, N. H. on the Day of Public Thanksgiving, Nov. 28, 1850. Concord, McFarland & Jenks, 1850. 30 p.

Boutwell, George Sewall. Emancipation: Its Justice, Expediency and Necessity, as the Means of Securing a Speedy and Permanent Peace. An Address Delivered by Hon. George S. Boutwell, in Tremont Temple, Boston, under the Auspices of the Emancipation League, December 16, 1861. [Boston, Wright & Potter, Printers, 1861.] 12 p.

Bowditch, William Ingersoll. Cass and Taylor on the Slavery Question. Boston, Damrell & Moore, 1848. 23 p. [Bowditch was a physician; strongly antislavery and active in aid to fugitives.]

Bowditch, William Ingersoll. The Anti-Slavery Reform, Its Principle and Method. Boston, Robert F. Wallcut, 1850. 19 p.

[Bowditch, William Ingersoll]. God or Our Country. Review of the Rev. Dr. Putnam's Discourse, Delivered on Fast Day, Entitled God and Our Country. Boston, I. R. Butts, 1847. 23 p.

Bowditch, William I. The Rendition of Anthony Burns. Boston, Robert F. Wallcut, 1854. 40 p.

Bowditch, William I. Slavery and the Constitution. Boston, Robert F. Wallcut, 1849. 156 p.

Bowen, Elias. Slavery in the Methodist Episcopal Church. Auburn, William J. Moses, Printer, 1859. 317 p.

Bowen, Nathaniel. A Pastoral Letter, on the Religious Instruction of the Slaves of Members of the Protestant Episcopal Church in the State of South Carolina, Prepared at the Request of the Convention of the Churches of the Diocese. To Which Is Appended a Table of Scripture Lessons, Prepared in Conformity with the Resolution of the Convention. By Nathaniel Bowen, D.D., Bishop of the Pro. Epis. Church in South Carolina. Charleston, A. E. Miller, 1835. 30 p.

Boyle, James. A Letter from James Boyle to William

Lloyd Garrison, Respecting the Clerical Appeal, Sectarianism, True Holiness, etc. Also, Lines on Christian Rest, by Mr. Garrison. Boston, Isaac Knapp, 1838. 43 p.

Bradburn, Miss E. W. Pity Poor Africa: A Dialogue for Children. In Three Parts. Second Edition. London, John Mason, 1831. 48 p.

Bradburn, Samuel. An Address to the People Called Methodists; Concerning the Evil of Encouraging the Slave Trade. Manchester, T. Harper, 1792. 24 p.

Bradburn, Samuel. An Address to the People Called Methodists; Concerning the Criminality of Encouraging Slavery. Fifth Edition. London, M. Gurney. 16 p.

Branagan, Thomas. Avenia, or a Tragical Poem, on the Oppression of the Human Species; and Infringement on the Rights of Man. In Five Books. With Notes Explanatory and Miscellaneous. Written in Imitation of Homer's Iliad. A New Ed. To Which Is Added the Constitution of the State of Pennsylvania. Philadelphia, Silas Engles, 1805. 358 p.

Same. Philadelphia, J. Cline, 1810. 324 p.

Branagan, Thomas. The Guardian Genius of the Federal Union: or, Patriotic Admonitions on the Signs of the Times, in Relation to the Evil Spirit of Party, Arising from the Root of All Our Evils, Human Slavery. Being the First Part of the Beauties of Philanthropy. By a Philanthropist. New York, the Author, 1839. 104, 288 p.

Branagan, Thomas. The Penitential Tyrant: Or, The Slave Trader Reformed: A Pathetic Poem in Four Cantos. Second Edition. New York, Samuel Wood, 1807. 290 p.

Branagan, Thomas. A Preliminary Essay, on the Oppression of the Exiled Sons of Africa. Consisting of Animadversions on the Impolicy and Barbarity of the Deleterious Commerce and Subsequent Slavery of the Human Species; to Which Is Added, a Desultory Letter Written to Napoleon Bonaparte, Anno Domini, 1801. By Thomas Branagan, Late Slave Trader from Africa. Philadelphia, John W. Scott, 1804. 282 p.

Branagan, Thomas. Serious Remonstrances, Addressed to the Citizens of the Northern States, and Their Representatives: Being an Appeal to Their Natural Feelings & Common Sense: Consisting of Speculations and Animadversions, on the Recent Revival of the Slave Trade, in the American Republic: with an Investigation Relative to the Consequent Evils Resulting to the Citizens of the Northern States from That Event. Interspersed with a Simplified Plan for Colonizing the Free Negroes of the North, in Conjunction with Those Who Have, or May Emigrate from the Southern States, in a Distant Part of the National Territory; Considered as the Only Possible Means of Avoiding the Deleterious Evils Attendant on Slavery in a Republic. By Thomas Branagan. Philadelphia, Thomas T. Stiles, 1805. 133 p.

Breckinridge, Robert Jefferson. An Address Delivered before the Colonization Society of Kentucky, at Frankfort, on the 6th Day of January, 1831. By Robert J. Breckinridge. Frankfort, K., A. G. Hodges, Printer, 1831. 24 p.

Breckinridge, Robert Jefferson. Speech of Robert J. Breckinridge, Delivered in the Courthouse Yard at Lexington, Ky., on the 12th Day of October, 1840, in Reply to "The Speech of Robert Wickliffe, Delivered in the Court-House in Lexington, on the 10th Day of August, 1840, upon the Occasion of Resigning His Seat as Senator from the County of Fayette"; and in Defence of His Personal Character, His Political Principles and His Religious Connexions: More Particularly in Regard to the Questions of the Power of the Legislature on the Subject of Slavery, the Importation of Slaves, of Abolitionism, of British Influence, of Religious Liberty, etc. Second Edition. Baltimore, R. J. Matchett, 1841. 32 p.

Brief Considerations on Slavery, and the Expediency of Its Abolition. With Some Hints on the Means Whereby It May Be Gradually Effected. Recommended to the Serious Attention of All, and Especially of Those Entrusted with the Powers of Legislation. Burlington, Isaac Collins, 1783. 16 p.

Brisbane, William H. Slaveholding Examined in the Light of the Holy Bible. Philadelphia, William Harned, 1847. 222 p.

Same. New York, American and Foreign Anti-Slavery Society, 1849. 222 p.

Same. Philadelphia [U. S. Job Printing Office] 1847. 222 p.

Brisbane, William Henry. Speech of the Rev. Wm. H. Brisbane, Lately a Slaveholder in South Carolina; Containing an Account of the Change of His Views on the Subject of Slavery. Delivered before the Ladies' Anti-Slavery Society of Cincinnati, Feb. 12, 1840. Hartford, S. S. Cowles, 1840. 12 p.

Brissot de Warville, Jaques Pierre. An Oration, upon the Necessity of Establishing at Paris, a Society to Cooperate with Those of America and London, Toward the Abolition of the Slave Trade and Slavery of the Negroes. Delivered the 19th of February, 1788, in a Society of a Few Friends, Assembled at Paris, at the Request of the Committee of London. Philadelphia, Francis Bailey, 1788. 159 p.

Bristol and Clifton Ladies' Anti-Slavery Society, Bristol, Eng. Statements Respecting the American Abolitionists; by Their Opponents and Their

Friends: Indicating the Present Struggle between Slavery and Freedom in the United States of America. Comp. by the Bristol and Clifton Ladies' Anti-Slavery Society. Dublin, Webb and Chapman, 1852. 24 p.

British and Foreign Anti-Slavery Society, *London*. American Slavery. Address of the Committee of the British and Foreign Anti-Slavery Society to the Moderator, Office Bearers, and Members of the General Assembly of the Free Church of Scotland. [London, 1846.] 12 p.

British and Foreign Anti-Slavery Society, *London*. The Crisis in the United States [Address of the Committee of the British and Foreign Anti-Slavery Society] London, 1862. 4 p.

British and Foreign Anti-Slavery Society. (Invitation to a General Conference in London to Commence on June 12, 1840 *in re* Slave Trade. John H. Tredgold, Secretary.)

British and Foreign Anti-Slavery Society, *London*. Slavery and the Internal Slave Trade in the United States of North America; Being Replies to Questions Transmitted by the Committee of the British and Foreign Anti-Slavery Society, for the Abolition of Slavery and the Slave Trade Throughout the World. Presented to the General Anti-Slavery Society, for the Abolition of Slavery and the Slave Trade Throughout the World. Presented to the General Anti-Slavery Convention, Held in London, June, 1840. By the Executive Committee of the American Anti-Slavery Society. London, T. Ward and Co., 1841. 280 p.

Broad, Amos, Defendant. The Trial of Amos Broad and His Wife, on Three Several Indictments for Assaulting and Beating Betty, a Slave, and Her Little Female Child Sarah, Aged Three Years. Had at the Court of Special Sessions of the Peace, Held in and for the City and County of New York, at the City Hall, of the Said City, on Tuesday, the 28th Day of February, 1809. New York, H. C. Southwick, 1809. 31 p.

Broadway Tabernacle Anti-Slavery Society. Proceedings of a Meeting to Form the Broadway Tabernacle Anti-Slavery Society, with the Constitution, etc., and Address to the Church. New York, W. S. Dorr, 1838. 42 p.

Brooke, Samuel. The Slave-Holder's Religion. Cincinnati, Sparhawk and Lytle, 1845. 47 p.

Brooke, Samuel. Slavery, and the Slaveholder's Religion; as Opposed to Christianity. Cincinnati, the Author, 1846. 72 p.

Brooks, Jehiel, Compiler. Fugitive Slave Laws; a Compilation of the Laws of the United States and of States in Relation to Fugitives from Labor, with the Clauses of the Constitution of the United States Involved in the Execution of the Same. Washington, Taylor & Maury, 1860. 32 p.

Brown, Benjamin Gratz. Speech of the Hon. B. Gratz Brown, of St. Louis, on the Subject of Gradual Emancipation in Missouri; Delivered in the House of Representatives [Missouri] February 12, 1857. St. Louis, Missouri, Democrat Book and Job Office, 1857. 26 p. [Brown was a lawyer, editor of the Free Soil-Republican *Missouri Democrat,* and governor of Missouri. He was a native of Kentucky.]

Brown, Charles. Speech of Charles Brown, of Pennsylvania, on Abolition and Slavery: Delivered in the House of Representatives, February 3 and 7, 1849. Washington, Congressional Globe Office, 1849. 15 p.

Brown, David Paul. Eulogium upon Wilberforce; with a Brief Incidental Review of the Subject of Colonization. Delivered, at the Request of the Abolition Society, March 10, 1834. Philadelphia, T. K. Collins & Co., 1834. 40 p.

Brown, David Paul. An Oration, Delivered by Request, before the Anti-Slavery Society of New York, on the Fourth of July, 1834. Philadelphia, T. K. Collins & Co., 1834. 30 p.

Brown, Henry Box. Narrative of Henry Box Brown, Who Escaped from Slavery Enclosed in a Box 3 Feet Long and 2 Wide. Written from a Statement of Facts Made by Himself. With Remarks upon the Remedy for Slavery. By Charles Stearns. Boston, Brown & Stearns [1849]. 90 p.

[Brown, John]. Provisional Constitution and Ordinances for the People of the United States. [St. Catherines, Ontario, William Howard Day, 1858]. 15 p.

Brown, John Thompson. The Speech of John Thompson Brown, in the House of Delegates of Virginia, on the Abolition of Slavery. Delivered Wednesday, January 18, 1832. Richmond, T. W. White, 1832. 32 p.

Brown, Josephine. Biography of an American Bondsman [William Wells Brown]. By His Daughter. Boston, R. F. Wallcut, 1856. 104 p.

Brown, Thomas. Brown's Three Years in the Kentucky Prisons, from May 30, 1854 to May 18, 1857. Indianapolis, Journal Co., 1858. 19 p. Same. 1858. 21 p.

Brown, Thomas Cilaven. Examination of Mr. Thomas C. Brown, a Free Colored Citizen of South Carolina, as to the Actual State of Things in Liberia in the Years 1833 and 1834 at the Chatham Street Chapel, May 9, 10, 1834. New York, S. W. Benedict & Co., 1834. 40 p.

Brown, William B. Religious Organizations, and Slavery. Oberlin, J. M. Fitch, 1850. 32 p.

Brown, William Wells, *comp.* The Anti-Slavery Harp: A Collection of Songs for Anti-Slavery Meetings. Boston, B. Marsh, 1848. 47 p.

Brown, William Wells. The Black Man, His Antecedents, His Genius, and His Achievements. New York, T. Hamilton [etc.], 1863. 288 p.

Brown, William Wells. A Lecture Delivered before the Female Anti-Slavery Society of Salem, at Lyceum Hall, Nov. 14, 1847. By William W. Brown, a Fugitive Slave. Reported by Henry M. Parkhurst. Boston, Massachusetts Anti-Slavery Society, 1847. 22 p.

Brown, William Wells. Narrative of William W. Brown, a Fugitive Slave. Written by Himself. Boston, the Anti-Slavery Office, 1847. 110 p.

Brown, William Wells. Clotil; or, The President's Daughter; a Narrative of Slave Life in the United States, with a Sketch of the Author's Life. London, Partridge & Oakey, 1853. 245 p.

Buchanan, George (Member of American Philosophical Society). An Oration upon the Moral and Political Evil of Slavery. Delivered at a public Meeting of the Maryland Society, for Promoting the Abolition of Slavery, and the Relief of Free Negroes, and Others Unlawfully Held in Bondage, Baltimore, July 4th, 1791. Baltimore, Philip Edwards, 1793. 20 p.

Buckingham, G. The Bible Vindicated from the Charge of Sustaining Slavery. Columbus, Ohio, Temperance Advocate Office, 1837. 24 p.

Buffinton, James. Position of Massachusetts on the Slavery Question. Speech of Hon. James Buffinton, of Massachusetts, in the House of Representatives, April 30, 1856. [Washington, D. C., Buell & Blanchard, 1856.] 7 p.

Buffum, Arnold. Lecture Showing the Necessity for a Liberty Party, and Setting Forth Its Principles, Measures, and Object. Cincinnati, Caleb Clark, 1844. 15 p.

Bulkley, C. H. A. Removal of Ancient Landmarks, or the Causes and Consequences of Slavery Extension. A Discourse Preached to the Second Congregational Church of West Winsted, Conn., March 5, 1854. Hartford, Case, Tiffany & Co., 1854. 23 p.

[Burgess, Ebenezer]. Address to the American Society for Colonizing the Free People of Colour of the United States, Read in Washington, November 21st, 1818. Washington, Davis and Force, 1818. 56 p.

Burgess, Thomas. Considerations on the Abolition of Slavery and the Slave Trade, upon Grounds of Natural, Religious, and Political Duty. Oxford, D. Prince and J. Cooke, 1789. 166 p.

Burke, Edmund. An Important Appeal to the People of the United States. Slavery and Abolitionism. Union and Disunion. By Edmund Burke, of New Hampshire. [n.p., 1856?] 16 p.

Burleigh, Charles Calistus. No Slave Hunting in the Old Bay State. Speech of Charles C. Burleigh at the Annual Meeting of the Massachusetts A. S.

Society, Friday, January 28, 1859. Boston, Massachusetts Anti-Slavery Society, 1859. 32 p.

[Burleigh, Charles Calistus]. Reception of George Thompson in Great Britain. Compiled from Various British Publications. Boston, I. Knapp, 1836. 238 p.

Burlingame, Anson. Defence of Massachusetts. Speech of Hon. Anson Burlingame, of Massachusetts, in the House of Representatives, June 21, 1856. Washington [D. C.], Buell & Blanchard, [1856.] 8 p.

Burnap, George W. Review of the Life, Character, and Writings of Elias Hicks. Reprinted from the Christian Examiner for November. Cambridge, 1851. 32 p.

Burnap, Uzziah Cicero. Bible Servitude. A Sermon Delivered in the Appleton Street Church, Lowell, on the Day of Annual Thanksgiving, November 30, 1843. Lowell, A. E. Newton & A. O. Ordway, 1843. 20 p.

Burns, Barnabas. Speech of Mr. Burns of Richland on the Several Resolutions on the Subject of the "Fugitive Slave Law" in the [Ohio State] Senate, Jan. 17, 1850. Columbus, O., Ohio Statesman Print, 1851. 8 p.

Burritt, Elihu. A Plan of Brotherly Copartnership of the North and South, for the Peaceful Extinction of Slavery. New York, Dayton and Burdick, 1856. 48 p. [Burritt, an advocate of compensated emancipation, was editor of the Philadelphia *Citizen of the World*.]

Burt, Jairus. The Law of Christian Rebuke, a Plea for Slave-Holders; a Sermon Delivered at Middletown, Conn., Before the Anti-Slavery Convention of Ministers and Other Christians, Oct. 18, 1843. Hartford, N. W. Goodrich & Co., 1843. 20 p.

Bushnell, Horace. The Census and Slavery; a Thanksgiving Discourse, Delivered in the Chapel at Clifton Springs, N. Y., November 29, 1860. Hartford, L. E. Hunt, 1860. 24 p. [One of the Lane rebels; Presbyterian minister at Delhi, Ohio.]

Bushnell, Horace. A Discourse on the Slavery Question. Delivered in the North Church, Hartford, Thursday Evening, Jan. 10, 1839. Hartford, Case, Tiffany & Co., 1839. 32 p.

Same. Second Edition: Hartford, Case, Tiffany & Co., 1839. 32 p.

Buxton, Sir Thomas Fowell. The African Slave Trade. Second Edition. London, J. Murray, 1839. 240 p.

Same. London, J. Murray, 1840. 236 p.

Same. First American from Second London Edition. With Appendix. Philadelphia, Merrihew & T. Gunn, Printers, 1839. 188 p.

[Byrnes, Daniel]. A Short Address to the English Colonies in North America. [Wilmington, 1775.] 2 p. [Mockery of fast day for success in war against England, while slavery was continued.]

Cabinet of Freedom. Under the Supervision of the Hon. William Jay, Rev. Prof. Bush of the University of New York, and Gerrit Smith, Esq. 4 Vols. New York, John S. Taylor, 1836.
Volumes I–III. The History of the Rise, Progress and Accomplishment of the Abolition of the African Slave Trade, by the British Parliament: Thomas Clarkson.
Volume IV. Adventures of Charles Ball.

[Cabot, George]. Boreas [pseud.]. Slave Representation. Awake! O Spirit of the North. [New Haven] 1812. 23 p.

Cadwalader, John. Speech of Hon. John Cadwalader, of Pennsylvania, on the Legislation of the United States upon the Subject of Slavery in the Territories. Delivered in the House of Representatives, March 5, 1856. Washington [D. C.], Congressional Globe Office, 1856. 16 p.

Caffrey, Andrew. An Essay on Slavery, with a Reasonable Proposition Made How to Dispense with It. With a Brief Investigation of What is Termed Civilized Life, Showing Unmasked, Without Colouring, a Picture of Some of Its Practices and Results. [Philadelphia? 1859.] 4 p.

Cairnes, John Elliot. The Revolution in America: A Lecture Delivered Before the Young Men's Christian Association in Connexion with the United Church of England and Ireland, in the Metropolitan Hall, October 30th, 1862. Dublin, Hodges, Smith and Co., 1862. 43 p.
Same. Second Edition. Dublin [n.d.]. 43 p.
Same. Third Edition. Dublin. 47 p.
Same. Fifth Edition. Dublin. 48 p.
Same. Seventh Edition. Dublin. 48 p.
Same. New York, T. J. Crowen, 1862. 15 p.

Cairnes, John Elliott. The Slave Power: Its Character, Career, and Probable Designs; Being an Attempt to Explain the Real Issues Involved in the American Contest. London, Parker, Son, and Bourn, 1862. 304 p.
Same. Second Edition. New York, Carleton, 1862. 171 p.
Same. Second English Edition. London, Macmillan & Co., 1863. 410 p.
Same. Third Edition. New York, Follett, Foster & Co., 1863. 171 p.

Campbell, Lewis Davis. Kansas and Nebraska—Georgia and Ohio—Free Labor and Slave Labor. Speech of Hon. Lewis D. Campbell, of Ohio, in the House of Representatives, December 14, 1854. [Washington, D. C., Congressional Globe Office, 1854.] 16 p.

Campbell, Lewis Davis. Speech of Hon. Lewis D. Campbell, of Ohio, in Reply to Mr. Stephens, of Georgia, Delivered in the House of Representatives, February 28, 1855. Washington [D. C.], Congressional Globe Office, 1855. 15 p.

Campbell, Lewis Davis. Speech of Hon. L. D. Campbell, of Ohio, on Southern Aggression, the Purposes of the Union, and the Comparative Effects of Slavery and Freedom. Delivered in the House of Representatives, Feb. 19, 1850. [Washington, D. C.] Buell & Blanchard [1850]. 16 p.

Campbell, Lewis Davis. Supremacy of the Constitution and Laws. Speech of Hon. Lewis D. Campbell, of Ohio, in the House of Representatives, in Reply to His Colleague, Mr. J. R. Giddings, the Senate's Amendments to the Deficiency Bill Being under Consideration. [Washington, D. C., Buell & Blanchard, 1856.] 8 p.

Campbell, Lewis Davis. "Union for the Cause of Freedom." Letter of Hon. L. D. Campbell, of Ohio, to the Hon. Daniel R. Tilden, as to the Proper Means of Securing Freedom to the Territories. [Washington, D. C.] Buell & Blanchard [1850]. 8 p.

Cambridge, Mass., Citizens Meeting. The Sumner Outrage; a Full Report of the Speeches at the Meeting of Citizens in Cambridge, June 2, 1856, in Reference to the Assault on Senator Sumner, in the Senate Chamber at Washington. Cambridge, John Ford, 1856. 33 p.

Canadian Anti-Slavery Baptist Association. Constitution, By-Laws, Minutes, Circular Letter. Declaration of Faith. [Chatham, 1854.] 14 p.

Canadian Anti-Slavery Society. First Annual Report, Presented to the Anti-Slavery Society of Canada, by Its Executive Committee, March 24th, 1852. Toronto, Brown's Printing Establishment, 1852. 24 p.

Canadian Anti-Slavery Society. Second Annual Report Presented to the Anti-Slavery Society of Canada, by Its Executive Committee, March 23rd, 1853. Toronto, Brown's Printing Establishment, 1853. 42 p.

Canadian Anti-Slavery Society. Sixth Annual Report of the Anti-Slavery Society of Canada, Presented at the Annual Meeting, Held on the 29th April, 1857. Toronto, Globe Book and Job Office, 1857. 14 p.

Canning, George. Speech of the Right Hon. George Canning, Secretary of State for Foreign Affairs, on Laying Before the House of Commons the Papers in Explanation of the Measures Adopted by His Majesty's Government with a View of Ameliorating the Condition of the Negro Slaves in the West Indies, on Wednesday, the 17th of March, 1824. To Which Is Added, an Order in Council, for Improving the Condition of the Slaves in Trinidad. London, Lupton Relfe, 1824. 78 p.

[Carey, Mathew]. A Calm Address to the People of the Eastern States, on the Subject of the Representation of Slaves; the Representation in the Senate; and the Hostility to Commerce Ascribed to the Southern States. By the Author of the Olive Branch. Philadelphia, M. Carey, 1814. 47 p. Same. Boston, Rowe and Hooper, 1814. 50 p. [Mathew Carey was a strong colonizationist.]

Carey, Mathew. Letters on the Colonization Society; and of Its Probable Results, under the Following Heads: The Origin of the Society; Increase of the Coloured Population; Manumission of Slaves in This Country; Declarations of Legislatures, and Other Assembled Bodies, in Favour of the Society; Situation of the Colonists at Monrovia, and Other Towns; Moral and Religious Character of the Settlers; Soil, Climate, Productions, and Commerce of Liberia; Advantages to the Free Coloured Population, by Emigration to Liberia; Disadvantages of Slavery to the White Population; Character of the Natives of Africa Before the Irruptions of the Barbarians; Effects of Colonization on the Slave Trade with a Slight Sketch of That Nefarious and Accursed Traffic. Addressed to the Hon. C. F. Mercer, N.H.R.U.S.
Same. Second Edition. Hartford, P. B. Gleason & Co., 1832. 32 p.
Same. Third Edition. Philadelphia, Young, 1832. 32 p.
Same. Thirteenth Edition. Philadelphia, 1838. 32 p.

Carey, Mathew. Reflections on the Causes that Led to the Formation of the Colonization Society: With a View of Its Probable Results: Under the Following Heads: The Increase of the Coloured Population. The Origin of the Colonization Society. The Manumission of Slaves in This Country. The Declarations of Legislatures, and Other Assembled Bodies, in Favour of the Society. The Situation of the Colonists at Monrovia and Other Towns. Moral and Religious Character of the Settlers. The Soil and Climate of Liberia. Its Productions and Commerce. The Advantages to the Free Coloured Population by Emigration to Liberia. The Character of the Natives of Africa, Before the Irruption of the Barbarians. The Effects of the Colonization on the Slave Trade—with a Slight Sketch of That Nefarious and Accursed Traffic. By M. Carey. Philadelphia, W. F. Geddes, 1832. 19 p.

[Carey, Mathew]. Hamilton, [pseud.]. Universal Emancipation. Second Edition. [Philadelphia, 1827.] 8 p.

Carman, Adam. An Oration Delivered at the Fourth Anniversary of the Abolition of the Slave Trade, in the Methodist Episcopal Church, in Second Street, New York, January 1, 1811. New York, Totten, 1811. 23 p.

Carpenter, Russell Lant. Observations on American Slavery, after a Year's Tour in the United States. London, Edward T. Whitfield, 1852. 69 p.

Carroll, Daniel Lynn. Sermons and Addresses on Various Subjects. Philadelphia, Lindsay & Blakiston, 1846. 372 p. [Including: "A Permanent Remedy for the African Slave Trade."]

Cartwright, S. A. The Dred Scott Decision. Opinion of Chief Justice Taney, with an Introduction by Dr. J. H. Van Evrie. Also, an Appendix Containing an Essay on the Natural History of the Prognathous Race of Mankind, Originally Written for the New York Day-Book. New York, Van Evrie, Horton & Co., 1860. 48 p.

Case of the Slave-Child, Med. Report of the Arguments of Counsel, and of the Opinion of the Court, in the Case of Commonwealth vs. Aves; Tried and Determined in the Supreme Judicial Court of Massachusetts. Boston, Isaac Knapp, 1836. 40 p.

Case of the Slave Isaac Brown. An Outrage Exposed. [n.p., 1847?] 8 p.

Caulkins, Nehemiah. Narrative of Nehemiah Caulkins. An Extract from "American Slavery as It Is." New York, American and Foreign Anti-Slavery Society, 1849. 22 p.

Cecil, pseud. See Fisher, Charles Edward.

Chalmers, Rev. Thomas. A Few Thoughts on the Abolition of Colonial Slavery. Glasgow, Chalmers & Collins, 1826. 16 p.

Chamberlain, Ebenezer Mattoon. Speech of Hon. E. M. Chamberlain, of Indiana, Against the Repeal of the Missouri Compromise Act; Delivered in the House of Representatives, Monday, March 13, 1854. Washington [D. C.], A. O. P. Nicholson, 1854. 23 p.

Chamberovzow, L. A. Slave Life in Georgia; a Narrative of the Life, Sufferings, and Escape of John Brown, a Fugitive Slave, Now in England. London, W. M. Watt, 1855. 250 p.

Chambers, William. American Slavery and Colour. London, W. & R. Chambers, 1857. 216 p.

Chandler, Elizabeth Margaret. Essays, Philanthropic and Moral, by Elizabeth Margaret Chandler, Principally Relating to the Abolition of Slavery in America. Philadelphia, 1845.
Same: Philadelphia, L. Howell, 1836. 120 p.

Chandler, Elizabeth Margaret. The Poetical Works of Elizabeth Margaret Chandler; with a Memoir of Her Life and Character, by Benjamin Lundy. Philadelphia, 1836. 180 p.
Same. Philadelphia, T. E. Chapman, 1845. 120 p.

Chandler, John A. The Speech of John A. Chandler (of Norfolk County), in the House of Delegates of Virginia, on the Policy of the State with Respect to Her Slave Population. Delivered January 17, 1832. Richmond, Thomas W. White, 1832. 10 p.

Chandler, Zachariah. Kansas-Lecompton Constitution. Speech of Hon. Z. Chandler, of Michigan. Delivered in the Senate of the United States,

March 12th, 1858. Washington, D. C., Buell & Blanchard, 1858. 14 p.

Channing, William Ellery. Emancipation. Boston, E. P. Peabody, 1840. 111 p.

Same. New York, American Anti-Slavery Society, 1841. 71 p.

Same. Philadelphia, Eastern Pennsylvania Anti-Slavery Society, Merrihew & Thompson, 1841. 95 p.

Channing, William Ellery. Dr. Channing's Last Address, Delivered at Lenox, on the First of August, 1842, the Anniversary of Emancipation in the British West Indies. Boston, Oliver Johnson, 1842. 24 p.

Same. Lenox, Mass., J. G. Stanley, 1842. 38 p.

Channing, William Ellery. The Duty of the Free States; or, Remarks Suggested by the Case of the Creole. Boston, William Crosby & Company, 1842. 54 p.

Same. Glasgow, Hedderwick & Son, 1842. 27 p.

Same. London, J. Green, 1842. 40 p.

Channing, William E. Letter of William E. Channing to James G. Birney. Boston, James Munroe & Co., 1837. 36 p.

Same. Cincinnati, A. Pugh, 1836. 14 p.

Channing, William Ellery. A Letter to the Abolitionists. Boston, Isaac Knapp, 1837. 32 p. First Published with Comments in the Liberator, December 22, 1837.

Channing, William Ellery. A Letter to the Hon. Henry Clay, on the Annexation of Texas to the United States. Boston, James Munroe & Co., 1837. 72 p. [Six editions, without change, by the same publisher in one year.]

Channing, William Ellery. Remarks on the Slavery Question, in a Letter to Jonathan Phillips, Esq. Boston, Munroe and Company, 1839. 91 p.

Same. Bristol, Philip and Evans; London, J. Green, 1839. 68 p. [Eight editions in two years.]

Channing, William Ellery. Slavery. Boston, James Munroe & Company, 1835. 167 p.

Same. Second Edition, Revised. Boston, Munroe, 1836. 183 p.

Same. Third Edition. Boston, Munroe, 1836. 183 p.

Same. Fourth Edition. Boston, Munroe, 1836. 187 p.

Chaplin Committee. Boston. The Case of William L. Chaplin; Being an Appeal to All Respecters of Law and Justice, Against the Cruel and Oppressive Treatment to Which, under Color of Legal Proceedings, He Has Been Subjected, in the District of Columbia and the State of Maryland. Boston, Pub. by the Chaplin Committee, 1851. 54 p. [Chaplin was a lawyer; arrested in Washington, D. C. on charge of aiding fugitives.]

Chapman, Maria Weston, Ed. The Liberty Bell. By Friends of Freedom, 15 vols. Boston, Massachusetts Anti-Slavery Fair, 1839–1846; National Anti-Slavery Bazaar, 1847–1858. None Published in 1840, 1850, 1854, 1855, 1857. [Volume dated 1841 was actually published in 1840. Mrs. Chapman edited the annual reports of the Boston Female Anti-Slavery Society under the title Right and Wrong in Boston.]

[Chapman, Mrs. Maria Weston]. Songs of the Free, and Hymns of Christian Freedom. Boston, I. Knapp, 1836. 227 p.

A Chapter of American History. Five Years' Progress of the Slave Power; a Series of Papers First Published in the Boston "Commonwealth," in July, August, and September, 1851. Boston, Benjamin B. Mussey and Company, 1852. 84 p.

Charleston Insurrection. An Account of the Late Intended Insurrection among a Portion of the Blacks of This City. Charleston, A. E. Miller, 1822. 46 p.

Charleston Citizens Meeting. Proceedings of the Citizens of Charleston, on the Incendiary Machinations, Now in Progress against the Peace and Welfare of the Southern States. Pub. by Order of Council. Charleston, A. E. Miller, 1835. 12 p.

Charter Oak. An Anti-Slavery Family Newspaper. Monthly and Weekly. Hartford, Conn. February 28, 1838–1848. Edited by George S. Shepherd and Erastus Hudson, 1846–1847. Published by Connecticut Anti-Slavery Society. Christian Freeman, 1843–1845, edited by William H. Burleigh.

Chase, Ezra B. Teachings of Patriots and Statesmen; or, The "Founders of the Republic" on Slavery. Philadelphia, J. W. Bradley, 1860. 495 p.

Chase, Henry, and Sanborn, Charles W. The North and South: A Statistical View of the Condition of the Free and Slave States. Compiled from Official Documents. Boston, John P. Jewett and Company [etc.], 1856. 134 p.

Same. Boston, J. P. Jewett and Company; Cleveland, O., H. P. B. Jewett, 1857. 191 p.

Chase, Lucien Bonaparte. English Serfdom and American Slavery; or, Ourselves, as Others See Us. New York, H. Long & Brother, [1854]. 259 p.

Chase, Salmon P. The Address [by A. J. Gordon] and Reply, on the Presentation of a Testimonial, to S. P. Chase, by the Colored People of Cincinnati. With Some Account of the Case of Samuel Watson [tried as a fugitive slave]. Cincinnati, H. W. Derby & Co., 1845. 36 p.

Chase, S. P. Maintain Plighted Faith. Speech of Hon. S. P. Chase, of Ohio, the Senate, February 3, 1854, Against the Repeal of the Missouri Prohibition of Slavery North of 36°30'. Washington [D. C.], John T. and Lem. Towers, 1854. 30 p.

Chase, Salmon Portland. The Radical Democracy of New York, and the Independent Democracy:

Letter of Senator Chase of Ohio, to Hon. B. F. Butler of New York, July 15, 1852. [1852]. 8 p.

Chase, Salmon Portland. Reclamation of Fugitives from Service; an Argument for the Defendant Submitted to the Supreme Court of the United States, at the December Term, 1846, in the Case of Wharton Jones vs. John Vanzandt. Cincinnati, R. P. Donogh & Co., 1847. 108 p.

Chase, Salmon Portland. Speech of Hon. Salmon P. Chase, Delivered at the Republican Mass Meeting in Cincinnati, August 21, 1855; Together with Extracts from His Speeches in the Senate on Kindred Subjects. Columbus, Printed by the Ohio State Journal Company, 1855. 20 p.

Chase, Salmon Portland. Speech of Senator Chase, Delivered at Toledo, May 30, 1851, Before a Mass Convention of the Democracy of Northwestern Ohio. [Cincinnati ?] Printed at Ben Franklin's Book and Job Office [1851]. 8 p.

Chase, Salmon P. Speech of Salmon P. Chase in the Case of the Colored Woman, Matilda, Who Was Brought Before the Court of Common Pleas of Hamilton County, Ohio, by Writ of Habeas Corpus, March 11, 1837. Cincinnati, Pugh & Dodd, 1837. 40 p.

Chase, Salmon P. Union and Freedom, without Compromise. Speech of Mr. Chase, of Ohio, on Mr. Clay's Compromise Resolutions. In Senate, March 26, 1850. Washington, D. C., Buell & Blanchard, 1850. 16 p.
Same. Washington [D. C.], Congressional Globe Office, 1850. 24 p.

Chase, Salmon Portland, and Cleveland, Charles Dexter. Anti-Slavery Addresses of 1844 and 1845. London, Sampson Low, Son, and Marston; Philadelphia, J. A. Bancroft and Co., 1867. 167 p.

Cheever, George B[arrell]. The Commission from God, of the Missionary Enterprise, Against the Sin of Slavery; and the Responsibility on the Church and Ministry for Its Fulfilment. An Address, Delivered in Tremont Temple, Boston, Thursday, May 27th, 1858, Before the American Missionary Association. Boston, John P. Jewett and Company, [etc.], 1858. 35 p. (Tracts for Thinking Men and Women, No. 3.) [Congregational clergyman; fearless champion of Negro citizenship.]

Cheever, George B[arrell]. The Fire and Hammer of God's Word Against the Sin of Slavery. Speech of George B. Cheever at the Anniversary of the American Abolition Society, May, 1858. New York, American Abolition Society, 1858. 16 p.

Cheever, George B[arrell]. God Against Slavery: and the Freedom and Duty of the Pulpit to Rebuke It, as a Sin Against God. Cincinnati, American Reform Tract and Book Society [1857]. 272 p.

Same. New York, Joseph H. Ladd, 1857. 272 p.

Cheever, George Barrell. God's Way of Crushing the Rebellion. A Sermon by George B. Cheever in the Church of the Puritans, New York, Sept. 29, 1861. New York, 1861. 16 p.

Cheever, George Barrell. The Guilt of Slavery and the Crime of Slaveholding, Demonstrated from the Hebrew and Greek Scriptures. Boston, John P. Jewett & Company, 1860. 472 p.
Same. New York, Smith & McDougall, 1860. 472 p.

Cheever, George B[arrell]. Rights of the Coloured Race to Citizenship and Representation; and the Guilt and Consequences of Legislation against Them. A Discourse Delivered in the Hall of Representatives of the United States, in Washington, D. C., May 29, 1864, by Rev. George B. Cheever, D.D., Pastor of the Church of the Puritans, in the City of New York. New York, Francis & Loutrel, 1864. 28 p.

Cheever, George Barrell. The Sin of Slavery, the Guilt of the Church, and the Duty of the Ministry. An Address Delivered Before the Abolition Society at New York, on Anniversary Week, 1858. By Rev. George B. Cheever, D.D. Boston, J. P. Jewett and Company; Cleveland, H. P. B. Jewett, 1858. 23 p. (Tracts for Thinking Men and Women, No. 1.)

Cheever, Henry Theodore. A Tract for the Times, on the Question, Is It Right to Withhold Fellowship from Churches or from Individuals That Tolerate or Practice Slavery? Read by Appointment, Before the Congregational Ministers' Meeting, of New London County, Ct. New York, John A. Gray, 1859. 23 p.

Chickering, Jesse. Letter Addressed to the President of the United States on Slavery, Considered in Relation to the Constitutional Principles of Government in Great Britain and in the United States; by an American Citizen. Boston, Redding and Company, 1855. 91 p.

Child, David L. The Despotism of Freedom; or the Tyranny and Cruelty of American Republican Slave-Masters, Shown to Be the Worst in the World; in a Speech, Delivered at the First Anniversary of the New England Anti-Slavery Society, 1833. Boston, Boston Young Men's Anti-Slavery Association for the Diffusion of Truth, 1833. 72 p. Abolitionists' Library. No. 1.

Child, David L. Oration in Honor of Universal Emancipation in the British Empire, Delivered at South Reading, August First, 1834. Boston, Garrison & Knapp, 1834. 38 p.

Child, David Lee, and Others. Remonstrance. [To Massachusetts Legislature, against repeal of the

Personal Liberty Law.] Massachusetts Legislature, House [Doc.] No. 121. March, 1861. 36 p.

Child, David Lee. Rights and Duties of the United States Relative to Slavery under the Laws of War. No Military Power to Return Any Slave. "Contraband of War" Inapplicable Between the United States and Their Insurgent Enemies. Boston, R. F. Wallcut, 1861. 48 p. Republished with Notes from the Liberator.

Child, David Lee. The Taking of Naboth's Vineyard; or, History of the Texas Conspiracy, and an Examination of the Reasons Given by the Hon. J. C. Calhoun, Hon. R. J. Walker, and Others, for the Dismemberment and Robbery of the Republic of Mexico. New York, S. W. Benedict & Co., 1845. 32 p.

Child, Lydia Maria *Francis.* Anti-Slavery Catechism. Newburyport, Charles Whipple, 1836. 36 p.
Same. Second Edition. Newburyport, Chas. Whipple, 1839. 36 p.

Child, Mrs. Lydia Maria *Francis.* An Appeal in Favor of That Class of Americans Called Africans. Boston, Allen & Ticknor, 1833. 232 p.
Same. New York, John S. Taylor, 1836. 216 p.

Child, Mrs. Lydia Maria *Francis.* Authentic Anecdotes of American Slavery. Second Edition. Newburyport, Charles Whipple, 1838. 23 p.

Child, Lydia Maria *Francis.* Correspondence Between Lydia Maria Child and Gov. Wise and Mrs. Mason, of Virginia. Boston, The American Anti-Slavery Society, 1860. 28 p.

Child, Lydia Maria *Francis.* The Evils of Slavery, and the Cure of Slavery; the First Proved by the Opinions of Southerners Themselves, the Last Shown by Historical Evidence. Newburyport, Charles Whipple, 1836. 19 p.
Same. Second Edition. Newburyport, Charles Whipple, 1839. 23 p.

Child, Mrs. Lydia Maria *Francis.* The Fountain, for Every Day in the Year. New York, John S. Taylor, 1836. 208 p.

Child, Lydia Maria *Francis.* Isaac T. Hopper: A True Life. Boston, J. P. Jewett and Company, 1853. 493 p.

Child, Lydia Maria *Francis,* ed. The Oasis. Boston, Benjamin C. Bacon, 1834. 276 p.

Child, Mrs. Lydia Maria *Francis.* The Patriarchal Institution, as Described by Members of Its Own Family. Comp. by L. Maria Child. New York, American Anti-Slavery Society, 1860. 55 p.

Child, Lydia Maria *Francis.* The Right Way the Safe Way, Proved by Emancipation in the British West Indies, and Elsewhere. New York, 5 Beekman St., 1860. 96 p.
Same. New York, American Anti-Slavery Society, 1862. 108 p.

Child, Lydia Maria, and Others. In Memoriam. Testimonials to the Life and Character of the Late Francis Jackson. Boston, R. F. Wallcut, 1861. 39 p.

The *Child's* Anti-Slavery Book. Containing a Few Words about American Slave Children and Stories of Slave-Life. New York, Carlton & Porter, 1859. 158 p.

The *Child's* Book on Slavery: or, Slavery Made Plain. Cincinnati, American Reform Tract & Book Society, 1857. 143 p.

Christian Anti-Slavery Convention. Minutes of the Convention Held July 3rd, 4th, and 5th, 1851, at Chicago, Illinois. Chicago, Office of the Western Citizen, 1851. 31 p.

Christian Anti-Slavery Convention. The Minutes of the Christian Anti-Slavery Convention Assembled April 17th–20th, 1850. Cincinnati, Ben Franklin Book & Job Rooms, 1850. 84 p.

Christian Witness. Weekly. Pittsburgh, Pa. 1836–1840. Edited by William H. Burleigh from 1837 to 1840. [Organ of the Pennsylvania State Anti-Slavery Society, Western Branch.]

Christy, David. African Colonization by the Free Colored People of the United States, an Indispensible Auxiliary to African Missions. A Lecture, by David Christy, Agent of the American Colonization Society for Ohio, with an Address to the Clergymen of Ohio, by the Ohio Colonization Committee. Cincinnati, J. A. & U. P. James, 1854. 64 p. [Christy was the ablest of all the Colonization lecturers.]

Christy, David. Ethiopia: Her Gloom and Glory, as Illustrated in the History of the Slave Trade and Slavery, the Rise of the Republic of Liberia, and the Progress of African Missions. By David Christy. With an Introduction. By W. P. Strickland. Cincinnati, Rickey, Mallory & Webb, 1857. 255 p.

Christy, David. Facts for Thinking Men: Showing the Necessity of African Colonization to Secure the Success of Tropical Free Labor. By David Christy, Agent of the American Colonization Society for Ohio. [Columbus, J. H. Riley & Co., 1853.] 15 p.

Christy, David. A Lecture on African Colonization. Including a Brief Outline of the Slave Trade, Emancipation, the Relation of the Republic of Liberia to England, &c. Delivered in the Hall of the House of Representatives of the State of Ohio. By David Christy. Cincinnati, Printed by J. A. & U. P. James, 1849. 56 p.

Christy, David. A Lecture on African Civilization. Including a Brief Outline of the Social and Moral Condition of Africa; and the Relations of American Slavery to African Civilization. Delivered in the Hall of the House of Representatives of the State of Ohio, January 19, 1850. Columbus, J. H. Riley & Co., 1853. 52 p.

Christy, David. A Lecture on the Present Relations of Free Labor to Slave Labor, in Tropical and Semi-Tropical Countries: Presenting an Outline of the Commercial Failure of West India Emancipation, and Its Effects upon Slavery and the Slave Trade, Together with Its Final Effect upon Colonization to Africa. Addressed to the Constitutional Convention of the State of Ohio, 1850. By David Christy. Cincinnati, Printed by J. A. & U. P. James, 1850. 72 p.

Same. Columbus, J. H. Riley & Co., 1853. 72 p.

Christy, David. Pulpit Politics; or, Ecclesiastical Legislation on Slavery, in Its Disturbing Influences on the American Union. Fifth Edition. Cincinnati, Farran & McLean, 1853 [1863]. 624 p.

[Christy, David]. Republic of Liberia. Facts for Thinking Men: Showing the Present Condition of Slave Labor and Free Labor, in Tropical and Semi-Tropical Countries; and the Indispensable Necessity of African Colonization; Being Letters Originally Addressed to the Citizens of Cleveland, Ohio, Through the Herald and the Plain Dealer, Daily Papers of This City.—Feb. 1852. [Cleveland, O., Harris, Fairbanks & Co., Printers, 1852.] 8 p.

Chronotype. Daily. Boston, Mass. February 1, 1846–January 1, 1851. Edited by Elizur Wright. [Supported by John A. Andrew, Dr. S. G. Howe, Henry Wilson, and Frank W. Bird—all ardent Free Soilers.]

Church Anti-Slavery Society. Proceedings of the Convention Which Met at Worcester, Mass. March 1, 1859. New York, John F. Trow, 1859. 31 p.

Church Anti-Slavery Society of United States. Circular—Declaration of Principles and Constitution. Worcester, 1859. 8 p.

Clark, George Washington. The Liberty Minstrel. New York, Benedict, 1844. 184 p.

Same. Fourth Edition. New York, Benedict, 1845. 184 p.

Same. Sixth Edition. New York, Author, 1846. 215 p.

Same. Seventh Edition. New York, Author, 1848. 215 p.

Clark, George Washington (Comp.). The Free Soil Minstrel. New York, Martyn & Ely, 1848. 228 p.

Clark, George Washington. The Harp of Freedom. New York, Miller, Orton & Mulligan, 1856. 335 p.

Clark, Rufus Wheelwright. Conscience and Law. A Discourse Preached in the North Church, Portsmouth, New Hampshire, on Fast Day, April 3, 1851, by Rufus W. Clark, Pastor. Boston, Tappan & Whittemore; Portsmouth, S. A. Badger, 1851. 25 p.

Clark, Rufus Wheelright. A Review of the Rev. Moses Stuart's Pamphlet on Slavery, Entitled Conscience and the Constitution. Boston, C. C. P. Moody, 1850. 103 p.

Clarke, James Freeman. Causes and Consequences of the Affair at Harper's Ferry. A Sermon Preached in the Indiana Place Chapel, on Sunday Morning, November 6, 1859. Boston, Walker, Wise, & Co., 1859. 14 p. [Clarke was a Congregational clergyman of Cincinnati; editor of the *Western Messenger*, 1836–1839.]

Clarke, James Freeman. Present Condition of the Free Colored People of the United States. New York, and Boston, American Anti-Slavery Society, 1859. 27 p.

Clarke, James Freeman. The Rendition of Anthony Burns. Its Causes and Consequences. A Discourse on Christian Politics, Delivered in Williams Hall, Boston, on Whitsunday, June 4, 1854. Boston, Crosby, Nichols & Co., and Prentiss & Sawyer, 1854. 28 p.

Same. Second Edition. Boston, Crosby, Nichols & Co., 1854. 28 p.

Clarke, James Freeman. Slavery in the United States. A Sermon Delivered in Amory Hall, on Thanksgiving Day, November 24, 1842. By James Freeman Clarke. (Printed by Friends for Gratuitous Distribution.) Boston, Benjamin H. Greene, 1843. 25 p.

Clarke, Lewis Garrard. Narrative of the Sufferings of Lewis Clarke, During a Captivity of More Than Twenty-five Years, among the Algerines of Kentucky, One of the So-Called Christian States of North America. Dictated by Himself. Boston, David H. Ela, 1845. 108 p.

Clarke, Lewis Garrard. Narratives of the Sufferings of Lewis and Milton Clarke, Sons of a Soldier of the Revolution, During a Captivity of More Than Twenty Years among the Slaveholders of Kentucky, One of the So-Called Christian States of North America. Boston, B. Marsh, 1846. 144 p.

Clarke, Walter. The American Anti-Slavery Society at War with the Church. A Discourse, Delivered Before the First Congregational Church and Society, in Canterbury, Conn., June 30, 1844. Same. Second Edition. Hartford, Elihu Geer, 1844. 21 p.

Clarkson, Thomas. The *Cries* of Africa, to the Inhabitants of Europe; or, A Survey of That Bloody Commerce Called the Slave-Trade. London, Harvey and Darton [1822]. 50 p.

Clarkson, Thomas. An *Essay* on the Impolicy of the African Slave Trade. London, J. Phillips, 1788. 134 p.

Same. Second Edition. London, J. Phillips, 1788. 138 p.

Clarkson, Thomas. An Essay on the Comparative

Efficiency of Regulation or Abolition, as Applied to the Slave Trade. Shewing That the Latter Only Can Remove the Evils to Be Found in That Commerce. London, James Phillips, 1789. 80 p.

Clarkson, Thomas. An Essay on the Impolicy of the African Slave Trade. In Two Parts. By the Rev. T. Clarkson. To Which Is Added, an Oration, upon the Necessity of Establishing at Paris, a Society to Promote the Abolition of the Trade and Slavery of the Negroes. By J. P. Brissot de Warville. Philadelphia, Francis Bailey, 1788. 159 p.
Same. Philadelphia, Francis Bailey, 1789. 155 p.

Clarkson, Thomas. An Essay on the Slavery and Commerce of the Human Species, Particularly the African, Translated from a Latin Dissertation, Which Was Honoured with the First Prize in the University of Cambridge, for the Year 1785, with Additions. London, J. Phillips, 1786. 256 p.
Same. Second Edition. London, J. Phillips, 1788. 167 p.
Same. Philadelphia, Joseph Crukshank, 1786. 155 p.
Same. Georgetown, Ky., David Barrow, 1816. 175 p.
Same. Third Edition. Philadelphia, 1787.

Clarkson, Thomas. The *History* of the Rise, Progress, and Accomplishment of the Abolition of the African Slave-Trade by the British Parliament. 2 vols. London, R. Taylor and Co., 1808. First American from the London Edition. 2 vols. Philadelphia, James P. Parke, 1808.
Same. Abridged by Evan Lewis. Wilmington, R. Porter, 1816. 348 p.
Same. 3 Vols. New York, John S. Taylor, 1836.
Same. Abridged by P. A. Brinsmad, with a View of the Present State of the Slave-Trade and of Slavery. 2 vols. Augusta, Me., 1830.
Same. [Cabinet of Freedom, Vols. 1–3.] New York, 1836.
Same. With Prefatory Remarks on the Subsequent Abolition of Slavery. London, 1839. viii, 36–615 p.

Clarkson, Thomas. A Letter to the Clergy of Various Denominations, and to the Slave-Holding Planters, in the Southern Parts of the United States of America. By Thomas Clarkson. London, Johnston and Barrett, 1841. 64 p.
Same. Second Edition. London, Johnston and Barrett. 48 p.

Clarkson, Thomas. Letters on the Slave Trade, and the State of the Natives in Those Parts of Africa Which Are Contiguous to Fort St. Louis and Goree; Written at Paris in December, 1789, and January, 1790. London, James Phillips, 1791. 81 p.

Clarkson, Thomas. Thoughts on the Necessity of Improving the Condition of the Slaves in the British Colonies, with a View to Their Ultimate Emancipation; and on the Practicability, the Safety, and the Advantages of the Latter Measure. London, Richard Taylor, 1823. 60 p.
Second Edition. London, Richard Taylor, 1823. 57 p.
First American Edition. New York, 1823. 64 p.

Clay, Cassius M[arcellus]. Appeal of Cassius M. Clay to Kentucky and the World. Boston, J. M. Macomber & E. L. Pratt, 1845. 35 p. [Clay, a Kentuckian, became an ardent opponent of slavery while at Yale (1832). He entered politics in Kentucky, published an antislavery paper at Lexington, and met the violence of slaveholders in kind, but was never driven out.]

Clay, Cassius Marcellus, Cassius M. Clay, and Gerrit Smith. A Letter of Cassius M. Clay, of Lexington, Ky., to the Mayor of Dayton, O., with a Review of It by Gerrit Smith, of Peterboro, N. Y. [Utica, N. Y.] Jackson & Chaplin [1844]. 12 p.

Clay, Cassius M[arcellus]. Letters of Cassius M. Clay. Slavery: The Evil—the Remedy. New York, Greeley & McElrath, 1844. 8 p.

Clay, Cassius Marcellus. Speech of C. M. Clay, of Fayette, in the House of Representatives of Kentucky, January, 1841, upon the Bill to Repeal the Law of 1835, "To Prohibit the Importation of Slaves into This State." [Washington ? 1841]. 20 p.
Same. Frankfort, 1841. 16 p.

Clay, Cassius Marcellus. Speech of Cassius M. Clay, Against the Annexation of Texas to the United States of America, in Reply to Col. R. M. Johnson and Others, in a Mass Meeting of Citizens of the Eighth Congressional District, at the White Sulphur Springs, Scott County, Ky., on Saturday, Dec. 30, 1843. Lexington, Observer and Reporter Office, 1844. 22 p.

Clay, Cassius Marcellus. Speech of C. M. Clay, at Lexington, Ky. Delivered August 1, 1851. [n.p., 1851]. 20 p.

Clay, Cassius Marcellus. Speech of Cassius M. Clay, at Frankfort, Ky., from the Capitol Steps, January 10, 1860. [Cincinnati ? 1860]. 20 p.

Clay, Cassius Marcellus. Speech of Cassius M. Clay before the Law Department of the University of Albany, N. Y., February 3, 1863. Second Edition. New York, Wynkoop, Hallenbeck & Thomas, 1863. 24 p.

Clay, Cassius Marcellus. The Writings of Cassius Marcellus Clay: Including Speeches and Addresses. Ed., with a Preface and Memoir, by Horace Greeley. New York, Harper & Brothers, 1848. 535 p.

Clay, Cassius Marcellus. To the People of Kentucky [on the Slave Question]. Lexington, Ky., 1845. 8 p.

Clay, Henry. Speech of Henry Clay, on Abolition Petitions. Delivered in the Senate of the United States on the 7th of February, 1839. Utica, Jackson & Chaplin, 1839. 16 p.

Cleland, Philip S. A Sermon, Delivered, Sabbath, July 4th, 1841, in the Presbyterian Church, Greenwood, Indiana, by Rev. P. S. Cleland. Greenwood, Executive Committee of the Greenwood and Vicinity Anti-Slavery Society, 1841. 13 p.

Clericus, pseud. See George Smith

Cleveland, Charles Dexter. Anti-Slavery Addresses of 1844 and 1845. By Salmon Portland Chase and Charles Dexter Cleveland. London, S. Low, Son, and Marston; Philadelphia, J. A. Bancroft and Co., 1867. 167 p. [First published as: Address of the Liberty Party of Pennsylvania to the People of the State, 1844; and, The Address of the Southern and Western Liberty Convention Held at Cincinnati, June 11 and 12, 1845. Cleveland was sometime professor of Latin and Greek at Dickinson College.]

Cleveland, C. D. [Appeal to Liberty Party Members for Funds to Purchase a German Newspaper in Philadelphia.] Philadelphia, Nov. 25, 1844.

Cleveland, Chauncey F. The California Question. Speech of Hon. Chauncey F. Cleveland, of Connecticut, in the House of Representatives, April 19, 1850. [Washington, D. C.] Congressional Globe Office [1850]. 8 p.

Cleveland, Chauncey Fitch. The Homestead Bill—The Fugitive Slave Bill—The Compromise Measures. Speech by C. F. Cleveland of Connecticut in the House of Representatives, April 1, 1852. [Washington, D. C., 1852.] 8 p.

Coffin, Joshua. An Account of Some of the Principal Slave Insurrections, and Others, Which Have Occurred, or Been Attempted, in the United States and Elsewhere, during the Last Two Centuries. With Various Remarks. Collected from Various Sources by Joshua Coffin. New York, The American Anti-Slavery Society, 1860. 36 p. [Coffin was present at the founding of both the American Anti-Slavery Society and the New England Anti-Slavery Society. He was active in Negro education in Boston.]

Coggeshall, S. W. An Anti-Slavery Address, Delivered in the M. E. Church, Danielsonville, Conn., July 4th, 1849. West Killingly, E. B. Carter, 1849. 58 p.

Coleman, Elihu. A Testimony Against That Anti-Christian Practice of Making Slaves of Men. Wherein It Is Shewed to Be Contrary to the Dispensation of the Law and Time of the Gospel, and Very Opposite Both to Grace and Nature. Printed in the Year 1733. New Bedford, Reprinted for Abraham Sherman, Jun., 1825. 24 p. [Signed

Elihu Coleman. Nantucket, the 20th of the 11th Mo. 1729–30. Coleman was a Quaker minister.]

Coleman, Elihu. To the Reader. [A Testimony Against Making Slaves.] Nantucket, 1829–30. 18 p.

Colfax, Schuyler. The "Laws" of Kansas. Speech of Schuyler Colfax, of Indiana, in the House of Representatives, June 21, 1856. Washington, D. C., Buell & Blanchard, 1856. 16 p.

Colfax, Schuyler. Kansas—The Lecompton Constitution. Speech of Hon. Schuyler Colfax, of Indiana, in the House of Representatives, March 20, 1858. Washington, D. C., Buell & Blanchard, 1858. 14 p.

Collamer, Jacob. The President's Message. Speech of Hon. J. Collamer, of Vermont. Delivered in the Senate of the United States, December 9, 1856. [Washington, D. C.] Congressional Globe Office [1856]. 16 p.

Collamer, Jacob. Report of the Kansas Conference Committee. Speech of Hon. Jacob Collamer, of Vermont. Delivered in the Senate of the United States, April 27, 1858. Washington, D. C., Buell & Blanchard, 1858. 7 p.

Collamer, Jacob. Speech of Hon. Jacob Collamer, of Vermont, on Affairs in Kansas. Delivered in the Senate of the United States, April 3 and 4, 1856. Washington [D. C.], Congressional Globe Office, 1856.

Collamer, Jacob. Speech of Hon. Jacob Collamer, of Vermont, on Slavery in the Territories, Delivered in the Senate of the United States, March 8, 1860. [Washington, D. C.] L. Towers [1860]. 24 p.

A Collection of Valuable Documents, Being Birney's Vindication of Abolitionists—Protest of the American A. S. Society—To the People of the United States, or, To Such Americans as Value Their Rights—Letter from the Executive Committee of the N. Y. A. S. Society, to the Exec. Com. of the Ohio State A. S. S. at Cincinnati—Outrage upon Southern Rights. Boston, I. Knapp, 1836. 80 p.

College for Colored Youth. An Account of the New Haven City Meeting and Resolutions, with Recommendations of the College, and Strictures upon the Doings of New Haven. New York, Published by the Committee, 1831. 24 p.

Collins, John A. The Anti-Slavery Picknick; A Collection of Speeches, Poems, Dialogues and Songs; Intended for Use in Schools and Anti-Slavery Meetings. By John A. Collins. Boston, H. W. Williams; New York, Amer. A. S. Soc., 1842. 144 p.

Collins, John A. The Monthly Offering. [Songs with Music.] 2 vols. Boston, Anti-Slavery Office, 1841–1842. [No numbers published March–August, 1841, inclusive.]

Collins, John A. To the Abolitionists of Massachusetts. Boston, Dow & Jackson, [184-] 3 p. [Forms and directions for Anti-Slavery petitions to Congress and the Massachusetts legislature.]

Collins, John A. Right and Wrong amongst the Abolitionists of the United States. With an Introductory Letter by Harriet Martineau, and an Appendix. Second Edition, Glasgow, G. Gallie; [etc., etc.] 1841. 76 p.

Colored American. Weekly. New York, N. Y. January 7, 1837–1842. Edited by Rev. Samuel E. Cornish. Appeared in January and February, 1837 as Weekly Advocate.

A Colored American. The Late Contemplated Insurrection in Charleston, S. C., with the Execution of Thirty-Six of the Patriots; the Death of William Irving, the Provoked Husband, and Joe Devaul, for Refusing to be the Slave of Mr. Roach; with the Capture of the American Slaver Trading between the Seat of Government and New Orleans, Together with an Account of the Capture of the Spanish Schooner Amistad. New York, Printed for the Publisher. [Signed:] A Colored American. Philadelphia, 1850.

Colored Citizens of California. Proceedings of the First State Convention of the Colored Citizens of the State of California, Held in Sacramento, Nov. 20th, 21st, and 22nd, in the Colored Methodist Church. Sacramento, Democratic State Journal, 1855. 27 p.

Colored Citizens of Connecticut. Proceedings of the Connecticut State Convention of Colored Men, Held at New Haven, on September 12th & 13th, 1849. New Haven, William H. Stanley, 1849. 24 p.

Colored Citizens of Ohio. Minutes and Address of the State Convention of the Colored Citizens of Ohio, Convened at Columbus, January 10th, 11th, 12th, & 13th, 1849. Oberlin, J. M. Fitch, 1849. 28 p.

Colored Citizens of Ohio. Address to the Constitutional Convention of Ohio, from the State Convention of Colored Citizens, Held in the City of Columbus, Jan. 15th, 16th, 17th, and 18th, 1851. E. Glover, Printer [1851]. 8 p.

Colored Citizens of Pennsylvania. Minutes of the State Convention of the Colored Citizens of Pennsylvania, Convened at Harrisburg, December 13th and 14th, 1848. Philadelphia, Merrihew and Thompson, 1848. 24 p.

Colored Freemen of Pennsylvania. Proceedings of the State Convention of the Colored Freemen of Pennsylvania, Held in Pittsburgh on the 23rd, 24th, and 25th of August, 1841, for the Purpose of Considering Their Condition and the Means of Its Improvement. Pittsburgh, Matthew M. Grant, 1841. 16 p.

Colored National Convention, Cleveland, 1848. Report of the Proceedings of the Colored National Convention, Held at Cleveland, Ohio, on Wednesday, September 6, 1848. Rochester, J. Dick, at the North Star Office, 1848. 20 p.

Colored National Convention, Rochester, N. Y., 1853. Proceedings of the Colored National Convention, Held in Rochester, July 6th, 7th and 8th, 1853. Rochester, Office of F. Douglass' Paper, 1853. 57 p.

Colored National Emigration Convention. Proceedings of the National Emigration Convention of Colored People; Held at Cleveland, Ohio, on Thursday, Friday, and Saturday, 1854. Pittsburgh, A. A. Anderson, 1854. 77 pp.

Colored People of Providence. Will the General Assembly Put Down Caste Schools? [Providence] December, 1857. 15 p. [A petition of the colored people of Providence, Newport, and Bristol to the General Assembly of Rhode Island for equal privilege in the schools.]

Columbiana County [Ohio] Anti-Slavery Society. An Address of the Board of Managers, of the Columbiana County Anti-Slavery Society, to the Citizens of Ohio. [n.p., n.d.] 8 p.

Columbus, pseud. [Benjamin Lundy]. The Origin and True Causes of the Texas Insurrection, Commenced in the Year 1835. [Originally published in Philadelphia National Gazette.] Philadelphia, 1836. 32 p.

Colver, Nathaniel. The Fugitive Slave Bill; or God's Laws Paramount to the Laws of Men. A Sermon, Preached on Sunday, October 20, 1850, by Rev. Nathaniel Colver, Pastor of the Tremont St. Church. Published by the Request of the Church. Boston, J. M. Hewes & Co., 1850. 24 p. [Colver was a Baptist clergyman, one of the "Seventy."]

Colver, Nathaniel. A Review of the Doings of the Baptist Board of Foreign Missions, and of the Triennial Convention at Baltimore, April, 1841; Originally Published in the Christian Reflector, in Dec., 1841. [Boston] 1841. 36 p.

Colver, Nathaniel. "Slavery or Freedom Must Die." The Harper's Ferry Tragedy: A Symptom of a Disease in the Heart of the Nation; or the Power of Slavery to Destroy the Liberties of the Nation, from Which There Is No Escape but in the Destruction of Slavery Itself. A Sermon, Preached . . . December 11, 1859, by Rev. Nathaniel Colver. Published by Request of the Congregation. Cincinnati, Office of the Christian Luminary, 1860. 16 p.

Committee of Correspondence. Report of the Committee of Correspondence with Southern Ecclesiastical Bodies on Slavery; to the General Association of Massachusetts. Salem, John P. Jewett and Company, 1844. 23 p.

Concord Abolition Society. A Circular Letter, from

Concord Abolition Society, to the Inhabitants of Kentucky, in Which, the Society, by a Concise Appeal to First Principles, and Facts, Plainly Shows That It Would Be Sound Policy, to Make a Law Declaring All Africans, Who Should Be Born in a Servile Condition after the Passing of That Act, Free at a Certain Age. [Concord, N. H.] Printed for Concord Abolition Society, 1814. 12 p.

Concord Female Anti-Slavery Society. Concord, N. H. The Constitution of the Society, Organized 15 November, 1834 with a List of the Names of Members. Concord, A. M'Farland, 1837. 8 p.

Condemnation of the Slave Trade; Being an Investigation of the Origin and Continuation of That Inhuman Traffic: Humbly Inscribed to the Citizens of the United States. By a Friend to Humanity. New York, Printed for the Author, 1794. 20 p.

Conder, Josiah. Wages or the Whip. An Essay on the Comparative Cost and Productiveness of Free and Slave Labour. By Josiah Conder. London, Hatchard and Son [etc.] 1833. 91 p.

Congregational Church Council. Proceedings of a Council of Congregational Churches, Relative to the Privileges of Members of the Church of the Puritans, New York. New York, Edward O. Jenkins, 1859. 92 p.

Congregational Church (Fourth) of Hartford, Conn. The Unanimous Remonstrance of the Fourth Congregational Church, Hartford, Conn., against the Policy of the American Tract Society on the Subject of Slavery. Hartford, Silas Andrus & Son, 1855. 34 p.

Congregational Churches in Maine—*General Conferences.* Slavery vs. the Bible; a Correspondence Between the General Conference of Maine and the Presbytery of Tombecbee, Mississippi. With a Brief Appendix by Cyrus P. Grosvenor. Worcester, Mass., Spooner and Howland, 1840. 158 p.

Congregational Churches in Massachusetts. *General Association.* Report of the Committee of Correspondence with Southern Ecclesiastical Bodies on Slavery; to the General Association of Massachusetts. Pub. by Vote of the Association. Salem, J. P. Jewett and Company, 1844. 23 p.

[Congregational Home Missionary Society]. Home Missions and Slavery: A Reprint of Several Articles, Recently Pub. in the Religious Journals; with an Appendix. New York, J. A. Gray, 1857. 48 p.

Congregational Ministers of Massachusetts. Report of the Committee on Slavery, to the Convention of Congregational Ministers of Massachusetts. Presented May 30, 1849. Boston, T. R. Marvin, 1849. 92 p.

Congregational Union of Scotland. Address of the Congregational Union in Scotland to Their Fellow Christians in the United States, on the Subject of American Slavery. New York, American and Foreign Anti-Slavery Society, 1840. 12 p.

Conkling, Charles. Slavery Abolished. Its Relation to the Government. Oberlin, Shankland, & Co., 1862. 20 p.

Conkling, Roscoe. The Supreme Court of the United States. Speech of Roscoe Conkling, of New York. Delivered in the House of Representatives, April 16, 1860. [Washington, 1860.] 8 p.

Connecticut Society for Promotion of Freedom [Etc.]. The Constitution of the Connecticut Society for the Promotion of Freedom and the Relief of Persons Unlawfully Holden in Bondage, as Revised and Enlarged on the 13th Day of September, 1792. New Haven, 1792. 3 p.

Connecticut Union Meeting, New Haven, 1850. The Proceedings of the Union Meeting, Held at Brewster's Hall, New Haven, Conn., Oct. 24, 1850. Published by Order of the "Union Safety Committee." New Haven, W. H. Stanley, 1851. 48 p.

Considerations on the Abolition of Slavery and the Slave Trade, upon Grounds of Natural, Religious, and Political Duty. Oxford, D. Prince and J. Cooke, 1789. 166 p.

Considerations on the Present Crisis of Affairs, as It Respects the West India Colonies, and the Probable Effects of the French Decree for Emancipating the Negroes, Pointing Out a Remedy for Preventing the Calamitous Consequences in the British Islands. London, J. Johnson, 1795. 76 p.

Considerations on the Slave Trade; and the Consumption of West Indian Produce. London, Darton and Harvey, 1791. 16 p.

Constitution for Anti-Slavery Societies. Constitution of the ———— Anti-Slavery Society. [Printed form for use in the organization of Local Societies]. Declaration of the Anti-Slavery Convention Assembled in Philadelphia, Dec. 4, 1833. [Abridged] Constitution of the American Anti-Slavery Society. [Abridged] Constitution of the Massachusetts Anti-Slavery Society. Boston, Isaac Knapp, 1838. 12 p.

Constitution of a Society for Abolishing the Slave Trade. With Acts of the Legislatures of Massachusetts, Connecticut, and Rhode Island for That Purpose. Providence, Printed by J. Carter, 1789. 19 p.

Continental Club, New York City. Lyrics for Freedom, and Other Poems. Composed by the Younger Members of the Club. New York, Carleton, 1862. 243 p.

Controversy between New York Tribune and Gerrit Smith. New York, John A. Gray, 1855. 32 p.

Conventions for the Improvement of the Free People of Color. Minutes and Proceedings of the Third Annual Convention, for the Improvement of the Free People of Colour in These United States, Held by Adjournments in the City of Philadelphia, from the 3d to the 13th of June Inclusive, 1833. New York by Order of the Convention, 1833. 40 p.

Convention of Abolitionists, West Bloomfield, N. Y., 1847. An Address from the American Abolitionists, to the Friends of the Slave in Great Britain. [Newcastle-on-Tyne, Printed at the Guardian Office, 1847.] 11 p.

Convention of Congregational Ministers of Massachusetts. Report of the Committee on Slavery, to the Convention of Congregational Ministers of Massachusetts. Presented May 30, 1849. Boston, T. R. Marvin, 1849. 92 p.

Convention of the Friends of Freedom in the Eastern and Middle States, Boston, 1845. Proceedings of the Great Convention of the Friends of Freedom in the Eastern and Middle States, Held in Boston, Oct. 1, 2, & 3, 1845. Lowell, Pillsbury and Knapp, 1845. 34 p.

Conway, Martin Franklin. Shall the War Be for Union and Freedom, or Union and Slavery? Speech of Hon. M. F. Conway, of Kansas, Delivered in the House of Representatives, Thursday, December 12, 1861. Washington, D. C., Scammell & Co., 1861. 14 p.

Conway, Moncure Daniel. The Golden Hour. Boston, Ticknor & Fields, 1862. 160 p. [Conway was the son of a Virginia slaveholder; a Methodist, then Unitarian minister; and a strong antislavery writer].

Conway, Moncure Daniel. The One Path; or, The Duties of the North and South; a Discourse in the Unitarian Church, Washington, Jan. 26, 1856. [Washington, 1856.] 8 p.

[Conway, Moncure Daniel]. The Rejected Stone; or Insurrection vs. Resurrection in America, by a Native of Virginia. Boston, Walker, Wise & Co., 1861. 132 p.
Same. Second Edition. Boston, Walker, Wise & Co., 1862. 131 p.
Same. Third Edition. Boston, Walker, Wise & Co., 1862. 161 p.

Conway, Moncure Daniel. Testimonies Concerning Slavery. By M. D. Conway, a Native of Virginia. 2d ed. London, Chapman and Hall, 1865. 140 p.

[Cooper, David]. A Mite Cast into the Treasury; or, Observations on Slave-Keeping. Philadelphia, Printed 1772. To Be Had at Most of the Booksellers in Town. 24 p.

[Cooper, David]. A Serious Address to the Rulers of America, on the Inconsistency of Their Conduct Respecting Slavery: Forming a Contrast Between the Encroachments of England on American Liberty and American Injustice in Tolerating Slavery. Trenton, Printed; London, Reprint by J. Phillips, 1783. 24 p.

Cooper, Thomas. Facts Illustrative of the Condition of the Negro Slaves in Jamaica: With Notes and an Appendix. London, J. Hatchard and Son, 1824. 64 p.

Cooper, Thomas. Negro Slavery; or, A View of Some of the More Prominent Features of That State of Society, as It Exists in the United States of America and in the Colonies of the West Indies, Especially in Jamaica. Fourth Edition. London, Printed by R. Taylor, for the Society for the Mitigation and Gradual Abolition of Slavery throughout the British Dominions, 1824. 92 p.

Copley, Esther Hewlett. History of Slavery and Its Abolition. London, 1836. 634 p.
Same. Second Edition. London, Houlston & Stoneman, 1839. 648 p.
Same. Third Edition. London, 1852. 648 p.

Copp, Joseph A. (Rev.). Discourse on American Liberty and Its Obligations, Delivered in Broadway Church, Chelsea, Mass., July 2, 1854. Boston, C. C. P. Moody, 1854. 24 p.

Cornish, Samuel E. The Colonization Scheme Considered, in Its Rejection by the Colored People—in Its Tendency to Uphold Caste—in Its Unfitness for Christianizing and Civilizing the Aborigines of Africa, and for Putting a Stop to the African Slave Trade: In a Letter to the Hon. Theodore Frelinghuysen and Hon. Benjamin F. Butler; by Samuel E. Cornish and Theodore S. Wright. Newark [N. J.], A. Guest, 1840. 26 p. [Cornish served on the executive committees of both the American and the American and Foreign Anti-Slavery Societies.]

The Correspondence between John Gladstone, Esq., M.P., and James Cropper, Esq., on the Present State of Slavery in the British West Indies and in the United States of America; and on the Importation of Sugar from the British Settlements in India, with an Appendix; Containing Several Papers on the Subject of Slavery. Liverpool, West India Association, 1824. 121 p.

Corwin, Thomas. Free Soil vs. Slavery. Speech of Mr. Corwin, of Ohio, Against the Compromise Bill, Delivered in the Senate of the United States, Monday, July 24, 1848. Washington [D. C.], Buell & Blanchard, 1848. 16 p.

Corwin, Thomas. State of the Union. Speech of Hon. Thomas Corwin, of Ohio. Delivered in the House of Representatives, Jan. 21, 1861. Washington [D. C.], Henry Polkinhorn, 1861. 16 p.

Corwin, Thomas. Speech of Hon. Thomas Corwin, of Ohio, in the House of Representatives, January 23 and 24, 1860. [Washington, D. C., Republican Congressional Committee, 1860]. 16 p.
Same. Washington, D. C., Buell & Blanchard, 1860. 30 p.

Cox, Samuel Hanson. Correspondence between the

Rev. Samuel H. Cox, D.D., of Brooklyn, L. I., and Frederick Douglass, a Fugitive Slave. New York, American Anti-Slavery Society, 1846. 16 p.

Crandall, Prudence. Report of the Arguments of Counsel in the Case of Prudence Crandall, Pltf. in Error vs. State of Connecticut, before the Supreme Court of Errors, at Their Session at Brooklyn, July Term, 1834. By a Member of the Bar. [Chauncey F. Cleveland] Boston, Garrison & Knapp, 1834. 34 p.

Crandall, Reuben. The Trial of Reuben Crandall, M.D., Charged with Publishing Seditious Libels, by Circulating the Publications of the American Anti-Slavery Society. Before the Circuit Court for the District of Columbia, Held at Washington, in April, 1836, Occupying the Court the Period of Ten Days. New York, H. R. Piercy, 1836. 62 p.

Crandall, Reuben (Defendant). The Trial of Reuben Crandall, M.D. Charged with Publishing and Circulating Seditious and Incendiary Papers, Etc. in the District of Columbia, with the Intent of Exciting Servile Insurrection. Carefully Reported, and Compiled from the Written Statements of the Court and the Counsel by a Member of the Bar. Washington City, Printed for the Proprietors, 1836. 48 p.

Crawford, Charles. Observations upon Negro Slavery. Philadelphia, Joseph Crukshank, 1784. 24 p. Same. Second Edition. Philadelphia, Eleazer Oswald, 1790. 125 p.

The Creole Case, and Mr. Webster's Despatch; with Comments of the N. Y. American. New York, Office of New York American, 1842. 39 p.

Cropper, James. The Extinction of the American Colonization Society, the First Step to the Abolition of American Slavery. London, S. Bagster, Jr., 1833. 24 p.

Cropper, James. A Letter Addressed to the Liverpool Society for Promoting the Abolition of Slavery, on the Injurious Effects of High Prices of Produce, and the Beneficial Effects of Low Prices, on the Condition of Slaves. Liverpool, James Smith, 1823. 32 p.

Cropper, James. A Letter to Thomas Clarkson, by James Cropper, and Prejudice Vincible; or, The Practicability of Conquering Prejudice by Better Means Than by Slavery and Exile; in Relation to the American Colonization Society. By C. Stuart. Liverpool, Printed by E. Smith and Co., 1832. Same: New York, 1833, 15 p. in *Anti-Slavery Reporter*, v. 1, No. 1. Also Reprinted from English Edition as Supplement to the *Emancipator*.

Cropper, James, and Others. Speeches at the Anti-Colonization Meeting, in Exeter Hall, London, July 13, 1833. By J. Cropper, W. L. Garrison, N.

Paul, D. O'Connell, Etc. Boston, Garrison & Knapp, 1833. 39 p.

Crosswhite Case (Giltner vs. Gorham, Hurd and Others). Marshall, Michigan, Jan. 1, 1849. Citizens Committee Report.

Crothers, Samuel. The Gospel of the Jubilee. An Explanation of the Typical Privileges Secured to the Congregation and Pious Strangers, by the Atonement on the Morning of the Jubilee. Lev. 25, 9–46. Samuel Crothers. Hamilton, O., I. M. Walters, 1837. 84 p. [*See also* James Gilliland]

Crothers, Samuel. The Gospel of the Jubilee. An Explanation of the Typical Privileges Secured to the Congregation and Pious Strangers, by the Atonement on the Morning of the Jubilee. *Lev.*, xxv, 9–46. Reprint from the Author's Edition of 1839. With an Introduction by Rev. John Rankin. Cincinnati, American Reform Tract and Book Society, 1856. 222 p.

Crothers, Samuel. The Gospel of the Typical Servitude; the Substance of a Sermon Preached in Greenfield, Jan. 1, 1834. Published by the Abolition Society of Paint Valley [Ohio], Hamilton, O., Gardner & Gibbon, 1835. 22 p.

Crothers, Samuel. Strictures on African Slavery. Published by the Abolition Society of Paint Valley [Ohio]. Rossville, Butler Co., Ohio, Taylor Webster, 1833. 46 p.

Crowell, John. Slavery in the District of Columbia. Speech of Mr. Crowell, of Ohio, on Slavery in the District of Columbia Delivered in the House, July 26, 1848. [Washington, D. C.] J. & G. S. Gideon [1848]. 16 p.

Crummell, Rev. A[lexander]. The Man: The Hero: The Christian! A Eulogy on the Life and Character of Thomas Clarkson: Delivered in the City of New York, December, 1846. By the Rev. Alexander Crummell, Together with Freedom, a Poem, Read on the Same Occasion by Charles L. Reason. New York, Egbert, Hovey & King, 1847. 44 p.

Crummell, Alexander. The Relations and Duties of Free Colored Men in America to Africa. A Letter to Charles B. Dunbar, M.D., Esq. of New York City. Hartford, Case, Lockwood & Co., 1861. 54 p.

Curtis, George C. Prospects Before the Country. A Discourse Delivered in Adrian, Michigan, June 25, 1854, by Geo. C. Curtis, Pastor of the First Presbyterian Church of That City. Adrian, Jermain & Brothers, 1854. 14 p.

Curtis, George Ticknor. The Constitutional Power of Congress over the Territories. An Argument Delivered in the Supreme Court of the United States, December 18, 1856, in the Case of Dred Scott, Plaintiff in Error, vs. John F. A. Sandford. Boston, Little, Brown and Company, 1857. 42 p.

Curtis, George Ticknor. The Just Supremacy of Congress over the Territories. Boston, A. Williams and Company, 1859. 44 p.

[Curtis, George Ticknor]. Observations on the Rev. Dr. Gannett's Sermon, Entitled "Relation of the North to Slavery." Republished from the Editorial Columns of the Boston Courier, of June 28th and 30th, and July 6th, 1854. Boston, Redding and Company, 1854. 29 p.

Cushing, Caleb. An Oration Pronounced at Boston before the Colonization Society of Massachusetts, on the Anniversary of American Independence, July 4, 1833. Boston, Lyceum Press, G. W. Light & Co., 1833. 24 p.

Cushing, Caleb. Speech Delivered in Faneuil Hall, —Boston, October 27, 1857. Also, Speech Delivered in City Hall,—Newburyport, October 31, 1857. By Caleb Cushing. [Boston] Office of the Boston Post, 1857. 48 p.

Cushing, Caleb. Speech of Mr. Cushing, of Massachusetts, on the Right of Petition, as Connected with Petitions for the Abolition of Slavery and the Slave Trade in the District of Columbia: In the House of Representatives, January 25, 1836. Washington [D. C.], Gales & Seaton, 1836. 15 p.

Cutting, Sewall Sylvester. Influence of Christianity on Government and Slavery: A Discourse, Delivered in the Baptist Church, in West Boylston, Mass., January 15, 1837. By Sewall S. Cutting, Pastor. Worcester, H. J. Howland, 1837. 14 p.

Daggs, Ruel vs. Frazier, Elihu, et als. Fugitive Slave Case. District Court of the United States for the Southern Division of Iowa. Burlington, June Term, 1850: Ruel Daggs vs. Elihu Frazier, et als. Trespass on the Case. Reported by Geo. Frazee. Burlington, Morgan & M'Kenny, 1850. 40 p.

Dana, James. The African Slave Trade. A Discourse Delivered in the City of New Haven, September 9, 1790, Before the Connecticut Society for the Promotion of Freedom, by James Dana, D.D., Pastor of the First Congregational Church in Said City. New Haven, Thomas & Samuel Green, 1791. 33 p.

Dana, Richard H. Remarks of Richard H. Dana, Jr., Esq., Before the Committee on Federal Relations, on the Proposed Removal of Edward G. Loring, Esq., from the Office of Judge of Probate, March 5, 1855. Boston, Alfred Mudge & Son, 1855. 28 p.

Damrell, W. S. Assault on Mr. Sumner. Speech of Hon. W. S. Damrell, of Massachusetts, in the House of Representatives, July 12, 1856. Washington, D. C., Buell and Blanchard, 1856. 8 p.

[Darlington, William]. Desultory Remarks on the Question of Extending Slavery into Missouri: As Enunciated During the First Session of the Sixteenth Congress, by the Representative from Chester County, State of Pennsylvania. Extracted from the American Republican Newspaper of 1819–20. West Chester, Pa., L. Marshall, 1856. 37 p.

Davenport, J. A Chapter in the History of Abolitionism at Syracuse: Together with a Glance at the Principles of Abolitionism. [Syracuse, 1839.] 8 p.

Davis, Charles G. United States vs. Charles G. Davis. Report of the Proceedings at the Examination of Charles G. Davis, Esq., on a Charge of Aiding and Abetting in the Rescue of a Fugitive Slave, Held in Boston, in February, 1851. Boston, White and Potter, 1851. 44 p.

Davis, Owen. Sketches of Sermons, Delivered by Rev. Owen Davis, in the First Free Bethel Church, in West Centre Street, Boston. Boston, Printed for the Author, 1837. 12 p.

Dawes, Henry Laurens. The Lecompton Constitution Founded neither in Law nor the Will of the People. Speech of Hon. Henry L. Dawes, of Massachusetts. Delivered in the U. S. House of Representatives, March 8, 1858. Washington, Buell & Blanchard, 1858. 8 p.

Dawes, Henry Laurens. The New Dogma of the South—"Slavery a Blessing." Speech of Hon. Henry L. Dawes, of Mass. Delivered in the House of Representatives, April 12, 1860. [Washington, 1860.] 7 p.

Day, Thomas. The Dying Negro, a Poem by the Late Thomas Day and John Bicknell, Esquires. To Which is Added, a Fragment of a Letter on the Slavery of Negroes. London, John Stockdale, 1793. 82 p.

Day, Thomas. Four Tracts: Reflections upon the Present State of England, and the Independence of America. Reflections upon the Peace, the East-India Bill, and the Present Crisis. A Dialogue between a Justice of the Peace and a Farmer. Fragment of an Original Letter on the Slavery of the Negroes. By Thomas Day. London, John Stockdale, 1785.

Day, Thomas. Fragment of an Original Letter on the Slavery of the Negroes, Written in the Year 1776. By Thomas Day, Esquire. London, Printed by John Stockdale, 1784. vi, 11–40 p. Boston, Reprinted by Garrison and Knapp, 1831. 12 p.

Day, Thomas. Fragments of an Original Letter on the Slavery of the Negroes; Written in the Year 1776 by Thomas Day, Esq. Philadelphia, Printed by Francis Bailey, at Yorick's Head, 1784. Broadside, 1 p. 34 × 42 cm.

[Day, Thomas]. A Letter from Thomas Day in London, to His Friend in America, on the Subject of the Slave-Trade; Together with Some Extracts, from Approved Authors of Matters of Fact, Confirming the Principles Contained in Said Letter. New York, S. Loudon, 1784. 28 p.

Day, William. Slavery in America Shown to Be Peculiarly Abominable, Both as a Political Anomaly and an Outrage on Christianity. London, Hamilton, Adams, and Co., 1841. 84 p.

Dean, Paul. A Discourse Delivered Before the African Society, at Their Meetinghouse, in Boston, Mass. on the Abolition of the Slave Trade by the Government of the United States of America, July 14, 1819. By Paul Dean, Pastor of the First Universal Church in Boston. Boston, Nathaniel Coverly, 1819. 16 p.

DeCharms, Richard. A Discourse on the True Nature of Freedom and Slavery; Delivered Before the Washington Society of the New Jerusalem, in View of the One Hundred and Eighteenth Anniversary of Washington's Birth. Philadelphia, J. H. Jones, 1850. 63 p.

Delaware Anti-Slavery Society. Memorial, to the Citizens and Legislature of the State of Delaware on the Subject of Slavery. [Wilmington, 1846.] 8 p.

Delaware Society for Promoting the Abolition of Slavery. Constitution of the Delaware Society for Promoting the Abolition of Slavery; and for the Relief and Protection of Free Blacks and People of Colour Unlawfully Held in Bondage or Otherwise Oppressed. Wilmington, Bonsal and Niles, 1801. 8 p.

DeTocqueville, Alexis. Report Made to the Chamber of Deputies on the Abolition of Slavery in the French Colonies, by Alexis DeTocqueville, July 23, 1839. Boston, James Munroe and Company, 1840. 54 p.

DeVinne, Daniel. The Methodist Episcopal Church and Slavery. A Historical Survey of the Relation of the Early Methodists to Slavery. New York, Francis Hart, 1857. 95 p.

Dewey, Rev. Orville. An Address Delivered under the Old Elm Tree in Sheffield, with Some Remarks on the Great Political Question of the Day. New York, C. S. Francis & Co., 1836. 26 p.

Dewey, Orville. A Discourse on Slavery and the Annexation of Texas. New York, Charles S. Francis and Company, 1844. 18 p.

Dewey, Orville. The Laws of Human Progress and Modern Reforms. A Lecture Delivered Before the Mercantile Library Association of the City of New York. New York, C. S. Francis & Co., 1852. 35 p.

Dewey, Orville. On Patriotism. The Conditions, Prospects, and Duties of the American People. A Sermon Delivered on Fast Day at Church Green, Boston. Boston, Ticknor & Fields, 1859. 39 p.

A Dialogue Concerning the Slavery of the Africans; Shewing It to Be the Duty and Interest of the American States to Emancipate All Their African Slaves. With an Address to the Owners of Such Slaves. Dedicated to the Honourable, the Continental Congress. To Which Is Prefixed, the Institution [sic] of the Society, in New York, for Promoting the Manumission of Slaves, and Protecting Such of Them as Have Been, or May Be Liberated. Norwich, Judach P. Spooner, 1776. New York: Re-printed for Robert Hodge, 1785. 71 p.

A Dialogue, Containing Some Reflections on the Late Declaration and Remonstrance, of the Black Inhabitants of the Province of Pennsylvania. With a Serious and Short Address, to Those Presbyterians, Who (to Their Dishonor) Have Too Much Abetted, and Conniv'd at the Late Insurrection. By a Member of That Community. Philadelphia, Printed: and Sold by All the Pamphlet Sellers, 1764. 16 p.

Dick, David. All Modern Slavery Indefensible; Intended for All Places Where Slavery Does Exist, and for All Legislative Powers by Whom It Is Allowed. Montrose, P. Milne, 1836. 323 p.

Dickey, Rev. James H. A Review of a Summary of Biblical Antiquities, Compiled for the Use of Sunday School Teachers, and for the Benefit of Families; by J. W. Nevin, Late Assistant Teacher in the Theol. Seminary of Princeton. By James H. Dickey, Pastor of the Church at Salem, Ross County, Ohio. Ripley, Campbell & Palmer, 1834. 36 p.

Dickinson, James Taylor. A Sermon, Delivered in the Second Congregational Church, Norwich, on the Fourth of July, 1834, at the Request of the Anti-Slavery Society of Norwich and Vicinity. Norwich, [Conn.], Anti Slavery Society, 1834. 40 p. Same: Rochester, Hoyt & Porter, 1835. 33 p.

[Dillwyn, William]. Brief Considerations on Slavery, and the Expediency of Its Abolition. With Some Hints on the Means Whereby It May Be Gradually Effected. Recommended to the Serious Attention of All, and Especially of Those Entrusted with the Powers of Legislation. Burlington, Isaac Collins, 1773. 16 p.

Directors of the African School [James Richards, Pres.]. An Address to the Public on the Subject of the African School, Lately Established under the Care of the Synod of New-York and New-Jersey. By the Directors of the Institution. New York, J. Seymour, 1816. 8 p.

Discipline of Earth and Time for Freedom and Immortality. Four Books of an Unpublished Poem. Boston, 1854. 147 p.

Dix, John Adams. Speech of Hon. John A. Dix, of New York, in Relation to Territories Acquired from Mexico. Delivered in the Senate of the United

States, February 28, 1849. Washington, D. C., 1849. 14 p.

Doggett, Simeon. Two Discourses on the Subject of Slavery. Boston, Published by Author, 1835. 28 p.

Dorchester Female Anti-Slavery Society. First Annual Report of the Dorchester Female Anti-Slavery Society. December, 1837. Boston, D. Clapp, 1838. 23 p.

[Douglas, Mrs. R.]. Reflections on the Conservatory Elements of the American Republic; by a Lady. Chillicothe, O., S. W. Ely, 1842. 55 p.

[Douglass, Frederick]. Abolition Fanaticism in New York. Speech of a Runaway Slave from Baltimore, at an Abolition Meeting in New York, Held May 11, 1847. [Baltimore] 1847. 8 p.

Douglass, Frederick. The Anti-Slavery Movement. A Lecture by Frederick Douglass, before the Rochester Ladies Anti-Slavery Society. Rochester, Lee, Mann & Co., 1855. 44 p.

Douglass, Frederick. The Claims of the Negro Ethnologically Considered. An Address Before the Literary Societies of Western Reserve College, at Commencement, July 12, 1854. Rochester, Lee, Mann & Co., 1854. 37 p.

Douglass, Frederick. Lectures on American Slavery. By Frederick Douglass. Delivered at Corinthian Hall, Rochester, N. Y. Buffalo, G. Reese & Co's Power Press, 1851. 32 p.

Douglass, Frederick. My Bondage and My Freedom. Part I: Life as a Slave. Part II: Life as a Freeman. By Frederick Douglass. With an Introduction. By Dr. James M'Cune Smith. New York, Miller, Orton & Mulligan, 1855. 464 p.

Douglass, Frederick. Narrative of the Life of Frederick Douglass, an American Slave; Written by Himself. Boston, Pub. at the Anti-Slavery Office, 1845. 125 p.

Douglass, Frederick. Oration, Delivered in Corinthian Hall, Rochester, by Frederick Douglass, July 5th, 1852. Rochester, Lee, Mann & Co., 1852. 39 p.

Douglass, Frederick. Two Speeches: One on West India Emancipation, Delivered at Canandaigua, Aug. 4, and the Other on the Dred Scott Decision, Delivered in New York, on the Occasion of the Anniversary of the American Abolition Society, May, 1857. Rochester, N. Y., C. P. Dewey [1857]. 46 p.

Douglass, Frederick, [and others]. Arguments, Pro and Con, on the Case for a National Emigration Convention, to Be Held in Cleveland, Ohio, August, 1854, by Frederick Douglass, W. J. Watkins, & J. M. Whitfield, with a Short Appendix of the Statistics of Canada West, West Indies, Central and South America. Detroit, George E. Pomeroy & Co., 1854. 34 p.

Douglass, H. Ford. Speech of H. Ford Douglass, in Reply to Mr. J. M. Langston, Before the Emigration Convention, at Cleveland, Ohio, Delivered on the Evening of the 27th of August, 1854. Chicago, Wm. H. Worrell, 1854. 16 p.

Douglass, Margaret. Educational Laws of Virginia. The Personal Narrative of Mrs. Margaret Douglass, a Southern Woman, Who Was Imprisoned for One Month in the Common Jail of Norfolk, under the Laws of Virginia, for the Crime of Teaching Free Colored Children to Read. Boston, John P. Jewett & Co., 1854. 65 p.

Douglass, William. Annals of the First African Church, in the United States of America, Now Styled the African Episcopal Church of St. Thomas, Philadelphia, in Its Connection with the Early Struggles of the Colored People to Improve Their Condition, with the Cooperation of Friends, and Other Philanthropists; Partly Derived from the Minutes of a Beneficial Society, Established by Absalom Jones, Richard Allen and Others, in 1787, and Partly from the Minister of the Aforesaid Church. Philadelphia, King & Baird, 1862. 172 p.

Drake, Richard. Revelations of a Slave Smuggler: Being the Autobiography of Capt. Rich'd Drake, an African Trader for Fifty Years—from 1807 to 1857; During Which Period He Was Concerned in the Transportation of Half a Million Blacks from African Coasts to America. With a Preface by His Executor, Rev. Henry Byrd West. New York, R. M. DeWitt [1860]. 100 p.

Drayton, Daniel. Personal Memoir of Daniel Drayton, for Four Years and Four Months a Prisoner (for Charity's Sake) in Washington Jail. Including a Narrative of the Voyage and Capture of the Schooner Pearl. Boston, Bela Marsh, 1855. 122 p.

Dresser, Amos. The Narrative of Amos Dresser, with Stone's Letters from Natchez,—an Obituary Notice of the Writer, and Two Letters from Tallahassee, Relating to the Treatment of Slaves. New York, American Anti-Slavery Society, 1836. 42 p.

Dresser, Amos. Narrative of the Arrest, Lynch Law Trial, and Scourging of Amos Dresser at Nashville, Tennessee, August, 1835. Oberlin, Dresser, 1849. 24 p.

Drew, Benjamin. The Refugee: or, The Narrative of Fugitive Slaves in Canada, Related by Themselves, with an Account of the History and the Condition of the Colored Population of Upper Canada. Boston, John P. Jewett & Company, 1856. 387 p.

[Dublin Anti-Slavery Society]. To Irish Emigrants Who Are Going to the United States. Dublin, R. D. Webb [n.d.]. 4 p.

Dublin Ladies Anti-Slavery Society. Rules and Resolutions of the Dublin Ladies' Anti-Slavery Society, with Lists of the District Treasurers, Committee and Secretaries; and of the Subscribers. Dublin, R. Napper, 1828. 24 p.

[Dudley, Miss Mary]. Scripture Evidence of the Sinfulness of Injustice and Oppression; Respectfully Submitted to Professing Christians, in Order to Call Forth Their Sympathy and Exertions on Behalf of the Much-Injured Africans. London, Harvey and Darton, 1828. 26 p.

Duffield, George. A Sermon on American Slavery: Its Nature, and the Duties of Christians in Relation to It. By George Duffield. Detroit, J. S. and S. A. Bagg, 1840. 32 p. [Presbyterian minister of Detroit; sometime secretary of the Pennsylvania Anti-Slavery Society.]

Duncan, James. The Slaveholder's Prayer. New York, American Anti-Slavery Society, 4 p. [Taken from Duncan, a Treatise on Slavery Published in Indiana, in 1824.]

Duncan, James. A Treatise on Slavery. In Which Is Shown Forth the Evil of Slaveholding Both from the Light of Nature and Divine Revelation. Vevay, Indiana Register Office, 1824. 88 p.
Same. New York, American Anti-Slavery Society, 1840. 136 p.
Same. Cincinnati, Cincinnati Anti-Slavery Society, 1840. 136 p.

Dupré, Lewis. A Political View of the Evils of Slavery; by Way of Appendix to a System of Progressive Emancipation. By L. Dupré . . . [Raleigh? N. C.] Printed for the Author, 1810. 24 p.

Dupré, Lewis. A Rational & Benevolent Plan for Averting Some of the Calamitous Consequences of Slavery, Being a Practicable, Seasonable and Profitable Institution for the Progressive Emancipation of Virginia and Carolina Slaves. [n.p.], 1810. 32 p.

Dupré, L[ewis]. An Admonitory Picture, and a Solemn Warning: Principally Addressed to Professing Christians in the Southern States of North America. Being an Introduction to the Establishment of a System of Progressive Emancipation. [Philadelphia] Published by the Author, 1810. 44 p.

Durkee, Charles. The Fugitive Slave Law, Etc. Speech of Charles Durkee, of Wisconsin, in the House of Representatives, August 6, 1852, on the Fugitive Slave Law as a "Finality," and the Present Position of Parties. Washington, D. C., Buell & Blanchard, 1852. 15 p.

Durkee, Charles. Speech of Charles Durkee, of Wisconsin, on the California Question. Made in the House of Representatives, June 10, 1850. [n.p., n.d.] 15 p.

Dwight, Theodore. An Oration, Spoken Before "The Connecticut Society, for the Promotion of Freedom and the Relief of Persons Unlawfully Holden in Bondage." Convened in Hartford, on the 8th Day of May, A.D., 1794. Hartford, Hudson and Goodwin, 1794. 24 p.

Dwight, Timothy. Dissertation on the History, Eloquence, and Poetry of the Bible, Delivered at the Public Commencement at New Haven. New Haven, Thomas and Samuel Green, 1772. 16 p.

Dyer, Frederick N. The Slave Girl: A Tale of the Nineteenth Century; in Five Cantos. London, Houlston and Stoneman, 1848. 224 p.

Dyer, Oliver. Oliver Dyer's Phonographic Report of the Proceedings of the National Free Soil Convention at Buffalo, N. Y., August 9th and 10th, 1848. Buffalo, G. H. Derby & Co., 1848. 32 p.

Earle, Thomas. The Life, Travels and Opinions of Benjamin Lundy, Including His Journeys to Texas and Mexico; with a Sketch of Contemporary Events, and a Notice of the Revolution in Hayti. Compiled under the Direction, and on Behalf of His Children. Philadelphia, William D. Parrish, 1847. 316 p.

Eastern Pennsylvania Anti-Slavery Society. Captains Drayton and Sayres; or the Way in Which Americans Are Treated, for Aiding the Cause of Liberty at Home. Philadelphia. 4 p.

Eastern Pennsylvania Anti-Slavery Society. Tracts, No. 4. The Political Economy of Slavery. [Philadelphia, Eastern Pennsylvania Anti-Slavery Society.] Pp. 13–16.

Eastman, David C., and Roebucke, Hugh. Examination of the Proceedings of the Ohio Annual Conference of the Methodist Episcopal Church, on Abolition and Colonization, at Its Meeting in Springfield, Clark County, Ohio, August, 1835; by Two Members of That Church Residing in Fayette County, O. Washington, Robert R. Lindsey, 1836. 28 p. [Eastman was secretary of the Ohio Anti-Slavery Society.]

Easton, Hosea. A Treatise on the Intellectual Character, and Civil and Political Conditions of the Colored People of the U. States, and the Prejudice Exercised Towards Them: With a Sermon on the Duty of the Church to Them. Boston, I. Knapp, 1837. 54 p.

Edge, Frederick Milnes. Slavery Doomed: or, The Contest Between Free and Slave Labour in the United States. By Frederick Milnes Edge. London, Smith, Elder and Co., 1860. 224 p.

Edgerton, Sidney. The Irrepressible Conflict. Speech of Hon. Sidney Edgerton, of Ohio, Delivered in the House of Representatives, February 29, 1860. [Washington, D. C.] Republican Executive Congressional Committee [1860]. 8 p.

Edgerton, Walter. A History of the Separation in Indiana Yearly Meeting of Friends; Which Took

Place in the Winter of 1842 and 1843, on the Anti-Slavery Question; Containing a Brief Account of the Rise, Spread, and Final Adoption by the Society, of Its Testimony Against Slavery; Together with a Record of Some of the Principal Facts and Circumstances Relating to That Separation; Embracing the Documents Issued by Both Parties Relative Thereto; and Some Account of the Action of Other Yearly Meetings of Friends, Touching the Controversy, Especially That of London, Etc. By Walter Edgerton. Cincinnati, A. Pugh, 1856. 352 p.

[Edinburgh Emancipation Society]. A Voice to the United States of America, from the Metropolis of Scotland; Being an Account of Various Meetings Held in Edinburgh on the Subject of American Slavery, upon the Return of Mr. George Thompson, from His Mission to That Country. Edinburgh, W. Oliphant and Son, 1836. 51 p. [The Edinburgh Ladies Anti-Slavery Society sent George Thompson to the United States.]

Edwards, Jonathan. The Injustice and Impolicy of the Slave-Trade, and of the Slavery of the Africans: Illustrated in a Sermon Preached before the Connecticut Society for the Promotion of Freedom, and for the Relief of Persons Unlawfully Holden in Bondage, at Their Annual Meeting in New Haven, September 15, 1791. By Jonathan Edwards. To Which Is Added, a Short Sketch of the Evidence for the Abolition of the Slave-Trade, Delivered before a Committee of the British House of Commons. Providence, J. Carter, 1792. 60 p.

Edwards, Jonathan. The Injustice and Impolicy of the Slave Trade, and of the Slavery of the Africans: Illustrated in a Sermon Preached before the Connecticut Society for the Promotion of Freedom, and for the Relief of Persons Unlawfully Holden in Bondage, at Their Annual Meeting in New Haven, September 15, 1791. New Haven, Thomas & Samuel Green, 1791. 37 p.
Same. Second Edition. Boston, Wells and Lilly, 1822. 40 p.
Same. Third Edition. New Haven, New Haven Anti-Slavery Society, 1833. 32 p.
Same. Fourth Edition. Newburyport, Charles Whipple, 1834. 24 p.

Elliott, Charles. The Bible and Slavery: In Which the Abrahamic and Mosaic Discipline Is Considered in Connection with the Most Ancient Forms of Slavery; and the Pauline Code on Slavery as Related to Roman Slavery and the Discipline of the Apostolic Churches. Cincinnati, L. Swarmstedt & A. Poe, for the Methodist Episcopal Church, 1859. 354 p.

Elliott, Charles. Sinfulness of American Slavery; Proved from Its Evil Sources; Its Injustice; Its Wrongs; Its Contrariety to Many Scriptural Commands, Prohibitions, and Principles, and to the Christian Spirit; and from Its Evil Effects; Together with Observations on Emancipation, and the Duties of American Citizens in Regard to Slavery. 2 Vols. Edited by Rev. B. F. Tefft. Cincinnati, L. Swarmstedt & J. H. Power, 1850.
Same: Cincinnati, L. Swarmstedt & J. H. Power, 1851.

Ely, Ezra Stiles. The Duty of Christian Freeman to Elect Christian Rulers: A Discourse Delivered on the Fourth of July, 1827, in the Seventh Presbyterian Church, in Philadelphia. With an Appendix, Designed to Vindicate the Liberty of Christians, and of American Sunday School Union. Philadelphia, W. F. Geddes, 1828. 32 p.

Emancipator. Weekly. New York, N. Y. 1833–December 3, 1841. Boston, Mass. December 10, 1841–1850. 1833–1850. Principal Editor: Joshua Leavitt. Edited by William Goodell from 1834 to 1836. Organ of the American Anti-Slavery Society.

Emerson, Ralph Waldo. An Address Delivered in the Court-House in Concord, Massachusetts, on 1st August, 1844, on the Anniversary of the Emancipation of the Negroes in the British West Indies. Boston, James Munroe & Co., 1844. 34 p.

Encroachments of the Slave Power, upon the Rights of the North. By a Northern Man. Boston, B. Marsh, 1848. 36 p.

England, John. Letters of the Late Bishop England to the Hon. John Forsyth, on the Subject of Domestic Slavery: To Which Are Prefixed Copies, in Latin and English, of the Pope's Apostolic Letter, Concerning the African Slave Trade. Baltimore, John Murphy, 1844. 156 p.

English Clergyman. Letter to a Member of the Congress of the United States of America, from an English Clergyman; Including a Republication, with Considerable Additions, of the Tract Entitled 'Every Man His Own Property.' London, Whittaker, Treacher, and Arnot, 1835. 30 p.

The Envoy from Free Hearts to the Free. Pawtucket, R. I., Juvenile Emancipation Society, 1840. 112 p. [A collection of poems and sketches relating to slavery.]

Essex County Anti-Slavery Convention, Danvers, Mass., 1838. Proceedings of the Essex County Anti-Slavery Convention, Held at Danvers, October 24, 1838, with an Address to the Voters, on Their Duties to the Enslaved. Salem, Gazette Office, 1838. 12 p.

Estlin, John Bishop. A Brief Notice of American Slavery and the Abolition Movement. Bristol, H. C. Evans, 1840. 40 p. [To stimulate contributions to the bazaars of the Boston F. A. S. S.]

Second Edition. Revised. London, William Tweedie, 1853. 98 p.

Estlin, John Bishop. Reply to a Circular Issued by the Glasgow Association for the Abolition of Slavery Recommending a Discontinuance of British Support to the Boston Anti-Slavery Bazaar. Paris, E. Brière, 1850. 8 p.

Estwick, Samuel. Considerations on the Negro Cause Commonly So Called, Addressed to the Right Honourable Lord Mansfield, Lord Chief Justice of the Court of King's Bench. Second Edition. London, J. Dodsley, 1773. 95 p.

Evangelical Union Anti-Slavery Society of the City of New York. Address to the Churches of Jesus Christ, by the Evangelical Union Anti-Slavery Society, of the City of New York, Auxiliary to the Am. A. S. Society. With the Constitution, Names of Officers, Board of Managers, and Executive Committee, April, 1839. New York, American Anti-Slavery Society, 1839. 54 p.

Exposition of the Proceedings of John P. Darg, Henry W. Merritt, and Others, in Relation to the Robbery of Darg, the Elopement of His Alleged Slave, and the Trial of Barney Corse, Who Was Unjustly Charged as an Accessory. New York, Isaac T. Hopper, 1840. 39 p.

Facts for the People. Monthly. Cincinnati, Washington, D. C. Edited by Gamaliel Bailey.
New Series. Volume 1. 1843.
No. 3. March. (17–24) Official Statistics of the Distribution of the Offices of the Federal Government. William Birney.
No. 4. April. (25–33). Cassius M. Clay's Pamphlet. [Extracts from Article by C. M. Clay, First Published in Lexington (Ky.) Intelligencer.]
No. 5. May (34–40). Address to the Non-Slaveholders of the South.
No. 6. June (41–48). Address to the Non-Slaveholders of the South [concluded].
No. 7. July. (49–56). Speech of Daniel O'Connell before the Repeal Association, on Occasion of the Reception of a Communication from the Pennsylvania Anti-Slavery Society.
No. 8. August. (57–64). Letter from the Hon. John Quincy Adams. [To Asa Walker, etc., of Bangor, July 4, 1843.]
No. 11. November. (81–88). Daniel O'Connell's Letter.
No. 12. December. (89–96). The O'Connell Letter. [Letter of Salmon P. Chase and Others to the Secretary of the Loyal National Repeal Association, November 30, 1843.]
New Series (Washington, D. C., 1855–1856). Volume 1.

No. 12. February. (145–160). Territorial Aggrandizement and War: The North and the South.

Fall River Female Anti-Slavery Society. Report of a Delegate to the Anti-Slavery Convention of American Women, Held in Philadelphia, May, 1838; Including an Account of Other Meetings Held in Pennsylvania Hall, and of the Riot. Addressed to the Fall River Female Anti-Slavery Society, and Published by Its Request. Boston, I. Knapp, 1838. 24 p.

Fawcett, Benjamin. A Compassionate Address to the Christian Negroes in Virginia, and Other British Colonies in North America. With an Appendix, Containing Some Account of the Rise and Progress of Christianity among That Poor People. Second Edition. Salop, Printed by F. Eddowes and F. Cotton, 1756. 40 p.

Featherstonhaugh, George William. Excursion through the Slave States, from Washington on the Potomac, to the Frontier of Mexico; with Sketches of Popular Manners and Geological Notices. 2 Vols. London, John Murray, 1844.
Same. New York, Harper and Brothers, 1844. 168 p.

Fee, John Gregg. An Anti-Slavery Manual, Being an Examination, in the Light of the Bible, and of Facts, into the Moral and Social Wrongs of American Slavery, with a Remedy for the Evil, by John G. Fee. Maysville, Ky., Herald Office, 1848. 230 p.
Same. Second Edition. New York, William Harned, 1851. 178 p. [Fee was a native of Kentucky. He attended Lane Seminary, then gave his life to the antislavery cause. He was clubbed, stoned, and shot at many times, but managed to remain in Kentucky until 1859. He founded Berea College.]

Fee, John Gregg. The Sinfulness of Slaveholding Shown in Appeals to Reason and Scripture. By John G. Fee, Minister of the Gospel in Kentucky. New York, John A. Gray, 1851. 36 p.

Fee, John Gregg. Non-Fellowship with Slaveholders, the Duty of Christians. New York, John A. Gray, 1851. 24 p.
Same. New York, John A. Gray, 1855. 68 p.

The Fellowship of Slaveholders Incompatible with a Christian Profession. New York, American Anti-Slavery Society, 1859. 20 p.

Female Anti-Slavery Society of Chatham Street Chapel. Constitution and Address of the Female Anti-Slavery Society of Chatham Street Chapel. New York, William S. Dorr, 1834. 16 p.

Fessenden, William Pitt. Speech of W. P. Fessenden, of Maine, against the Repeal of the Missouri Prohibition, North of 36°30′. Delivered in the Senate of the United States, March 3, 1854, on the Bill to Establish Territorial Governments in Nebraska and Kansas. [Washington, D. C.] Buell & Blanchard [1854]. 16 p.

Fessenden, William Pitt. Speech of Mr. Fessenden, of Maine, on the President's Message, Delivered in the Senate of the United States, December 4, 1856. Washington, Printed at the Capital City Office, 1856. 16 p.

Fessenden, William Pitt. Speech of Mr. Fessenden, of Maine, on the Message of the President Transmitting the Lecompton Constitution, Delivered in the United States Senate, February 8, 1858. Washington, D. C., Buell & Blanchard, 1858. 24 p.

Filton, Theodore. The American Board and American Slavery. Speech of Theodore Filton in Plymouth Church, Brooklyn, January 28, 1860. Reported by William Henry Burr. [New York, John A. Gray, 1860.] 44 p.

Fish, Henry Clay. Freedom or Despotism. The Voice of Our Brother's Blood: Its Source and Its Summons. A Discourse Occasioned by the Sumner and Kansas Outrages. Preached in Newark, June 8th and 15th, 1856. Newark, N. J. Douglass & Starbuck, 1856. 24 p.

[Fisher, ———]. Slavery in the United States; a Narrative of the Life and Adventures of Charles Ball, a Black Man Who Lived Forty Years in Maryland, South Carolina, and Georgia as a Slave. Lewistown, Pa., John W. Shugert, 1836. 400 p. Same. In "Cabinet of Freedom," New York, 1837. 517 p.

[Fisher, Charles Edward]. Cecil, pseud. Kanzas and the Constitution. Boston, Damrell & Moore, 1856. 16 p. [Sometimes wrongly ascribed to S. G. Fisher.]

[Fisher, Sidney George]. The Law of the Territories. Philadelphia, C. Sherman & Sons, 1859. 127 p.

[Fisher, Thomas]. The Negroe's Memorial, or, Abolitionist's Catechism; by an Abolitionist. London, Hatchard and Co., 1825. 127 p.
Same. Abridged. Bristol, Wright & Bagnall, 1830. 16 p.

Fitch, Charles. An Address, Delivered on the Fourth of July, 1836, at Pine Street Church, Boston, in the Morning, and at Salem, in the Afternoon. By Request of the Friends to the Immediate Abolition of Slavery. Boston, I. Knapp, 1836. 27 p.

Fitch, Charles. Slaveholding Weighed in the Balance of Truth and Its Comparative Guilt Illustrated. Boston, I. Knapp, 1837. 36 p. [Congregational minister of Boston; a powerful anti-Garrisonian.]

FitzGerald, John. Christian Slaveholders Disobedient to Christ; or, Ten Thousand English Christians Invited to Protest Actively Against the Sin of the Church in the United States: And to Cease from Purchasing the Produce of Slave Labour. London, W. H. Dalton, 1854. 114 p.

Fitzgerald, W. P. N. A Scriptural View of Slavery and Abolition. New Haven, 1839. 24 p.

Follen, Mrs. Eliza Lee *Cabot*. The Liberty Cap. Boston, L. C. Bowles, 1846. 36 p. [Widow of Prof. Charles Follen of Harvard, who had indoctrinated many workers of the movement by his lectures on moral philosophy.]

Foot, Samuel A. An Examination of the Case of Dred Scott Against Sanford, in the Supreme Court of the United States, and a Full and Fair Exposition of the Decision of the Court, and of the Opinions of the Majority of the Judges, Prepared at the Request of, and Read Before, "The Geneva Literary and Scientific Association" on Tuesday Evening, 28th December, 1858. New York, Wm. C. Bryant & Co., 1859. 19 p.

Foot, Samuel Alfred. Reasons for Joining the Republican Party. Reasons of Hon. Samuel A. Foot, Late Judge of the Supreme Court of New York, and Now a Member of the Assembly, for Accepting a Republican Nomination. [Washington, D. C.] Buell & Blanchard [1855]. 7 p.

Foote, Commander Andrew Hull. Africa and the American Flag. New York, D. Appleton & Co., 1854. 390 p. [Commander Foote, of Civil War fame, was zealous in his suppression of the African slave trade.]

Foote, Charles C. American Women Responsible for the Existence of American Slavery: A Conversation Between an Anti-Slavery Lecturer and a Lady. Third Edition. Rochester, E. Shepard, 1846. 24 p.

Forbes, Alexander C., Defendant. The State of Ohio vs. Forbes and Armitage, Arrested upon the Requisition of the Government of Ohio, on Charge of Kidnapping Jerry Phinney, and Tried Before the Franklin Circuit Court of Kentucky, April 10, 1846. [n.p., 1846.] 41 p.

Forman, Jacob Gilbert. The Christian Martyrs; or, The Conditions of Obedience to the Civil Government: A Discourse by J. G. Forman, Minister of the Second Congregational Church in Nantucket; until Recently Minister of the First Church and Congregation in West Bridgewater, Mass. To Which Is Added, a Friendly Letter to Said Church and Congregation on the Pro-Slavery Influences That Occasioned His Removal. Boston, W. Crosby and H. P. Nichols, 1851. 51 p.

Forman, Jacob Gilbert. The Fugitive Slave Law; a Discourse Delivered in the Congregational Church in West Bridgewater, Mass., on Sunday, November 17th, 1850. Boston, Wm. Crosby and H. P. Nichols, 1850. 36 p.

Forten, James, Jr. An Address Delivered before the Ladies' Anti-Slavery Society of Philadelphia, on the Evening of the 14th of April, 1836. Philadelphia, Printed by Merrihew & Gunn, 1836. 16 p.

Foss, A. T., and Mathews, E. Facts for Baptist Churches, Collected, Arranged and Reviewed by A. T. Foss, of New Hampshire, and E. Mathews, of Wisconsin. Utica, American Baptist Free Mission Society, 1850. 408 p.

Foster, Aaron. Liberty, the Nation, the Occasion. Greenfield, Mass., C. J. J. Ingersoll, 1854. 50 p.

Foster, Daniel. An Address on Slavery, Delivered in Danvers, Mass., in Compliance with the Request of the Voters of Danvers. Boston, Bela Marsh, 1849. 44 p.

Foster, Daniel. The Constitution of the United States, with a Lecture, by Daniel Foster, Showing That a Fair Interpretation and Application of Said Constitution Will Abolish Slavery and Establish Liberty. Springfield, 1855, Samuel Bowles & Company, 1855. 60 p.

Foster, Daniel. Our Nation's Sins and the Christian's Duty. A Fast Day Discourse, by Daniel Foster, Minister in Charge of the Congregational Church of Concord, Mass., Delivered April 10th, 1851. Boston, White & Potter, Printers, 1851. 34 p.

Foster, Eden Burroughs. A North-Side View of Slavery. A Sermon on the Crime Against Freedom, in Kansas and Washington. Preached at Henniker, N. H., August 31, 1856. By Eden B. Foster, Pastor of St. John Church, Lowell, Mass. Concord, Jones & Cogswell, 1856. 39 p.

Foster, Eden B[urroughs]. The Rights of the Pulpit, and Perils of Freedom. Two Discourses Preached in Lowell, Sunday, June 25th, 1854. Lowell, Mass., J. J. Judkins, 1854. 72 p.

Foster, Stephen Symonds. The Brotherhood of Thieves; or, A True Picture of the American Church and Clergy: A Letter to Nathaniel Barney of Nantucket. Boston, Anti-Slavery Office [1843]. 72 p.
Same. New London, W. Bolles, 1843. 68 p.
Same. New London, W. Bolles, 1843. 64 p.
Same. Concord, N. H., P. Pillsbury, 1886. 75 p.
Same. Boston, 1844. 72 p.

Franklin [pseud.]. An Examination of Mr. Bradish's Answer to the Interrogatories Presented to Him by a Committee of the State Anti-Slavery Society, October 1, 1838. Albany, Hoffman & White, 1838. 30 p.

Free Church Anti-Slavery Society. The Sinfulness of Maintaining Christian Fellowship with Slaveholders. Strictures on the Proceedings of the Last General Assembly of the Free Church of Scotland, Regarding Communion with the Slave-Holding Churches of America, Respectfully Addressed to the Office-Bearers and Members of That Church. From the Committee of the Free Church Anti-

Slavery Society. Edinburgh, C. Ziegler, 1846. 32 p.

Free Produce Association of Friends of New York, Yearly Meeting. Report of the Board of Managers of the Free Produce Association of Friends of New York, Yearly Meeting, 1854. New York, Collins, Bowne & Co. [1854]. 9 p.

Free Produce Association of Friends of Ohio, Yearly Meeting, 1850. Address of Farmington Quarterly Meeting (New York) to the Monthly Meetings Constituting It, and to the Members of the Same Generally. [Mount Pleasant, Ohio] Enoch Harris, [1850.] 8 p.

Free Produce Association of Friends of Ohio, Yearly Meeting. Extracts from the Minutes of the Annual Meeting of the Free Produce Association of Ohio Yearly Meeting, Held 3d of Ninth Month, 1850, with the Report of the Board of Managers. Constitution, Etc. Mount Pleasant, Ohio, E. Harris, 1851. 12 p.

Free Produce Association of Friends of Ohio Yearly Meeting, 1850. Stolen Goods; or, The Gains of Oppression, by Le Mabbett; and Comparison of Stolen Goods with Slave Labor Produce by Elihu Burritt. [Mount Pleasant] Enoch Harris [1850]. 4 p.

Free Produce Association of Friends of Ohio Yearly Meeting, 1850.
No. 1. Considerations on Abstinence from the Use of the Products of Slave Labor; Addressed to the Members of the Ohio Yearly Meeting. Mount Pleasant, Enoch Harris, [1850.] 8 p.
Same. Mountpleasant [sic], Enoch Harris, 1851. 12 p.
No. 2. The Plea of Necessity. Mountpleasant [sic], Enoch Harris, 1851. 12 p.

Free Produce Association of Friends of Ohio, Yearly Meeting. Second Annual Report of the Board of Managers of the Free Produce Association of Friends of Ohio Yearly Meeting, Held 9th of Ninth Month, 1851. Mountpleasant, Ohio, Enoch Harris, 1851. 8 p.

Free Produce Association of Friends of Philadelphia. An Address to Our Fellow Members of the Religious Society of Friends on the Subject of Slavery and the Slave-Trade in the Western World, by Philadelphia Free Produce Association of Friends. Philadelphia, 1849. 16 p.

Free Produce Society of Pennsylvania. Constitution of the Free Produce Society of Pennsylvania. Philadelphia, D. & S. Neall, [1827]. 12 p.

Free Remarks on the Spirit of the Federal Constitution, the Practice of the Federal Government, and the Obligations of the Union, Respecting the Exclusion of Slavery from the Territories and New States. By a Philadelphian. Philadelphia, Published by A. Finley, N.E. Corner of Chestnut and Fourth Streets. Wm. Fry, 1819. 116 p. [Probably by Robert Walsh.]

Free Soil Association of the District of Columbia. Address of the Free Soil Association of the District of Columbia to the People of the United States; Together with a Memorial to Congress, of 1060 Inhabitants of the District of Columbia, Praying for the Gradual Abolition of Slavery. Washington, Buell & Blanchard, 1849. 16 p.

Free State Rally and Texan Chainbreaker. Weekly. Boston, Mass. Volume 1, Nos. 1–6. Nov. 15, 1845– Jan. 12, 1846. No more published. Edited by Massachusetts State Texas Committee: Charles F. Adams, Henry I. Bowditch, etc.

Freedom's Journal. Weekly. New York, N. Y. Volumes 1–2. March 16, 1827–March 28, 1829. Edited by S. E. Cornish and J. B. Russwurm. [Probably first paper published by Negroes in United States.]

Friend of Humanity [pseud.]. Remarks on the Constitution, on the Subject of Slavery. Philadelphia, Office of Evening Star, 1836. 12 p.

Friend of Man. Weekly. Utica, New York. Volumes 1–6, No. 11. Numbers 1–287. June 23, 1836– January 11, 1842. Edited by William Goodell, 1836–1842. Organ of New York State Anti-Slavery Society. Published as Liberty Press, 1843–1849.

A Friend to Mankind. Arguments from Scripture, for and Against the African Slave Trade, as Stated in a Series of Letters Lately Published in the Glasgow Courier. Glasgow, 1792. 27 p.

Friends of Freedom in the Eastern and Middle States. Proceedings of the Great Convention of Friends of Freedom in the Eastern and Middle States Held in Boston, Oct. 1, 2, & 3, 1845. Lowell, Pillsbury & Knapp, 1845. 24 p.

Friends, Association of. *Extracts* from Writings of Friends, on the Subject of Slavery. Pub. by the Direction of the "Association of Friends for Advocating the Cause of the Slave, and Improving the Condition of the Free People of Color." Philadelphia, Merrihew and Thompson, 1839. 24 p.

Friends, Association for Advocating the Cause of the Slave, Etc. Annual Report of the Association of Friends for Promoting the Abolition of Slavery, and Improving the Condition of the Free People of Color. Philadelphia, T. E. Chapman, 1848. 11 p.

Friends, Association for Promoting the Abolition of Slavery. Annual Report of the Association of Friends for Promoting the Abolition of Slavery and Improving the Condition of Free People of Color; for the Year 1851. Philadelphia, T. Ellwood Chapman, 1851. 11 p.

Friends, Baltimore Yearly Meeting. Extracts from the Minutes of the Yearly Meeting of Friends Held at Lombard Street in the City of Baltimore, 1842. Baltimore, Wm. Wooddy, 1842. 21 p.

Friends, Farmington Quarterly Meeting. An Address from the Farmington Quarterly Meeting of Friends to Its Members on Slavery. Rochester, N. Y., Hoyt & Porter, 1836. 8 p.

Friends, Germantown, Pa. Germantown Friends' Protest Against Slavery, 1688. Facsimile. Broadside, 1 p. 25 × 35 cm.

Friends, Germantown, Pa. Protest Against Slavery by the Society of Germantown Friends. Minutes Read at Yearly Meeting Held at Burlington, the 5th Day of the 7th Month, 1688.

Friends, Indiana Yearly Meeting, 1844. An Appeal on the Iniquity of Slavery and the Slave-Trade; Issued by the Yearly Meeting of the Religious Society of Friends, Held in London, 1844. Re-Published for General Circulation, by Indiana Yearly Meeting of Friends, Held at Whitewater, in Wayne County, Indiana, 1844. Cincinnati, A. Pugh & Co., 1844. 9 p.

Friends Indiana Yearly Meeting, 1848. Address to the Citizens of the State of Ohio, Concerning What Are Called the Black Laws. Issued in Behalf of the Society of Friends Indiana Yearly Meeting, by Their Meeting for Sufferings, Representing the Said Yearly Meeting in Its Recess. (A Large Portion of the Members Reside in the State of Ohio). Cincinnati, A. Pugh, 1848. 15 p.

Friends, London Yearly Meeting, 1783. The Case of Our Fellow Creatures, the Oppressed Africans, Respectfully Recommended to the Serious Consideration of the Legislature of Great Britain, by the People Called Quakers. [Signed]: John Ady. London, James Phillips, 1783. 16 p.
Same. Philadelphia, Reprinted by Joseph Crukshank, 1784. 13 p.

Friends, London Yearly Meeting, 1822. An Address to the Inhabitants of Europe on the Iniquity of the Slave Trade; Issued by the Religious Society of Friends, Commonly Called Quakers, in Great Britain and Ireland. London, W. Phillips, 1822. 15 p.

Friends, London Yearly Meeting, 1844. An Appeal on the Iniquity of Slavery and the Slave Trade: Issued by the Yearly Meeting of the Religious Society of Friends, Held in London, 1844. London, Edward Marsh, 1844. 10 p.

Friends, London Yearly Meeting, 1849. Address on the Slave Trade and Slavery, to Sovereigns, and Those in Authority in the Nations of Europe, and Other Parts of the World Where the Christian Religion Is Professed, from the Yearly Meeting of Friends in London, Held in 1849. Richmond, Indiana, Published by Central Committee & Tract Committee of Friends [1849]. 8 p.

Friends, London Yearly Meeting, 1854. Proceedings in Relation to the Presentation of the Address of the Yearly Meeting of the Religious Society of Friends, on the Slave-Trade and Slavery, to Sovereigns and Those in Authority in the Nations of Europe, and in Other Parts of the World, Where the Christian Religion is Professed. London, Printed by Edward Newman, 1854. 62 p. Cincinnati, E. Morgan and Sons, 1855. 62 p. New York, J. Egbert, 1856. 48 p.

Friends, New England Yearly Meeting, 1837. Address of the Yearly Meeting of Friends for New England, Held on Rhode Island, in the Sixth Month, 1837, to Its Own Members, and Those of Other Christian Communities. Published by Direction of Said Meeting. New Bedford, J. C. Parmenter, Printer, 1837. 7 p.

Friends, New England Yearly Meeting, 1842. An Appeal to the Professors of Christianity, in the Southern States and Elsewhere, on the Subject of Slavery: by the Representatives of the Yearly Meeting of Friends for New England. Providence, Knowles & Vose, 1842. 24 p.

Friends, New England Yearly Meeting, 1847. Testimony of the Religious Society of Friends, against Slavery; Revived by the Representatives of New England Yearly Meeting. Boston, S. N. Dickinson & Co., 1847. 12 p.

Friends, New York Yearly Meeting, 1837. Address to the Citizens of the United States of America on the Subject of Slavery, from the Yearly Meeting of the Religious Society of Friends, (called Quakers) Held in New York, Mahlon Day, 1837. 11 p.

Friends, New York Yearly Meeting, 1844. An Address of Friends of the Yearly Meeting of New York, to the Citizens of the United States, Especially to Those of the Southern States, upon the Subject of Slavery. New York, M. Day & Co., 1844. 16 p.

Friends, New York Yearly Meeting, 1852. Address of the Yearly Meeting of the Religious Society of Friends, Held in the City of New York in the Sixth Month, 1852, to the Professors of Christianity in the United States on the Subject of Slavery. New York, R. Craighead, 1852. 10 p.

Friends, New York Yearly Meeting, 1862. Report of a Committee of Representatives of New York Yearly Meeting of Friends upon the Condition and Wants of the Colored Refugees. [New York, 1862.] 30 p.

Friends, Ohio Yearly Meeting, 1852. Proceedings of the Ohio Yearly Meeting of Progressive Friends Held in Salem, from the 5th to the 7th of Ninth Month, Inclusive. Including an Address to the Public. Salem, G. P. Smith, 1852. 20 p.

Friends, Pennsylvania, New Jersey, Delaware. An Exposition of the African Slave Trade, from the Year 1840, to 1850, Inclusive. Prepared from Official Documents, and Published by Direction of the Representatives of the Religious Society of Friends, in Pennsylvania, New Jersey, and Delaware. Philadelphia, J. Rakestraw, 1851. 160 p.

Friends, Pennsylvania, New Jersey, Delaware. Facts and Observations Relative to the Participation of American Citizens in the African Slave Trade. Published by Direction of a Meeting Representing the Religious Society of Friends in Pennsylvania, New Jersey, etc. Philadelphia, Joseph & William Kite, 1841. 36 p.

Friends, Pennsylvania, New Jersey, Delaware. Memorial of the Society of Friends in Pennsylvania, New Jersey and Delaware, on the African Slave Trade. Philadelphia, Joseph and William Kite, 1840. 7 p.

Friends, Pennsylvania and New Jersey Yearly Meeting, 1754. An Epistle of Caution and Advice, Concerning the Buying and Keeping of Slaves. Philadelphia, James Chattin, 1754. 8 p.

Friends, Pennsylvania, New Jersey, Delaware. A View of the Present State of the African Slave Trade; Published by Direction of a Meeting Representing the Religious Society of Friends in Pennsylvania, New Jersey, etc. Philadelphia, William Brown, 1824. 69 p.

Friends, Philadelphia Yearly Meeting, 1837. Address of the Representatives of the Religious Society of Friends, Commonly Called Quakers, in Pennsylvania, New Jersey, Delaware, Etc. to the Citizens of the United States. Philadelphia, Joseph and William Kite, 1837. 15 p.

Friends, Philadelphia Yearly Meeting, 1839. An Address to the Quarterly, Monthly and Preparative Meetings and Members Thereof, Composing the Yearly Meeting of Friends, Held in Philadelphia, by the Committee Appointed at the Late Yearly Meeting to Have Charge of the Subject of Slavery. Philadelphia, J. Richards, 1839. 12 p.

Friends, Philadelphia Yearly Meeting, 1843. The Ancient Testimony of the Religious Society of Friends, Commonly Called Quakers, Respecting Some of Their Christian Doctrines and Practices: Revived and Given Forth by the Yearly Meeting, Held in Philadelphia in the Fourth Month, 1843. Philadelphia, Joseph Rakestraw, 1843. 84 p.

Friends, Philadelphia Yearly Meeting, 1858. The Appeal of the Religious Society of Friends in Pennsylvania, New Jersey, Delaware, etc., to Their Fellow Citizens of the United States on Behalf of the Coloured Races. Philadelphia, Friends Book Store, 1858. 48 p.

Friends, Philadelphia Yearly Meeting, 1843. A Brief

Statement of the Rise and Progress of the Testimony of the Religious Society of Friends, against Slavery and the Slave Trade. Pub. by Direction of the Yearly Meeting, Held in Philadelphia, in the Fourth Month, 1843. Philadelphia, J. and W. Kite, 1843. 59 p.

Friends, Philadelphia Yearly Meeting, 1839. Extracts and Observations on the Foreign Slave Trade. Published by the Committee Appointed by the Yearly Meeting of Friends Held in Philadelphia in 1839, on the Subject of Slavery. Philadelphia, Printed for the Committee, 1839. 12 p.

Friends, Philadelphia Yearly Meeting, 1839. Slavery and the Domestic Slave Trade, in the United States. By the Committee Appointed by the Late Yearly Meeting of Friends, Held in Philadelphia in 1839. Philadelphia, Printed by Merrihew and Thompson, 1841. 46 p.

Friends, Philadelphia Yearly Meeting, 1799. To Our Fellow Citizens of the United States of North America and Others to Whom It May Concern. [Philadelphia, 1799.] 3 p.

Friends, Tract Association. No. 85. Considerations on the Keeping of Negroes; Recommended to the Professors of Christianity of Every Denomination. Philadelphia, J. & W. Kite, 1754. 12 p.

Frothingham, Frederick. Significance of the Struggle between Liberty and Slavery in America. A Discourse by Rev. Frederick Frothingham at Portland, Maine, on Fast Day, April 16th, 1857. New York, American Anti-Slavery Society, 1857. 21 p.

Frothingham, Octavius Brooks. The Last Signs. A Sermon Preached at the Unitarian Church in Jersey City, on Sunday Morning, June 1, 1856. New York, John A. Gray, 1856. 22 p.

Frothingham, Octavius Brooks. The New Commandment: A Discourse Delivered in the North Church, Salem, on Sunday, June 4, 1854. Salem, Printed at the Observer Office, 1854. 21 p.

Frothingham, Octavius Brooks. Speech of the Rev. O. B. Frothingham, before the American Anti-Slavery Society, in New York, May 8th, 1856. New York, Anti-Slavery Society, 1856. 26 p.

The Fugitive Slave Bill, Enacted by the United States Congress, and Approved by the President, Millard Fillmore, September 18, 1850. Boston, 145 Hanover St., 1854. 8 p. [Printed in mourning. Deep black edges on pamphlet.]

The Fugitive Slave Bill: Its History and Unconstitutionality; with an Account of the Seizure and Enslavement of James Hamlet, and His Subsequent Restoration to Liberty. New York, William Harned, 1850. 86 p.

The Fugitive Slave Law. Unconstitutionality of the Fugitive Slave Act. Decisions of the Supreme Court of Wisconsin in the Cases of Booth and

Rycraft. Milwaukee, Rufus King & Co., 1856. 218 p.

Fuller, Edward J. A Fast Sermon Delivered April 7, 1836, before the Calvinistic Church and Society in Hardwick, Mass. Brookfield, Mass., E. and L. Merriam, 1836. 15 p.

Furman, Richard. Rev. Dr. Richard Furman's Exposition of the Views of the Baptists, Relative to the Coloured Population of the United States, in a Communication to the Governor of South Carolina. Charleston, A. E. Miller, 1823. 24 p. [Furman was the spokesman for Southern Baptists.]

Furness, William Henry. An Address Delivered Before a Meeting of the Members and Friends of the Pennsylvania Anti-Slavery Society during the Annual Fair December 19, 1849. By W. H. Furness. Philadelphia, Merrihew & Thompson, 1850. 16 p. [Unitarian clergyman; Harvard graduate; antislavery as early as 1824.]

Furness, William Henry. The Blessings of Abolition. A Discourse Delivered in the First Congregational Unitarian Church, Sunday, July 1, 1860. Philadelphia, C. Sherman & Son, 1860. 26 p.

Furness, William Henry. Christian Duty. Three Discourses Delivered in the First Congregational Unitarian Church of Philadelphia May 28th, June 4th and June 11th, 1854, by W. H. Furness, with Reference to the Recent Execution of the Fugitive Slave Law in Boston and New York. Philadelphia, Merrihew & Thompson, 1854. 42 p.

Furness, William Henry. A Discourse Occasioned by the Boston Fugitive Slave Case, Delivered in the First Congregational Unitarian Church, Philadelphia, April 13, 1851. Philadelphia, Merrihew & Thompson, 1851. 15 p.

Furness, William Henry. The Moving Power. A Discourse Delivered in the First Congregational Unitarian Church in Philadelphia, Sunday Morning, Feb. 9, 1851, after the Occurrence of a Fugitive Slave Case. Philadelphia, Merrihew and Thompson, 1851. 16 p.

Furness, William Henry. Put Up Thy Sword. A Discourse Delivered before Theodore Parker's Society, at the Music Hall, Boston, Sunday, March 11, 1860. Boston, R. F. Wallcut, 1860. 23 p.

Furness, William Henry. The Right of Property in Man. A Discourse Delivered in the First Congregational Unitarian Church, Sunday, July 3, 1859. Philadelphia, C. Sherman & Son, 1859. 23 p.

Furness, William Henry. A Sermon Occasioned by the Destruction of Pennsylvania Hall, and Delivered the Lord's Day Following, May 20, 1838, in the First Congregational Unitarian Church, by the Pastor. Philadelphia, John C. Clark, 1838. 12 p.

Garnet, Henry Highland. Walker's Appeal, with a Brief Sketch of His Life; and, also, Garnet's Address to the Slaves of the United States of America. New York, J. H. Tobitt, 1848. 96 p.

Garrettson, Freeborn. A Dialogue between Do-Justice and Professing-Christian. Dedicated to the Respective and Collective Abolition Societies, and to All Other Benevolent, Humane Philanthropists, in America. By Freeborn Garrettson. Wilmington, P. Brynberg [1820?]. 58 p. [Garrettson, an itinerant Methodist preacher, was a former slaveholder. He had freed his slaves and crusaded vigorously against the institution. He died in 1827.]

Garrison, William Lloyd. An Address before the Old Colony Anti-Slavery Society, at South Scituate, Mass., July 4, 1839. Boston, Dow & Jackson, 1839. 40 p.

Garrison, William Lloyd. An Address Delivered at the Broadway Tabernacle, New York, August 1, 1838. By Request of the People of Color of That City, in Commemoration of the Complete Emancipation of 600,000 Slaves on That Day, in the British West Indies. Boston, I. Knapp, 1838. 46 p.

Garrison, William Lloyd. An Address, Delivered Before the Free People of Color, in Philadelphia, New York and Other Cities, during the Month of June, 1831. Boston, Stephen Foster, 1831. 24 p.
Same. Second Edition. Boston, S. Foster, 1831. 24 p.
Same. Third Edition. Boston, S. Foster, 1831. 24 p.

Garrison, William Lloyd. Address Delivered in Boston, New York and Philadelphia, Before the Free People of Colour, in April, 1833. By William Lloyd Garrison. Pub. by Request. New York, Printed for the Free People of Color, 1833. 23 p.

Garrison, William Lloyd. An Address Delivered in Marlboro' Chapel, Boston, July 4, 1838. Boston, Isaac Knapp, 1838. 48 p.

Garrison, William Lloyd. An Address on the Progress of the Abolition Cause; Delivered Before the African Abolition Freehold Society of Boston, July 16, 1832. Boston, Garrison and Knapp, 1832. 24 p.

Garrison, William Lloyd. A Brief Sketch of the Trial of William Lloyd Garrison, for an Alleged Libel on Francis Todd of Newburyport, Massachusetts. Boston, Garrison and Knapp, 1834. 24 p.

Garrison, William Lloyd. Juvenile Poems, for the Use of Free American Children of Every Complexion. Boston, Garrison & Knapp, 1835. 72 p.

[Garrison, William Lloyd]. The Loyalty and Devotion of Colored Americans in the Revolution and War of 1812. Boston, R. F. Wallcut, 1861. 24 p.

Garrison, William Lloyd. Letter to Louis Kossuth, Concerning Freedom and Slavery in the United States. In Behalf of the American Anti-Slavery Society. Boston, R. F. Wallcut, 1852. 112 p.

[Garrison, William Lloyd]. A Friend of Liberty. The Maryland Scheme of Expatriation Examined by a Friend of Liberty. Boston, Garrison & Knapp, 1834. 20 p.

Garrison, William Lloyd. 'No Fetters in the Bay State!' Speech of Wm. Lloyd Garrison, before the Committee on Federal Relations, in Support of the Petitions Asking for a Law to Prevent the Recapture of Fugitive Slaves, Thursday, Feb. 24, 1859. Boston, R. F. Wallcut, 1859. 24 p.

Garrison, William Lloyd. Proceedings of a Crowded Meeting of the Colored Population of Boston, Assembled the 15th July, 1846, for the Purpose of Bidding Farewell to William Lloyd Garrison, on His Departure for England; with His Speech on the Occasion. Dublin, Webb & Chapman, 1846. 16 p.

Garrison, William Lloyd. Selections from the Writings and Speeches of William Lloyd Garrison. With an Appendix. Boston, R. F. Wallcut, 1852. 416 p.

Garrison, William Lloyd. Sonnets and Other Poems. Boston, Oliver Johnson, 1843. 96 p.

Garrison, William Lloyd. A Selection of Anti-Slavery Hymns, for the Use of the Friends of Emancipation. Boston, Garrison & Knapp, 1834. 36 p.

Garrison, William Lloyd. Thoughts on African Colonization; or, An Impartial Exhibition of the Doctrines, Principles, and Purposes of the American Colonization Society. Together with the Resolutions, Addresses and Remonstrances of the Free People of Color. Boston, Garrison & Knapp, 1832. 78 p.

General Anti-Slavery Convention, London, 1840. Minutes of the Proceedings of the General Anti-Slavery Convention, Called by the Committee of the British and Foreign Anti-Slavery Society, Held in London on the 12th of June, 1840, and Continued by Adjournments to the 23rd of the Same Month. London, Johnston & Barrett, 1840. 32 p.

General Assembly of the Presbyterian Church. Testimony of the General Assembly of the Presbyterian Church in the United States of America on the Subject of Slavery. Philadelphia, Presbyterian Publication Committee, 1858. 31 p.

General Conference of the Methodist Episcopal Church. Debate on "Modern Abolitionism" in the General Conference of the Methodist Episcopal Church, Held in Cincinnati, May, 1836. Cincinnati, Ohio Anti-Slavery Society, 1836. 91 p.

General Emancipation Society, Missouri. Constitution and By-Laws of the General Emancipation Society of the State of Missouri. Adopted at St. Louis, April 8th, 1862. St. Louis, Democrat Book and Job Office, 1862. 16 p.

A General View of the African Slave-Trade, Demonstrating Its Injustice and Impolicy: with Hints Towards a Bill for Its Abolition. London, R. Faulder, 1788. 39 p.

Genesee County Anti-Slavery Society. Proceedings of the First Annual Meeting of the Genesee Co. Anti-Slavery Society, Commenced at Batavia, March 16, and Concluded at Warsaw, March 23, 1836; with the Report of the Executive Committee for the Preceding Year. Warsaw, Printed for the Executive Committee, 1836. 24 p.

Genius of Universal Emancipation. Monthly. Greenville, Tennessee. Volumes 1–4. 1821–September, 1825. Edited by Benjamin Lundy.

Genius of Universal Emancipation and Baltimore Courier. Weekly. Baltimore, Maryland. Volumes 1–2. September 5, 1825–June 23, 1827. Edited by Benjamin Lundy.

The Genius of Universal Emancipation, or Anti-Slavery Journal, and Register of News. Weekly. Baltimore, Maryland. New Series. Volumes 1–3, July 4, 1827– [Old Series. Volumes 7–9] January 3, 1829. Edited by Benjamin Lundy.

Genius of Universal Emancipation. Weekly. Baltimore, Maryland. New Series, Volume 4, September 2, 1829– [Old Series, Volume 10] March 5, 1830. Editor: Benjamin Lundy. Co-Editor: William Lloyd Garrison.

Genius of Universal Emancipation. Monthly. Baltimore, Maryland. Third Series, Volume 1, No. 1–9. [Old Series, Volume 11, No. 1–9] April, 1830–December, 1830. Baltimore and Washington, D. C. Third Series, Volume 1, No. 10–Volume 2, No. 7, January, 1831–[Old Series, Volume 11, No. 10–Volume 12, No. 7] December, 1831. Washington, D. C. Third Series, Volume 2, No. 8–Volume 3, No. 12. January, 1832–October, 1833.

The Genius of Universal Emancipation, a Monthly Periodical Work, Containing Original Essays, Documents, and Facts, Relative to the Subject of African Slavery. Fourth Series. Volume 1—Philadelphia, Penn. January, 1834–December, 1836 ? Edited by Benjamin Lundy.

The Genius of Universal Emancipation and Quarterly Anti-Slavery Review. Fifth Series. Volume 1—July, 1837.

Giddings, Joshua Reed. Amistad Claim. History of the Case; Decision of the Judiciary; Comity of the Various Departments of Government; Construction of Treaties; Law of Nations; Natural Rights of Persons; Duty of All to Sustain the Doctrines on Which Our Government Was Founded. Speech of Mr. Giddings, of Ohio, in the House of Representatives, Dec. 21, 1853, in Committee of the Whole [etc.]. [n.p., n.d.] 7 p.

Giddings, Joshua Reed. Baltimore Platforms—Slavery Question. Speech of Hon. Joshua R. Giddings,

of Ohio, in the House of Representatives, June 23, 1852. [Washington, D. C.] Buell & Blanchard, [1852]. 8 p.

Giddings, Joshua R. The Conflict Between Religious Truths and American Infidelity. Speech of Mr. Giddings, of Ohio, upon the Issues Pending before the American People in Regard to Freedom and Slavery. Delivered in Committee of the Whole House on the State of the Union, February 26, 1858. Washington, D. C., Buell & Blanchard, 1858. 8 p.

Giddings, Joshua Reed. The Exiles of Florida: or, The Crimes Committed by Our Government against the Maroons, Who Fled from South Carolina and Other Slave States Seeking Protection under Spanish Laws. Columbus, Ohio, Follett & Foster, 1858. 338 p.

Giddings, Joshua Reed. The Florida War. Speech of Mr. Giddings, of Ohio, Delivered in the House of Representatives, February 9, 1841. Hallowell, Published by the Bangor Female Anti-Slavery Society, 1841. 24 p.

Giddings, Joshua R. The Issue—Its History. Speech of Hon. Joshua R. Giddings, of Ohio, Delivered in the House of Representatives, January 12, 1859. Washington, D. C., Buell & Blanchard, 1859. 8 p.

Giddings, Joshua Reed. A Letter from Hon. J. R. Giddings upon the Duty of Anti-Slavery Men in the Present Crisis. Ravenna, Ohio, William Wadsworth, 1844. 16 p.

Giddings, Joshua Reed. Moral Responsibility of Statesmen. Speech of Hon. J. R. Giddings, of Ohio, on the Bill Organizing Territorial Governments in Kansas and Nebraska, in Committee of the Whole on the State of the Union, May 17, 1854. Washington, D. C., Buell & Blanchard, [1854]. 8 p.

Giddings, Joshua Reed. Our Domestic Policy. Speech of Hon. J. R. Giddings, on the Reference of the President's Message. Made, December 9, 1850, in Committee of the Whole on the State of the Union. [Washington, D. C.] Buell & Blanchard [1850]. 8 p.

Giddings, Joshua Reed. Pacificus: The Rights and Privileges of the Several States in Regard to Slavery; Being a Series of Essays, Published in the Western Reserve Chronicle, (Ohio), after the Election of 1842. By a Whig of Ohio. Cincinnati, [1843]. 16 p.

Giddings, Joshua Reed. Payment for Slaves. Speech of Mr. J. R. Giddings, of Ohio, on the Bill to Pay the Heirs of Antonio Pacheco for a Slave Sent West of the Mississippi with the Seminole Indians in 1838. Made in the House of Representatives, Dec. 28, 1848, and Jan. 6, 1849. Washington, Buell & Blanchard, 1849. 14 p.

Giddings, Joshua R. The Rights and Duties of Representatives. Speech of Mr. Joshua R. Giddings, of Ohio, in the House of Representatives, December 27, 1849. [Washington, D. C.] Congressional Globe Office [1849].

[Giddings, Joshua Reed]. The Rights and Privileges of the Several States in Regard to Slavery; Being a Series of Essays, Published in the Western Reserve Chronicle, (Ohio) after the Election of 1842. By a Whig of Ohio. [Warren? O., 1843?] 16 p.

[Giddings, Joshua]. The Rights of the Free States Subverted, or, An Enumeration of the Most Prominent Instances in Which the Federal Constitution Has Been Violated by Our National Government, for the Benefit of Slavery. By a Member of Congress. [n.p., 1844.] 16 p.

Giddings, Joshua Reed. Slavery in the Territories. Speech of Hon. J. R. Giddings, of Ohio, in the House of Representatives, Monday, March 18, 1850, in Committee of the Whole on the State of the Union, on the President's Message Transmitting the Constitution of California. [Washington, D. C.] Buell & Blanchard [1850]. 8 p.

Giddings, Joshua Reed. Speech of Hon. J. R. Giddings, of Ohio, on Cuban Annexation. Delivered in the House of Representatives, December 14, 1852. Washington, D. C., Buell & Blanchard [1852]. 12 p.

Giddings, Joshua Reed. Speech of Mr. Giddings, of Ohio, in the House of Representatives, upon a Proposition of Mr. Thompson, of South Carolina, to Appropriate One Hundred Thousand Dollars, for the Removal, Subsistence and Benefit of Such of the Seminole Chiefs and Warriors as May Surrender for Emigration. Delivered Feb. 9, 1841. [Washington, 1841.] 15 p.

Giddings, Joshua. Speech of Mr. Giddings, of Ohio, upon Adopting the Rules of the House Excluding Petitions in Relation to Slavery. House of Representatives, February 13, 1844. Washington, D. C., J. & G. S. Gideon, 1844. 8 p.

Giddings, Joshua Reed. Speech of the Hon. J. R. Giddings, of Ohio, on the Compromise Measures. Delivered in the House of Representatives, March 16, 1852. [Washington, D. C.] Buell & Blanchard [1852]. 8 p.

[Gilbert, Olive]. Narrative of Sojourner Truth, a Northern Slave, Emancipated from Bodily Servitude by the State of New York, in 1828. With a Portrait. Boston, Printed for the Author, 1850. 144 p.
Same. Boston, Printed for the Author, 1853. 144 p.
Same. Battle Creek, Mich., 1878. 320 p. [Susan B. Anthony wrote in the copy now in the Rare Book Room of the Library of Congress: "This most wonderful woman—born in New York—40 years a slave there—and the remainder of her 50 or more years in freedom—had she been educated—no woman could have matched her. Jan. 1, 1903."]

Gillette, Francis. National Slavery and National Responsibility. Speech of Hon. Francis Gillette, of Connecticut, in the Senate of the United States, February 23d, 1855. Washington, D. C., Buell & Blanchard, 1855. 15 p. [Candidate for governor in Connecticut on Liberty ticket in 1841. Elected to Congress on Free Soil ticket, 1854.]

Gillette, Francis. A Review of the Rev. Horace Bushnell's Discourse on the Slavery Question, Delivered in the North Church, Hartford, January 10, 1839. Hartford, S. S. Cowles, 1839. 44 p.

Gilliland, James, and Crothers, Samuel. Two Letters on the Subject of Slavery from the Presbytery of Chillicothe, to the Churches under Their Care. Hillsborough, Whetstone and Buxton, 1830. 50 p.

Gilmore, H. S., (Comp.). A Collection of Miscellaneous Songs from the Liberty Minstrel and Mason's Juvenile Harp; for the Use of the Cincinnati High School; Compiled and Published by the Principal. Cincinnati, Sparhawk & Lytle, 1845. 46 p.

Glasgow Emancipation Society. Address by the Committee of the Glasgow Emancipation Society to the Ministers of Religion in Particular and the Friends of Negro Emancipation in General on American Slavery. Glasgow, Aird & Russell, 1836. 8 p.

Glasgow Emancipation Society. The American Board of Commissioners for Foreign Missions, and the Rev. Dr. Chalmers, on Christian Fellowship with Slaveholders: An Address by the Glasgow Emancipation Society, to Christians of All Denominations, but Especially to Members of the Free Church of Scotland. Glasgow, D. Russell, 1845. 11 p.

Glasgow Emancipation Society. Britain and America United in the Cause of Universal Freedom: Being the Third Annual Report of the Glasgow Emancipation Society. Glasgow, Aird & Russell, 1837. 144 p.

Glasgow Emancipation Society. Report of the Speeches, and Reception of the American Delegates, at the Great Public Meeting of the Glasgow Emancipation Society, Held in Dr. Wardlaw's Chapel, on the Evening of Mon., the 27th July, 1840. Glasgow, John Clark, 1840. 24 p.

Glasgow Female Anti-Slavery Society. An Appeal to the Ladies of Great Britain, in Behalf of the American Slave, by the Committee of the Glasgow Female Anti-Slavery Society. With the Constitution of the Society. Glasgow, J. M'Leod [etc., etc.], 1841. 16, 2 p.

Glasgow Ladies Auxiliary Emancipation Society. Three Years' Female Anti-Slavery Effort, in Britain and America: Being a Report of the Proceedings of the Glasgow Ladies Auxiliary Emancipation Society, Since Its Formation in January, 1834: Containing a Sketch of the Rise and Progress of the American Female Anti-Slavery Societies; and Valuable Communications Addressed by Them, Both to Societies and Individuals in This Country. Glasgow, Aird & Russell [etc.], 1837. 72 p.

Gloucester, Jeremiah. An Oration Delivered on January 1, 1823, in Bethel Church, on the Abolition of the Slave Trade. Philadelphia, John Young, 1823. 16 p.

Goodell, William. Address of the Macedon Convention, by William Goodell; and Letters of Gerrit Smith. Albany, S. W. Green, Patriot Office, 1847. 16 p.

[Goodell, William]. Address Read at the New York State Liberty Convention, Held at Port Byron, on Wednesday and Thursday, July 25, and 26, 1845. Albany Patriot-Extra. 14 p.

Goodell, William. The American Slave Code in Theory and Practice: Its Distinctive Features Shown by Its Statutes, Judicial Decisions, and Illustrative Facts. New York, American and Foreign Anti-Slavery Society, 1853. 431 p.
Same. Second, Third, and Fourth Editions: New York, American and Foreign Anti-Slavery Society, 1853. 431 p.

Goodell, William. American Slavery a Formidable Obstacle to the Conversion of the World. New York, American and Foreign Anti-Slavery Society, 1854. 24 p.

Goodell, William. Come-Outerism. The Duty of Secession from a Corrupt Church. New York, American Anti-Slavery Society, 1845. 38 p.

[Goodell, William]. The Constitutional Duty of the Federal Government to Abolish American Slavery. An Exposé of the Position of the Abolition Society of New York City and Vicinity. New York, Abolition Society of New York City, 1855. 16 p.

[Goodell, William]. The Kansas Struggle of 1856 in Congress and in the Presidential Campaign with Suggestions for the Future. New York, American Abolition Society, 1857. 80 p.

Goodell, William. Origins of American Slavery. Extracts from "Slavery and Anti-Slavery." New York, William Goodell, 1855. 31 p.

Goodell, William. Our National Charters: for the Millions. I. The Federal Constitution of 1788–9. II. The Articles of Confederation, 1788. III. The Declaration of Independence, 1776. IV. The Articles of Association, 1774. With Notes, Showing Their Bearing on Slavery, and the Relative Powers of the State and National Governments. New York, J. W. Alden, 1864. 144 p.
Same. New York, W. Goodell, 1860. 144 p.

Goodell, William. Slavery and Anti-Slavery; a History of the Great Struggle in Both Hemispheres, with a View of the Slavery Question in the United States. New York, Wm. Harned, 1852. 604 p.
3d Edition. New York, Wm. Goodell, 1855. 606 p.

Goodell, William. Views of American Constitutional Law, in Its Bearing upon American Slavery. Utica, N. Y., Jackson & Chaplin, 1844. 160 p.
Second Edition, with Additions. Utica, N. Y., Lawson & Chaplin, 1845. 163 p.

Goodell, William, and Others. Call for a National Nominating Convention, [June 8–20, 1847, at Macedon Lock, N. Y.]. 8 p.

Goodloe, Daniel Reaves. Is It Expedient to Introduce Slavery into Kansas? A Tract for the Times. Respectfully Inscribed to the People of Kansas. Cincinnati, American Reform Tract & Book Society, [n.d.]. 24 p. [Goodloe was the North Carolina exile who succeeded Bailey as editor of the National Era.]

[Goodloe, Daniel Reaves]. The South and the North, Being a Reply to a Lecture on the North and the South by Elwood Fisher, Delivered Before the Young Men's Mercantile Library Association of Cincinnati, Jan. 16, 1849. By a Carolinian. Washington, Buell & Blanchard, 1849. 32 p.

Goodloe, Daniel R. The Southern Platform: or, Manual of Southern Sentiment on the Subject of Slavery. Boston, John P. Jewett & Co., 1858. 80 p.
Same. Boston, J. P. Jewett & Co., 1858. 95 p.

Goodrich, John Z. Non-Extension of Slavery the Policy of the "Fathers of the Republic."—Slavery Allowed, Though Disapproved, in the Old States, but Absolutely Prohibited in the Territories and New States.—Effect of This Policy, and Its Bearing upon the Modern Doctrine of State Rights and State Equality, Stated and Considered. Speech of Hon. J. Z. Goodrich, of Mass., Delivered in the Peace Convention in Washington, February, 1861. Boston, J. E. Farwell and Company, 1864. 31 p.

The Grand Bill of Abominations Commonly Called the Compromise Act, or a Compromise with Sin —a Covenant with Destruction—an Agreement with Hell—a Treaty of Peace, Amity, and Commerce with the Infernal Powers—You May Here Find the Names of the Thirty-four Northern Delinquents, Who Voted in Congress for the Compromise, Fugitive Slave Bill, and Ten Millions Paid for Nothing to Texas. [1850.] Broadside. Printed on Linen.

[Grandy, Moses]. Narrative of the Life of Moses Grandy; Late a Slave in the United States of America. Sold for the Benefit of His Relations Still in Slavery. First American from the last London Edition. Boston, Oliver Johnson, 1844. 145 p.

Granger, Amos Phelps. Slavery Unconstitutional. Speech of Hon. Amos P. Granger, of New York, in the House of Representatives, April 4, 1856, the House Being in Committee of the Whole on the State of the Union. Washington, D. C., Buell & Blanchard, 1856. 8 p.

Granger, Amos Phelps. State Sovereignty—the Constitution—Slavery. Remarks of Hon. A. P. Granger, of New York, in the House of Representatives, February 17, 1859. [Washington? 1859.] 8 p.

Grattan, Peachy R. Speech of Peachy R. Grattan, Esq., in the General Assembly at Cleveland, June 2, 1857. Richmond, H. K. Ellyson, 1857. 22 p.

Gray, Edgar Harkness. Assaults upon Freedom! or, Kidnapping an Outrage upon Humanity and Abhorrent to God. A Discourse Occasioned by the Rendition of Anthony Burns. Shelburne Falls, Mass., D. B. Gunn, 1854. 22 p.

Gray, Horace. A Legal Review of the Case of Dred Scott, as Decided by the Supreme Court of the United States. From the Law Reporter for June, 1857. Boston, Crosby and Nichols Co., 1857. 62 p.

Gray, Thomas, D.D. A Sermon, in Boston, Before the African Society, 14th of July, 1818; the Anniversary of the Abolition of the Slave Trade. Boston, Parmenter and Norton, 1818. 16 p.

[Gray, William Farley]. Letter to His Excellency Wm. H. Seward, Governor of the State of New-York, Touching the Surrender of Certain Fugitives from Justice. New-York, W. Osborn, 1841. 100 p.

Greeley, Horace. A History of the Struggle for Slavery Extension or Restriction in the United States, from the Declaration of Independence to the Present Day. Mainly Compiled and Condensed from the Journals of Congress and Other Official Records, and Showing the Vote by Yeas and Nays on the Most Important Divisions in Either House. New York, Dix, Edwards & Co., 1856. 164 p.

[Greeley, Horace]. The North and the South. Reprinted from the New York Tribune. New York, Office of the Tribune, 1854. 40 p.

Greeley, Horace, and Cleveland, John. Political Textbook for 1860: Comprising a Brief Review of the Presidential Nominations and Elections, Including All the National Platforms Ever Yet Adopted. Also, a History of the Struggle Respecting Slavery in the Territories, and the Action of Congress as to the Freedom of Public Lands, with the Most Notable Speeches and Letters of Messrs. Lincoln, Douglas, Bell, Seward, Everett, Etc., Touching the Questions of the Day. New York, Tribune Association, 1860. 248 p.

Green, Beriah. Belief Without Confession: A Sermon, Preached at Whitesboro, N. Y[ork.] Utica, R. W. Roberts, 1844. 15 p.

Green, Beriah. The Chattel Principle and Abhorrence of Jesus Christ and the Apostles: or, No Refuge for American Slavery in the New Testament. New York, American Anti-Slavery Society, 1839. 71 p.

Green, Beriah. The Church Carried Along; or, The Opinions of a Doctor of Divinity on American Slavery. New York, W. R. Dorr, 1836. 61 p.

Green, Beriah. The Counsel of Caiphas: A Sermon. [n.p., n.d.] 8 p.

Green, Beriah. Four Sermons, Preached in the Chapel of the Western Reserve College, on Lord's Days, November 18th and 25th, and December 2nd and 9th, 1832. Cleveland, Office of the Herald, 1833. 52 p.

Green, Beriah. Iniquity and a Meeting. A Discourse Delivered in the Congregational Church, Whitesboro [N. Y.], Lord's Day. Jan. 31, 1841. 7 p.

Green, Beriah. The Martyr. A Discourse, in Commemoration of the Martyrdom of the Rev. Elijah P. Lovejoy, Delivered in Broadway Tabernacle, New York; and in the Bleecker Street Church, Utica. By Beriah Green, President of Oneida Institute. [New York] American Anti-Slavery Society, 1838. 18 p.

Green, Beriah. Miscellaneous Writings. Whitesboro, Published by the Oneida Institute, 1841. 408 p.

Green, Beriah. Sketches of the Life and Writings of James Gillespie Birney. Utica, N. Y., Jackson & Chaplin, 1844. 119 p.

Green, Beriah. Things for Northern Men to Do: A Discourse Delivered Lord's Day Evening, July 17, 1836, in the Presbyterian Church, Whitesboro, N. Y. New York, Published by Request, 1836. 22 p.

Green, Beriah. Work and Wages. A Sermon Preached in Whitesboro, N. Y., November, 1840, by Beriah Green. [n.p., n.d.] 8 p.

Green, Charles C. The Nubian Slave. [A Poem] Boston, Bela Marsh, 1845.

Green, William, Slave. Narrative of Events in the Life of William Green (Formerly a Slave.) Written by Himself. Springfield [Mass.], L. M. Guernsey, 1853. 23 p.

Gregoire, H. An Enquiry Concerning the Intellectual and Moral Faculties and Literature of Negroes; Followed with an Account of the Life and Works of Fifteen Negroes & Mulattoes, Distinguished in Science, Literature and the Arts. Translated by D. B. Worden, Secretary to the American Legation at Paris. Brooklyn, Thomas Kirk, 1810. 253 p.

Gregory, John. The Life and Character of John Brown; a Sermon Preached at the Wesleyan Methodist Church, Pittsburgh, Pa., on Sunday Morning, December 4, 1859. Pittsburgh, A. A. Anderson, 1860. 16 p.

Greville, Robert Kaye. Slavery and the Slave Trade in the United States of America; and the Extent to Which the American Churches Are Involved in Their Support. Edinburgh, W. Oliphant and Sons, 1845. 24 p.

Griffith, William. Address of the President of the New Jersey Society, for Promoting the Abolition of Slavery, to the General Meeting at Trenton, on Wednesday the 26th of September, 1804. Trenton, Sherman & Merchon, 1804. 12 p.

Griffiths, Julia, ed. Autographes for Freedom. Auburn and Rochester, Rochester Ladies Anti-Slavery Society, 1853. 263 p.
Same. Auburn and Rochester, Rochester Ladies Anti-Slavery Society, 1854. 309 p.

Griffiths, Mattie. Autobiography of a Female Slave. New York, Redfield, 1857. 401 p.

Grimes, William. Life of William Grimes, the Runaway Slave. Written by Himself. New York, 1825. 68 p.

Grimké, Angelina Emily. Appeal to the Christian Women of the South. New York [1836]. 36 p.

Grimké, Angelina Emily. Letters to Catherine E. Beecher, in Reply to an Essay on Slavery and Abolitionism, Addressed to A. E. Grimké. Revised by the Author. Boston, Isaac Knapp, 1838. 130 p.

Grimké, Angelina E. Slavery and the Boston Riot [A Letter to W. L. Garrison]. Philadelphia, August 30, 1835. Broadside. 22 × 33 cm.

Grimké, Angelina Emily. Slavery in America. A Reprint of an Appeal to the Christian Women of the Slave States of America. By Angelina E. Grimké, of Charleston, South Carolina. With Introduction, Notes, and Appendix, by George Thompson. Recommended to the Special Attention of the Anti-Slavery Females of Great Britain. Edinburgh, Oliphant and Son, 1837. 56 p.

[Grimké, Sarah]. The Christian Economy: Translated from the Original Greek of an Old Manuscript, Found in the Island of Patmos, Where St. John Wrote His Book of the Revelation. New York, Williams and Whiting, 1809. 95 p.

Grimké, Sarah Moore. An Epistle to the Clergy of the Southern States. New York, 1836. 20 p.

[Grimké, Sarah]. Letters on the Equality of the Sexes and the Condition of Woman. Addressed to Mary Parker, President of the Boston Female Anti-Slavery Society. Boston, Isaac Knapp, 1838. 128 p.

Grimké, Thomas S. A Letter to the Honorable John C. Calhoun, Vice President of the United States, Robert Y. Hayne, Senator of the United States, George M'Duffie, of the House of Representatives of the United States, and James Hamilton, Jr., Governor of the State of South Carolina. Philadelphia, Thomas Kite & Co., 1832.

Grimké, Thomas S. Oration on the Principal Duties of Americans; Delivered before the Washington Society, and Other Citizens of Charleston; in the Second Presbyterian Church, on Thursday, the 4th of July. With the Farewell Address of Hon. William Drayton, to the Washington Society, Delivered on the Same Day, at Their Anniversary Dinner. Charleston, William Estill, 1833. 39 p.

Gross, Ezra Carter. Speech of Mr. Gross, of New York, on the Restriction of Slavery in Missouri. Delivered in the House of Representatives of the United States, February 1, 1820. [Washington, 1820.] 14 p.

Grosvenor, Cyrus Pitt. Address Before the Anti-Slavery Society of Salem and the Vicinity, in the South Meeting-House, in Salem, February 24, 1834. Salem, W. & S. B. Ives, 1834. 48 p.

Gruber, Jacob, Defendant. Trial of the Rev. Jacob Gruber, Minister in the Methodist Episcopal Church, at the March Term, 1819, in the Frederick County Court, for a Misdemeanor. [The charge was preaching in such manner as to incite slave insurrection.] Fredericktown, Md., David Martin, 1819. 111 p.

Gulliver, J. P. The Lioness and Her Whelps: A Sermon on Slavery, Preached in the Broadway Congregational Church, Norwich, Ct., December 18, 1859. Norwich, Manning, Perry & Co., 1860. 12 p.

[Gunn, Lewis Carstairs]. Address to Abolitionists. Philadelphia, Merrihew and Gunn, 1838. 16 p.

Gurney, Joseph John. Free and Friendly Remarks, on a Speech Lately Delivered to the Senate of the United States, by Henry Clay of Kentucky, on the Subject of the Abolition of North American Slavery. New York, Mahlon Day & Co., 1839. 24 p.

Gurowski, Adam. Slavery in History. New York, A. B. Burdick, 1860. 260 p.

Hale, John Parker. Kansas and the Supreme Court. Speech of John P. Hale, of New Hampshire. Delivered in the United States Senate, January 19 and 21, 1858. [Washington, D. C., Buell & Blanchard, 1858.] 16 p.

Hale, John Parker. Speech of Hon. John P. Hale upon the Slavery Resolutions in the House of Representatives, June 25th, 1846. 15 p.

Hale, John Parker. Speech of Mr. Hale, of New Hampshire, on the Territorial Question. Delivered in the Senate of the United States, Tuesday, March 19, 1850. [Washington, D. C.] Buell & Blanchard [1850]. 16 p.

Hale, John Parker. The Wrongs of Kansas. Speech of Hon. John P. Hale, of New Hampshire. In the United States Senate, February [26] 1856. Washington, D. C., Buell & Blanchard, [1856]. 16 p.

Hale, John Parker. Speech of John P. Hale, of New

Hampshire, in the Senate of the United States, February 14, 1860. [Washington, D. C., 1860.] 15 p.

Hale, John Parker. Speech of John P. Hale, of New Hampshire, on the Abolition of Slavery in the District of Columbia. Delivered in the Senate of the United States, March 18, 1862. [Washington, D. C., L. Towers & Co., 1862.] 8 p.

Hall, Marshall. The Facts of the Two-Fold Slavery of the United States, Carefully Collected During a Personal Tour in the Years 1853 and 1854; with a Project of Self-Emancipation and the Conversion of the Slave into Free Peasantry. London, Adam Scott, 1854. 159 p.

Hall, Nathaniel. The Iniquity: A Sermon Preached in the First Church, Dorchester, on Sunday, Dec. 11, 1859. Boston, J. Wilson & Son, 1859. 37 p.

Hall, Nathaniel. The Limits of Civil Obedience. A Sermon Preached in the First Church, Dorchester, January 12, 1851. Boston, W. Crosby and H. P. Nichols, 1851. 26 p.

Hall, Nathaniel. Righteousness and the Pulpit; A Discourse Preached in the First Church, Dorchester, on Sunday, Sept. 30, 1855. Boston, Crosby, Nichols & Company, 1855. 27 p.

Hall, Nathaniel. Two Sermons on Slavery and Its Hero Victim. Boston, John Wilson & Son, 1859. 37 p.
[1.] The Iniquity, a Sermon Preached in the First Church, Dorchester, on Sunday, Dec. 11, 1859.
[2.] The Man, the Deed, the Event: A Sermon Preached in the First Church, Dorchester, on Sunday, Dec. 4, and Repeated Dec. 11, 1859.

Hall, P. W. Thoughts and Inquiry on the Principles and Tenur[e] of the Revealed and Supreme Law, Shewing the Utter Inconsistency and Injustice of Our Penal Statutes, and the Illicit Traffic and Practice of Modern Slavery. With Some Grounds of a Plan for Abolishing the Same. To Which Is Added a Letter to a Clergyman on the Same Subject. London, J. Ridgway, 1792. 304 p.

Hamilton, William. Address to the Fourth Annual Convention of the Free People of Color of the United States. Delivered at the Opening of Their Session in the City of New York, June 2, 1834. New York, S. W. Benedict & Co., 1834. 8 p.

Hamilton, William. An Oration Delivered in the African Zion Church, on the Fourth of July, 1827, in Commemoration of the Abolition of Domestic Slavery in This State. By William Hamilton. New York, Gray & Bunce, 1827. 16 p.

Hamlin, Hannibal. Speech of Hon. Hannibal Hamlin, of Maine, on the Proposition to Admit California as a State into the Union. Delivered in the Senate of the United States, March 5, 1850. Washington, [D. C.] Congressional Globe Office, 1850. 14 p.

[Law partner of Fessenden; senator and vice-president of the United States.]

Hamlin, Hannibal. Speech of Hon. Hannibal Hamlin, of Maine, in the United States Senate, March 9 and 10, 1858, in Reply to Governor Hammond, and in Defense of the North and Northern Laborers. [Washington, D. C., 1858.] 16 p.

[Hammon, Jupiter]. An Address to the Negroes, in the State of New York. By Jupiter Hammon, Servant of John Lloyd, Jun., Esq. of the Manor of Queen's Village, Long-Island. New-York Printed; Philadelphia, Re-Printed by Daniel Humphreys, 1787. 15 p.

Hammond, Stephen Hallet. Freedom National—Slavery Sectional. Speech of the Hon. S. H. Hammond, of the Twenty-Seventh Senate District, on the Governor's Message. In Senate, February, 1860. Albany, Weed, Parsons, & Co., 1860. 16 p.

Hanaford, Mrs. Joseph H. (Phebe Anne Coffin). Lucretia, the Quakeress; or, Principle Triumphant. Boston, J. Buffum, 1853. 172 p.

Hancock, Pseud. [William Jay]. A Letter to the Hon. Samuel A. Eliot, Representative in Congress from the City of Boston, in Reply to His Apology for Voting for the Fugitive Slave Bill. Boston, William Crosby & H. P. Nichols, 1851. 57 p.

Hanway, Castner (Defendant). A History of the Trial of Castner Hanway and Others, for Treason, at Philadelphia in November, 1851, with an Introduction upon the History of the Slave Question. By a Member of the Philadelphia Bar. Philadelphia, Uriah Hunt & Sons, 1852. 86 p.

Hanway, Castner, Defendant. Report of the Trial of Castner Hanway for Treason, in the Resistance of the Execution of the Fugitive Slave Law of September, 1850. Before Judges Grier and Kane, in the Circuit Court of the United States, for the Eastern District of Pennsylvania. Held in Philadelphia in November and December, 1851. To Which Is Added an Appendix, Containing the Laws of the United States on the Subject of Fugitives from Labor, and the Charges of Judge Kane to the Grand Juries in Relation Thereto, and a Statement of the Points of Law Decided by the Court During the Trial. By James J. Robbins. From the Notes of Arthur Cannon and Samuel B. Dalrymple, Phonographic Reporters Appointed by the Court for This Case. Philadelphia, King & Baird, 1852. 275 p.

Harding, Aaron. Emancipation of Slaves in Rebel States; Speech in the House of Representatives, Dec. 17, 1861, on the Joint Resolution Relative to the Right and Duty of the President in Regard to Persons Held as Slaves in Any Military District in a State of Insurrection. [Washington, D. C.] 16 p.

Hargrave, Francis. An Argument in the Case of

James Sommersett, a Negro. Wherein It Is Attempted to Demonstrate the Present Unlawfulness of Domestick Slavery in England. To Which Is Prefixed, a State of the Case. By Mr. Hargrave, One of the Counsel for the Negro. London, Printed for the Author, 1772. 82 p.
Same. Second Edition. London, Printed for the Author, 1775.
Same. Third Edition. London, Printed for the Author; and Sold by T. Cadell, 1783. 65 p.

Harlan, James. Shall the Territories Be Africanized? Speech of Hon. James Harlan, of Iowa. Delivered in the Senate of the United States, January 4, 1860. [Washington, D. C.] Buell & Blanchard, 1860. 8 p. [Printed also in German.] Soll Man die territorien Afrikanis iren? Rede des ehrb. James Harlan, von Iowa. Gehalten im Senat am 4. Januar 1860.

Harlan, Mary B. Ellen; or, The Chained Mother; and Pictures of Kentucky Slavery. Drawn from Real Life. By Mary B. Harlan. Cincinnati, for the Author, by Applegate & Co., 1853. 259 p.

Harris, Thaddeus Mason. A Discourse Delivered Before the African Society in Boston, 15th of July, 1822, on the Anniversary Celebration of the Abolition of the Slave Trade. Boston, Phelps and Farnham, 1822. 27 p.

Harris, Thomas L. Letter of Hon. Thomas L. Harris of Illinois upon the Repeal of the Fugitive Slave Law. Washington, D. C., Jno. T. Towers, 1851. 12 p.

Harris, William Logan. The Constitutional Powers of the General Conference, with a Special Application to the Subject of Slave Holding. Cincinnati, Methodist Book Concern, 1860. 156 p.

[Harrison, Jesse Burton]. Review of the Slave Question, Extracted from the American Quarterly Review, Dec. 1832; Based on the Speech of Th. Marshall, of Fauquier: Showing That Slavery Is the Essential Hindrance to the Prosperity of the Slave-Holding States; with Particular Reference to Virginia. Though Applicable to Other States Where Slavery Exists. By a Virginian. Richmond, T. W. White, 1833. 48 p.

Hart, Levi, D.D. Liberty Described and Recommended; in a Sermon, Preached to the Corporation of Freemen in Farmington, September 20, 1774. Hartford, Watson, 1775. 23 p.

Hartford Convention. The Proceedings of a Convention of Delegates from the States of Massachusetts, Connecticut, and Rhode Island; the Counties of Cheshire and Grafton in the State of New Hampshire; and the County of Windham, in the State of Vermont; Convened at Hartford, in the State of Connecticut, December 15th, 1814. Third Edition.

Corrected and Improved. Boston, Wills and Lilly, 1815. 32 p.

Hastings, Samuel D. Speech of Samuel D. Hastings, of Walworth County, in the Assembly, in Committee of the Whole, in Support of the Resolutions Reported by Him as Chairman of the Select Committee to Whom the Subject Had Been Referred. January 27, 1849. Milwaukee, S. M. Booth, 1849. 16 p.

Hatfield, Edwin Francis, Comp. Freedom's Lyre: or, Psalms, Hymns, and Sacred Songs, for the Slave and His Friends. Comp. by Edwin F. Hatfield. New York, S. W. Benedict, 1840. 265 p.

Hawker, Rev. Robert. An Appeal to the Common Feelings of Mankind in Behalf of Negroes, in the West-India Islands, More Especially Addressed to the Subjects of the British Empire: Through the Medium of a Letter to William Wilberforce [etc.] [Added: a Plan for Giving Relief in the Purchase of Plantations.] London, A. A. Paris, 1823. 24 p.

Hawkins, Joseph. A History of a Voyage to the Coast of Africa, and Travels into the Interior of That Country; Containing Particular Descriptions of the Climate and Inhabitants, and Interesting Particulars Concerning the Slave Trade. Philadelphia, Printed for the Author, by S. C. Ustick & Co., 1797. 179 p.
Same. Second Edition. Troy, 180 p. [Prefatory endorsement by Benjamin Rush.]

Hawley, H. H., Publisher. Songs for Freemen; a Collection of Campaign and Patriotic Songs for the People, Adapted to Familiar and Popular Melodies and Designed to Promote the Cause of "Free Speech, Free Press, Free Soil, Free Men, and Fremont." Utica, H. H. Hawley, 1856. 48 p.

Hear Him and His Neighbors. Letters and Documents of Distinguished Citizens of Tennessee, on the Buying and Selling of Human Beings. New York, Sickles, 1828. 16 p.

Hebbard, William Wallace. The Night of Freedom: An Appeal, in Verse, against the Great Crime of Our Country, Human Bondage! By William Wallace Hebbard. Boston, S. Chism, 1857. 42 p.

Hedge, Frederick Henry. Conscience and the State. A Discourse, Preached in the Westminster Church, Providence, Sunday, April 27, 1851. Providence, Joseph Knowles, 1851. 22 p.

Helper, Hinton Rowan. The Impending Crisis of the South: How to Meet It. By Hinton Rowan Helper. 13th Thousand. New York, Burdick Brothers, 1857. 419 p.
Same. 15th Thousand. New York, A. B. Burdick, 1860. 420 p.

[Henry, C. S.]. Politics and the Pulpit: A Series of Articles Which Appeared in the Journal of Commerce and in the Independent during the Year 1850. To Which Is Added an Article from the Independent of Feb. 21, 1850, Entitled "Shall We Compromise?" New York, William Harned, 1851. 63 p.

Henry, Joseph. A Statement of Facts Respecting the Condition & Treatment of Slaves, in the City of Vicksburgh and Its Vicinity, in the State of Mississippi, in 1838 & '39. By Joseph Henry. Medina, O., 1839. 24 p.

Henson, Josiah. The Life of Josiah Henson, Formerly a Slave, Now an Inhabitant of Canada, as Narrated by Himself. Boston, Arthur D. Phelps, 1849. 76 p.

Henson, Josiah. Truth Stranger than Fiction. Father Henson's Story of His Own Life with an Introduction by Mrs. H. B. Stowe. Boston, John P. Jewett & Co., 1858. xii, 212 p.

Herald of Freedom. Weekly. Concord, N. H. March 7, 1835–October 23, 1846. Organ of New Hampshire Anti-Slavery Society. Edited by Joseph H. Kimball (1836–1837); N. P. Rogers (1839–1844); Parker Pillsbury (1845–1846).

Herald of Freedom. Weekly. Lawrence, Kansas. October 21, 1854–1860. Edited by Augustus Wattles.

Hersey, John. An Appeal to Christians, on the Subject of Slavery. By John Hersey. 2d ed. Baltimore, Armstrong & Plaskitt, 1833. 124 p.

[Heyrick, Mrs. Elizabeth]. Apology for Ladies' Anti-Slavery Associations, by the Author of "Immediate, Not Gradual Abolition, etc." London, J. Hatchard, 1828. 16 p.

[Heyrick, Mrs. Elizabeth]. Immediate, Not Gradual Abolition; or, An Inquiry into the Shortest, Safest, and Most Effectual Means of Getting Rid of West Indian Slavery. London, Printed 1824; Philadelphia, Reprinted by Joseph Rakestraw, 1824. 24 p.
Same. New York, James V. Seaman, 1825. 24 p.
Same. Second American Edition. Philadelphia, Merrihew & Gunn, 1836. 24 p.
Same. Philadelphia, Anti-Slavery Society, 1837.
Same. Boston, Isaac Knapp, 1838. 35 p.

Hicks, Elias. Observations on the Slavery of the Africans and Their Descendants. Recommended to the Serious Perusal, and Impartial Consideration of the Citizens of the United States of America, and Others Concerned. New York, Samuel Wood, 1811. 24 p. [Hicks secured the complete emancipation of slaves in New York, 1827.]

Hicks, Elias. Observations on the Slavery of the Africans and Their Descendants, and on the Use of the Produce of Their Labour. Recommended to the Serious Perusal, and Impartial Consideration of the Citizens of the United States of America, and Others Concerned. New York, Samuel Wood, 1814. 23 p.

Higginson, Thomas Wentworth. "Man Shall Not Live by Bread Alone." A Thanksgiving Sermon, Preached in Newburyport, Nov. 30, 1848. Second Edition. Newburyport, Charles Whipple, 1848. 12 p. [This sermon cost Higginson his pulpit.]

Higginson, Thomas Wentworth. Massachusetts in Mourning. A Sermon Preached in Worcester, on Sunday, June 4, 1854, by Thomas W. Higginson, Reprinted by Request, from the Worcester Daily Spy. Boston, James Munroe & Co., 1854. 15 p. [The Anthony Burns case.]

Higginson, Thomas Wentworth. The New Revolution; A Speech Before the American Anti-Slavery Society at Their Annual Meeting in New York, May 12, 1857. Boston, R. F. Wallcut, 1857. 16 p.

Hildreth, Richard. Brief Remarks on Miss Catharine E. Beecher's Essay on Slavery and Abolitionists. By the Author of Archy Moore. Boston, I. Knapp, 1837. 28 p.

[Hildreth, Richard]. Despotism in America: or, An Inquiry into the Nature and Results of the Slave-Holding System in the United States. Boston, Whipple & Damrell, 1840. 186 p.
Same. Second Edition. Boston, Massachusetts Anti-Slavery Society, 1840. 186 p.

Hildreth, Richard. Despotism in America; an Inquiry into the Nature, Results, and Legal Basis of the Slaveholding System in the United States. Boston, John P. Jewett & Co., 1854. 307 p.

Hildreth, Richard. The Slave; or, Memoirs of Archy Moore. Boston, John H. Eastburn, 1836. Third Edition. Two Volumes in One. Boston, Massachusetts Anti-Slavery Society; New York, American Anti-Slavery Society, 1840. [There were, also, five French editions.]
Same: The White Slave; or Memoirs of a Fugitive. Boston, Tappan and Whittemore, 1852. 408 p.

Hill, Isaac. Speech of Mr. Hill, of New Hampshire, on the Motion of Mr. Calhoun That the Senate Refuse to Receive a Petition from the Society of Friends, in the State of Pennsylvania, to Abolish Slavery in the District of Columbia. In Senate, February 12, 1836. [Washington, 1836] 8 p.

Hill, Pascol Grenfell (Chaplain, H.M.S. *Cleopatra*). Fifty Days on Board a Slave-Vessel in the Mozambique Channel, in April and May, 1843. New York, J. Winchester, [1844]. 29 p.

[Hill, Rev. Thomas]. Christmas, and Poems on Slavery, for Christmas, 1843. Dedicated to Eliza Lee Follen. Cambridge, Published by the Author for the Massachusetts Anti-Slavery Fair, 1843. 16 p.

[Hill, at a later date, was president of Antioch and then of Harvard.]

[Hillard, Isaac]. To the Honorable the General Assembly of the State of Connecticut, to Be Holden at Hartford, on the Second Thursday of May Next. The Memorial of Harry, Cuff, and Cato, Black Men, Now in Slavery in Connecticut, in Behalf of Ourselves and the Poor Black People of Our Nation in Like Circumstances. [n.p., 1797?] 12 p.

[Hillhouse, William]. Pocahontas; a Proclamation: With Plates. [New Haven, J. Clyme, 1820.] 16 p. [Satire on Virginia and slavery.]

[Hillhouse, William]. The Crisis, No. 1–2; or, Thoughts on Slavery Occasioned by the Missouri Question. New Haven, A. H. Maltby & Co., 1820.

Hinchman, Morgan. The Hinchman Conspiracy Case, in Letters to the New York Home Journal, with an Abstract of the Evidence for the Defence, Furnishing a Complete Explanation of This Most Extraordinary Case. By an American Citizen. Philadelphia, Stokes & Brother, 1849. 58 p.

Hingham Anti-Slavery Society, and Weymouth Anti-Slavery Society. Celebration of West India Emancipation, by the Hingham and Weymouth Anti-Slavery Societies. In Hingham, August 1, 1842. [Hingham, Mass., 1842.] 12 p.

History and Record of the Proceedings of the People of Lexington and Its Vicinity; in the Suppression of the True American, from the Commencement of the Movement on the 14th of August, 1845, to Its Final Termination on Monday, the 18th of the Same Month. Lexington, Virden, 1845. 35 p.

A History of the Trial of Castner Hanway and Others, for Treason, at Philadelphia, in November, 1851. With an Introduction upon the History of the Slave Question. By a Member of the Philadelphia Bar. Philadelphia, U. Hunt & Sons, 1852. 86 p.

Hoar, Ebenezer Rockwood. Charge to the Grand Jury, at the July Term of the Municipal Court, in Boston, 1854. Boston, Little, Brown & Co., 1854. 22 p.

Hoar, Samuel. Remarks by Samuel Hoar of Massachusetts, on the Resolutions Introduced by Mr. Jarvis, of Maine, and Mr. Wise, of Virginia, Delivered in the House of Representatives, Thursday, January 21, 1836. Washington, National Intelligencer Office, 1838. 13 p.

Hodgson, Adam. A Letter to M. Jean-Baptiste Say, on the Comparative Expense of Free and Slave Labour. New York, Reprinted for the Manumission Society, by Mahlon Day, 1823. 50, 14 p. Second Edition. Liverpool, Halotard & Son, 1823. 60 p.

Holden Anti-Slavery Society, Holden, Mass. Report of the Holden Slave Case, Tried at the January Term of the Court of Common Pleas, for the County of Worcester, A.D. 1839. Worcester, 1839. 32 p. [Case of Anne, slave of Mrs. Olivia Eames.]

Holley, Myron. Address Delivered Before the Rochester Anti-Slavery Society, on the 19th January, and Again, by Request of Several Citizens, at the Court House, in Rochester, on the 5th February, 1837. Rochester, Hoyt & Porter, 1837. 22 p.

Holley, Myron. An Address Delivered at Perry, N. Y., July 4, 1839. Perry, Mitchell & Warren, 1839. 16 p.

Holly, Joseph C. Freedom's Offering; A Collection of Poems. Rochester, Chas. H. McDonnell, 1853. 38 p.

Holmes, Daniel. Dialogue on Slavery, and Miscellaneous Subjects, Based on the Word of God, by Daniel Holmes. Dayton [O.] Gazette Book and Job Rooms, 1854. 29 p.

Home Missions and Slavery: A Reprint of Several Articles Recently Published in Religious Journals, with an Appendix. New York, John A. Gray, 1857. 48 p. [Introduction signed:] A.D.S.

[Hopkins, Samuel]. A Dialogue Concerning the Slavery of the Africans; Shewing It to Be the Duty and Interest of the American States to Emancipate All Their African Slaves. With an Address to the Owners of Such Slaves. Dedicated to the Honourable the Continental Congress. To Which Is Prefixed, the Institution of the Society, in New York, for Promoting the Manumission of Slaves, and Protecting Such of Them as Have Been, or May Be, Liberated. Norwich [Conn.], Judah P. Spooner, 1776. New York, Re-printed for Robert Hodge, 1785. 72 p.

Hopkins, Samuel. A Discourse upon the Slave Trade and the Slavery of the Africans. Delivered in the Baptist Meeting-House at Providence, before the Providence Society for Abolishing the Slave-Trade &c. At Their Annual Meeting, on May 17, 1793. Providence, J. Carter, 1793. 28 p.

[Hopper, Isaac Tatem]. Exposition of the Proceedings of John P. Darg, Henry W. Merritt, and Others, in Relation to the Robbery of Darg, the Elopement of His Alleged Slave, and the Trial of Barney Corse, Who Was Unjustly Charged as an Accessory. New York, Isaac T. Hopper, 1840. 39 p. [Hopper was pre-eminent in the rescue of fugitives, and in the legal protection of free Negroes. His entire life was devoted to protection of helpless persons against kidnapping and other forms of oppression.]

Hopper, Isaac Tatem. Narrative of the Life of Thomas Cooper. New York, Isaac T. Hopper, 1832. 36 p.

Fourth Edition, N. Y., Hopper, 1837. 35 p.

Hopper, Isaac Tatem. A Narrative of the Proceedings of the Monthly Meeting of New York and Their Subsequent Confirmation by the Quarterly and Yearly Meetings in the Case of I. T. Hopper. New York, Printed for the Author, 1843. 126 p.

Horsmanden, Daniel. The New York Conspiracy; or, A History of the Negro Plot; with the Journal of the Proceedings Against the Conspirators at New York, in the Years 1741–2. Together with Several Interesting Tables Containing the Names of the White and Black Persons Arrested on Account of the Conspiracy—the Times of Their Trials—Their Sentences—Their Executions by Burning and Hanging—Names of Those Transported, and Those Discharged. With a Variety of Other Useful and Highly Interesting Matter. New York, Southwick & Pelsue, 1812. 385 p.

[First Published in New York, 1744.]

[Second Edition, 1810.]

[Horton, George Wm.]. Poems by a Slave. [George, Property of James Horton, Chatham County, North Carolina]. A Reprint of the Hope of Liberty. By George M. Horton. Raleigh, Gales & Son, 1829.

Hossack, John. Report of the Trial of John Hossack, Indicted for Rescuing a Fugitive Slave from the U. S. Deputy Marshal at Ottawa, October 20th, 1859. R. B. Hitt, Reporter. Chicago, Press and Tribune Office, 1860. 265 p.

Hovey, Sylvester. Letters from the West Indies; Relating Especially to the Danish Island St. Croix, and the British Islands Antigua, Barbadoes, and Jamaica. New York, Gould and Newman, 1838. 212 p.

Howard, Benjamin C. Report of the Decision of the Supreme Court of the United States, and the Opinions of the Judges Thereof, in the Case of Dred Scott versus John F. A. Sandford. December Term, 1856. Washington, Cornelius Wendell, 1857. 239 p.

Howard, Hope. The Man Hunt. An American Ballad. Journeymen Printers Association. No. 5 Harmony Court. [8 p.].

Howe, S. G. The Refugees from Slavery in Canada West. Report to the Freedman's Inquiry Commission. Boston, Wright & Potter, 1864. 110 p.

Howe, Samuel Gridley. Slavery at Washington: Narrative of the Heroic Adventures of Drayton, an American Trader in "The Pearl," Coasting Vessel, Which Was Captured by American Citizens, near the Mouth of the Potomac, Having on Board Seventy-Seven Men, Women, and Children, Endeavoring to Escape from Slavery in the Capital of the American Republic. London, Printed by Order of the Council of the Anti-Slavery League, 1848. 24 p.

Human Rights. Monthly. New York, N. Y. July, 1835–June, 1839. Edited by Elizur Wright. Organ of the American Anti-Slavery Society.

Humanitas [pseud.]. Reflections on Slavery; with Recent Evidence of Its Inhumanity. Occasioned by the Melancholy Death of Romain, a French Negro. By Humanitas. Philadelphia, Printed for the Author, 1803. 40 p.

Humphrey, Heman. The Missouri Compromise. An Address Delivered before the Citizens of Pittsfield. By Rev. Heman Humphrey, D.D., in the Baptist Church. On Sabbath Evening, Feb. 26, 1854. Pittsfield, Reid, Hull & Perison, 1854. 32 p.

Humphrey, Heman. Parallel Between Intemperance and the Slave Trade. An Address. Delivered at Amherst College, July 4, 1828, by Heman Humphrey, D.D., President of the College. Amherst, J. S. & C. Adams, 1828. 40 p.

Hurd, John Codman. The Law of Freedom and Bondage in the United States. 2 Vols. Boston, Little, Brown & Co., 1858–1862.

Hurd, John Codman. Topics of Jurisprudence Connected with Conditions of Freedom and Bondage. New York, D. Van Nostrand, 1856. 113 p.

Hutchinson, A. B. The Granite Songster; Comprising the Songs of the Hutchinson Family, Without the Music. Boston, Charles Holt, 1847. 69 p.

Hymns and Songs for the Friends of Freedom. Middletown, C. H. Pelton, 1842. 40 p.

Hymns and Songs for the Anti-Slavery Celebration of the Declaration of Independence, at Farmington, July 4, 1855. Boston, Prentiss & Sawyer, 1855. Broadside.

Hymns and Songs for the Anti-Slavery Celebration of the Declaration of Independence, at Farmington, July 5, 1858. Boston, Prentiss, Sawyer & Co., 1858. Broadside.

Hymns for the New England Anti-Slavery Convention, Wednesday and Thursday, May 25th and 26th, 1859. Broadside.

Illinois Anti-Slavery Society. Alton Observer—Extra. Proceedings of the Illinois Anti-Slavery Convention Held at Upper Alton on the Twenty-Sixth, Twenty-Seventh, and Twenty-Eighth October, 1837. Alton, Parks and Breath, 1838. 36 p.

Important Act of the Legislature of South Carolina Passed at the Session in December, 1823, to Prevent Free Negroes and Persons of Colour from Entering This State. Every Master or Commander of a Vessel, Entering into, or Sailing from This Port, Ought to Be Provided with a Copy of This Act. Charleston, A. E. Miller, 1824. 8 p.

In Memoriam. Testimonials to the Life and Character of the Late Francis Jackson. Boston, R. F. Wallcut, 1861. 36 p.

The Independent. Politics and the Pulpit: A Series of Articles Which Appeared in the Journal of Commerce and in the Independent, during the Year 1850. To Which Is Added an Article from the Independent of Feb. 21, 1850, Entitled "Shall We Compromise?" New York, W. Harned, 1851. 63 p.

Independent Democrats in Congress. Appeal of the Independent Democrats in Congress, to the People of the United States. Shall Slavery Be Permitted in Nebraska? [Washington, Towers, 1854.] 8 p.

Indiana Anti-Slavery Society. Proceedings of the Indiana Convention Assembled to Organize a State Anti-Slavery Society Held in Milton, Wayne Co., Sept. 12, 1838. Cincinnati, Sam'l A. Alley, 1838. 238 p.

Indiana (Ter.) Governor, 1801–1812 [Harrison]. Letter from William Henry Harrison, Governor of the Indiana Territory, Inclosing Certain Resolutions Passed by the Legislative Council and House of Representatives of the Said Territory, Relative to a Suspension, for a Certain Period, of the Sixth Article of Compact Between the United States and the Territories and States, Northwest of the River Ohio, Made 13 July, 1787. City of Washington: A. & G. Way, 1807. 7 p.

Infidelity Unmasked. Bi-Weekly. Cincinnati, Ohio. Volume 1. June 5, 1831–April 22, 1832. Edited by Dyer Burgess. [Whole title:] Anti-Conspirator, or, Infidelity Unmasked; Being a Development of the Principles of Free Masonry; to Which Is Added, Strictures on Slavery, as Existing in the Church.

Inhabitants of Dumbarton and the Vale of Levan. Remonstrance on the Subject of American Slavery. Glasgow, 1837. 8 p.

Interesting Correspondence. Letter of Commodore Stockton on the Slavery Question. New York, S. W. Benedict, 1850. 23 p.

Irish, David. Observations on a Living and Effectual Testimony against Slavery. Introduced with Some Remarks upon Excess and Superfluity, Recommended to the Consideration of the Members of the Society of Friends. New York, Printed for the Author, 1836. 30 p.

Irish Unitarian Christian Society. Address of the Irish Unitarian Christian Society to Their Brethren in America. Boston, Office of the Christian World, 1846. 7 p.

Ivimey, Joseph. The Utter Extinction of Slavery an Object of Scripture Prophecy: A Lecture the Substance of Which Was Delivered at the Annual Meeting of the Chelmsford Ladies' Anti-Slavery Association, in the Friend's Meeting House, on Tuesday, the 17th of April, 1832. London, G. Wightman [etc.], 1832. 74 p.

Jack, A Negro Man. In the Court for the Correction of Errors. Jack a Negro Man, Against Mary Martin. Case on the Part of the Plaintiff in Error. New York, J. Van Norden, 1834. 37 p.

Jackson, Andrew. Narrative and Writings of Andrew Jackson, of Kentucky; Containing an Account of His Birth, and Twenty-Six Years of His Life While a Slave; His Escape; Five Years of Freedom, Together with Anecdotes Relating to Slavery; Journal of One Year's Travels; Sketches, Etc. Narrated by Himself; Written by a Friend. Syracuse, Daily and Weekly Star Office, 1847. 120 p.

Jackson, James C[aleb]. The Duties and Dignities of American Freemen. By James C. Jackson. [Boston, New England Anti-Slavery Tract Association, 1843?] 12 p. (Tract No. 6).

Jackson, James Caleb. The Condition of Living— "Liberty is Not Life, but the Condition of Living." [New York, 1844] 8 p. N. Y. State A. S. Society, *Monthly Tracts*, No. 8.

[Jackson, John]. Considerations on the Impropriety of Friends Participating in the Administration of Political Governments. Philadelphia, 1840. 12 p.

Jackson, William. View of Slavery, in Its Effects on the Wealth, Population, and Character of Nations. By William Jackson, of Chester Co., Pennsylvania. Philadelphia, Junior Anti-Slavery Society, 1838. 12 p.

Jacobs, Mrs. Harriet Brent. Incidents in the Life of a Slave Girl. Written by Herself. Edited by L. Maria Child. Boston, Published for the Author, 1861. 306 p.

Jagger, William. To the People of Suffolk Co. Information, Acquired from the Best Authority, with Respect to the Institution of Slavery. New York, R. Craighead, 1856. 28 p.

James, Horace. Our Duties to the Slave. A Sermon, Preached Before the Original Congregational Church and Society, in Wrentham, Mass., on Thanksgiving Day, November 28, 1846. Boston, Richardson & Filmer, 1847. 23 p.

James, Mrs. Mary *Prince*. The History of Mary Prince, a West Indian Slave. Related by Herself. With a Supplement by the Editor [T. Pringle]. To Which Is Added, the Narrative of Asa-Asa, a Captured African. Third Edition, F. Westley and A. H. Davis, 1831. 44 p.

Jamieson, Rev. John. The Sorrows of Slavery, a Poem. Containing a Faithful Statement of the Facts Respecting the African Slave Trade. London, J. Murray, 1789. 80 p.

Jay, John. America Free, or America Slave. An Address on the State of the Country. Delivered by John Jay, Esq., at Bedford, Westchester County, New York, October 8th, 1856. New York, New York Tribune, [1856]. 20 p.

[Jay, John]. Caste and Slavery in the American Church. By a Churchman. New York, Wiley and Putnam, 1843. 51 p.

Jay, John. Correspondence Between John Jay, Esq., and the Vestry of St. Matthew's Church, Bedford, N. Y. [Bedford? N. Y.] 1862. 16 p.

Jay, John. The Great Conspiracy. An Address Delivered at Mt. Kisco, West Chester County, New York, on the 4th of July, 1861, the 86th Anniversary of American Independence. New York, Roe Lockwood & Son, 1861. 50 p.

Jay, John. The Progress and Results of Emancipation in the English West Indies. A Lecture Delivered Before the Philomathian Society of the City of New York. New York, Wiley and Putnam, 1842. 39 p.

Jay, John. Thoughts on the Duty of the Episcopal Church, in Relation to Slavery: Being a Speech Delivered in N. Y. A. S. Convention, February 12, 1839. By John Jay. New York, Piercy & Reed, 1839. 11 p.

[Jay, William]. The Condition of the Free People of Colour in the United States of America. Reprinted from No. XIII of the Anti-Slavery Examiner, Published at New York, 1839. To Which Are Added, Resolutions Passed at the Late Meeting of the Anti-Slavery Convention, Held in London, in June, 1840, on the Same Subject. London, Thomas Ward and Co., 1841. 22 p.

[Jay, William]. The Creole Case, and Mr. Webster's Despatch; with the Comments of the N. Y. American. New York, Office of the New York American, 1842. 39 p.

Jay, William. An Examination of the Mosaic Laws of Servitude. New York, W. M. Dodd, 1854. 56 p.

Jay, William. An Inquiry into the Character and Tendency of the American Colonization and American Anti-Slavery Societies. First Edition. New York, Leavitt, Lord & Co., 1835. 202 p.
Same. Second Edition. New York, Leavitt, Lord & Co., 1835. 206 p.
Same. Third Edition. New York, Leavitt & Lord, 1835. 206 p.
Same. Fourth Edition. New York, R. G. Williams, 1837. 206 p.
Same. Sixth Edition. New York, R. G. Williams for American Anti-Slavery Society, 1838. 206 p.
Same. Tenth Edition. New York, American Anti-Slavery Society, 1840. 206 p.

Jay, William. Letter of the Hon. William Jay to Hon. Theodore Frelinghuysen [on slavery]. New York, 1844. 8 p.

[Jay, William]. Letter to the American Tract Society. New York, February 14, 1853. 16 p.

Jay, William. A Letter to the Committee Chosen by the American Tract Society, to Inquire into the Proceedings of Its Executive Committee, in Relation to Slavery. [New York, 1857.] 38 p.

Jay, William. A Letter to the Right Rev. L[evi] Silliman Ives, Bishop of the Protestant Episcopal Church in the State of North Carolina Occasioned by His Late Address to the Convention of His Diocese. Washington, Buell & Blanchard, 1846. Third Edition. New York, W. Harned, 1848. 32 p.

Jay, William. Letters Respecting the American Board of Commissioners for Foreign Missions and the American Tract Society. New York, Lewis J. Bates, 1853. 16 p.

Jay, William. Miscellaneous Writings on Slavery. Boston, J. P. Jewett, 1853. 670 p.

Jay, William. Reply to Remarks of Rev. Moses Stuart, Late of Andover Theological Seminary, on Hon. John Jay, and an Examination of His Scriptural Exegesis Contained in His Recent Pamphlet Entitled, "Conscience and the Constitution." New York, J. A. Gray, 1850. 22 p.

Jay, William. A Reply to Webster, in a Letter from Hon. William Jay to Hon. Wm. Nelson, M. C. Boston, W. Crosby and H. P. Nichols, 1850. 12 p.

Jay, William. A Review of the Causes and Consequences of the Mexican War. Boston, Benjamin B. Mussey & Co., 1849. 333 p.
Same: Fourth Edition. Boston, Benjamin B. Mussey & Co., 1849. 333 p.

Jay, William. A View of the Action of the Federal Government, in Behalf of Slavery. New York, J. S. Taylor, 1839. 217 p.
Same: Second Edition. New York, American Anti-Slavery Society, 1839. 240 p.
Same: Utica, New York, J. C. Jackson for New York Anti-Slavery Society, 1844. 112 p.
Same: With an Appendix by Joshua Leavitt. Utica, Jackson & Chaplin, 1844. 112 p. [Appendix: Amistad and Creole Cases].

Jeffrey, Rev. George. The Pro-Slavery Character of the American Churches, and the Sin of Holding Christian Communion with Them: A Lecture by Rev. George Jeffrey, Glasgow, Edinburgh, Charles Ziegler, 1847. 19 p.

Jeremie, John. Four Essays on Colonial Slavery. London, J. Hatchard and Son, 1831. 123 p.
Same: Second Edition. London, J. Hatchard, and Son, 1832. 125 p.

Jeremie, John. A Letter to T. Fowell Buxton, Esq. on Negro Emancipation and African Colonization. London, J. Hatchard & Son, 1840. 52 p.

Jessup, Lewis. God's Honor; or, The Christian Statesman. A Sermon, Preached in Millsbury, Sunday, June 15th, 1856. Worcester, Chas. Hamilton, 1856. 12 p.

[Jocelyn, Simeon S.]. College for Colored Youth. An Account of the New Haven City Meeting and

Resolutions, with Recommendations of the College, and Strictures upon the Doings of New Haven. New York, Published by the Committee, 1831. 24 p.

Johnson, Lyman H. Sin of Slavery. A Discourse, First Preached in the N. S. Presbyterian Church, Rockford, Ill., July 15, 1860, by Its Pastor, Lyman H. Johnson. Also at the Congregational Church, Southampton, and at the Third Cong. Church, Chicopee, Mass. New York, John P. Prall, 1860. 24 p.

Johnson, Oliver. An Address Delivered in the Congregational Church, in Middlebury, by Request of the Vermont Anti-Slavery Society, on Wednesday Evening, February 18, 1835. Montpelier, Knapp and Jewett, 1835. 32 p.

Johnson, Oliver, and White, George. Correspondence Between Oliver Johnson and George F. White, a Minister, of the Society of Friends. With an Appendix. New York, Oliver Johnson, 1841. 48 p.

Johnson, Samuel. The Crisis of Freedom. A Sermon, Preached at the Free Church, in Lynn, on Sunday, June 11, 1854. By Samuel Johnson, Pub. by Request of the Society. Boston, Crosby, Nichols & Co., 1854. 21 p.

Johnston, Robert. Four Letters to Rev. J. Caughey, Methodist Episcopal Minister, on the Participation of the American Methodist Episcopal Church in the Sin of American Slavery: Three from R. Johnston, Member of the Methodist Society, Dublin, and One from R. Allen, Secretary of the Hibernian Anti-Slavery Society. Dublin, Samuel J. Machen, 1841. 28 p.

Johnston, William. Speech of Wm. Johnston, Esq., Before the Franklin Circuit Court of Kentucky. April 10, 1846, Before the Hon. Mason Brown, Circuit Judge. The State of Ohio v. Forbes and Armitage. [n.p., n.d.] 23 p.

Johnston, William. The State of Ohio vs. Forbes and Armitage, Arrested upon the Requisition of the Government of Ohio, on Charge of Kidnapping Jerry Phinney, and Tried Before the Franklin Circuit Court of Kentucky, April 10, 1846. [n.p.] 1846. 41 p.

Jones, Absalom. A Thanksgiving Sermon, Preached January 1, 1808, in St. Thomas's, or the African Episcopal Church, Philadelphia: On Account of the Abolition of the African Slave Trade, on That Day, by the Congress of the United States. Philadelphia, Fry and Kammerer, 1808. 22 p.

Jones, Absalom, & Allen, Richard. A Narrative of the Proceedings of the Black People, During the Late Awful Calamity in Philadelphia, in the Year 1793; and a Refutation of Some Censures, Thrown upon Them in Some Late Publications. 1794. [In reply to a vicious attack upon Negroes by Mathew Carey, colonizationist.]

[Jones, Benjamin S.]. Abolitionrieties: or Remarks on Some of the Members of the Pennsylvania State Anti-Slavery Society for the Eastern District, and the American Anti-Slavery Society, Most of Whom Were Present at the Annual Meetings, Held in Philadelphia and New York in May, 1840. [n.p., n.d.]

Jones, J[ane] Elizabeth. The Young Abolitionists; or, Conversations on Slavery. Boston, Anti-Slavery Office, 1848. 131 p.

Jones, Thomas H. The Experience of Thomas H. Jones, Who Was a Slave for Forty-Three Years. Written by a Friend, as Given to Him by Brother Jones. Boston, D. Laing, Jr., 1850. 47 p.
Same: Worcester, Howland, 1857. 48 p.
Same: Boston, Bazin & Chandler, 1862. 48 p.

Judson, Andrew Thompson. Andrew T. Judson's Remarks to the Jury, on the Trial of the Case, State v. P. Crandall, Superior Court, Oct. Term, 1833, Windham County Ct. Hartford, John Russell, 1833. 32 p.

[Judson, Elisha]. Epistles from the Old Man of the Hills to the People of the Valley. Kingsboro [N. Y.], The Author, 1859. 46 p.

Julian, George Washington. Confiscation and Liberation. Speech of Hon. Geo. W. Julian, of Indiana, in the U. S. House of Representatives, Friday, May 23, 1862. Washington, D. C., Scammell & Co., 1862. 8 p.

Julian, George Washington. The Slavery Question. Speech of George W. Julian, of Indiana, Delivered in the House of Representatives, May 14, 1850, in Committee of the Whole on the State of the Union, on the President's Message Transmitting the Constitution of California. [Washington, D. C.] Buell & Blanchard [1850]. 16 p.

Julian, George Washington. Speech of Hon. George W. Julian, of Indiana, on the Slavery Question, Delivered in the House of Representatives, May 14, 1850. Washington, Congressional Globe Office, 1850. 15 p.

Juvenile Poems. For the Use of Free American Children of Every Complexion. Boston, Garrison & Knapp, 1835. 72 p.

Kane, John Kintzing. District Court of the United States for the Eastern District of Pennsylvania: United States of America, ex relatione Wheeler vs. Williamson. Opinion of Judge Kane on the Suggestion of Jane Johnson, October 12, 1855. Philadelphia, Crissy & Markley, 1855. 20 p.

[Keith, George]. An Exhortation & Caution to Friends

Concerning Buying or Keeping Negroes, Given the 13th Day of the 8th Month, 1693. [Philadelphia, William Bradford, 1693.] 15 p.

Kelley, William D., and Others. The Equality of All Men before the Law Claimed and Defended; in Speeches by Hon. William D. Kelley, Wendell Phillips, & Frederick Douglass, and Letters from Elizur Wright and Wm. Heighton. Boston, Geo. C. Rand & Avery, 1865. 41 p.

Kelsey, William H. Speech of Hon. W. H. Kelsey, of New York, on the Slavery Question; Delivered in the House of Representatives, July 29, 1856. Washington, Printed at the Congressional Globe Office, 1856. 8 p.

Kennedy, John Herron. Sympathy, Its Foundation and Legitimate Exercise Considered, in Special Relation to Africa: A Discourse Delivered on the Fourth of July, 1828, in the Sixth Presbyterian Church, Philadelphia. Philadelphia, W. F. Geddes, 1828. 11 p.

Kennedy, Lionel H., and Thomas Parker. An Official Report of the Trials of Sundry Negroes Charged with an Attempt to Raise an Insurrection in South Carolina, Preceded by an Introduction and Narrative, and in an Appendix, a Report of the Trials of Four White Persons on Indictment for Attempting to Excite the Slaves to Insurrection. Charleston, 1822. 188 + 14 p.

Kenrick, John. Horrors of Slavery. In Two Parts. Part I: Containing Observations, Facts and Arguments, Extracted from the Speeches of Wilberforce, Grenville, Pitt, Burke, Fox, Martin, Whitehead, and Other Distinguished Members of the British Parliament. Part II: Containing Extracts, Chiefly American, Compiled from Authentic Sources; Demonstrating That Slavery Is Impolitic, Antirepublican, Unchristian, and Highly Criminal; and Proposing Measures for Its Complete Abolition Through the United States. Cambridge, Hilliard and Metcalf, 1817. 59 p. [Kenrick was president of the New England Anti-Slavery Society in 1832. He gave substantial sums of money to the cause.]

Kentucky Anti-Slavery Society. Proceedings of the Kentucky Anti-Slavery Society, Auxiliary to the American Anti-Slavery Society, at Its First Meeting in Danville, Ky., March 19th, 1835. [n.p., n.d.] 8 p.

Kentucky Colonization Society. The Fourth Annual Report of the Kentucky Colonization Society, with an Address Delivered at the Request of the Society, by Rev. John C. Young. Frankfort, Ky., 1833. 32 p.

Kentucky Society for the Gradual Relief of the State from Slavery. "Constitution and Address of the Kentucky Society for the Gradual Relief of the

State from Slavery" in Olive Branch, Danville, December 24, 1833.

Kettell, George F. A Sermon on the Duty of Citizens, with Respect to the Fugitive Slave Law, by Rev. G. F. Kettell, of the Methodist Episcopal Society, Poughkeepsie, New York. White Plains, N. Y., Eastern State Journal, 1851. 20 p.

Key, Francis Scott. A Part of a Speech Pronounced by Francis S. Key, Esq., on the Trial of Reuben Crandall, M.D., Before the Circuit Court of the District of Columbia, at the March Term Thereof, 1836, on an Indictment for Publishing Libels with Intent to Excite Sedition and Insurrection among the Slaves and Free Coloured People of Said District. Washington, 1836. 15 p.

Key, Francis Scott. Speech of F. S. Key, before the Colonization Convention, May 9, 1842. [Washington, D. C.] Alexander & Barnard [1842]. 17 p.

King [Rufus]. Papers Relative to the Restriction of Slavery. Speeches of Mr. King in the Senate, and of Messrs. Taylor and Talmadge in the House of Representatives, of the United States, on the Bill for Authorizing the People of the Territory of Missouri to Form a Constitution and State Government, and for the Admission of the Same into the Union; in the Session of 1818–1819. With a Report of a Committee of the Abolition Society of Delaware. Philadelphia, Hall and Atkinson, 1819. 35 p.

Kingsbury, Harmon. The Fugitive Slave Bill: Its History and Unconstitutionality; with an Account of the Seizure and Enslavement of James Hamlet, and His Subsequent Restoration to Liberty. Third Edition. New York, American and Foreign Anti-Slavery Society, 1850. 36 p.

Kingsbury, Harmon. The Slavery Question Settled. Man-Stealing, Legitimate Servitude, Etc. New York, Gray, 1862. 36 p.

Kingsbury, Harmon. Thoughts on the Fugitive Slave Law and Nebraska Bill. New York, Printed for the Author, 1855. 26 p.

Kirk, Rev. Edward Norris. Speech of Rev. E. N. Kirk, at the Second Anniversary of the American Anti-Slavery Society, Held in the City of New York, on the 12th of May, 1835. [n.p., n.d.] 4 p.

Kitchel, Harvey Denison. An Appeal for Discussion and Action on the Slavery Question. By H. D. Kitchel. Hartford, L. Skinner, 1840. 28 p.

Knibb, Rev. William, and Borthwick, Peter. Colonial Slavery. Defense of the Baptist Missionaries from the Charge of Inciting the Late Rebellion in Jamaica; in a Discussion Between the Rev. William Knibb and Mr. P. Borthwick, at the Assembly Rooms, Bath, on Saturday, December 15, 1832.

Second Edition, London, Published at the Tourist Office, 1832. 30 p.

Knight, P. Human Rights and the Way to Protect Them. A Tract for the People. Cortland, N. Y., Stedman & Clisbe, 1847. 16 p.

Knox, William. Three Tracts Respecting the Conversion and Instruction of the Free Indians and Negroe Slaves in the Colonies. Addressed to the Venerable Society for Propagation of the Gospel in Foreign Parts, in the Year 1768. A New Ed. London, J. Debrett, 1789. 39 p.

Kramer, John Theophilus. The Slave Auction. Boston, Robert F. Wallcut, 1859. 48 p.

Krebs, John Michael. The American Citizen. A Discourse on the Nature and Extent of Our Religious Subjection to the Government under Which We Live; Including an Inquiry into the Scriptural Authority of That Provision of the Constitution of the United States, Which Requires the Surrender of Fugitive Slaves. Delivered in the Rutgers Street Presbyterian Church in the City of New York, on Thanksgiving Day, Dec. 12, 1850. Afterwards at Their Request as a Lecture Before Young Men's Assoc. of Albany & Waterford, N. Y., on Jan. 14 & 15, 1851. New York, Charles Scribner, 1851 40 p.

Ladd, Elizabeth. Some Account of Lucy Cardwell, a Woman of Colour, Who Departed This Life on the 25th of the 3rd Month, 1824—Aged 39 Years. Philadelphia, Benjamin & Thomas Kite, 1824. 4 p.

Ladies' Association for the Relief of Destitute Colored Fugitives. The First Annual Report of the Ladies' Association for the Relief of Destitute Colored Fugitives. Toronto, Brown's Printing Establishment, 1852. 15 p.

Ladies' New York City Anti-Slavery Society. First Annual Report of the Ladies' New York Anti-Slavery Society. New York, William S. Dorr, 1836. 19 p.

Lafon, Thomas. The Great Obstruction to the Conversion of Souls at Home and Abroad. An Address by Rev. Thomas Lafon, M.D., Late a Missionary of the American Board at the Sandwich Islands. New York, Union Missionary Society, 1843. 23 p.

Lame, J. S. Maryland Slavery and Maryland Chivalry. Containing the Letters of "Junius," Originally Published in Zion's Herald; Together with a Brief History of the Circumstances That Prompted the Publication of Those Letters. Also a Short Account of the Persecution Suffered by the Author at the Hands of Southern Slaveholders. Philadelphia, Collins, 1858. 59 p.

Lane, Lunsford. The Narrative of Lunsford Lane, Formerly of Raleigh, North Carolina. Published by Himself. Boston, J. G. Torrey, 1842. 54 p.

Lane Seminary. Fourth Annual Report of the Trustees of the Cincinnati Lane Seminary; Together with a Catalogue of the Officers and Students. Lane Seminary, Students Typographical Association, 1834. 28 p.

Lane Seminary. Fifth Annual Report of the Trustees of the Cincinnati Lane Seminary; Together with the Laws of the Institution, and a Catalogue of the Officers and Students. Cincinnati, Corey & Fairbank, November, 1834. 47 p. [Contains statement by faculty concerning the late troubles with students over slavery.]

Lane Seminary. General Catalogue of Lane Theological Seminary, 1828–1881. Cincinnati, Elm Street Printing Co., 1881. 69 p.

Lane Seminary Anti-Slavery Society. Preamble and Constitution of the Anti-Slavery Society of Lane Seminary. From the Standard—Extra. Broadside 1 p. 20½ × 33½ cm.

Lane Seminary Students [Theodore D. Weld]. A Statement of the Reasons Which Induced the Students of Lane Seminary to Dissolve Their Connection with That Institution. Cincinnati, 1834. 28 p.

Langston, Charles H. Should Colored Men Be Subject to the Pains and Penalties of the Fugitive Slave Law? Speech of C. H. Langston, before the U. S. District Court for the Northern Dis. of Ohio, May 12, 1859. Delivered When about to Be Sentenced for Rescuing a Man from Slavery. Cleveland, O., E. Cowles & Co., 1859. 20 p.

Larned, Edwin Channing. Argument of E. C. Larned, Esq., Counsel for the Defense, on the Trial of Joseph Stout, Indicted for Rescuing a Fugitive Slave from the United States Deputy Marshal, at Ottawa, Ill., Oct. 20, 1859; Delivered in the United States District Court, in the Northern District of Illinois, Monday & Tuesday, March 12 & 13, 1860. R. R. Hitt, Reporter. Chicago, Press & Tribune Book and Job Printing Office, 1860. 43 p.

Larned, Edwin Channing. The New Fugitive Slave Law. Speech of Edwin C. Larned, Esq. at the City Hall in the City of Chicago, on the Evening of Oct. 25th, 1850, in Reply to Hon. S. A. Douglas. Chicago, Printed at the Democrat Office, 1850. 16 p.

Laurens, Henry. A South Carolina Protest Against Slavery: Being a Letter from Henry Laurens, Second President of the Continental Congress, to His Son, Colonel John Laurens; Dated Charleston, S. C., August 14th, 1776. Now First Published from the Original. New York, G. P. Putnam, 1861. 34 p.

Law, William. An Extract from a Treatise on the Spirit of Prayer, or the Soul Rising Out of the Vanity of Time into the Riches of Eternity, with

Some Thoughts on War; Remarks on the Nature and Bad Effects of the Use of Spirituous Liquors. And Considerations on Slavery. Philadelphia, Joseph Crukshank, 1780. 84 p.

Lawrence, John. A Brief Treatise on American Slavery. Second Edition. Circleville, O., Printed at the Telescope Office, 1851. 64 p.

Lawrence, John. The Slavery Question. Dayton, Ohio, Conference Printing Establishment of the United Brethren, 1854. 224 p.

Same. Second Edition. Dayton, Ohio, Vonnieda & Kimler, 1854. 224 p.

Lay, Benjamin. All Slave-Keepers That Keep the Innocent in Bondage, Apostates Pretending to Lay Claim to the Pure and Holy Christian Religion; of What Congregation So Ever; but Especially in Their Ministers, by Whose Example the Filthy Leprosy and Apostacy Is Spread Far and Near; It Is a Notorious Sin, Which Many of the True Friends of Christ, and His Pure Truth, Called Quakers, Has Been for Many Years, and Still Are Concern'd to Write and Bear Testimony Against; as a Practice So Gross and Hurtful to Religion, and Destructive to Government, Beyond What Words Can Set Forth, or Can Be Declared of by Men or Angels, and Yet Lived in by Ministers and Magistrates in America. The Leaders of the People Cause Them to Err. Written for a General Service, by Him That Truly and Sincerely Desires the Present and Eternal Welfare and Happiness of All Mankind, All the World Over, of All Colours, and Nations, as His Own Soul. Philadelphia, Printed for the Author, 1737. 271 p.

Leach, DeWitt Clinton. The Amistad Case. Men Not Recognised as Property by the Constitution. Speech of Hon. DeWitt C. Leach, of Michigan. Delivered in the House of Representatives, January 27, 1858. [Washington, D. C., Buell & Blanchard, 1858]. 8 p.

Learned, Joseph D. A View of the Policy of Permitting Slaves in the States West of the Mississippi; Being a Letter to a Member of Congress. Baltimore, J. Robinson, 1820. 47 p.

Leavitt, Joshua. The Financial Power of Slavery. The Substance of an Address Delivered in Ohio, in September, 1840. [n.p., n.d.] 4 p.

Lee, Luther. Slavery: A Sin Against God. Syracuse, Wesleyan Methodist Book Room, 1853. 24 p.

Lee, Luther. Slavery Examined in the Light of the Bible. Syracuse, N. Y., Wesleyan Methodist Book Room, 1855. 185 p.

Lee, Rev. Luther. The Supremacy of the Divine Law. A Sermon Preached on the Occasion of the Death of Rev. Charles Turner Torrey. [n.p., n.d.] 8 p.

Leeds Anti-Slavery Association. Juvenile Anti-Slavery Series. 1856. [Exceedingly fine woodcuts.]

No. 1. A Short History of Slavery. 24 p.
No. 2. Who Would Not Be an Abolitionist. 12 p.
No. 3. The Story of Helen, George, and Lucy. 24 p.
No. 4. The Anti-Slavery Alphabet. 12 p.
No. 5. Won't It Wash Off. 36 p.
No. 6. Uncle Tom's Cabin—Abridged. 36 p.
No. 7. Hunting Slaves with Bloodhounds. 12 p.
No. 8. Singular Escape from Slavery. 12 p.
No. 9. The Negro Mother, or Christian Steadfastness. 12 p.
No. 10. Malem-Boo, the Brazilian Slave. 24 p.
No. 11. Branding Slaves with Hot Irons. 12 p.
No. 12. Address from the Women of England. 12 p.
No. 13. Sale of a Family of Slaves. 12 p. [All Published]

Leggett, William. A Collection of the Political Writings of William Leggett, Selected and Arranged, with a Preface, by Theodore Sedgwick, Jr. 2 Volumes. New York, Taylor and Dodd, 1840.

Lemmon, Jonathan. New York Court of Appeals. Report of the Lemmon Slave Case. Containing Points and Arguments of Counsel on Both Sides, and Opinions of All the Judges. New York, Horace Greeley & Co., 1861. 146 p.

[Lester, Charles Edwards]. Chains and Freedom: or, The Life and Adventures of Peter Wheeler, a Colored Man Yet Living. By the Author of the 'Mountain Wild Flower.' New York, E. S. Arnold & Co., 1839. 260 p.

Letter from the Inhabitants of Bridgewater, Somersetshire, England, to the Inhabitants of Bridgewater, Massachusetts, New England, America, Dated Sept. 10, 1846; with the Reply of the Latter, Dated Feb. 10, 1847. Boston, Andrews & Prentiss, 1847. 39 p.

Letter to a Member of the Congress of the United States of America, from an English Clergyman; Including a Republican, with Considerable Additions, of the Tract Entitled, 'Every Man His Own Property.' London, Whittaker, Treacher and Arnot, 1835. 30 p.

A Letter to John Bull: To Which Is Added the Sketch of a Plan for the Safe, Speedy, and Effectual Abolition of Slavery. By a Free Born Englishman. London, J. Hatchard and Son, 1823. 32 p.

A *Letter* to Philo Africanus, upon Slavery; in Answer to His of the 22d of November, in the General Evening Post; Together with the Opinions of Sir John Strange, and Other Eminent Lawyers upon This Subject, with the Sentence of Lord Mansfield, in the Case of Som[m]erset[t] and Knowles, 1772, with His Lordship's Explanation of That Opinion in 1786. London, Printed; Newport (Rhode Island), Reprinted by Peter Edes [1788]. 23 p.

Letters on American Slavery from Victor Hugo, de

Tocqueville, Emile de Girardin, Carnot, Passy, Mazzini, Humboldt, O. Lafayette—&c. Boston, American Anti-Slavery Society, 1860. 24 p.

Levering, Robert E. H. The Kingdom of Slavery: Or the Ark of Liberty in the Phillistian Hands of Two Hundred and Fifty Thousands Slaveholders: Also an Appeal to the American Churches for the Free Discussion of Slavery in Their Periodicals: The Whole Spiced with Liberty Songs. First Edition. Circleville, Ohio, Religious Telescope Office, 1844. 16 p.

[Lewis, Evan]. An Address to Christians of All Denominations, on the Inconsistency of Admitting Slave-Holders to Communion and Church Membership. Philadelphia, S. C. Atkinson, 1831. 19 p.

Lewis, Evan. Address to the Coloured People of Philadelphia. Delivered at Bethel Church, 12th of March, 1833. Philadelphia, J. Richards, 1833. 22 p.

Lewis, Graceanna. An Appeal to Those Members of the Society of Friends Who, Knowing the Principles of the Abolitionists, Stand Aloof from the Anti-Slavery Enterprise. [n.p., n.d.] 8 p.

Lewis, John W. Life, Labors, and Travels of Elder Charles Bowles of the Free Will Baptist Denomination. Together with an Essay on the Character and Condition of the African Race by the Same. Also an Essay on the Fugitive Slave Law of the U. S. Congress of 1850; by Rev. Arthur Dearing. Watertown, Ingall's and Stowell's Steam Press, 1852. 285 p.

Lewis County Anti-Slavery Society. Sketch of Proceedings of the Lewis County Anti-Slavery Society: Convened in the Village of Lowville, January 10, 1837. Watertown, Knowlton & Rice, 1837. 16 p.

Lexington, Ky., Anti-Slavery Meeting, May 12, 1850. To the People Who Wish to Do Right. [Notice of meeting in Lexington Court House, to discuss a system of gradual emancipation for the state.] Broadside. 1 p. 29 × 43 cm.

Liberator. Weekly. Boston, Mass. January 1, 1831–December 29, 1865. Edited by William Lloyd Garrison.

Liberia Unmasked; or, The Incompatibility of the Views and Schemes of the American Colonization Society, with Those of the Real Friends of the Immediate Abolition of Slavery, Proved by Facts. Edinburgh, W. Oliphant [Etc., Etc.], 1833. 19 p.

The Liberty Bell. By Friends of Freedom. [Gift book collections of antislavery poems & prose sketches]. 15 Vols. Boston, 1839–1858. No volumes issued for 1840, 1850, 1854, 1855, 1857. Edited by Maria Weston Chapman from 1843 to 1858. Published by American Anti-Slavery Society, 1839; by Massachusetts Anti-Slavery Fair, 1841–1846; by National Anti-Slavery Bazaar, 1847–1858.

Liberty Chimes. [Verses and Prose Sketches]. Providence, R. I., Ladies' Anti-Slavery Society, 1845. 148 p.

Liberty or Slavery; the Great National Question. Three Prize Essays on American Slavery. Boston, Congregational Board of Publications, 1857. 138 p.
Rev. R. B. Thurston: The Error and the Duty in Regard to Slavery.
Rev. A. C. Baldwin: Friendly Letters to a Christian Slaveholder.
Timothy Williston: Is American Slavery an Institution Which Christianity Sanctions and Will Perpetuate?

Liberty Standard. Weekly. Hallowell, Me. July 12, 1841–August 24, 1848. Edited by Joseph C. Lovejoy. Published as Free Soil Republican from August 24, 1848–June 7, 1849.

Liberty Tracts. Boston, J. W. Alden, 1843–1844.
No. 1. Stowe, Harriet B. The Two Altars.
No. 2. The Right Sort of Politics. 4 p.
No. 3. [A Teller of the Truth.] The Influence of the Slave Power. 4 p. Emancipator Extra, Sept. 21, 1843.
No. 4. Don't Throw Away Your Vote. 4 p. Emancipator Extra, September 28, 1843.
No. 5. Liberty Incomplete—Letter from John Quincy Adams. 8 p. Emancipator Extra, October 5, 1843.
No. 6. The Tyrant Paupers; or, Where the Money Goes. 4 p. Emancipator Extra, October 12, 1843.
No. 7. Bible Politics. 4 p.
No. 9. The Compact; or, What Have Our State Politics to Do with Slavery? 4 p. Emancipator Extra, November 2, 1843.
No. 11. Remedy for Duelling. A Sermon Delivered before the Presbytery of Long Island, at the Opening of Their Session at Aquebogue, April 16, 1806, by Rev. Lyman Beecher. Boston, Leavitt & Alden [1844]. 16 p.
No. 12. The Alliance of Jehoshaphat and Ahab. A Sermon, Preached on the Annual Fast, April 4, 1844, at Cambridgeport, by Rev. J. C. Lovejoy. [Boston, Leavitt & Alden, 1844.] 7 p.
No. 14. Duty of Christians to Suppress Duelling. A Sermon Preached at Annual Fast, April 4, 1844, at South Boston, by Rev. W. W. Patton. Boston, Leavitt & Alden [1844]. 8 p.

Liberty Tracts. Utica, Jackson & Chaplin, 1844.
No. 1. Slavery and the Slave Trade at the Nation's Capital. 12 p.
No. 2. The Cause of the Hard Times. 4 p. Liberty Press. Extra.

No. 3. Stewart, Alvin. The Creed of the Liberty Party Abolitionists. 8 p.

No. 4. The Lawlessness of Slavery. 4 p. Liberty Press Extra.

No. 7. Jackson, James C. The Duties and Dignities of American Freemen. 8 p. Liberty Press Extra.

No. 9. Stewart, Alvin. The Great Whig Tract against the Liberty Party Exposed. Its Wickedness and Sophistry Revealed. 12 p.

Lincoln, Abraham. Republican Principles. Speech of Hon. Abraham Lincoln, of Illinois, at the Republican State Convention, Held at Springfield, Illinois, June 16, 1858. [Albany, Albany Journal, 1860.] 6 p. (*Evening Journal* Tracts, No. 7)

Lincoln, Abraham. Speech of Hon. Abraham Lincoln, before the Republican State Convention, June 16, 1858. Sycamore [Ill.], O. P. Basset, 1858. 16 p.

Lincoln, Enoch. The Village [A Poem] with an Appendix [Containing "Origin of Slavery," "Manner of Obtaining Slaves," Etc.]. Portland, 1816. 180 p.

Lincoln, Jairus. Anti-Slavery Melodies: For the Friends of Freedom; Prepared for the Hingham Anti-Slavery Society. Hingham, [Mass.], Elijah B. Gill, 1843. 96 p.

Lincoln, Levi. Speech of Mr. Lincoln, of Massachusetts: Delivered in the House of Representatives of the United States, Feb. 7, 1837, on the Resolution to Censure the Hon. John Q. Adams, for Inquiring of the Speaker, Whether a Paper, Purporting to Come from Slaves, Came Within the Resolution Laying on the Table All Petitions Relating to Slavery. Washington, Gales and Seaton, 1837. 9 p.

Lincoln, William S. Alton Trials: Of Winthrop S. Gilman, Who Was Indicted with Enoch Long, Amos B. Roff, George H. Walworth, George H. Whitney, William Harned, John S. Noble, James Morss, Jr., Henry Tanner, Royal Weller, Reuben Gerry, and Thaddeus B. Hurlbut, for the Crime of Riot; Committed on the Night of the 7th of November, 1837, While Engaged in Defending a Printing Press, from an Attack Made on It at That Time, by an Armed Mob. Also, the Trial of John Solomon, Levi Palmer, Horace Beall, Josiah Nutter, Jacob Smith, David Butler, William Carr, and James M. Rock, Indicted with James Jennings, Solomon Morgan, and Frederick Bruchy, for a Riot Committed in Alton, on the Night of the 7th of November, 1837, in Unlawfully and Forcibly Entering the Warehouse of Godfrey, Gilman & Co., and Breaking up and Destroying a Printing Press. Written out from Notes Taken at the Time of Trial by William S. Lincoln, a Member of the Bar of the Alton Municipal Court. New York, John F. Trow, 1838. 158 p.

Little, Mrs. Sophia Louise *Robbins*. The Branded Hand: A Dramatic Sketch, Commemorative of the Tragedies at the South in the Winter of 1844–45. Pawtucket, R. I., R. W. Potter, 1845. 46 p.

[Little, Mrs. Sophia Louise *Robbins*]. A Picture of Slavery for Youth; by the Author of "The Branded Hand," and "Chattelized Humanity." Boston, 24 p.

Little, Mrs. Sophia Louise *Robbins*. Thrice Through the Furnace; A Tale of the Times of the Iron Hoof. Pawtucket, R. I., A. W. Pearce, 1852. 190 p.

Liverpool Society for Promoting the Abolition of Slavery. Declaration of the Objects of the Liverpool Society for Promoting the Abolition of Slavery, 25th March, 1823. Liverpool, James Smith, 1823. 14 p.

Lloyd, Elizabeth. An Appeal for the Bondwoman, to Her Own Sex. [A Poem] Philadelphia, Merrihew and Thompson, 1846. 36 p.

Loguen, Jermain Wesley. The Rev. J. W. Loguen, as a Slave and as a Freeman. A Narrative of Real Life. Syracuse, N. Y., J. G. K. Truair & Co., 1859. 454 p.

London Anti-Slavery Society. Food and Other Maintenance and Allowances under the Apprenticeship System; Extracted from the Appendix to a Report Recently Published by the Committee of the London Anti-Slavery Society, on Negro Apprenticeship in the British Colonies. London, London Anti-Slavery Society, 1838. 34 p.

London Public Meeting. American Slavery; Report of a Public Meeting Held at Finsbury Chapel, Moorfields, to Receive Frederick Douglass, the American Slave, on Friday, May 22, 1846. London, Christopher B. Christian & Co., 1846. 24 p.

Long, John Dixon. Pictures of Slavery in Church and State; Including Personal Reminiscences, Biographical Sketches, Anecdotes, etc., with an Appendix, Containing the Views of John Wesley and Richard Watson on Slavery. Philadelphia, the Author, 1857. 414 p.

Longfellow, Henry Wadsworth. Poems on Slavery. Cambridge, John Owen, 1842. 31 p.

Same. Second Edition. Cambridge, John Owen, 1842. 31 p.

Looker On [pseud.]. Slavery Rhymes, Addressed to the Friends of Liberty Throughout the United States. New York, John S. Taylor, 1837. 84 p.

Lounsbury, Thomas. Pro-Slavery Overthrown; and the True Principles of Abolitionism Declared; or, A Series of Lectures in Answer to the Question "What Do the Scriptures Teach on the Subject of Slavery?" Second Edition, Geneva, N. Y., Geo. H. Derby & Co., 1847. 155 p.

Lounsbury, Rev. Thomas. The Touchstone of Truth, Applied to Modern Abolition; or, Seven Lectures in Answer to the Question, "What Do the Scriptures Teach on the Subject of Slavery." Geneva, N. Y., Scotten & Van Brunt, 1844. 155 p.

[Love, Horace Thomas]. Slavery in Its Relation to God. A Review of Rev. Dr. Lord's Thanksgiving Sermon, in Favor of Domestic Slavery, Entitled the Higher Law, in Its Application to the Fugitive Slave Bill. By a Minister of the Gospel, in Massachusetts. Written by Special Request. Buffalo, A. M. Clapp & Co., 1851. 56 p.

Love, Wm. De Loss. Obedience to Rulers—The Duty and Its Limitations. A Discourse Delivered December 22d, 1850, on the Two Hundred and Thirtieth Anniversary of the Landing of the Pilgrims. New Haven, Storer & Stone, 1851. 16 p.

Lovejoy, Joseph Cammett. Memoir of Rev. Charles T. Torrey Who Died in the Penitentiary of Maryland, Where He Was Confined for Showing Mercy to the Poor. Boston, J. P. Jewett, 1847. 364 p.

Lovejoy, Joseph Cammett, and Lovejoy, Owen. Memoir of the Rev. Elijah P. Lovejoy Who Was Murdered in Defense of the Liberty of the Press, at Alton, Illinois, November 7, 1837. With an Introduction by John Quincy Adams. New York, J. S. Taylor, 1838. 382 p.

Lovejoy, Joseph Cammett. The North and the South! Letter from J. C. Lovejoy, Esq., to His Brother, Hon. Owen Lovejoy, M.C., with Remarks by the Editor of the Washington Union. [n.p., 1859.] 8 p.

Lovejoy, Joseph Cammett. The Robbers of Adullam; or, A Glance at "Organic Sins." A Sermon, Preached at Cambridgeport, November 27, 1845. By J. C. Lovejoy. Boston, D. H. Ela, 1845. 22 p.

Lovejoy, Owen. The Barbarism of Slavery. Speech by Owen Lovejoy Delivered in the United States House of Representatives, April 5, 1860. Washington [D. C.], Buell & Blanchard, 1860. 8 p.

Lovejoy, Owen. Human Beings Not Property. Speech of Hon. Owen Lovejoy, of Illinois. Delivered in the U. S. House of Representatives, February 17, 1858. [Washington, D. C., Buell & Blanchard, 1858]. 8 p.

Lovejoy, Owen. State of the Union. Speech of Hon. Owen Lovejoy, of Illinois, Delivered in the House of Representatives, January 23, 1861. Washington, D. C., H. Polkinhorn, [1861]. 8 p.

Lovewell, Lyman. A Sermon on American Slavery Preached in New Hudson, Michigan, June 18, 1854. Detroit, Baker and Conover, 1854. 22 p.

Ludlow, James R. The Address of James R. Ludlow, Esq., Junior Counsel for the United States, in Summing up the Evidence for the Prosecution, upon the Trial of Castner Hanway, Indicted for High Treason. Delivered in the United States Circuit Court, for the Eastern District of Pennsylvania, upon the 5th Day of December, A.D., 1851. 8 p.

Lundy, Benjamin. The Life, Travels and Opinions of Benjamin Lundy, Including His Journeys to Texas and Mexico, with a Sketch of Contemporary Events, and a Notice of the Revolution in Hayti. Compiled under the Direction and on Behalf of His Children. Philadelphia, W. D. Parrish, 1847. 316 p. [Compiled by Thomas Earle.]

[Lundy, Benjamin]. The War in Texas; A Review of Facts and Circumstances, Showing That This Contest Is the Result of a Long Premeditated Crusade Against the Government, Set on Foot by Slaveholders, Land Speculators, Etc., with the View of Re-Establishing, Extending, and Perpetuating the System of Slavery and the Slave Trade in the Republic of Mexico, by a Citizen of the United States. Philadelphia, Merrihew & Gunn, 1836. 56 p.
Same: Second Edition, Revised and Enlarged. Philadelphia, Merrihew & Gunn, 1837. 64 p.

McKeen, Rev. Silas. A Scriptural Argument in Favor of Withdrawing Fellowship from Churches and Ecclesiastical Bodies Tolerating Slaveholding among Them. New York, American and Foreign Anti-Slavery Society, 1848. 37 p.

McLeod, Alexander. Negro Slavery Unjustifiable. A Discourse, by Alexander McLeod, A.M., Pastor of the Reformed Presbyterian Congregation in the City of New York. New York, T. & F. Swords, 1802. 42 p.
Same. Tenth Edition, New York, Alexander McLeod, 1860. 46 p.
Same. Eleventh Edition, New York, 1863. 48 p.

[Macaulay, Zachary]. Negro Slavery; or, A View of Some of the More Prominent Features of That State of Society, as It Exists in the United States of America and in the Colonies of the West Indies, Especially in Jamaica. London, R. Taylor, 1823. 92 p.

Macbeth, James. The Church and the Slaveholder; or, Light and Darkness: An Attempt to Prove, from the Word of God and from Reason, That to Hold Property in Man Is Wholly Destitute of Divine Warrant, Is a Flagrant Crime, and Demands Excommunication. Earnestly and Respectfully Addressed to the Members of the Approaching Assembly of the Free Church of Scotland, and to the Churches Generally. Edinburgh, J. Johnstone [Etc., Etc., 1850]. 36 p.

Macbeth, James. No Fellowship with Slaveholders: A Calm Review of the Debate on Slavery, in the Full Assembly of 1846; Addressed Respectfully to the Assembly of 1847, and to the Members and Kirk Sessions of the Free Church. Edinburgh, C. Ziegler, 1846. 34 p.

Mack, Rev. Enoch. The Revolution Unfinished; or American Independence Begun; Illustrated in an Address Before the Anti-Slavery Societies of Dover and Great Falls, New Hampshire, on the Fourth of July, 1838. Dover, Dover and Great Falls Anti-Slavery Societies, 1838. 15 p.

Madden, R. R. Letter to W. E. Channing, D.D., on the Subject of the Abuse of the Flag of the United States in the Island of Cuba, and the Advantage Taken of Its Protection in Promoting the Slave Trade. Boston, William D. Ticknor, 1839. 32 p.

Mahan, John B. Trial of Rev. J. B. Mahan, for Felony, in the Mason Circuit Court of Kentucky, Commencing on Tuesday, the 13th, and Terminating on Monday, the 19th of November, 1838. Reported by Joseph B. Reid & Henry R. Reeder. Cincinnati, Samuel A. Alley, 1838. 88 p.

Maine Anti-Slavery Society. Fourth Annual Report of the Maine Anti-Slavery Society, with the Minutes of the Anniversary Meeting, Held in Augusta, on the 7th and 8th of February, 1839. Brunswick, Thomas W. Newman, 1839. 56 p.

Maine Anti-Slavery Society. Fifth Annual Report of the Executive Committee of the Maine Anti-Slavery Society, with the Minutes of the Anniversary Meeting, Held in Hallowell, on the 6th and 7th of February, 1840. Brunswick, Joseph Guffin, 1840. 48 p.

Maine Union in Behalf of the Colored Race. Proceedings of the Convention Which Formed the Maine Union in Behalf of the Colored Race. With the Address of the Executive Committee to the Public. Portland, Merrill and Byram, 1835. 16 p.

Mann, Horace. The Fugitive Slave Law. Speech of Mr. Horace Mann, of Mass., Delivered in the House of Representatives, in Committee of the Whole on the State of the Union, Friday, February 28, 1851, on the Fugitive Slave Law. [Washington, D. C.] Congressional Globe Office [1851]. 24 p.

Mann, Horace. Horace Mann's Letters on the Extension of Slavery into California and New Mexico; and the Duty of Congress to Provide the Trial by Jury for Alleged Fugitive Slaves. Republished with Notes. Washington [D. C.], Buell & Blanchard, 1850. 32 p.

Mann, Horace. New Dangers to Freedom, and New Duties for Its Defenders: A Letter by the Hon. Horace Mann to His Constituents, May 3, 1850. Boston, Redding and Company, 1850. 32 p.

Mann, Horace. Slavery. Letters and Speeches, by Horace Mann. Boston, B. B. Mussey & Co., 1851. 564 p.
Same: Boston, B. B. Mussey & Co., 1853. 564 p.

Mann, Horace. Speech of Horace Mann, of Massachusetts, in the House of Representatives, Feb. 23, 1849; on Slavery in the United States, and the Slave Trade in the District of Columbia. Boston, W. B. Fowle, 1849. 15 p.

Mann, Horace. Speech of Hon. Horace Mann, of Massachusetts, on the Institution of Slavery. Delivered in the House of Representatives, August 17, 1852. Washington, D. C., Buell & Blanchard, 1852. 24 p.
Same. Boston, Charles List & Co., 1852. 23 p.

Mann, Horace. Speech of Mr. Horace Mann, on the Right of Congress to Legislate for the Territories of the United States, and the Duty to Exclude Slavery Therefrom. Delivered in the House of Representatives, in Committee of the Whole, June 30, 1848. Revised Edition. Boston, William B. Fowle, 1848. 31 p.

Mann, Horace. Speech of Hon. Horace Mann, on the Right of Congress to Legislate for the Territories of the United States, and Its Duty to Exclude Slavery Therefrom; Delivered in the House of Representatives, in Committee of the Whole, June 30, 1848. To Which Is Added, a Letter from Hon. Martin Van Buren, and Rev. Joshua Leavitt. Boston, J. Howe, 1848. 48 p.

Mann, Horace. Speech of Horace Mann, of Massachusetts, on the Subject of Slavery in the Territories, and the Consequences of a Dissolution of the Union. Delivered in the United States House of Representatives, February 15, 1850. Boston, Redding and Company, 1850. 35 p.
Same: Washington, Gideon and Co., 1850. 13 p.

Manumission Society of North Carolina. An Address to the People of North Carolina, on the Evils of Slavery by the Friends of Liberty and Equality. Greenborough, N. C., William Swain, 1830. 68 p.

March, Daniel. The Crisis of Freedom. Remarks on the Duty Which All Christian Men and Good Citizens Owe to Their Country in the Present State of Public Affairs. Nashua, N. H., Dodge & Noyes, 1854. 20 p.

Marcus [pseud.]. An Examination of the Expediency and Constitutionality of Prohibiting Slavery in the State of Missouri. New York, C. Wiley & Co., 1819. 22 p.

Marriott, Charles. An Address to the Members of the Religious Society of Friends, on the Duty of Declining the Use of the Products of Slave Labour. New York, Isaac T. Hopper, 1835. 18 p.

Mars, James. Life of James Mars, a Slave Born and

Sold in Connecticut. Written by Himself. Hartford, Case, Lockwood & Co., 1865. 36 p.
Same. 6th Edition, 1868. 38 p.

Marsh, Roswell. Comparison of the Present with the Former Doctrines of the General Government, on the Subject of Slavery, the Territories, Internal Improvements, Domestic Manufactures, and the Veto. Steubenville, O., Daily Herald Office, 1856. 23 p.

Marsh, Rev. William H. God's Law Supreme. A Sermon, Aiming to Point Out the Duty of a Christian People in Relation to the Fugitive Slave Law: Delivered at Village Corners, Woodstock, Conn., on the Day of the Annual Thanksgiving, Nov. 28, 1850; and Subsequently Repeated, by Request, in Southbridge, Mass. Worcester, Henry J. Howland, 1850. 30 p.

Marshall, Thomas. The Speech of Thomas Marshall, (of Fauquier) in the House of Delegates of Virginia, on the Policy of the State in Relation to Her Colored Population: Delivered January 14, 1832. Richmond, T. W. White, 1832. 52 p.

Martin, Rev. David. Trial of the Rev. Jacob Gruber, Minister in the Methodist Episcopal Church, at the March Term, 1819, in the Frederick County Court, for a Misdemeanor. Fredericktown, Md., David Martin, 1819. 111 p.

[Martineau, Harriet]. The 'Manifest Destiny' of the American Union. Reprinted from Westminster Review, July, 1857. New York, American Anti-Slavery Society, 1857. 72 p.

Martineau, Harriet. The Martyr Age of the United States. Boston, Weeks, Jordan & Co., 1839. 84 p.
Same: New York, 1839. 36 p.

[Martineau, Harriet]. The Martyr Age of the United States of America, with an Appeal on Behalf of the Oberlin Institute in Aid of the Abolition of Slavery. Republished from the London and Westminster Review, by the Newcastle upon Tyne Emancipation and Aborigines Protection Society. Newcastle upon Tyne, Finlay and Charlton [Etc., Etc.], 1840. 44 p.

Martineau, Harriet. Views of Slavery and Emancipation; from "Society in America." New York, Piercy & Reed, 1837. 79 p.

Marvin, Abijah Perkins. Fugitive Slaves: A Sermon, Preached in the North Congregational Church, Winchendon, on the Day of the Annual Fast, April 11, 1850. Boston, J. P. Jewett & Co., 1850. 24 p.

Maryland. Board of Managers for Removing the Free People of Color. Colonization of the Free Colored Population of Maryland, and of Such Slaves as May Hereafter Become Free. Statement of Facts, for the Use of Those Who Have Not Yet Reflected on This Important Subject. Baltimore, Managers Appointed by the State of Maryland, 1832. 16 p.

Maryland Society for Promoting the Abolition of Slavery. Constitution of the Maryland Society for Promoting the Abolition of Slavery, and the Relief of Free Negroes, and Others, Unlawfully Held in Bondage. Baltimore, William Goddard and James Angell, 1789.

Maryland Society for Promoting the Abolition of Slavery. Report of the Committee of Grievances, in Consequence of the Complaint of Messrs. Ezekiel John, and Edward Dorsey, Together with the Memorial Presented to the General Assembly by This Society, and the Resolves to the House of Delegates, upon the Said Report and Memorial. Accompanied with an Address to the Public, in Vindication of the Conduct of This Society from the Charges Contained in Those Resolves of the House of Delegates. [Baltimore, W. Goddard and J. Angell, 1792.] 8 p.

Mason, William Powell. A Report of the Case of the Jeune Eugenie, Determined in the Circuit Court of the United States, for the First Circuit, at Boston, December, 1821; with an Appendix. Boston, Wells and Lilly, 1822. 108 p.

Massachusetts, [pseud.]. The New States; or, A Comparison of the Wealth, Strength, and Population of the Northern and Southern States; as Also of Their Respective Powers in Congress; with a View to Expose the Injustice of Erecting New States at the South. Boston, J. Belcher, 1813. 36 p.

Massachusetts Abolition Society. Formation of the Massachusetts Abolition Society. [Boston? 1839?] 36 p.

Massachusetts Abolition Society. The Second Annual Report of the Massachusetts Abolition Society: Together with the Proceedings of the Second Annual Meeting, Held at Tremont Chapel, May 25, 1841. Boston, David H. Ela, 1841. 58 p.

Massachusetts Abolition Society. The True History of the Late Division in the Anti-Slavery Societies, Being Part of the Second Annual Report of the Executive Committee of the Massachusetts Abolition Society. Boston, D. H. Ela, Printer, 1841. 45 p.

MASSACHUSETTS ANTI-SLAVERY SOCIETY

Fourth Annual Report of the Board of Managers of the Massachusetts Anti-Slavery Society with Some Account of the Annual Meeting, January 20, 1836. Boston, Isaac Knapp, 1836. 72 p. [Reports for 1833, 1834, and 1835 were by New England Anti-Slavery Society. Titles of reports do not change through twenty-first (1853).]

Proceedings of the Massachusetts Anti-Slavery Society at the Annual Meetings Held in 1854, 1855 & 1856; with the Treasurer's Reports and General Agent's Annual Statements. Boston, Office of Massachusetts Anti-Slavery Society, 1856. 67 p.

An Account of the Interviews Which Took Place on the Fourth and Eighth of March, Between a Committee of the Massachusetts Anti-Slavery Society, and the Committee of the Legislature. Boston, Massachusetts Anti-Slavery Society, 1836. 26 p.

Address to the Abolitionists of Massachusetts. Boston, February 27, 1839.

An Address to the Abolitionists of Massachusetts, on the Subject of Political Action. By the Board of Managers of the Mass. A. S. Society. [Boston? 1838.] 20 p.

Anti-Slavery Petitions. [Blank Form Petitions to Congress Concerning (1) Commercial and Diplomatic Relations with Hayti; (2) Abolition of Slavery in the District of Columbia; (3) Admission of Florida or Other Slave States; (4) Enforcement of Fugitive Slave Act and Suppression of Insurrections; and to the Legislature of Massachusetts Concerning the Repeal of the Laws, (1) Excluding Negroes from Public Conveyances; and (2) Prohibiting Inter-Marriage of Persons of Different Colors.] Broadside, 1 p. 36 × 44 cm.

Constitution of the New England Anti-Slavery Society: With an Address to the Public. Boston, Garrison and Knapp, 1832. 16 p.

A Full Statement of the Reasons Which Were in Part Offered to the Committee of the Legislature of Massachusetts, on the Fourth and Eighth of March, Showing Why There Should Be No Penal Laws Enacted and No Condemnatory Resolutions Passed by the Legislature, Respecting Abolitionists and Anti-Slavery Societies. Boston, Massachusetts Anti-Slavery Society, 1836. 48 p.

Massachusetts Colonization Society. Proceedings at the Annual Meeting of the Massachusetts Colonization Society. Held in Park Street Church, Feb. 7, 1833. Together with the Speeches Delivered on That Occasion by Hon. Messrs. Everett, Todd, and Cushing, and Rev. Messrs. Stow and Blagden. Also the Letters of His Excellency Governor Lincoln, and the Hon. Samuel Lathrop, Communicated to the Meeting. Boston, Pierce & Parker, 1833. 28 p.

Massachusetts Convention on Proposed Annexation of Texas, 1845. Proceedings of a Convention of Delegates, Chosen by the People of Massachusetts, Without Distinction of Party, Assembled at Faneuil Hall, in the City of Boston, Wednesday, the 29th of January, A.D., 1845, to Take into Consideration the Proposed Annexation of Texas. Boston, Eastburn's Press, 1845. 18 p.

Massachusetts Female Emancipation Society. [Address] to the Public [Boston, 1841]. 4 p.

Massachusetts Female Emancipation Society. Third

Annual Report of the Massachusetts Female Emancipation Society. Boston, James Loring, 1843. 22 p. [This society was organized in 1839–40 as an ally of the Massachusetts Abolition Society. It was still holding meetings in 1848.]

Massachusetts Legislature. House Reports, 1837.
No. 51. Trial by Jury in Questions of Personal Freedom. 38 p.

Massachusetts Legislature. House Reports, 1839.
No. 28. Petitions Respecting Distinctions of Color. 16 p.
No. 38. Deliverance of Citizens Liable to Be Sold as Slaves. 36 p.
No. 74. Petition of S. P. Sanford and Others, Concerning Distinctions of Color. 34 p.

Massachusetts Legislature. House Reports, 1840.
No. 44. Slavery, and Admission of New States. 7 p.
No. 46. Interracial Marriages. 8 p.

Massachusetts Legislature. House Reports, 1843.
No. 9. Correspondence with Virginia in the Case of George Latimer. 22 p.
No. 35. Recovery of Citizens of Massachusetts Unlawfully Imprisoned in Southern States. 11 p.
No. 41. Fugitive Slaves in Massachusetts. 37 p.
No. 48. Imprisonment of Colored Seamen. 5 p.

Massachusetts Legislature. House Reports, 1855.
No. 93. [In re:] Removal of Edward Greeley Loring from His Office of Judge of Probate for the County of Suffolk. 43 p.

Massachusetts Legislature. Senate Reports, 1836.
No. 56. Reports and Resolves on the Subject of Slavery. 59 p. [Includes:] Report and Resolutions of North Carolina [on Incendiary Publications]. Report and Resolutions of South Carolina. Report and Resolutions of Georgia. Memorial and Resolutions of Alabama. Resolutions of Virginia.
No. 57. Memorial of the Anti-Slavery Society. 10 p.
No. 92. Colored Seamen in Southern Ports. 35 p.

Massachusetts Legislature. Senate Reports, 1838.
No. 50. Annexation of Texas to the United States. 39 p.
No. 86. Right of Petition. 20 p.
No. 87. Powers and Duties of Congress upon the Subject of Slavery and the Slave Trade. 36 p.

Massachusetts Legislature. Senate Reports, 1839.
No. 35. Foreign Slave Trade. 16 p.
No. 37. Domestic Slavery. 11 p.

Massachusetts Legislature. Senate Reports, 1842.
No. 63. Equal Rights in Railroad Accommodations. 13 p.

Massachusetts Legislature. Senate Reports, 1851.
No. 51. Joint Special Committee on So Much of the Governor's Address as Relates to Slavery and on Petitions Praying the Legislature to Instruct Their Senators and to Request Representatives in Congress to Endeavor to Procure a Repeal of the

Fugitive Slave Law. 19 p.

Massachusetts Legislature. Senate Reports, 1857. No. 100. Petition of Levi Baker, of Yarmouth, and the Petition of 100 Citizens of Yarmouth in Aid of the Same. 19 p.

Massachusetts State Disunion Convention. Proceedings of the State Disunion Convention Held at Worcester, Massachusetts, Jan. 15, 1857. Boston, Printed for the Committee, 1857. 19 p.

[Massachusetts State Texas Committee]. How to Settle the Texas Question. [Boston, E. Wright, Jr., 1845.] 11 p.

Massie, James William. The Slave: Hunted, Transported, and Doomed to Toil; a Tale of Africa. Manchester, James Lowndes, 1846. 176 p.

Massie, James William. Slavery the Crime and Curse of America: An Expostulation with the Christians of That Land. London, John Snow, 1852. 61 p.

Mathews, Edward. Anti-Slavery Labours in England of the Rev. Edward Mathews, Agent of the American Baptist Free Mission Society. Bristol, T. Mathews [185–]. 12 p.

Mathews, Edward. The Autobiography of the Rev. E. Mathews; the "Father Dickson" of Mrs. Stowe's "Dred"; Also a Description of the Influence of the Slave Party over the American Presidents, and the Rise and Progress of the Anti-Slavery Reform; with a Preface by Handel Cossham. New York, Baptist Free Mission Society, 1866. 444 p.

Mathews, Edward. The Shame and Glory of the American Baptists; or, Slaveholders *Versus* Abolitionists. Second Edition. Bristol, Thomas Mathews, [1852]. 23 p.

Mathews, Edward. Statistical Account of the Connection of the Religious Bodies in America with Slavery; Together with a Notice of Various Anti-Slavery Secessions. Presented by the Rev. Edward Mathews, of Wisconsin, Delegate of the American Baptist Free Mission Society, to the Committee of the Bristol and Clifton Ladies' Anti-Slavery Society. March, 1852. Bristol, 1852. 4 p.

Matlack, Lucius C. The History of American Slavery and Methodism, from 1780 to 1849; and History of the Wesleyan Methodist Connection of America. 2 Volumes in 1. New York, 1849.

Matlack, Lucius C. Narrative of the Anti-Slavery Experience of a Minister in the Methodist Episcopal Church, Who Was Twice Rejected by the Philadelphia Annual Conference, and Finally Deprived of License to Preach for Being an Abolitionist. Philadelphia, Merrihew & Thompson, 1845. 24 p.

Matlack, Lucius C. Secession. A Personal Narrative of Proscription, for Being an Abolitionist. Syracuse, New York, 1856. 63 p.

Mattison, Hiram. The Impending Crisis of 1860; or, The Present Connection of the Methodist Episcopal Church with Slavery, and Our Duty in Regard to It. New York, Mason Bros., 1859. 136 p.

May, George. A Sermon on the Connection of the Church with Slavery. Lowell [Mass.], W. H. Stevens, 1845. 24 p.

May, Samuel J[oseph]. Address of Rev. Mr. May, on Emancipation in the British West Indies; Delivered in the First Presbyterian Church in Syracuse, August 1, 1845. Syracuse, J. Barber, 1845. 24 p.

May, Samuel Joseph. A Discourse on Slavery in the United States, Delivered in Brooklyn, [Conn.] July 3, 1831. Boston, Garrison & Knapp, 1832. 29 p.

May, Rev. Samuel Joseph. A Discourse on the Life and Character of the Rev. Charles Follen, Who Perished, Jan. 13, 1840, in the Conflagration of the Lexington. Delivered before the Massachusetts Anti-Slavery Society, in the Marlborough Chapel, Boston, April 17, 1840. Boston, Henry L. Devereux, 1840. 30 p.

May, Samuel J[oseph]. Letter Addressed to the Editor of the Christian Examiner. Boston, Garrison & Knapp, 1835. 8 p.

May, Samuel Joseph. The Right of Colored People to Education Vindicated. Letters to Andrew T. Judson, Esq., and Others in Canterbury, Remonstrating with Them on Their Unjust and Unjustifiable Procedure Relative to Miss Crandall and Her School for Colored Females. Brooklyn, Advertiser Press, 1833. 24 p.

May, Samuel Joseph. Liberty or Slavery, the Only Question. Oration Delivered on the Fourth of July, 1856, at Jamestown, Chautauqua County, N. Y. Syracuse, J. G. K. Truair, 1856. 30 p.

May, Samuel J[oseph]. The Public Are Respectfully Invited to Peruse the Following Concise and Able Defense of Abolition Principles, Prepared and Published under Direction of the Providence Anti-Slavery Society. [n.p., n.d.] 12 p.

May, Samuel Joseph. Speech of Rev. Samuel J. May, to the Convention of Citizens of Onondaga County, in Syracuse, on the 14th of October, 1851, Called "To Consider the Principles of the American Government, and the Extent to Which They Are Trampled under Foot by the Fugitive Slave Law," Occasioned by an Attempt to Enslave an Inhabitant of Syracuse. Syracuse, Agan & Summers, 1851. 23 p.

May, Samuel J[oseph]. These Bad Times, the Product of Bad Morals. A Sermon Preached to the Second Church in Scituate, Mass., May 21, 1837. Boston, Isaac Knapp, 1837. 21 p.

Mayo, Amory Dwight. Herod, John and Jesus; or,

American Slavery and Its Christian Cure. A Sermon Preached in Division Street Church, Albany, N. Y. Albany, Weed, Parsons & Co., 1860. 29 p.

Mayo, Amory Dwight. The Capitol; or, The Higher Law. A Lecture Delivered in the Division St. Church, Albany, Sunday, February 21st, 1858. Albany, Evening Journal Office, 1858. 6 p.

Meigs, Henry. Speech of Mr. Meigs, of New York, on the Restriction of Slavery in Missouri. Delivered in the House of Representatives, January 25, 1820. [Washington, D. C., 1820.] 8 p.

Mellen, George W. F. An Argument on the Unconstitutionality of Slavery, Embracing an Abstract of the Proceedings of the National and State Conventions on This Subject. Boston, Saxton & Pierce, 1841. 440 p.

To the *Members* of the Kentucky Convention. [Lexington, Ky., 1849.] 8 p. Signed: The Author of the Ohio River Plan. Lexington, Ky., October 8th, 1849.

Meriden, Conn., Anti-Slavery Society. An Apology for Abolitionists: Addressed by the Anti-Slavery Society of Meriden, Conn., to Their Fellow-Citizens. [Signed:] Philo Pratt, Walter Webb, Isaac Tibbals. Second Edition. Middletown, C. H. Pelton, 1837. 32 p.

Methodist Episcopal Church. The Address of the General Conference of the Methodist Episcopal Church to All Their Brethren and Friends in the United States. "Dear Brethren: We the Members of the General Conference of the Methodist Episcopal Church Beg Leave to Address You with Earnestness on a Subject of First Importance. We Have Long Lamented the Great National Evil of Negro Slavery . . ." Baltimore, May 20, 1800. Broadside, 1 p. 40 × 38½ cm.

Methodist Episcopal Church. General Conference, 1836. Debate on "Modern Abolitionism," in the General Conference of the Methodist Episcopal Church, Held in Cincinnati, May, 1836. With Notes. Cincinnati, Ohio Anti-Slavery Society, 1836. 91 p.

Methodist Episcopal Church. Debates in the General Conference of the Methodist Episcopal Church, during Its Session in New York, 1844. [New York, 1844.] 240 p.

Methodist Episcopal Church. Report of Debates in the General Conference of the Methodist Episcopal Church, Held in the City of New York, 1844. By Robert Athon West, Official Reporter. New York, Carlton & Phillips, 1855. 240 p.

Methodist Episcopal Church. The Majority and Minority Reports of the Committee of Slavery at the General Conference, Buffalo, 1860. 20 p.

Michigan State Anti-Slavery Society. Report of the Meeting of the Michigan State Anti-Slavery Society, June 28th, 1837, Being the First Annual Meeting, Adjourned from June 1st, 1837. Detroit, Geo. L. Whitney, 1837. 20 p.

Michigan State Legislature. House Reports, 1849. No. 21. Slavery and the Slave Trade in the District of Columbia. 6 p.

Mifflin, Warner. The Defence of Warner Mifflin Against Aspersions Cast on Him on Account of His Endeavors to Promote Righteousness, Mercy and Peace, among Mankind. Philadelphia, Samuel Sansom, June 1796. 30 p.

[Mifflin, Warner]. A Serious Expostulation with the Members of the House of Representatives of the United States. Philadelphia, Printed by D. Lawrence, in the Year 1793. 16 p.
Same. Philadelphia. Printed, New Bedford, Reprinted by J. Spooner, 1793. 16 p.
Same. Philadelphia, Printed; Poughkeepsie, Duchess County, Reprinted by Nicholas Power, 1794. 23 p.

Miller, Samuel. A Discourse, Delivered April 12, 1797, at the Request of and before the New York Society for Promoting the Manumission of Slaves, and Protecting Such of Them as Have Been or May Be Liberated. New York, T. and J. Swords, 1797. 36 p.

Miller, Samuel. A Sermon, Preached at Newark, October 22d, 1823, Before the Synod of New Jersey, for the Benefit of the African School, under the Care of the Synod. Trenton, G. Sherman, 1823. 28 p.

Moody, Loring. Facts for the People; Showing the Relations of the United States Government to Slavery, Embracing a History of the Mexican War, Its Origins and Objects. Boston, Dow and Jackson Anti Slavery Press, 1847. 142 p.
Same. Second Edition, Boston, Bela Marsh, 1848. 120 p.

Moore, George Henry. Historical Notes on the Employment of Negroes in the American Army of the Revolution. New York, Chas. T. Evans, 1862. 24 p.

More, Hannah. Slavery, a Poem. London, T. Cadell, 1788. 20 p.

Morrill, Justin Smith. Modern Democracy. The Extension of Slavery in Our Own Territory or by the Acquisition of Foreign Territory Wrong Morally, Politically, and Economically. Speech of Hon. Justin S. Morrill, of Vermont. Delivered in the U. S. House of Representatives, June 6, 1860. [Washington, D. C., Republican Congressional Committee, 1860.] 8 p.

Morris, Benjamin Franklin, Ed. The Life of Thomas Morris; Pioneer and Long a Legislator of Ohio, and U. S. Senator from 1833 to 1839. Cincinnati,

Moore, Wilstach, Keys & Overend, 1856. 408 p.

Morris, Robert Desha. Slavery, Its Nature, Evils, and Remedy. A Sermon Preached to the Congregation of the Presbyterian Church, Newtown, Pennsylvania. On July 27, 1845. Philadelphia, W. S. Martien, 1845. 31 p.

Morris, Thomas. Speech of the Hon. Thomas Morris, of Ohio, in the Senate of the United States, February 6, 1839, in Reply to the Hon. Henry Clay. New York, Piercy & Reed, 1839. 36 p.

Morse, Jedidiah. A Discourse, Delivered at the African Meeting House, in Boston, July 14, 1808, in Grateful Celebration of the Abolition of the African Slave-Trade by the Governments of the United States, Great Britain, and Denmark. Boston, Lincoln & Edmands, 1808. 28 p.

Morse, Sidney Edwards. The Bible and Slavery. From the N. Y. Observer of Oct. 4, 1855. [New York, 1855.] 8 p.

[Morse, Sidney Edwards]. Letter on American Slavery, Addressed to the Editor of the "Edinburgh Witness," 8th July, 1846. By an American. New York, John Henry, 1847. 8 p.

Morse, Sidney Edwards. Premium Questions on Slavery, Each Admitting of a Yes or No Answer; Addressed to the Editors of the New York Independent and New York Evangelist, by Sidney E. Morse, Lately Editor of the New York Observer. New York, Harper & Brothers, 1860. 30 p.

Mortimer, George Ferris Whidborne. The Immediate Abolition of Slavery, Compatible with the Safety and Prosperity of the Colonies, in a Letter to the Representatives of the Southern Division of Northumberland, and of the Town and County of Newcastle-on-Tyne. Newcastle-upon-Tyne, J. Blackwell and Co., 1823. 24 p.

Mott, Mrs. Lucretia *Coffin*. A Sermon to the Medical Students, Delivered by Lucretia Mott, at Cherry Street Meetinghouse, Philadelphia, on First-Day Evening, Second Month 11th, 1849. Philadelphia, W. B. Zeiber [Etc.], 1849. 21 p.

Myers, Emanuel, Defendant. The Trial of Emanuel Myers, of Maryland, for Kidnapping Certain Fugitive Slaves, Had at Carlisle, Pennsylvania November, 1859. [Carlisle? 1859.] 10 p.

A Narrative of the Adventures and Escape of Moses Roper, from American Slavery; with a Preface by Rev. T. Price, D.D. Philadelphia, Merrihew and Gunn, 1838. 89 p.
Same. London, Harvey and Darton, 1844. 116 p.

Narrative of Dimmock Charlton, a British Subject, Taken from the Brig "Peacock" by the U. S. Sloop "Hornet," Enslaved While a Prisoner of War, and Retained Forty-Five Years in Bondage. [London, 1859.] 15 p.

Narrative of Facts in the Case of Passmore Williamson. Philadelphia, The Pennsylvania Anti-Slavery Society, 1855. 24 p.

The Narrative of Lunsford Lane, Formerly of Raleigh, N. C., Embracing an Account of His Early Life, the Redemption by Purchase of Himself and Family from Slavery, and His Banishment from the Place of His Birth for the Crime of Wearing a Colored Skin. Published by Himself. Second Edition. Boston, J. G. Torrey, Printer, 1842. 54 p.

The National Era. Weekly. Washington, D. C. 1847–1860. Edited by Gamaliel Bailey. J. G. Whittier, Contributing Editor.

National Anti-Slavery Bazaar. Report of the Twentieth National Anti-Slavery Bazaar. Boston, J. B. Yerrington, 1854. 33 p. Report of the Twenty-First National Anti-Slavery Bazaar. Boston, J. B. Yerrington, 1855. 34 p. [Reports, written by Anne W. Weston and Mrs. Maria Weston Chapman, were not usually published in pamphlet form, but only in some antislavery newspaper.]

National Anti-Slavery Standard. Weekly. New York, N. Y. June 11, 1840–April 16, 1870. Published by American Anti-Slavery Society. Edited by Sydney H. Gay from 1843 to 1857.

National Liberty Convention, Buffalo. Proceedings of the National Liberty Convention Held at Buffalo, N. Y., June 14th & 15th, 1848; Including the Resolutions and Addresses Adopted by That Body and Speeches of Beriah Green and Gerrit Smith on That Occasion. Utica, S. W. Green, 1848. 52 p.

National Philanthropist. Weekly. Boston, New York. Volumes 1–8, No. 24, March 4, 1826–December 25, 1833. Publication Began under William Goodell, and Prudence Crandall. Volumes 1–3, No. 37, March 4, 1826–January 9, 1829—National Philanthropist. Volume 4, Nos. 1–33, January 16–August, 1829—National Philanthropist and Investigator. August, 1829–December 25, 1833—Genius of Temperance, Philanthropist and Peoples Advocate.

Needles, Edward. An Historical Memoir of the Pennsylvania Society for Promoting the Abolition of Slavery, the Relief of Free Negroes Unlawfully Held in Bondage, and for Improving the Condition of the African Race. Compiled from the Minutes of the Society and Other Official Documents. Philadelphia, Merrihew and Thompson, 1848. 116 p.

Needles, Edward. Ten Years' Progress: or, A Comparison of the State and Condition of the Colored People in the City and County of Philadelphia from 1837 to 1847. Philadelphia, Merrihew & Thompson, 1849. 16 p.

The Negroes' Flight from American Slavery to British Freedom. The Brothers, Fugitives and Free.

Prefatory Remarks by George Thompson. London, John Snow, 1849. 16 p.

Negro Plot; An Account of the Late Intended Insurrection Among a Portion of the Blacks of the City of Charleston, South Carolina. Second Edition, Boston, Joseph W. Ingraham, 1822. 50 p.

Negro Slavery; or a View of Some of the More Prominent Features of That State of Society, as It Exists in the United States of America and in the Colonies of the West Indies, Especially in Jamaica. London, Hatchard and Son, 1823. 118 p.

Neilson, Peter. The Life and Adventures of Zamba, an African Negro King, and His Experience of Slavery in South Carolina. Written by Himself. Corrected and Arranged by P. Neilson. London, Smith, Elder and Co., 1847. 258 p.

Nell, William Cooper. Services of Colored Americans, in the Wars of 1776 and 1812. Boston, Prentiss & Sawyer, 1851. 24 p.
Second Edition. Boston, Prentiss & Sawyer, 1852. 40 p. [Nell was a protégé of Wendell Phillips. He devoted his life to equality of education for Negroes and was in large part responsible for integration in the Boston schools in 1851. He was said to have been the first Negro to enter the service of the federal government.]

Nell, William Cooper. The Colored Patriots of the American Revolution, with Sketches of Several Distinguished Colored Persons; to Which Is Added a Brief Survey of the Condition and Prospects of Colored Americans. By Wm. C. Nell. With an Introduction by Harriet Beecher Stowe. Boston, R. F. Wallcut, 1855. 369 p.

Nell, William Cooper. Property Qualifications or No Property Qualifications: A Few Facts from the Record of Patriotic Services of the Colored Men of New York, During the Wars of 1776 and 1812, with a Compendium of Their Present Business and Property Statistics. New York, Thomas Hamilton, 1860. 24 p.

Nelson, David. Letter from the Rev. David Nelson. Last Advice to My Old and Beloved Congregation, at Danville, Kentucky. In Western Luminary, Vol. XII, No. 19 [n.d.].

Nelson, David. To the Presbyterian Clergy of the United States. 20 p.

Nelson, Isaac. Slavery Supported by the American Churches, and Countenanced by Recent Proceedings in the Free Church of Scotland; A Lecture by Rev. Isaac Nelson, Belfast. Edinburgh, Charles Ziegler, 1847. 20 p.

The New England Anti-Slavery Almanac, for 1841. Being the 65th Year of American Independence. Calculated for Boston and the Eastern States. Boston, J. A. Collins, 1841. 36 p.

New England Anti-Slavery Society. Constitution of the New England Anti-Slavery Society; Together with Its By-Laws, and a List of Its Officers. Boston, Garrison and Knapp, 1832. 8 p.

New England Anti-Slavery Society. Constitution of the New England Anti-Slavery Society: With an Address to the Public [by Rev. Moses Thacher]. Boston, Garrison & Knapp, 1832. 16 p.

New England Anti-Slavery Society. First Annual Report of the Board of Managers of the New England Anti-Slavery Society, Presented January 9, 1833. Boston, Garrison & Knapp, 1833. 56 p. [Written by Garrison.]

New England Anti-Slavery Society. Second Annual Report of the Board of Managers of the New England Anti-Slavery Society, Presented January 15, 1834, with an Appendix. Boston, Garrison & Knapp, 1834. 48 p. [Written by Samuel Sewall.]

New England Anti-Slavery Society. Third Annual Report of the Board of Managers of the New England Anti-Slavery Society, Presented January 21, 1835. Boston, Garrison and Knapp, 1835. 23 p. [Written by Samuel Sewall.]

New England Anti-Slavery Society. Proceedings of the New England Anti-Slavery Convention Held in Boston on the 27th, 28th, and 29th of May, 1834. Boston, Garrison & Knapp. 72 p.

New England Anti-Slavery Society. Proceedings of the [Third] New England Anti-Slavery Convention; Held in Boston, May 24, 25, 26, 1836. Boston, Isaac Knapp, 1836. 76 p.

New England Anti-Slavery Society. Proceedings of the Fourth New England Anti-Slavery Convention, Held in Boston, May 30, 31, and June 1 and 2, 1837. Boston, Isaac Knapp, 1837. 124 p.

New England Anti-Slavery Convention. 10th, Boston, 1843. Address of the New England Anti-Slavery Convention to the Slaves of the United States; with an Address to President Tyler; Adopted in Faneuil Hall, May 31, 1843. Boston, O. Johnson, 1843. 16 p.

New England Anti-Slavery Society. Address to the People of the United States on the Subject of Slavery. [By a Committee of the New England Anti-Slavery Convention, Held in Boston on the 27th, 28th and 29th of May, 1834.] Boston, Garrison & Knapp, 1834. 16 p.

New England Anti-Slavery Tract Association. Tracts. Boston, J. W. Alden.
No. 1. Longfellow, H. W. Poems on Slavery. 8 p.
No. 2. Address of Loyal National Appeal Association. 12 p.
No. 3. Appleton, Gen. James. The Missouri Compromise; or, The Extension of the Slave Power. 4 p.
No. 4. Stewart, Alvan. The Cause of the Hard Times. Why Is This Country Periodically in Such

Deep Distress, without Famine, Pestilence, or War? 4 p.

No. 5. Weld, Theodore Dwight. Persons Held to Service, Fugitive Slaves, Etc. Boston, J. W. Alden, [n.d.]. 8 p.

No. 6. Jackson, James C. The Duties and Dignities of American Freemen. 12 p.

No. 7. Goodell, William. One More Appeal to Professors of Religion, Ministers and Churches Who Are Not Enlisted in the Struggle against Slavery. 8 p.

No. 8. Hildreth, Richard. What Can I Do for the Abolition of Slavery? 4 p.

No. 9. Hussey, Ebenezer. The Religion of Slavery. 4 p.

No. 10. Clarkson, Thomas. Letter to a Friend on the Ill-Treatment of the People of Color in the United States, on Account of the Color of Their Skin. 8 p.

No. 11. The Lawlessness of Slavery; from the Liberty Press. Extra. 4 p. [Signed:] Terrible Truth.

No. 12. Walker, A. Two Cents Postage. 4 p.

No. 14. Kendall, Rev. D. Jewish Servitude. 8 p.

New England Man, [pseud.—James Kirke Paulding]. An Attempt to Demonstrate the Practicability of Emancipating the Slaves of the United States of North America, and of Removing Them from the Country, Without Impairing the Right of Private Property, or Subjecting the Nation to a Tax. By a New England Man. New York, G. & C. Carvill, 1825. 75 p. [Paulding had a unique plan for colonizing Negroes in Santo Domingo and in the countries of South America, with the governments collecting and returning to the United States Government a portion of their wages.]

New Hampshire Anti-Slavery Convention, Concord, 1834. Proceedings of the N. H. Anti-Slavery Convention, Held in Concord, on the 11th & 12th of November, 1834. Concord, N. H., Eastman, Webster & Co., 1834. 36 p.

New Hampshire Anti-Slavery Society. First Annual Report of the New Hampshire Anti-Slavery Society. Presented at a Meeting of the Society, Held in Concord, June 4, 1835. Concord, Elbridge G. Chase, 1835. 48 p.

[New Jersey Society for Promoting the Abolition of Slavery]. Cases Adjudged in the Supreme Court of New Jersey; Relative to the Manumission of Negroes and Others Holden in Bondage. Burlington, Isaac Neale, 1794. 32 p.
Same. Buffalo, N. Y., Dennis & Co., 1840. 32 p.

New Jersey Society for Promoting the Abolition of Slavery. Constitution of the New Jersey Society for Promoting the Abolition of Slavery; to Which Is Annexed Extracts from a Law of New Jersey Passed the 2d March, 1786, and Supplement to the Same, Passed the 26th November, 1788. Burlington, Isaac Neale, 1793. 16 p.

New Jersey Society for Promoting the Abolition of Slavery. Address of the President [W. Griffith] of the New Jersey Society, for Promoting the Abolition of Slavery, to the General Meeting at Trenton, on Wednesday the 26th of September, 1804. Trenton, Sherman and Mershon, 1804. 12 p.

New Jersey State Abolitionist Convention. An Address to the People of New Jersey, by the Abolitionists of the State Favorable to Political Action Against American Slavery, in Convention at Paterson, Jan. 12, 1841. New York, Piercy & Reed, 1841. 7 p.

New York City Anti-Slavery Society. Address of the New York City Anti-Slavery Society to the People of the City of New York. New York, West & Trow, 1833. 46 p.

New York Committee of Vigilance. The First Annual Report of the New York Committee of Vigilance, for the Year 1837, Together with Important Facts Relative to Their Proceedings. New York, Piercy and Reed, 1837. 84 p.

New York Committee of Vigilance. Fifth Annual Report. New York, [1841]. 38 p.

New York Court of Appeals. Report of the Lemmon Slave Case: Containing Points and Arguments of Counsel on Both Sides, and Opinions of All the Judges. New York, W. H. Tinson, 1860. 146 p.
Same. New York, Horace Greeley & Co., 1860. 146 p.
Same. New York, Horace Greeley & Co., 1861. 146 p.

New York Evening Post. Daily. New York, N. Y. 1826–1868. Edited by William C. Bryant. [It was antislavery by 1838.]

New York Slave Laws. Laws Relative to Slaves and the Slave Trade. New York, Samuel Stansbury, 1806. 29 p.

New York Society for Promoting the Manumission of Slaves. The Constitution of the New York Society for Promoting the Manumission of Slaves, and Protecting Such of Them as Have Been, or May Be, Liberated. Revised, October, 1796. New York, Hopkins, Webb & Co., 1796. 19 p.

New York Society for Promoting the Manumission of Slaves. The Act of Incorporation, and Constitution of the New York Society for Promoting the Manumission of Slaves, and Protecting Such of Them as Have Been, or May Be Liberated. Revised and Adopted, 31st January, 1809. With the By-Laws of the Society Annexed. New York, Samuel Wood, 1810. 23 p.

New York Society for Promoting the Manumission of Slaves. Selections from the Revised Statutes of the State of New York; Containing All the Laws of the State Relative to Slaves, and the Law Relative to the Offence of Kidnapping; Which Several Laws Commenced and Took Effect January 1, 1830. Together with Extracts from the Laws of the United States, Respecting Slaves. New York, Vanderpool & Cole, 1830. 44 p.

New York State Anti-Slavery Society. Proceedings of the New York Anti-Slavery Convention, Held at Utica, October 21, and New York Anti-Slavery State Society, Held at Peterboro, October 22, 1835. Utica, Standard & Democrat Office, 1835. 48 p.

New York State Anti-Slavery Society. First Annual Report of the Proceedings of the New York State Anti-Slavery Society, Held at Peterboro, Oct. 22, 1835. Utica, Standard & Democrat Office, 1835. 48 p.

New York State Anti-Slavery Society. Proceedings of the First Annual Meeting of the New York State Anti-Slavery Society, Convened at Utica, October 19, 1836. Utica, N. Y., Pub. for the Society, 1836. 60 p.

New York State Anti-Slavery Society. Minutes of the First Annual Meeting, Utica, October 19, 1836. Utica, Published for the Society, 1836. 60 p.

New York State Anti-Slavery Society. Address of the Peterboro State Convention to the Slaves and Its Vindication. Cazenovia, R. L. Myrick, 1842. 23 p. [A miniature pamphlet for circulation in the slave states. Created great agitation because of advice to slaves to steal if necessary to escape.]

New York State Legislature. Senate Documents, 1841.
No. 71. Message from the Governor, Transmitting a Communication from the Honorable John M. Patton, Lieutenant Governor of Virginia, Together with a Copy of His Reply Thereto. 14 p.

New York State Legislature. Senate Documents, 1836.
Doc. 106. Report of the Joint Committee of the Senate and Assembly on So Much of the Governor's Message as Relates to Domestic Slavery. 5 p.

New York State Legislature. Select Committee on the Petitions to Prevent Slave Hunting. Report of the Select Committee on the Petitions to Prevent Slave Hunting in the State of New York. Transmitted to the Legislature, February 11, 1860. Albany, C. Van Benthuysen, 1860.

New York Young Men's Anti-Slavery Society. Preamble and Constitution of the New York Young Men's Anti-Slavery Society, Formed May 2, 1834. New York, W. T. Coolidge & Co., 1834. 11 p.

New York Young Men's Anti-Slavery Society. Address of the New York Young Men's Anti-Slavery Society, to Their Fellow Citizens. New York, W. T. Coolidge & Co., 1834. 40 p. [Contains constitution.]

New York Young Men's Anti-Slavery Society. First Annual Report of the New York Young Men's Anti-Slavery Society, Auxiliary to the American Anti-Slavery Society; with Addresses, Delivered at the Anniversary, May, 1835. New York, Coolidge & Lambert, 1835. 19 p.

New York Young Men's Anti-Slavery Society. Friends of Liberty! Read This before You Vote. New York, Nov. 3, 1838.

Newburyport Anti-Slavery Society. Constitution of the Anti-Slavery Society of Newburyport and Vicinity. Newburyport, Hiram Tozer, 1834. 40 p.

Newhall, Fales Henry. The Conflict in America. A Funeral Discourse Occasioned by the Death of John Brown of Ossawattomie, Who Entered into Rest, from the Gallows, at Charlestown, Virginia, Dec. 2, 1859. Preached at the Warren St. M.E. Church, Roxbury, Dec. 4, by Rev. Fales Henry Newhall, Pastor. Boston, J. M. Hewes, 1859. 22 p.

Newton, John. Thoughts upon the African Slave Trade. London, J. Buckland, 1788. 23 p.

Nickolls, Robert Boucher. A Letter to the Treasurer of the Society Instituted for the Purpose of Effecting the Abolition of the Slave Trade. From the Rev. Robert Boucher Nickolls, Dean of Middleham. A New Edition, with Additions. London, James Phillips, 1788. 35 p.

Niles, John Milton. Speech of Mr. Niles, of Connecticut, on the Petition of a Society of Friends in Pennsylvania, Praying for the Abolition of Slavery in the District of Columbia. In Senate, February 15, 1836. Washington, Blair and Rives, 1836. 14 p.

Nisbet, Richard. The Capacity of Negroes for Religious and Moral Improvement, Considered; with Cursory Hints, to Proprietors and to Government, for the Immediate Melioration of the Condition of Slaves in the Sugar Colonies: To Which Are Subjoined Short and Practical Discourses to Negroes, on the Plain and Obvious Principles of Religion and Morality. London, James Phillips, 1789. 207 p.

Nixon, Barnaby. A Serious Address, to the Rulers of America in General, and the State of Virginia in Particular. By Barnaby Nixon. Richmond, Seaton Grantland, 1806. 12 p.

The Non-Slaveholder. Philadelphia, Pa. Volumes 1–5, 1846–1850. New Series, Volumes 1–2, 1853–1854. Volumes 1–2 Edited by A. L. Pennock, S. Rhoads, & G. W. Taylor. Volume 3 Edited by S. Rhoads & G. W. Taylor. Volumes 4–5 Edited by S. Rhoads. New Series, Volumes 1–2, Edited by W. J. Allinson.

Northup, Solomon. Twelve Years a Slave. Narrative of Solomon Northup, a Citizen of New York, Kidnapped in Washington City in 1841, and

Rescued in 1853, from a Cotton Plantation Near the Red River in Louisiana. Buffalo, Derry, Orton & Mulligan, 1853. 336 p.

Northup, Solomon. Twelve Years a Slave: The Thrilling Story of a Free Colored Man, Kidnapped in Washington in 1841, Sold into Slavery, and After Twelve Years' Bondage, Reclaimed by State Authority from a Cotton Plantation in Louisiana. By S. Northup. Philadelphia, J. E. Potter and Company [18—]. 336 p.

North Star. Weekly. Rochester, New York. December 3, 1847–August, 1863. Founded and Edited by Frederick Douglass. Published as North Star, December 3, 1847–April, 1851; and as Frederick Douglass' Paper after April, 1851.

Nott, Samuel. Slavery, and the Remedy; or, Principles and Suggestions for a Remedial Code. Boston, Crocker and Brewster, 1856. 118 p.
Same. Second Edition. Boston, Crocker and Brewster; New York, Appleton & Co., 1856. 118 p.
Same. Fourth Edition. Boston, Crocker and Brewster, 1856. 120 p.
Same. Fifth Edition, with a Review of the Decision of the Supreme Court in the Case of Dred Scott. New York, D. Appleton & Company, 1857. 137 p.
Same. Sixth Edition. Boston, Crocker & Brewster, 1859. 137 p.

Nourse, James. Views of Colonization. Philadelphia, Merrihew & Gunn, 1837. 52 p.
Same: Second Edition. New York, American Anti-Slavery Society, 1839. 60 p.

[O'Connell, Daniel]. Address from the People of Ireland to Their Countrymen and Countrywomen in America. [n.p., 1847.] 32 p.

[O'Connell, Daniel]. Address of the Irish Liberator, to the Irish Repeal Association of Cincinnati, Ohio; with the Pope's Bull on Slavery and the Slave Trade. New York, Published at 128 Fulton St., 1843. 24 p.

Ober, Benjamin. Slavery: A Lecture Delivered Before the Lyceum in Attleborough, Jan. 4th, 1838. By Rev. Benjamin Ober. Published by Request. Pawtucket, Mass., R. Sherman, 1838. 28 p.

Observations on the Inslaving, Importing and Purchasing of Negroes. Second Edition. Germantown, C. Sower, 1760. 16 p.

[Odell, Margaret Matilda]. Memoir and Poems of Phillis Wheatley. Also, Poems by a Slave [G. M. Horton]. Third Edition. Boston, Isaac Knapp, 1838. 155 p.

Offley, Rev. G. W. A Narrative of the Life and Labors of the Rev. G. W. Offley, a Colored Man, and Local Preacher. Written by Himself. Hartford, Conn., 1860. 52 p.

Ohio Anti-Slavery Society. Proceedings of the Ohio Anti-Slavery Convention, Held at Putnam on the Twenty-Second, Twenty-Third, and Twenty-Fourth of April, 1835. [Putnam], Beaumont and Wallace, [1835]. 54 p.
Same. New York, American Anti-Slavery Society, 1835. 54 p.

Ohio Anti-Slavery Society. Report on the Condition of the People of Color in the State of Ohio. From the Proceedings of the Ohio Anti-Slavery Convention, Held at Putnam, on the 22d, 23d, and 24th of April, 1835. [n.p., n.d.] 24 p. Also [Putnam? 1835].
Same. Boston, Isaac Knapp, 1839. 48 p. [Written by Augustus Wattles, but signed by committee: A. Wattles, J. W. Alvord, S. Wells, H. Lyman, M. R. Robinson.]

Ohio Anti-Slavery Society. Memorial to the General Assembly of the State of Ohio. Cincinnati, 1838. Pugh & Dodd, 1838. 34 p.

Ohio Anti-Slavery Society. Narrative of the Late Riotous Proceedings Against the Liberty of the Press in Cincinnati, with Remarks and Historical Notices Relating to Emancipation. Addressed to the People of Ohio by Executive Committee of the Ohio Anti-Slavery Society. Cincinnati, 1836. 48 p.

Ohio Anti-Slavery Society. Report of the First Anniversary of the Ohio Anti-Slavery Society, Held Near Granville, on the Twenty-Seventh and Twenty-Eighth of April, 1836. Cincinnati, Ohio Anti-Slavery Society, 1836. 53 p.

Ohio Anti-Slavery Society. Report of the Second Anniversary of the Ohio Anti-Slavery Society, Held at Mt. Pleasant, Jefferson Co., Ohio, on the Twenty-Seventh of April, 1837. Cincinnati, the Anti-Slavery Society, 1837. 67 p.

Ohio Anti-Slavery Society. Report of the Third Anniversary of the Ohio Anti-Slavery Society, Held in Granville, Licking County, Ohio, on the 30th of May, 1838. Cincinnati, Ohio Anti-Slavery Society, 1838. 38 p.

Ohio Anti-Slavery Society. Report of the Fourth Anniversary of the Ohio Anti-Slavery Society, Held in Putnam, Muskingum County, Ohio, on the 29th of May, 1839. Cincinnati, Ohio Anti-Slavery Society, 1839. 63 p.

Ohio State Anti-Slavery Society. Report of the Fifth Anniversary of the Ohio State Anti-Slavery Society, Held in Massillon, Stark County, Ohio, May 27, 1840. [Cincinnati, 1840.] 20 p.

Ohio State Christian Anti-Slavery Convention. Proceedings of the Ohio State Christian Anti-Slavery Convention, Held at Columbus, August 10 and 11, 1859. [Columbus, Ohio] 1859. 28 p.

Ohio State Free Territory Convention. Addresses and Proceedings of the State Independent Free

Territory Convention of the People of Ohio, Held at Columbus, June 20 and 21, 1848. Cincinnati, Herald Office, 1848. 14 p.

Olcott, Charles. Two Lectures on the Subject of Slavery and Abolition. Compiled for the Special Use of Anti Slavery Lecturers and Debaters, and Intended for Public Reading. Massillon, Ohio, Printed for the Author, 1838. 128 p.

Olin, A. B. Emancipation. Speech of Hon. A. B. Olin, of New York, Delivered in the House of Representatives, Tuesday, March 11, 1862. Washington, D. C., Scammell & Co., 1862. 8 p.

Olmsted, Frederick Law. The Cotton Kingdom; a Traveller's Observations on Cotton and Slavery in the American Slave States. Based upon Three Former Volumes of Journeys and Investigations. 2 vols. New York, Mason Brothers [etc., etc.], 1861.

Olmsted, Frederick Law. A Journey in the Back Country. New York, Mason Brothers, 1860. 492 p.

Opie, Mrs. Amelia *Alderson*. The Negro Boy's Tale; a Poem, Addressed to Children. London, 1824. 16 p.

Osborn, Charles. Journal of That Faithful Servant of Christ, Charles Osborn, Containing an Account of Many of His Travels and Labors in the Work of the Ministry, and His Trials and Exercises in the Service of the Lord, and in Defense of the Truth, as It Is in Jesus. Cincinnati, A. Pugh, 1854. 472 p.

Osborn, Charles. A Testimony Concerning the Separation Which Occurred in Indiana Yearly Meeting of Friends, in the Winter of 1842–'43; Together with Sundry Remarks and Observations, Particularly on the Subjects of War, Slavery, and Colonization. By Charles Osborn. Centreville [Ind.?], R. Vaile, 1849. 54 p.

Oswego County Anti-Slavery Society. Address to the Democratic Editors of Oswego County, October 27, 1838.

The Outrage in the Senate; Proceedings of a Public Meeting of the Citizens of Providence, Held in Howard Hall, on the Evening of June 7th, 1856. Providence, Knowles, Anthony & Company, 1856. 12 p.

Owen, Robert Dale. Annexation of Texas; Speech of Mr. Owen Delivered in the House of Representatives, May 21, 1844, on the Right and Duty of the United States Not to Accept the Offer Made by Texas of Annexation. 8 p.

Paine, Byron, and Smith, A. D. Unconstitutionality of the Fugitive Act. Argument of Byron Paine, Esq., and Opinion of Hon. A. D. Smith, Associate Justice of the Supreme Court of the State of Wisconsin. Milwaukee, Free Democrat Office. 29 p.

Paine, Lewis W. Six Years in a Georgia Prison. Narrative of Lewis Paine, Who Suffered Imprisonment Six Years in Georgia for the Crime of Aiding the Escape of a Fellow-Man from That State, after He Had Fled from Slavery. Written by Himself. New York, Printed for the Author, 1851. 187 p. Same. Boston, Bela Marsh, 1852. 187 p.

Palfrey, John Gorham. A Chapter of American History. Five Years' Progress of the Slave Power; A Series of Papers, First Published in the Boston "Commonwealth," in July, August and September, 1851. Boston, B. B. Mussey & Co., 1852. 84 p.

Palfrey, John Gorham. Correspondence Between Nathan Appleton and John G. Palfrey, Intended as a Supplement to Mr. Palfrey's Pamphlet on the Slave Power. Boston, Eastburn's Press, 1846. 20 p.

Palfrey, John G[orham]. A Letter to a Friend. Cambridge, Mass., Metcalf and Company, 1850. 28 p.

Palfrey, John Gorham. Papers on the Slave Power, First Published in the "Boston Whig." Boston, Merrill, Cobb & Co., 1846. 91 p.
Same. Second Edition. Boston, Merrill, Cobb & Co. [1846]. 92 p.
Same. Third Edition. Boston, Merrill, Cobb & Co., [n.d.]. 92 p.

Palfrey, John Gorham. Speech of Mr. Palfrey, of Massachusetts, on the Political Aspects of the Slave Question. Delivered in the House of Representatives, January 26th, 1848. Washington, D. C., J. & G. S. Gideon, 1848. 16 p.

Palfrey, John Gorham. Speech of Mr. Palfrey, of Massachusetts, on the Bill Creating a Territorial Government for Upper California, Delivered in the House of Representatives of the United States, February 26, 1849. Washington, D. C., J. & G. S. Gideon, 1849. 10 p.

Palmer, William Pitt. Poem, Spoken July 4, 1828, Before the Anti-Slavery Society of Williams College. Williamstown, Ridley Bannister, 1828. 24 p.

Parker, Joel. Discussion Between Rev. Joel Parker, and Rev. A. Rood, on the Question "What Are the Evils Inseparable from Slavery?" Which Was Referred to by Mrs. Stowe, in "Uncle Tom's Cabin." Reprinted from the Philadelphia Christian Observer of 1846; New York, S. W. Benedict; Philadelphia, H. Hooper, 1852. 120 p. [Parker was professor of law, and a renowned jurist.]

Parker, Joel. Non-Extension of Slavery and Constitutional Representation. An Address Before the Citizens of Cambridge, October 1, 1856. Cambridge, James Munroe & Co., 1856. 92 p.

Parker, Joel. Personal Liberty Laws, and Slavery in the Territories [Case of Dred Scott]. Boston, Wright & Potter, 1861. 97 p.

Parker, Joel. The True Issue, and the Duty of the Whigs. An Address Before the Citizens of Cambridge, October 1, 1856. By Joel Parker. Cambridge, J. Munroe and Company, 1856. 88 p.

Parker, Theodore. An Address Delivered by the Rev. Theodore Parker, before the New York City Anti-Slavery Society, at Its First Anniversary, Held at the Broadway Tabernacle, May 12, 1854. New York, American Anti-Slavery Society, 1854. 46 p. [Parker was a renowned scholar and one of the most active and daring participants in the latter phases of the movement.]

Parker, Theodore. The Boston Kidnapping: A Discourse to Commemorate the Rendition of Thomas Simms, Delivered on the First Anniversary Thereof, April 12, 1852, Before the Committee on Vigilance at the Melodeon in Boston. By Theodore Parker. Boston, Crosby, Nichols, & Company, 1852. 72 p.

Parker, Theodore. Discourse Occasioned by the Death of Daniel Webster, Preached at the Melodeon on Sunday, October 31, 1852. Boston, Benjamin B. Mussey & Co., 1853. 108 p.

Parker, Theodore. A Discourse Occasioned by the Death of John Quincy Adams. Delivered at the Melodeon in Boston, March 5, 1848. Boston, Bela Marsh, 1848. 66 p.

Parker, Theodore. The Effect of Slavery on the American People. A Sermon Preached at the Music Hall, Boston, on Sunday, July 4, 1858. Revised by the Author. Boston, Wm. L. Kent & Co., 1858. 14 p.

Parker, Theodore. The Function and Place of Conscience, in Relation to the Laws of Men; A Sermon for the Times; Preached at the Melodeon, on Sunday, September 22, 1850. Boston, Crosby & Nichols, 1850. 40 p.

Parker, Theodore. The Great Battle Between Slavery and Freedom, Considered in Two Speeches Delivered Before the American Anti-Slavery Society, at New York, May 7, 1856. Boston, Benjamin H. Greene, 1856. 93 p.

Parker, Theodore. John Brown's Expedition, Reviewed in a Letter from Rev. Theodore Parker, at Rome, to Francis Jackson, Boston. Boston, Published by The Fraternity, 1860. 19 p.

Parker, Theodore. The Law of God and the Statutes of Men. A Sermon, Preached at the Music Hall, in Boston, on Sunday, June 18, 1854. By Theodore Parker. Phonographically Reported by Rufus Leighton. Boston, B. B. Mussey & Co., 1854. 32 p.

Parker, Theodore. A Letter to the People of the United States Touching the Matter of Slavery. Boston, James Munroe & Co., 1848. 120 p.

Parker, Theodore. The Nebraska Question. Some Thoughts on the New Assault upon Freedom in America, and the General State of the Country in Relation Thereunto, Set Forth in a Discourse Preached at the Music Hall, in Boston, on Monday, Feb. 12, 1854. Boston, Benjamin B. Mussey & Co., 1854. 72 p.

Parker, Theodore. The New Crime Against Humanity. A Sermon, Preached at the Music Hall, in Boston, on Sunday, June 4, 1854. Boston, Benjamin B. Mussey & Co., 1854. 76 p.

Parker, Theodore. A New Lesson for the Day: A Sermon Preached at the Music Hall, in Boston, on Sunday, May 25, 1856. By Theodore Parker. Phonographically Reported by Messrs. Yerrington and Leighton. Boston, B. H. Greene, 1856. 40 p.

Parker, Theodore. The Present Aspect of Slavery in America and the Immediate Duty of the North. A Speech Delivered in the Hall of the State House, in Boston, Before the Massachusetts Anti-Slavery Convention, on Friday Night, January 29, 1858. Boston, Bela Marsh, 1858. 44 p.

Parker, Theodore. The Relation of Slavery to a Republican Form of Government. A Speech Delivered at the New England Anti-Slavery Convention, Wednesday Morning, May 26, 1858. Boston, William L. Kent & Company, 1858. 21 p.

Parker, Theodore. A Sermon on Slavery, Delivered Jan. 31, 1841, Repeated June 4, 1843, and Now Published by Request. Boston, Thurston & Torrey, 1843. 24 p.

Parker, Theodore. A Sermon of the Dangers Which Threaten the Rights of Man in America; Preached at the Music Hall, on Sunday, July 2, 1854, by Theodore Parker. Boston, B. B. Mussey & Co., 1854. 56 p.

Parker, Theodore. A Sermon on the Mexican War; Preached at the Melodeon, on Sunday, June 25, 1848, by Theodore Parker, Minister of the XXVIII Congregational Church in Boston. Boston, Coolidge and Wiley, 1848. 56 p.

Parker, Theodore. Theodore Parker's Review of Webster. Speech of Theodore Parker, Delivered in the Old Cradle of Liberty, March 25, 1850. Boston, R. F. Wallcut, 1850. 26 p.

Parker, Theodore. Tribute to Theodore Parker, Comprising the Exercises at the Music Hall, on Sunday, June 17, 1860, with the Proceedings of the New England Anti-Slavery Convention at the Melodeon, May 31, and the Resolutions of the Fraternity and the Twenty-eighth Congregational Society. Boston, Published by the Fraternity, 1860. 60 p.

Parker, Theodore. Two Sermons Preached Before the Twenty-Eighth Congregational Society in Boston. On the 14th and 21st of November, 1852, on Leaving Their Old and Entering a New Place of

Worship. Boston, Crosby, Nichols & Company, 1853. 56 p.

Parker, Theodore. The State of the Nation, Considered in a Sermon for Thanksgiving Day, Preached at the Melodeon, Nov. 28, 1850. Boston, Wm. Crosby & H. P. Nichols, 1851. 38 p.

Parker, Theodore. The Trial of Theodore Parker for the "Misdemeanor" of a Speech in Faneuil Hall Against Kidnapping, before the Circuit Court of the United States, at Boston, April 3, 1855. With the Defence, by Theodore Parker, Minister of the Twenty-Eighth Congregational Society in Boston. Boston, Published for the Author, 1855. 221 p.

Parrish, Isaac. Brief Memoirs of Thomas Shipley and Edwin P. Atlee, Read Before the Pennsylvania Society for Promoting the Abolition of Slavery, Etc., Tenth Month, 1837. Philadelphia, Published by the Society. 40 p.

Parrish, John. Remarks on the Slavery of the Black People; Addressed to the Citizens of the United States, Particularly to Those Who Are in Legislative or Executive Stations in the General or State Governments; and Also to Such Individuals as Hold Them in Bondage. Philadelphia, Kimber, Conrad & Co., 1806. 66 p. [Successor to Benezet in Philadelphia.]

Parrott, Russell. An Oration on the Abolition of the Slave Trade, by Russell Parrott. Delivered on the First of January, 1812, at the African Church of St. Thomas. Philadelphia, James Maxwell, 1812. 10 p.

Parrott, Russell. An Address on the Abolition of the Slave-Trade, Delivered Before the Different African Benevolent Societies, on the 1st of January, 1816. Philadelphia, T. S. Manning, 1816. 12 p.

Parsons, Charles Grandison. Inside View of Slavery; or, A Tour Among the Planters by C. G. Parsons, M.D., with an Introductory Note by Mrs. Harriet Beecher Stowe. Boston, J. P. Jewett and Co.; Cleveland, O., Jewett, Proctor and Worthington, 1855. 318 p.

Parsons, Theodore, and Pearson, Eliphalet. A Forensic Dispute on the Legality of Enslaving the Africans, Held at the Public Commencement in Cambridge, New England, July 21st, 1773. By Two Candidates for the Bachelor's Degree. Boston, John Boyle, 1773. 48 p.

Paterson, Rev. Wm. C. A Discourse on the Sin of American Slavery, Delivered in the Baptist Church, E. Dedham, on Sabbath Evening, May 21, 1854. Boston, J. Howe, 1854. 16 p.

Patterson, James. A Sermon on the Effects of the Hebrew Slavery as Connected with Slavery in This Country. Preached in the 7th Presbyterian Church in the City of Philadelphia, at a United Meeting of Christians of Different Religious Persuasions to Celebrate Our National Independence, July 4, 1825. Philadelphia, S. Probasco, 1825. 36 p.

Patten, William. On the Inhumanity of the Slave-Trade, and the Importance of Correcting It. A Sermon, Delivered in the Second Congregational Church, Newport, Rhode Island, August 12, 1792. By William Patten, A.M., Minister of Said Church. Providence, J. Carter, 1793. 14 p.

Patton, William Weston. An Attempt to Prove that Pro-Slavery Interpretations of the Bible Are Productive of Infidelity. Hartford, W. H. Burleigh, 1846. 20 p.

Patton, William Weston. Conscience and Law; or, A Discussion of Our Comparative Responsibility to Human and Divine Government; with an Application to the Fugitive Slave Law. New York, Newman & Co., 1850. 64 p.

Patton, William Weston. Freedom's Martyr. A Discourse on the Death of the Rev. Charles T. Torrey. By Rev. Wm. W. Patton, Pastor of the Fourth Cong. Church, Hartford, Ct. Hartford, William H. Burleigh, 1846. 19 p.

Patton, William Weston. Slavery and Infidelity; or, Slavery in the Church Ensures Infidelity in the World. Cincinnati, American Reform Book & Tract Society, 1856. 70 p.

Patton, William Weston. Slavery—The Bible—Infidelity. Pro-Slavery Interpretations of the Bible, Productive of Infidelity; by William W. Patton. Second Edition. Hartford, W. H. Burleigh, 1847. 16 p.

Patton, William Weston. Thoughts for Christians, Suggested by the Case of Passmore Williamson: A Discourse Preached in the Fourth Congregational] Church, Hartford, Conn., October 7, 1855. Hartford, Conn., Montague & Co., 1855. 23 p.

Patton, William Weston. The Unanimous Remonstrance of the Fourth Congregational Church, Hartford, Conn., Against the Policy of the American Tract Society on the Subject of Slavery. Hartford, Silas Andrus & Son, 1855. 34 p.

Paul, Nathaniel. An Address, Delivered on the Celebration of the Abolition of Slavery, in the State of New York, July 5, 1827. By Nathaniel Paul, Pastor of the First African Baptist Society in the City of Albany. Pub. by the Trustees for the Benefit of Said Society. Albany, J. B. Van Steenbergh, 1827. 24 p.

Paulding, James K[irke]. Slavery in the United States. New York, Harper & Brothers, 1836. 312 p.

Paxton, John D. Letters on Slavery; Addressed to the Cumberland Congregation, Virginia. Lexington, Ky., Abraham T. Skillman, 1833. 207 p.

Peabody, Andrew Preston. Position and Duties of the North with Regard to Slavery. Reprinted from the

Christian Examiner of July, 1843. Newburyport, Charles Whipple, 1847. 22 p.

Peabody, E[phraim]. Slavery in the United States: Its Evils, Alleviations, and Remedies. Reprinted from the North American Review, October, 1851. Boston, Charles C. Little and James Brown, 1851. 36 p.

Peabody, William Bourne Oliver. The Duties and Dangers of Those Who Are Born Free. A Sermon Preached at the Annual Election of January 2, 1833, Before His Excellency Levi Lincoln, Governor, and His Honor Thomas L. Winthrop, Lieutenant-Governor, the Honorable Council and the Legislature of Massachusetts. Boston, Dutton and Wentworth, 1833. 31 p.

Pearson, Henry B. A Discourse Delivered in the First Congregational Church, at Harvard, Worcester Co., Mass., on the Day of the Annual Fast, April 6, 1848: by Henry B. Pearson; Published by Subscription, at the Request of the Hearers and Others. Boston, W. B. Fowle, 1848. 22 p.

Pearson, Henry B. Freedom Versus Slavery. Letters from Henry B. Pearson, Late of the Philadelphia Bar, to Hon. Rufus Choate, on His Letter to the Whig Committee of the State of Maine, Originally Written by Request, and Published in the Eastern Mail, Waterville, for August and September, A.D. 1856. Portland, Daley & Lufkin, 1856. 16 p.

Peck, George. Slavery and the Episcopacy: Being an Examination of Dr. Bascom's Review of the Reply of the Majority to the Protest of the Minority of the Late General Conference of the M.E. Church, in the Case of Bishop Andrew. New York, G. Lane & C. B. Tippett, 1845. 139 p.

Peck, Nathaniel, and Thomas S. Price. Report of Messrs. Peck and Price, Who Were Appointed at a Meeting of the Free Colored People of Baltimore, Held on the 25th November, 1839, Delegates to Visit British Guiana, and the Island of Trinidad; for the Purpose of Ascertaining the Advantages to Be Derived by Colored People Migrating to Those Places. Baltimore, Woods & Crane, 1840. 23 p.

Pennington, James W. C. Covenants Involving Moral Wrong Are Not Obligatory upon Man: A Sermon Delivered in the Fifth Congregational Church, Hartford, on Thanksgiving Day, Nov. 17th, 1842. Hartford, J. C. Wells, 1842. 12 p.

Pennington, James W. C. The Fugitive Blacksmith: or, Events in the History of James Pennington, Pastor of a Presbyterian Church, Formerly a Slave in the State of Maryland, United States. Third Edition. London, Charles Gilpin, 1850. 84 p.

Pennington, James W. C. The Reasonableness of the Abolition of Slavery at the South, a Legitimate Inference from the Success of British Emancipation:

An Address Delivered at Hartford, Connecticut, on the First of August, 1856. Hartford, Case, Tiffany & Co., 1856. 20 p.

Pennington, James W. C. A Text Book of the Origin and History, Etc., Etc., of the Colored People. Hartford, L. Skinner, 1841. 96 p.

Pennsylvania Free Produce Society. Constitution of the Free Produce Society of Pennsylvania. Philadelphia, D. & S. Neall, 1827. 12 p.

Pennsylvania Freeman. Weekly. Philadelphia, Pa. August 3, 1836–June 29, 1854. Edited by John Greenleaf Whittier from 1838 to 1844 and C. C. Burleigh and J. M. McKim from 1844 to 1854. Published as National Enquirer from 1836–March 8, 1838. Organ of Eastern Pennsylvania Anti-Slavery Society after 1849.

[Pennsylvania Hall Association]. History of Pennsylvania Hall, Which Was Destroyed by a Mob, on the 17th of May, 1838. Philadelphia, Merrihew & Gunn, 1838. 200 p. [Authorship attributed to Samuel Webb.]

PENNSYLVANIA SOCIETY FOR PROMOTING
THE ABOLITION OF SLAVERY

Act of Incorporation and Constitution of the Pennsylvania Society, for Promoting the Abolition of Slavery, and for the Relief of Free Negroes Unlawfully Held in Bondage, and for Improving the Condition of the African Race; Also, a List of Those Who Have Been Elected Members of the Society. Instituted 1775; Incorporated 1789. Philadelphia, Merrihew & Thompson, 1860. 36 p.

An Address from the Pennsylvania Society for Promoting the Abolition of Slavery, for the Relief of Free Negroes Unlawfully Held in Bondage, and for Improving the Condition of the African Race; on the Origin, Purposes and Utility of Their Institution. Philadelphia, Hall & Atkinson, 1819. 6 p.

Celebration of the Ninetieth Anniversary of the Organization of the Pennsylvania Society for Promoting the Abolition of Slavery, for the Relief of Free Negroes Unlawfully Held in Bondage, and for Improving the Condition of the African Race. Held at Concert Hall, Fourth Mo. [April] 14, 1865. Philadelphia, Merrihew & Son, 1866. 25 p.

Centennial Anniversary of the Pennsylvania Society, for Promoting the Abolition of Slavery, the Relief of Free Negroes Unlawfully Held in Bondage; and for Improving the Condition of the African Race. Philadelphia, Grant, Faires & Rodgers, Printers, 1875. 82 p.

Constitution and Act of Incorporation of the Pennsylvania Society, for Promoting the Abolition of Slavery, and the Relief of Free Negroes, Unlawfully Held in Bondage. And for Improving the Condition of the African Race. To Which Are

Added, the Acts of the General Assembly of Pennsylvania for the Gradual Abolition of Slavery, and the Acts of Congress of the United States, Respecting Slaves and the Slave Trade. Philadelphia, J. Ormond, 1800. 53 p.

Constitution and Act of Incorporation of the Pennsylvania Society for Promoting the Abolition of Slavery, and for the Relief of Free Negroes, Unlawfully Held in Bondage, and for the Improving the Condition of the African Race. To Which Are Added Abstracts of the Laws of the States of Pennsylvania, New York, New Jersey, Delaware and Maryland, and of the Acts of Congress, Respecting Slavery and the Slave Trade. Philadelphia, Hall & Atkinson, 1820. 31 p.

Constitution of the Pennsylvania Society for Promoting the Abolition of Slavery, and the Relief of Free Negroes, Unlawfully Held in Bondage. Begun in the Year 1774, and Enlarged on the Twenty-third of April, 1787. To Which Are Added, the Acts of the General Assembly of Pennsylvania, for the Gradual Abolition of Slavery. Philadelphia, Joseph James, 1787. 15 p.

The Constitution of the Pennsylvania Society, for Promoting the Abolition of Slavery, and the Relief of Free Negroes, Unlawfully Held in Bondage; Enlarged at Philadelphia, April 23d, 1787. [Philadelphia? 1788?] 29 p.

Five Years' Abstract of Transactions of the Pennsylvania Society for Promoting the Abolition of Slavery, the Relief of Free Negroes Unlawfully Held in Bondage, and for Improving the Condition of the African Race. Philadelphia, Merrihew & Thompson, 1853. 15 p.

An Historical Memoir of the Pennsylvania Society, for Promoting the Abolition of Slavery; the Relief of Free Negroes Unlawfully Held in Bondage, and for Improving the Condition of the African Race. Comp. from the Minutes of the Society and Other Official Documents, by Edward Needles, and Pub. by Authority of the Society. Philadelphia, Merrihew and Thompson, 1848. 116 p.

Memorials Presented to the Congress of the United States of America, by the Different Societies Instituted for Promoting the Abolition of Slavery, Etc., Etc., in the States of Rhode Island, Connecticut, New York, Pennsylvania, Maryland, and Virginia. Published by Order of the Pennsylvania Society for Promoting the Abolition of Slavery, and the Relief of Free Negroes Unlawfully Held in Bondage, and for Improving the Condition of the African Race. Philadelphia, Francis Bailey, 1792. 31 p.

Philadelphia 26 October, 1789. At a Meeting of the Pennsylvania Society for Promoting the Abolition of Slavery, &c. An Essay of a Plan for Improving the Condition of Free Negroes Was Presented by the Committee Appointed to Prepare It, Which After Deliberate Consideration Was Adopted as Follows. A Plan for Improving the Condition of the Free Blacks. Philadelphia, Francis Bailey, [1789]. Broadside. 20½ × 33½ cm.

The Present State and Condition of the Free People of Color, of the City of Philadelphia and Adjoining Districts, as Exhibited by the Report of a Committee of the Pennsylvania Society for Promoting the Abolition of Slavery. Read First Month, 5th, 1838. Philadelphia, Merrihew and Gunn, 1838. 40 p. [Joseph Parrish, M.D., Chm.]

Statistics of the Colored People of Philadelphia, Taken by Benjamin C. Bacon, and Published by Order of the Board of Concession of the Pennsylvania Society for Promoting the Abolition of Slavery. Philadelphia, 1856. 16 p.

To the People of Color in the State of Pennsylvania. Philadelphia, Merrihew and Gunn, 1838. 8 p.

————

Pennsylvania, Governor, 1848–1852 (William F. Johnston). Message of the Governor of Pennsylvania, Transmitting Resolutions Relative to Slavery, Passed by the Legislatures of Virginia and Georgia. Harrisburg, J. M. G. Lescure, 1850. 17 p.

Pennsylvania State Anti-Slavery Society. Proceedings of the Pennsylvania Convention, Assembled to Organize a State Anti-Slavery Society, at Harrisburg, on the 31st of January and 1st, 2d, and 3d of February, 1837. Philadelphia, Merrihew and Gunn, 1837. 97 p.

Pennsylvania State Anti-Slavery Society. Address to the Coloured People of the State of Pennsylvania. Philadelphia, Merrihew and Gunn, Printers, 1837. 7 p.

Pennsylvania State Anti-Slavery Society. Address of the Eastern Executive Committee of the State Anti-Slavery Society to the Citizens of Pennsylvania. Philadelphia, Merrihew & Gunn, 1838. 16 p.

Pennsylvania State Anti-Slavery Society. Address of the State Anti-Slavery Society, to the Ministers of the Gospel in the State of Pennsylvania; Read and Adopted Jan. 18, 1838. Philadelphia, Pennsylvania State Anti-Slavery Society, 1838. 11 p.

Pennsylvania State Anti-Slavery Society. Thirteenth Annual Report, Presented to the Pennsylvania State Anti-Slavery Society, by Its Executive Committee, October 15, 1850. With the Proceedings of the Annual Meeting. Philadelphia, Anti-Slavery Office, 1850. 56 p.

Pennsylvania State Anti-Slavery Society. Fifteenth Annual Report, Presented to the Pennsylvania Anti-Slavery Society, by Its Executive Committee,

October 25, 1852. With the Proceedings of the Annual Meeting. Philadelphia, Anti-Slavery Office, 1852. 57 p.

Pennsylvania State Anti-Slavery Society. Narrative of Facts in the Case of Passmore Williamson. Philadelphia, Merrihew & Thompson, 1855. 24 p.

Pennsylvania State Legislature. Report of the Committee on the Judiciary in Relation to the Repeal of an Act to Prevent Kidnapping, to Preserve the Peace, Etc. Mr. Porter, Chairman. Harrisburgh, J. M. G. Lescure, 1850. 9 p.

Pennsylvania State Legislature. Report of the Committee Appointed in the Senate of Pennsylvania, to Investigate the Cause of an Increased Number of Slaves Being Returned for That Commonwealth, by the Census of 1830, over That of 1820. Read in Senate, February 25, 1833. Samuel Breck, Chairman. Harrisburg, Henry Welsh, 1833. 7 p.

Pennsylvania State Legislature. Report of the Committee on the Judiciary, Relative to the Abolition of Slavery in the District of Columbia and in Relation to the Colored Population of This Country. Mr. Smith, of Franklin, Chairman. Read in the House of Representatives, June 24, 1839. Harrisburg, Boas & Coplan, 1839. 14 p.

Pennsylvania State Legislature. Resolutions Relative to Preventing the Introduction of Slavery into New States. [Harrisburg, 1819.]

Pennsylvania Statutes. An Act of the Legislature of Pennsylvania for the Gradual Abolition of Slavery. Passed March 1st, 1780. [Philadelphia, 1780.]

Pennsylvania Statutes. An Act to Explain and Amend an Act, Entitled, "An Act for the Gradual Abolition of Slavery"; Passed March 8, 1788. Philadelphia, T. Bradford, 1788. Broadside 32 × 19.2 cm.

Pennsylvania Statutes. An Act for the Entire Abolition of Slavery in Pennsylvania. [Philadelphia, 1826.] 4 p.

Pennsylvanian, A. Considerations on the Impropriety and Inexpediency of Renewing the Missouri Question. By a Pennsylvanian. Philadelphia, M. Carey & Son, 1820. 88 p.

Peoples Advocate. Weekly. Concord, N. H. August 12, 1841–1844. Edited by A. St. Clair.

[Perkins, Justin]. American Slavery in Connection with American Christianity. New York, H. B. Knight, 1854. 60 p.

Perkins, Justin. Our Country's Sin. A Sermon Preached to the Members and Families of the Nestorian Mission, at Oroomiah, Persia, July 3, 1853. New York, H. B. Knight, 1854. 24 p.
Same. Boston, Jewett, 1854. 40 p. [Author a missionary of A.B.C.F.M.]

Perry, John Jasiel. Freedom National—Slavery Sectional. Speech of Hon. John J. Perry, of Maine, on the Comparative Nationality and Sectionalism of the Republican and Democratic Parties. In the House of Representatives, May 1, 1856, in Committee of the Whole on the State of the Union. Washington, D. C., Buell & Blanchard, 1856. 15 p.

Perry, John Jasiel. Posting the Books Between the North and the South. Speech of Hon. John J. Perry, of Maine. Delivered in the U. S. House of Representatives, March 7, 1860. [Washington, D. C., Buell & Blanchard, 1860.] 16 p.

Peterson, Henry. An Address Delivered Before the Junior Anti-Slavery Society of the City and County of Philadelphia, December 23, 1836. Philadelphia, Merrihew and Gunn, 1837. 12 p.

Peterson, Henry. Address on American Slavery, Delivered Before the Semi-Annual Meeting of the Junior Anti-Slavery Society of Philadelphia, July 4, 1838. Philadelphia, the Society, 1838. 28 p.

Petition of People Called Quakers. To the Commons of Great Britain, in Parliament Assembled. The Petition of the People Called Quakers [Against Slavery in America]. Philadelphia, 1784. 3 p.

Phelps, Amos Augustus. Lectures on Slavery and Its Remedy. Boston, New England Anti-Slavery Society, 1834. 284 p.

Phelps, Amos Augustus. Letters to Prof. Stowe and Dr. Bacon on God's Real Method with Great Social Wrongs in Which the Bible Is Vindicated from Grossly Erroneous Interpretations. New York, American & Foreign Anti-Slavery Society, 1848. 168 p.

Philadelphia Anti-Slavery Convention, 1833. Proceedings of the Anti-Slavery Convention, Assembled at Philadelphia, December 4, 5, and 6, 1833. New York, Dorr & Butterfield, 1833. 28 p.

Philadelphia Anti-Slavery Society. Constitution of the Philadelphia Anti-Slavery Society. Instituted Fourth Month 30th, 1834. Philadelphia, T. Town, 1834. 12 p.

Philadelphia Anti-Slavery Society. Address of the Members of the Philadelphia Anti-Slavery Society to Their Fellow Citizens. Philadelphia, W. P. Gibbons, 1835. 24 p.

Philadelphia Anti-Slavery Society. First Annual Report of the Board of Managers of the Philadelphia Anti-Slavery Society, Read and Accepted at the Annual Meeting of the Society, July 4th, 1835. Philadelphia, Printed by Order of the Society, 1835. 16 p.

Philadelphia Association for the Moral and Mental Improvement of the People of Colour. Constitution and By-Laws of the Philadelphia Association for the Moral and Mental Improvement of the People of Colour. Philadelphia, 1835. 17 p.

Philadelphia Convention of the People of Colour. Minutes and Proceedings of the First Annual Convention of the People of Colour. Held by Adjournments in the City of Philadelphia, from the Sixth to the Eleventh of June, Inclusive, 1831. Philadelphia, Published by Order of the Committee of Arrangements, 1831. 16 p.

Philadelphia Female Anti-Slavery Society. Fifth Annual Report of the Philadelphia Female Anti-Slavery Society. January 10, 1839. Philadelphia, Merrihew and Thompson, 1839. 15 p. [Reports thereafter do not vary in title from year to year.]

Philadelphia Female Anti-Slavery Society. Address of the Female Anti-Slavery Society of Philadelphia, to the Women of Pennsylvania. With the Form of a Petition to the Congress of the U. States. Philadelphia, Merrihew and Gunn, 1836. 32 p.

Philadelphia Female Anti-Slavery Society. Tracts. No. 1. Extracts from the American Slave Code. [Philadelphia, 1829.] 4 p.

Philadelphia Society for Promoting the Abolition of Slavery. Remarks on the Slave Trade. [Reprint of the Plan of an African Slave Ship, with Extracts from a Pamphlet by a Society at Plymouth, Great Britain]. Printed and Sold by Samuel Wood. [Philadelphia, n.d.] Broadside. 21 × 33½ cm.

Philadelphia Union Meeting. The Union—"It Must and Shall Be Preserved!" Fanaticism Rebuked, in the Interchange of Patriotic Sentiments at the Philadelphia Union Meeting, December 7, 1859. Philadelphia, 1859. 59 p.

A Philadelphian, pseud. See Robert Walsh.

Philanthropist. Weekly. Mount Pleasant, O. August 29, 1817 to 1820. Edited by Charles Osborn.

Philanthropist. Weekly. New Richmond & Cincinnati. January 1, 1836–October 11, 1843. Edited by James G. Birney to September, 1837. Edited by Gamaliel Bailey, May, 1836–1847. Organ of Ohio Anti-Slavery Society. Published at New Richmond, January 1–April 8, 1836. Continued as Cincinnati Weekly Herald and Philanthropist after 1843.

Philanthropos, pseud. See David Rice.

Philleo, Mrs. Prudence Crandall vs. the State of Connecticut. Report of the Arguments of Council in the Case of Prudence Crandall, Plaintiff in Error vs. State of Connecticut, Before the Supreme Court of Errors, at Their Session at Brooklyn, July Term, 1834; by a Member of the Bar. Boston, Garrison and Knapp, 1834. 34 p.

Philleo, Mrs. Prudence Crandall vs. the State of Connecticut. Report of the Trial of Miss Prudence Crandall Before the County Court for Windham County, August Term, 1833, on an Information Charging Her with Teaching Colored Persons not Inhabitants of This State. Brooklyn, 1833. 22 p.

[Phillips, Samuel R.]. Nebraska; a Poem, Personal and Political. Boston, J. P. Jewett & Co., 1854. 42 p.

Phillips, Stephen Clarendon. An Address on the Annexation of Texas, and the Aspect of Slavery in the United States, in Connection Therewith; Delivered in Boston, Nov. 14 and 18, 1845. Boston, W. Crosby & H. P. Nichols, 1845. 56 p.

[Phillips, Stephen Clarendon]. An Appeal to the People of Massachusetts, on the Texas Question. Boston, Charles C. Little and James Brown, 1844. 20 p.

Phillips, Wendell. Argument of Wendell Phillips, Esq., Against the Repeal of the Personal Liberty Law, Before the Committee of the [Massachusetts] Legislature, Tuesday, January 29, 1861. Boston, R. F. Wallcut, 1861. 24 p.

Phillips, Wendell. Argument of Wendell Phillips, Esq., Before the Committee on Federal Relations (of the Massachusetts Legislature) in Support of the Petitions for the Removal of Edward Greeley Loring, from the Office of the Judge of Probate, February 20, 1855. Boston, J. B. Yerrington & Son, 1855. 43 p.

[Phillips, Wendell]. Can Abolitionists Vote or Take Office under the United States Constitution? Cincinnati, Sparhawk & Lytle, 1845. 36 p.

Phillips, Wendell, ed. The Constitution a Pro-Slavery Compact; or, Extracts from the Madison Papers, Etc. Selected by Wendell Phillips. Third Edition, Enlarged. New York, American Anti-Slavery Society, 1856. 208 p.

Phillips, Wendell. Disunion: Two Discourses at Music Hall, on January 20th, and February 17th, 1861. Boston, Robert F. Wallcut, 1861. 46 p.

Phillips, Wendell. The Lesson of the Hour. Lecture of Wendell Phillips Delivered at Brooklyn, N. Y., Tuesday Evening, November, 1859. [n.p., 1859,] 24 p.

Phillips, Wendell. No Slave-Hunting in the Old Bay State. Speech of Wendell Phillips, Esq., Before the Committee of Federal Relations, in Support of the Petitions Asking for a Law to Prevent the Recapture of Fugitive Slaves in the Hall of the House of Representatives, Thursday, February 17, 1859. J. M. W. Yerrington. Boston, R. F. Wallcut, 1859. 31 p.

Phillips, Wendell. Note [Relating to Dr. Lyman Beecher as President of Lane Seminary and resolutions of the Trustees forbidding discussions of slavery, Dated March 4, 1853]. 4 p.

Phillips, Wendell. Review of Lysander Spooner's Essay on the Unconstitutionality of Slavery. Reprinted from the "Anti-Slavery Standard," with Additions. Boston, Andrews & Prentiss, 1847. 95 p.

Phillips, Wendell. Review of Webster's Speech on Slavery. Boston, American A. S. Society, 1850. 44 p.

Phillips, Wendell. Speech in Vindication of the

Course Pursued by the American Abolitionists; Delivered in Boston, on Thursday, January 27, 1853, at the Twenty-First Annual Meeting of the Massachusetts Anti-Slavery Society. London, 1853. 36 p.

Phillips, Wendell. Speech of Wendell Phillips, at the Melodeon, Thursday Evening, Jan. 27, 1853. [Boston, American Anti-Slavery Society, 1853.] 32 p.

Phillips, Wendell. Speech of Wendell Phillips, Esq., at the Worcester Disunion Convention, Jan. 15, 1857. [Boston, American Anti-Slavery Society, 1857.] 16 p.

Phillips, Wendell. Speeches Before the Massachusetts Anti-Slavery Society, January, 1852. Boston, Robert F. Wallcut, 1852. 24 p.

Pickard, Mrs. Kate E. R. The Kidnapped and the Ransomed. Being the Personal Recollections of Peter Still and His Wife "Vina," after Forty Years of Slavery. By Mrs. Kate E. R. Pickard, with an Introduction, by Rev. Samuel J. May; and an Appendix by William H. Furness, D.D. Syracuse, W. T. Hamilton [Etc.], 1856. 409 p.
Same. New York, Muller, Orton, & Mulligan, 1856. 400 p.
Same. Third Edition. Syracuse, Wm. T. Hamilton [etc.], 1856. 409 p.

Pierpont, John. The Anti-Slavery Poems of John Pierpont. Boston, Oliver Johnson, 1843. 64 p.

Pierpont, John. A Discourse on the Covenant with Judas, Preached in Hollis Street Church, Nov. 6, 1842. Boston, C. C. Little & J. Brown, 1842. 39 p.

Pierpont, John. A Discourse Occasioned by the Death of William Ellery Channing. Preached in Hollis Street Church, Oct. 16, 1843. Boston, Oliver Johnson, 1842. 23 p.

Pierpont, John. Moral Rule of Political Action. A Discourse Delivered in Hollis Street Church, Sunday, January 27, 1839. Boston, James Munroe & Co., 1839. 24 p.

Pierpont, John. National Humiliation. A Sermon, Preached in Hollis Street Church, Fast Day Morning, April 2, 1840. Boston, Samuel N. Dickinson, 1840. 16 p.

Pierpont, John. Proceedings of a Meeting of Friends of Rev. John Pierpont, and His Reply to the Charges of the Committee, of Hollis Street Society, October 26th, 1839. Boston, S. N. Dickinson, 1839. 48 p.

Pierpont, Rev. John. Reply of the Friends of Rev. John Pierpont, to a Proposal for Dissolving the Pastoral Connexion between Him and the Society in Hollis Street. Boston, [Charles C. Little and James Brown] 1840. 8 p.

Pierson, Mrs. Emily Catharine. Jamie Parker, the Fugitive. Hartford, Brockett, Fuller, and Co., 1851. 192 p.

Pillsbury, Parker. The Church as It Is: or, the Forlorn Hope of Slavery. Second Edition, Revised and Improved. Boston, Bela Marsh, 1847. 90 p.

Pinkney, William. Speech of William Pinkney, Esq., in the House of Delegates of Maryland, at Their Session in November, 1789. Philadelphia, Joseph Crukshank, 1790. 22 p.

Pittsburgh Female Anti-Slavery Society. Review by a Pittsburger, of a Pamphlet, Entitled, "View of the Subject of Slavery," Contained in the Biblical Repertory for April, 1836, in Which the Scriptural Argument, It Is Believed, Is Very Clearly and Justly Exhibited. Pittsburgh, Female Anti-Slavery Society, 1836. 21 p.

The Planter's Victim; or, Incidents of American Slavery, with Illustrations. Philadelphia, Wm. White Smith, 1855. 365 p.

Platt, Smith H. The Martyrs, and the Fugitive; or, A Narrative of the Captivity, Sufferings, and Death of an African Family, and the Slavery and Escape of Their Son. New York, D. Fanshaw, 1859. 95 p.

Plumer, William. Speech of Mr. Plumer, of New Hampshire, on the Missouri Question, Delivered in the House of Representatives of the United States, February 21, 1820. [Washington? 1820.] 42 p.

[Plumer, William]. Cincinnatus. Freedom's Defence; or, A Candid Examination of Mr. Calhoun's Report on the Freedom of the Press, Made to the Senate of the United States, Feb. 4, 1836. Worcester, Dorr, Howland & Co., 1836. 24 p.

A Poetical Epistle to the Enslaved Africans, in the Character of an Ancient Negro, Born a Slave in Pennsylvania; but Liberated Some Years Since, and Instructed in Useful Learning, and the Great Truths of Christianity. With a Brief Historical Introduction, and Biographical Notices of Some of the Earliest Advocates for That Oppressed Class of Our Fellow Creatures. Philadelphia, Joseph Crukshank, 1790. 24 p.

Politics and the Pulpit: A Series of Articles Which Appeared in the Journal of Commerce and in the Independent, During the Year 1850. To Which Is Added an Article from the Independent of Feb. 21, 1850, Entitled "Shall We Compromise!" New York, William Harned, 1851. 63 p.

Porter, Noah. Civil Liberty. A Sermon Preached in Farmington, Connecticut, July 13, 1856. New York, Pudney & Russell, 1856. 22 p.

Porter, Noah. Two Sermons on Church Communion and Excommunication, with a Particular View to the Case of Slaveholders, in the Church. Hartford, Case, Tiffany and Co., 1853. 31 p.

Potter, Alonzo. Christian Philanthropy. A Discourse, Preached in St. George's Church, Schenectady, Sunday Evening, January 13, 1833, Before the

African School Society. Schenectady, [N. Y.], S. S. Riggs, 1833. 16 p.

The Prayer of One Hundred-Thousand. [Petition for emancipation of slaves, presented in Senate, Feb. 9th, 1863, by Charles Sumner.] 2 p.

Prentiss, Samuel. Speech of the Hon. Samuel Prentiss, of Vermont, upon the Question of Reception of the Vermont Resolutions, on the Subject of the Admission of Texas, the Domestic Slave Trade, and Slavery in the District of Columbia. Delivered in the Senate U. S., January 16, 1838. Washington, D. C., Gales and Seaton, 1838. 10 p.

Presbyterian Church, Connecticut. Minority Report, of a Committee of the General Association of Connecticut, on the Sin of Slavery. Presented, June, 1849, at the Meeting of the Association, at Salisbury, Conn. [1849.] 20 p.

Presbyterian Church, General Assembly. Testimony on Slavery. [Philadelphia? 1857.] 16 p.

Presbyterian Church, Synod of Cincinnati. An Address to the Churches, on the Subject of Slavery. Georgetown, Ohio, August 5, 1831. [Georgetown?] D. Ammen & Co. [1831]. 24 p.

Presbyterian Church, Synod of Indiana. "To the General Assembly of the Presbyterian Church in the United States, on the Subject of African Slavery, from the Synod of Indiana, Adopted at Their Meeting at Salem, Indiana, October, 1827" in the Western Luminary, Lexington, Kentucky, Wednesday, March 19, 1828. No. 38, Vol. IV. Thomas T. Skillman, Editor.

Presbyterian Church, Synod of Kentucky. An Address to the Presbyterians of Kentucky, Proposing a Plan for the Instruction and Emancipation of Their Slaves by a Committee of the Synod of Kentucky. Cincinnati, Taylor & Tracy, 1835. 64 p.

Presbyterian Church, Synod of Kentucky. An Address to the Presbyterians of Kentucky, Proposing a Plan for the Instruction and Emancipation of Their Slaves. By a Committee of the Synod of Kentucky. [Signed:] John Brown, Chairman; John C. Young, Secretary. Newburyport, Charles Whipple, 1836. 36 p.

Same. With Constitution of American Anti-Slavery Society. New York, 1838. 38 p.

Priestley, Joseph. A Sermon on the Subject of the Slave Trade. Delivered to a Society of Protestant Dissenters, at the New Meeting, in Birmingham, and Published at Their Request. Birmingham, Pearson and Rollason, 1788. 40 p.

Prigg, Edward, Plaintiff in Error. Report of the Case of Edward Prigg against the Commonwealth of Pennsylvania. Argued and Adjudged in the Supreme Court of the United States, at January Term, 1842. In Which It Was Decided That All the Laws of the Several States Relative to Fugitive Slaves Are Unconstitutional and Void; and That Congress Have the Exclusive Power of Legislation on the Subject of Fugitive Slaves Escaping into Other States. By Richard Peters, Reporter of the Decisions of the Supreme Court of the United States. Philadelphia, Stereotyped by L. Johnson, 1842. 140 p.

Prime, Nathaniel Scudder. The Year of Jubilee; but Not to Africans: A Discourse, Delivered July 4, 1825, Being the 49th Anniversary of American Independence. Salem, N. Y., Dodd & Stevenson, 1825. 24 p.

Prindle, Cyrus. Slavery Illegal. A Sermon, on the Occasion of the Annual Fast, April 12, 1850. Delivered in the Wesleyan Methodist Church, Shelburne, Vt. Burlington, Tuttle & Stacy, 1850. 28 p.

Providence Baptist Anti-Slavery Society. Constitution of the Baptist Anti-Slavery Society, Providence; Formed December 12, 1839; with an Address to the First, Second, Third, and Fourth Baptist Churches. Providence, H. H. Brown, 1840. 17 p.

Providence Anti-Slavery Society. The Report and Proceedings of the First Annual Meeting of the Providence Anti-Slavery Society. With a Brief Exposition of the Principles and Purposes of the Abolitionists. Providence, H. H. Brown, 1833. 16 p.

Providence Ladies Anti-Slavery Society. Liberty Chimes. Providence, 1845. 148 p.

Providence Public Meeting, 1854. Proceedings of a Public Meeting of the Citizens of Providence, Held in the Beneficent Congregational Church, March 7, 1854, to Protest Against Slavery in Nebraska; with the Addresses of the Speakers. Providence, Knowles, Anthony & Co., 1854. 32 p.

Providence Society for Abolishing the Slave-Trade. Constitution of the Providence Society for Abolishing the Slave Trade, with Several Acts of the Legislatures of the States of Massachusetts, Connecticut, and Rhode Island for That Purpose. Providence, John Carter, 1789. 19 p.

Pullen, William H. The Blast of a Trumpet in Zion, Calling upon Every Son and Daughter of Wesley, in Great Britain and Ireland, to Aid Their Brethren in America in Purifying Their American Zion from Slavery. By William H. Pullen. By Authority of the Anti-Slavery Societies of Great Britain and Ireland. London, Webb, Millington, & Co. [Etc.], 1860. 48 p.

Puritan, A. The Abrogation of the Seventh Commandment, by the American Churches. New York, D. Ruggles, 1835. 23 p.

Purvis, Robert. A Tribute to the Memory of Thomas Shipley, the Philanthropist. By Robert Purvis. Delivered at St. Thomas' Church, Nov. 23d, 1836. Published by Request. Philadelphia, Merrihew and Gunn, 1836. 18 p.

[Purvis, Robert]. Appeal of Forty Thousand Citizens,

Threatened with Disfranchisement, to the People of Pennsylvania. Philadelphia, Merrihew and Gunn, 1838. 18 p.

Putnam, George. God and Our Country. A Discourse Delivered in the First Congregational Church in Roxbury, on Fast Day, April 8, 1847. Boston, Wm. Crosby and H. P. Nichols, 1847. 29 p.

Putnam, George. Our Political Idolatry. A Discourse Delivered in the First Church in Roxbury, on Fast Day, April 6, 1843. Boston, William Crosby and Co., 1843. 16 p.

Putnam, George. The Signs of the Times. A Sermon Preached Sunday, March 6, 1836. Boston, Charles J. Hindee, 1836. 24 p.

Putnam, John Milton. An Address, Delivered at Concord, N. H., Dec. 25, 1835, Before the Female Anti-Slavery Society of That Place. Concord, N. H., Elbridge G. Chase, 1836. 15 p.

Quarterly Anti-Slavery Magazine. New York, N. Y. October, 1835–July, 1837. Edited by Elizur Wright from 1835 to 1837. Published by the American Anti-Slavery Society.

Quincy, Edmund. An Examination of the Charges of Mr. John Scoble & Mr. Lewis Tappan Against the American Anti-Slavery Society. Dublin, Webb and Chapman, 1852. 27 p.
Same. Second Edition. London, Whitfield, 1852. 34 p. [Quincy was corresponding secretary of the Massachusetts Anti-Slavery Society from 1844 to 1853. He was a nonresistant—Garrisonian.]

Quincy, Josiah. Address Illustrative of the Nature and Power of the Slave States, and the Duties of the Free States; Delivered at the Request of the Inhabitants of the Town of Quincy, Mass., on Thursday, June 5, 1856. Boston, Ticknor and Fields, 1856. 32 p.

Quincy, Josiah. Speech Delivered by Hon. Josiah Quincy, Senior, Before the Whig State Convention, Assembled at the Music Hall, Boston, Aug. 16, 1854. Boston, J. Wilson & Son, 1854. 8 p.

Quincy, Ill. Anti-Slavery Concert for Prayer, 1842. Narrative of Facts, Respecting Alanson Work, Jas. E. Burr & Geo. Thompson, Prisoners in the Missouri Penitentiary, for the Alleged Crime of Negro Stealing. Prepared by a Committee. Quincy, Ill., Quincy Whig Office, 1842. 37 p.

Radical Political Abolitionists. Proceedings of the Convention of Radical Political Abolitionists, Held at Syracuse, N. Y., June 26th, 27th, and 28th, 1855. New York, Central Abolition Board, 1855. 68 p.
Same. New York, Central Abolition Board, 1856. 68 p.

Ramsay, James. An Address on the Proposed Bill for the Abolition of the Slave Trade; Humbly Submitted to the Consideration of the Legislature. London, James Phillips, 1788. 41 p.

Ramsay, James. An Essay on the Treatment and Conversion of African Slaves in the British Sugar Colonies. London, James Phillips, 1784. 298 p.

Ramsay, James. Examination of the Rev. Mr. Harris' Scriptural Researches on the Licitness of the Slave-Trade, by the Rev. James Ramsay. London, James Phillips, 1788. 29 p.

[Ramsay, James]. An Inquiry into the Effects of Putting a Stop to the African Slave Trade, and of Granting Liberty to the Slaves in the British Sugar Colonies. By the Author of the Essay on the Treatment and Conversion of African Slaves in the British Sugar Colonies. London, James Phillips, 1784. 44 p.

Ramsay, James. Objections to the Abolition of the Slave Trade, with Answers. To Which Is Prefixed, Strictures on a Late Publication, Entitled "Considerations on the Emancipation of Negroes, and the Abolition of the Slave Trade by a West India Planter." London, James Phillips, 1788. 60 p.

Ramsay, James. A Reply to the Personal Invectives and Objections Contained in Two Answers, Published by Certain Anonymous Persons, to an Essay on the Treatment and Conversion of African Slaves, in the British Colonies, by James Ramsay, M.A., Vicar of Teston. London, James Phillips, 1785.

Rand, Asa. The Slave-Catcher Caught in the Meshes of Eternal Law. Cleveland, Smead and Cowles, 1852. 42 p.

Randall, Robert. Speech of Robert E. Randall, of Philadelphia, on the Laws of the State Relative to Fugitive Slaves, Delivered in the House of Representatives of Pennsylvania, January 16, 1861. [Philadelphia], Hamilton, 1861. 14 p.

Randolph, Peter. Sketches of Slave Life; or, Illustrations of the 'Peculiar Institution.' Second Edition, Boston, the Author, 1855. 82 p.

Randolph, Thomas Jefferson. The Speech of Thomas J. Randolph, (of Albemarle,) in the House of Delegates of Virginia, on the Abolition of Slavery: Delivered Saturday, Jan. 21, 1832. Second Edition, Richmond, T. W. White, 1832. 22 p.

Randolph County, Ill., Citizens. Memorial of Sundry Inhabitants of the Counties of Randolph and St. Clair, in the Indiana Territory. January 17, 1806. Referred to the Committee Appointed the 19th Ultimo, on a Letter from William Henry Harrison, Governor of the Indiana Territory. Washington, A. & G. Way, 1806. 12 p.

Rankin, John. An Address to the Churches in Relation to Slavery; Delivered at the First Anniversary of the Ohio State Anti-Slavery Society, with a Few Introductory Remarks by a Gentleman of the Bar. Medina [Ohio], Anti-Slavery Office, 1836. 8 p.

Rankin, John. Letters on American Slavery, Addressed to Mr. Thomas Rankin, Merchant at Middlebrook, Augusta County, Virginia. Boston, Garrison & Knapp, 1833. 118 p.

Same. Second Edition, Newburyport, Charles Whipple, 1837. 118 p.

Same. Third Edition, Newburyport, Charles Whipple, 1836. 118 p.

Same. Fifth Edition, Boston, I. Knapp, 1838. 109 p.

Rankin, John. The Soldier, the Battle, and the Victory; Being a Brief Account of the Work of Rev. John Rankin in the Anti-Slavery Cause; by the Author of Life and Writings of Samuel Crothers, Etc. Cincinnati, Western Tract & Book Society [1852]. 120 p.

Rantoul, Robert. The Fugitive Slave Law. Speech of Hon. Robert Rantoul, Jr., of Beverly, Mass., Delivered Before the Grand Mass Convention of the Democratic Voters of the Second Congressional District of Massachusetts, Holden at Lynn, Thursday, April 3, 1851. [Lynn? Mass., 1851.] 15 p.

Rantoul, Robert, Jr. Memoirs, Speeches and Writings, Edited by Luther Hamilton. Boston, J. P. Jewett & Co., 1854. 864 p.

Rantoul, Robert. Speech of Mr. Rantoul, of Massachusetts, on the Constitutionality of the Fugitive Slave Law, Delivered in the House of Representatives, June 11, 1852. [Washington, D. C.] Congressional Globe Office [1852]. 8 p.

Read, John M[eredith]. Speech of John M. Read of Pennsylvania at the Democratic Town Meeting in Favor of the Union and California. Delivered in the Hall of the Chinese Museum, Philadelphia, on Wednesday, March 13, 1850. 11 p.

Read, John Meredith. Speech of Hon. John M. Read, on the Power of Congress over the Territories, and in Favor of Free Kansas, Free White Labor, and of Fremont and Dayton. Delivered on Tuesday Evening, September 30, 1856, at Philadelphia. Philadelphia, C. Sherman & Son, 1856. 46 p.

Reeder, Robert S. A Letter from Robert S. Reeder, Esq., to Dr. Stouton W. Dent, on the Colored Population of Maryland, and Slavery; and a Speech on the Proposition to Call a Convention, by a Single Act of the Legislature, to Change the Constitution, at December Session, 1845. Port Tobacco [Md.], E. Wells, 1859. 58 p.

Reeder, Robert S. Reports, Speeches, and Fragmentary Reflections on the Colored Population of Maryland, and Slavery. Washington, Polkinhorn's Steam Job Office, 1857. 60 p.

Register of Trades of the Colored People in the City of Philadelphia, and Districts. Philadelphia, Merrihew & Gunn, 1838. 8 p.

Reid, James. King Slavery's Council; or, The Midnight Conclave: A Poem, by James Reid. Troy, Daily Whig Office, 1844. 58 p.

The *Reign* of Terror in Kansas: As Encouraged by President Pierce, and Carried Out by the Southern Slave Power: By Which Men Have Been Murdered and Scalped! Women Dragged from the Homes and Violated! Printing Offices and Private Houses Burned! Ministers of the Gospel Tarred and Feathered! Citizens Robbed and Driven from Their Homes! And Other Enormities Inflicted on Free Settlers by Border Ruffians. As Related by Eye Witnesses of the Events. Boston, C. W. Briggs, 1856. 34 p.

Religious Anti-Slavery Convention. The Declaration and Pledge Against Slavery, Adopted by the Religious Anti-Slavery Convention, Held at Marlboro Chapel, Boston, February 26, 1846. Boston, Devereaux & Seaman, 1846. 8 p.

Remsen, Cornelius. Slavery or Freedom: A Strange Matter, Truly! Letters from Remsen to Rynders. Pittston, Pa., Gazette and Journal Office, 1856. 24 p.

Report of the Proceedings of the Great Anti-Slavery Meeting Held in the Rev. Mr. Cairnes Church, on Wednesday, 23d September, 1846, Including the Speeches of Wm. Lloyd Garrison, Esq., and Frederick Douglass, Esq. Taken in Short Hand by Cincinnatus. [Boston, Alex Gardner, 1846.]

Requited Labor Convention, Philadelphia, 1838. Minutes of the Proceedings of the Requited Labor Convention, Held in Philadelphia, on the 17th and 18th of the Fifth Month, and by Adjournment on the 5th and 6th of the Ninth Month, 1838. Philadelphia, Merrihew and Gunn, 1838. 36 p. [Lewis C. Gunn: Address to Abolitionists, pages 22–36.]

Resolutions and Remonstrances of the People of Colour [of Philadelphia] Against Colonization on the Coast of Africa. [Philadelphia] 1818. 8 p.

A *Review* of the Official Apologies of the American Tract Society, for Its Silence on the Subject of Slavery. From the New York Daily Tribune. New York, American Abolition Society, 1856. 16 p.

A *Review* of the Report of a Select Committee of the House of Commons, on the State of the West India Colonies, Ordered to Be Printed, 13th April, 1832; or, The Interests of the Country and the Prosperity of the West India Planters Mutually Secured by the Immediate Abolition of Slavery. Liverpool, Egerton Smith and Co., 1833. 30 p.

[Rhoads, Samuel]. Considerations on the Use of the Productions of Slavery, Especially Addressed to the Religious Society of Friends Within the Limits of Philadelphia Yearly Meeting. Philadelphia, Merrihew and Thompson, 1844. 36 p.

Same. Second Edition. Philadelphia, Merrihew and Thompson, 1845. 36 p.

Rhode Island and Massachusetts Christian Conference, New Bedford. A Protest Against American Slavery, by One Hundred and Seventy-Three Unitarian Ministers. Boston, B. H. Greene, 1845. 20 p.

Rhode Island State Anti-Slavery Society. Proceedings of the Rhode-Island Anti-Slavery Convention, Held in Providence, on the 2d, 3d and 4th of February, 1836. Providence, H. H. Brown, 1836. 88 p.

Rhode Island State Legislature. Select Committee to Whom Were Referred the Resolutions of Mr. Wells, on Slavery. Mr. Whipple's Report, and Mr. Otis' Letter. Boston, Cassady and March, 1839. 30 p.

Rhode Island State Legislature. Reports of the Select Committee to Whom Were Referred the Resolutions of Mr. Wells, Touching Certain Resolutions of the House of Representatives of the U. States Relating to Petitions for the Abolition of Slavery, &c., &c.; Also the Petitions of Sundry Citizens of This State, Relative to the Right to Petition. [Providence, Printed by Order of the House of Representatives, 1839.] 8 p.

[Rice, David], Philanthropos, pseud. Slavery Inconsistent with Justice and Good Policy. Lexington, Ky., J. Bradford, 1792. 32 p.

Rice, Rev. David. Slavery Inconsistent with Justice and Good Policy; Proved by a Speech Delivered in the Convention at Danville, Kentucky. Philadelphia, Printed, 1792. London, Reprinted, and Sold by M. Gurney, 1793. 24 p.

Same. New York, Isaac Collins and Son, 1804. 36 p.

Same. New York, Samuel Wood, 1812. 13 p.

Richardson, Richard Higgins. "Wickedness in High Places." A Discourse Occasioned by the Bill for the Government of Kanzas and Nebraska, Passed by the Senate of the United States, March 4, 1854. Delivered in the North Presbyterian Church, of Chicago, March 5, 1854. Chicago, S. C. Griggs & Co., 1851. 43 p.

The *Right* of Petition. Remarks of Messrs. Seward, Hale, and Chase, with a Sketch of the Debate in the Senate on Various Petitions and Other Matters Connected with the Subject of Slavery. Washington, Buell & Blanchard, 1850. 15 p.

Right of Petition. New England Clergymen. Remarks of Messrs. Everett, Mason, Pettit, Douglas, Butler, Seward, Houston, Adams, Badger, on the Memorial from Some 3050 Clergymen of All Denominations and Sects in the Different States of New England, Remonstrating Against the Passage of the Nebraska Bill, Senate of the United States, March 14, 1854. Washington, D. C., Buell & Blanchard, 1854. 16 p.

The *Rights* of the Free States Subverted; or, An Enumeration of Some of the Most Prominent Instances in Which the Federal Constitution Has Been Violated by Our National Government, for the Benefit of Slavery. By a Member of Congress. [Washington, D. C., 1845.] 16 p.

Ritter, George. A Speech, Delivered on the 13th. January, 1802, Before the Society Called the Proficuous Judicatory; Concerning the Advantages That Would Be Derived from a Total Abolition of Slavery. Philadelphia, Printed for the Author, 1802. 20 p.

Roberts, William L. The Higher Law; or, The Law of the Most High; A Discourse, Delivered at the Baptist Church, in Sterling Centre, Wednesday Evening, Jan. 22d, 1851. Auburn, T. W. Brown, 1851. 31 p.

Robertson, D. F. National Destiny and Our Country. New York, E. French, 1851.

Robinson, John. The Testimony and Practice of the Presbyterian Church in Reference to American Slavery; with an Appendix, Containing the Position of the General Assembly (New School), Free Presbyterian Church, Reformed Presbyterian, Associate, Associate Reformed, Baptist, Protestant Episcopal, and Methodist Episcopal Churches. Cincinnati, John D. Thorpe, 1852. 256 p.

Robinson, Robert. Slavery Inconsistent with the Spirit of Christianity. A Sermon Preached at Cambridge, on Sunday, Feb. 10, 1788. Cambridge, J. Archdeacon, Printer to the University, 1788. 39 p.

Rogers, Charles. Speech of Mr. Charles Rogers of New York, on the Right of Petition, Delivered in the House of Representatives, February 23, 1844. Washington, [D. C.] J. & S. Gideon, 1844. 16 p.

[Rogers, Edward Coit]. Letters on Slavery, Addressed to the Pro-Slaverymen of America; Showing Its Illegality in All Ages and Nations; Its Destructive War upon Society and Government, Morals and Religions. By O. S. Freeman, [pseud.] Boston, Bela Marsh, 1855. 108 p.

Rogers, Nathaniel Peabody. An Address Delivered Before the Concord Female Anti-Slavery Society, at Its Annual Meeting, 25 Dec. 1837. By Nathaniel P. Rogers. To Which Is Added, the Third Annual Report of Said Society. Concord, N. H., W. White, 1838. 32 p.

Rogers, Nathaniel Peabody. A Collection from the Newspaper Writings of Nathaniel Peabody Rogers. Concord [N. H.], J. R. French, 1847. 380 p.

Rogers, Nathaniel Peabody. A Collection from the

Miscellaneous Writings of Nathaniel Peabody Rogers. Second Edition. Manchester, N. H., W. H. Fisk [Etc., Etc.], 1849. 380 p.

Root, David. The Abolition Cause Eventually Triumphant. A Sermon, Published Before the Anti-Slavery Society of Haverhill, Mass., Aug. 1836. Andover, Gould & Newman, 1836. 24 p.

Root, David. A Fast Sermon on Slavery, Delivered April 2, 1835 to the Congregational Church and Society in Dover, N. H. Dover, Enquirer Office, 1835. 22 p.

Root, David. A Memorial to the Martyred Lovejoy: In a Discourse by Rev. David Root. Delivered in Dover, N. H. Published by Request. [Dover, 1837.] 16 p.

Root, David.
No. 1. A Tract for the Times and for the Churches; Being the Substance of a Discourse Delivered at South Boston, June, 1845. Boston, A. J. Wright [1845]. 16 p.

Root, Joseph Mosley. California and New Mexico. Speech of Hon. Joseph M. Root, of Ohio, in the House of Representatives, February 15, 1850. [Washington, D. C.] Congressional Globe Office [1850]. 7 p.

Roper, Moses. A Narrative of the Adventures and Escape of Moses Roper, from American Slavery; with a Preface, by the Rev. T. Price. 1st American, from the London Ed. Philadelphia, Merrihew and Gunn, 1838. 72 p.
Same. Philadelphia, Merrihew and Gunn, 1838. 89 p.
Same. Berwick-upon-Tweed, The Author, 1846. 88 p.

Roy, Joseph Edwin. Kansas—Her Struggle and Her Defence. A Discourse Preached in the Plymouth Congregational Church of Chicago, Sabbath Afternoon, June 1, 1856, by the Pastor. Chicago, Wright, Medill, Day & Co., 1856. 34 p.

Ruffner, Henry. Address to the People of West Virginia; Shewing That Slavery Is Injurious to the Public Welfare, and That It May Be Gradually Abolished Without Detriment to the Rights and Interests of Slaveholders. By a Slaveholder of West Virginia. Lexington, R. C. Noel, 1847. 40 p.

Ruggles, David. An Antidote for a Poisonous Combination Recently Prepared by a 'Citizen of New York,' Alias Dr. Reese, Entitled "An Appeal to the Reason and Religion of American Christians." New York, William Stuart, 1838. 32 p.

Ruggles, David. The "Extinguisher" Extinguished! or David M. Reese, M.D. "Used Up." By David Ruggles, a Man of Color. Together with Some Remarks upon a Late Production Entitled "An Address on Slavery and Against Immediate Emancipation with a Plan of Their Being Gradually Emancipated and Colonized in Thirty-Two Years. By Heman Howlett." New York, D. Ruggles, 1834. 48 p.

Ruggles, David. A Plea for "A Man and a Brother," Made on the 18th July, 1839, Before a Public Meeting Held at the Hall, 245 Spring Street. Also, Extracts from the Speeches of Messrs. Philip A. Bell & William P. Johnson; with Notes and Remarks. New York, Office of the Mirror of Liberty, 1839. 16 p.

Rules for the Regulation of the Society for the Relief of Free Negroes, and Others, Unlawfully Held in Bondage, Instituted in Philadelphia in the Year 1784. To Which Are Prefixed, the Acts of the General Assembly of Pennsylvania, Respecting the Gradual Abolition of Slavery. Philadelphia, Joseph Crukshank, 1784. 16 p.

[Rush, Benjamin]. An Address to the Inhabitants of the British Settlements in America, upon Slave-Keeping. New York, Hodge and Shober, 1773. 36 p.
Same: Philadelphia, J. Dunlap, 1773. 30 p.
Same: Norwich, Judah P. Spooner, 1775. 24 p.

[Rush, Benjamin]. A Vindication of the Address, to the Inhabitants of the British Settlements, on the Slavery of the Negroes in America, in Answer to a Pamphlet Entitled, "Slavery Not Forbidden by Scripture; or, A Defence of the West-India Planters from the Aspersions Thrown Out Against Them by the Author of the Address." By a Pennsylvanian. Philadelphia, Printed by J. Dunlap, 1773. 54 p.

Rushton, Edward. Expostulatory Letter to George Washington, of Mount Vernon, in Virginia, on His Continuing to Be a Proprietor of Slaves. Liverpool, Printed 1797. 24 p.
Same. Lexington, John Bradford, 1797. 16 p.

Saffin, John. A Brief and Candid Answer to a Late Printed Sheet, Entitled, The Selling of Joseph. Whereunto Is Annexed, a True and Particular Narrative by Way of Vindication of the Author's Dealing with and Prosecution of His Negro Man Servant, for His Vile and Exorbitant Behaviour Towards His Master, and His Tenant Thomas Shepard; Which Hath Been Wrongfully Represented to Their Prejudice and Defamation. Boston, 1701. 12 p.

Salem, Massachusetts, Anti-Slavery Society. Constitution of the Anti-Slavery Society of Salem and Vicinity. Salem, Massachusetts, W. & S. B. Ives, 1834. 8 p. [Society organized Jan. 27, 1834.]

[Sandiford, Ralph]. A Brief Examination of the Practice of the Times, by the Foregoing and the Present Dispensation . . . [Philadelphia] Printed for the Author [by Franklin and Meredith], 1729. 74 p.

[Sandiford, Ralph]. The Mystery of Iniquity; in a Brief Examination of the Practice of the Times, by the Foregoing and the Present Dispensations. Second Editions, with Additions. Philadelphia, Franklin and Meredith, 1730. 111 p.

Sawyer, Leicester Ambrose. A Dissertation on Servitude; Embracing an Examination of the Scripture Doctrines on the Subject, and an Inquiry into the Character and Relations of Slavery. New Haven, Durrie & Peck, 1837. 108 p.

Schurz, Carl. The Irrepressible Conflict and the Dissolution of the Union. Speech of Carl Schurz, of Wisconsin, at Verandah Hall, St. Louis, Missouri, August 1, 1860. [n.p., 1860.] 14 p.
Same. Published as: Slavery at War with the Moral Sentiment of the World. Albany, Weed, Parsons & Co., 1860. 12 p. Evening Journal, Tracts No. 11.

Scoble, John. Texas: Its Claims to Be Recognized as an Independent Power, by Great Britain; Examined in a Series of Letters. London, Harvey and Darton, 1839. 56 p.

Scott, Dred (Plaintiff in Error). A Legal Review of the Case of Dred Scott, as Decided by the Supreme Court of the United States. From the Law Reporter for June, 1857. Boston, Crosby, Nichols & Co., 1857. 62 p.

Scott, Orange. Address to the General Conference of the Methodist Episcopal Church, by the Rev. O. Scott, a Member of That Body; Presented During Its Session in Cincinnati, Ohio, May 19, 1836. To Which Is Added the Speech of the Rev. Mr. Scott, Delivered on the Floor of the General Conference, May 27th, 1836. New York, H. R. Piercy, 1836. 24 p.

Scott, Orange. The Grounds of Secession from the M.E. Church: or, Book for the Times; Being an Examination of Her Connection with Slavery, and Also of Her Form of Government; Revised and Corrected. To Which Is Added Wesley upon Slavery. New York, L. C. Mallock, 1851. 229 p. [Scott, and others, withdrew from the Methodist Church in 1841 and formed the Wesleyan Methodist Connection of America.]

Scott, Orange. The Methodist E. Church and Slavery. Containing Also the Views of the English Wesleyan Methodist Church with Regard to Slavery, and a Treatise on the Duty of Seceding from All Pro-Slavery Churches. Boston, Orange Scott, 1844. 128 p.

Scott, Orange. The Wesleyan Anti-Slavery Review, Containing an Appeal to the Methodist Episcopal Church. No. 1, 1838. Boston, David H. Ela, 1838. 156 p. [Only issue published.]

[Sedgwick, Theodore]. The Practicability of the Abolition of Slavery: A Lecture, Delivered at the Lyceum in Stockbridge, Massachusetts, February, 1831. New York, J. Seymour, 1831. 48 p.

[Sedgwick, Theodore]. Thoughts on the Proposed Annexation of Texas to the United States. First Published in the New York Evening Post under the Signature of Veto. New York, D. Fanshaw, 1844. 55 p.

Senate Chamber, U. S. A. Conclusion of Clay's Speech in Defense of Slavery. [New York, 1839.] Broadside. [Cartoon with quotations, representing Calhoun and Clay grasping hands and both trampling upon a prostrate Negro.]

Sergeant, John. Speech of Mr. Sergeant on the Missouri Question, in the House of Representatives of the United States, February 1820. [n.p., n.d.] 48 p.

[Sewall, Samuel]. The Selling of Joseph; A Memorial. Boston of the Massachusetts, Bartholomew Green and John Allen, June 24, 1700. 3 p.

[Sewall, Samuel Edmund]. Remarks on Slavery in the United States. From the Christian Examiner, Vol. IV. No. III. Boston, Bowles and Dearborn, 1827. 28 p. [Sewall, a young Boston lawyer, contributed to the financial support of the Liberator.]

Sewall, Samuel Edmund, and John A. Andrew. Argument on Behalf of Thaddeus Hyatt, Brought Before the Senate of the United States on a Charge of Contempt for Refusing to Appear as a Witness before the Harper's Ferry Committee. [n.p., n.d.] 20 p.

Seward, William H. [Albany] Evening Journal Tracts. No. 12. The National Divergence and Return. Speech of William H. Seward, at Detroit, September 4, 1860.
Destiny of the United States. Speech Delivered by William H. Seward, at St. Paul, September 18, 1860.
The West: Its Destiny and Its Duty. Speech Delivered by William H. Seward at Dubuque, September 21, 1860.

Seward, William H. California, Union, and Freedom. Speech of William H. Seward, on the Admission of California. Delivered in the Senate of the United States, March 11, 1850. [Washington, D. C.] Buell & Blanchard [1850]. 14 p.

Seward, William Henry. The Dangers of Extending Slavery, and the Contest and the Crisis. Two Speeches of William H. Seward. [Washington, D. C., The Republican Association, 1856.] 16 p.

Seward, William Henry. Freedom and Public Faith. Speech of William H. Seward, on the Abrogation of the Missouri Compromise, in the Kansas and Nebraska Bills. Senate of the United States, February 17, 1854. Washington, D. C., Buell & Blanchard, 1854. 16 p.

Seward, William H. Freedom and the Union. Speech

of William H. Seward, in the Senate of the United States, in Vindication of Freedom and the Union, Wednesday, February 29, 1860. Albany, Weed, Parsons & Co., 1860. 12 p.

Seward, William Henry. Freedom in Kansas. Speech of William H. Seward, in the Senate of the United States, March 3, 1858. Washington, D. C., Buell & Blanchard, 1858. 15 p.

Seward, William H. Immigrant White Free Labor, or Imported Black African Slave Labor. Speech of Hon. William H. Seward at Oswego, New York, November 3, 1856. Washington [D. C.], Republican Association, 1856. 7 p.

Seward, William H. In the Supreme Court of the United States. John Van Zant, ad Sectum Wharton Jones. Argument for the Defendant. Albany, Weed and Parsons, 1847. 40 p.

Seward, William Henry. The Irrepressible Conflict. A Speech by William H. Seward, Delivered at Rochester, Monday, October 25, 1858. [New York] New York Tribune [1860]. 15 p.

Seward, William H. The Slaveholding Class Dominant in the Republic. Speech of William H. Seward at Detroit, October 2, 1856. Washington, D. C., Buell & Blanchard, 1857. 14 p.
Same. Washington, D. C., The Republican Association of Washington, 1857. 14 p.

Seward, William Henry. Speech of William H. Seward, on Emancipation in the District of Columbia. Delivered in the Senate of the United States, September 11, 1850. Washington [D. C.], Buell & Blanchard, 1850. 8 p.

Seward, William Henry. Speech of the Hon. W. H. Seward, on the Admission of California, and the Subject of Slavery; Delivered in the United States Senate, on Monday, March 11, 1850. Boston, Redding & Company, 1850. 26 p.

Seward, William H. Speech of William H. Seward, for the Immediate Admission of Kansas into the Union. Senate of the United States, April 9, 1856. Washington, D. C., Buell & Blanchard, 1856. 14 p.

Seward, William Henry. Speeches of Hon. William H. Seward, and Hon. Lewis Cass, on the Subject of Slavery. Delivered in the Senate of the United States, March, 1850. New York, Stringer & Townsend, 1850. 32 p.

Seward, William H. The State of the Country. Speech of William H. Seward, in the United States Senate, February 29, 1860. [n.p., n.d.] 8 p.

Seward, William H. The Admission of Kansas. Speech of William H. Seward, of New York, Delivered in the Senate of the United States, Feb. 29, 1860. New York, Tribune Office, 1860. 14 p. Tribune Tracts No. 3.

Seward, William Henry. The Usurpations of Slavery. Speech of William H. Seward, in the Senate of the United States, on the Bill to Protect Officers of the United States. February 23, 1855. [Washington, D. C., Buell & Blanchard, 1855.] 7 p.

Sharp, Granville. An Essay on Slavery, Proving from Scripture Its Inconsistency with Humanity and Religion, in Answer to a Late Publication, Entitled, "The African Trade for Negro Slaves Shewn to Be Consistent with Principles of Humanity, and with the Laws of Revealed Religion." By Granville Sharp, Esq. With an Introductory Preface, Containing the Sentiments of the Monthly Reviewers on That Publication; and the Opinion of Several Eminent Writers on the Subject. To Which Is Added, An Elegy on the Miserable State of an African Slave, by the Celebrated and Ingenious William Shenstone, Esq. Burlington, Isaac Collins, 1773. 17–28 p.

Sharp, Granville. A Representation of the Injustice and Dangerous Tendency of Tolerating Slavery; or of Admitting the Least Claim of Private Property in the Persons of Men, in England. London, Benjamin White and Robert Horsfield, 1769. 167 p.

Sharp, Granville. Extract from a Representation of the Injustice and Dangerous Tendency of Tolerating Slavery, or Admitting the Least Claim of Private Property in the Persons of Men in England. London, 1769. Philadelphia, Reprinted by Joseph Crukshank, 1771. 44 p.

[Sharp, Granville]. Extract of a Letter to a Gentleman in Maryland; Wherein Is Demonstrated the Extreme Wickedness of Tolerating the Slave Trade, in Order to Favour the Illegalities of Our Colonies, Where the Two First Foundations of English Law (Two Witnesses of God), Are Supplanted by Opposite (and, of Course, Illegal) Ordinances, Which Occasions a Civil Death of the English Constitution, So That These Two Witnesses May Be Said to Lie Dead in All the West India Islands! Originally Printed in America. First Printed in London in 1793. Third Edition. London, J. Phillips and Son, 1797. 14 p.

Sharp, Granville. The Just Limitations of Slavery in the Laws of God Compared with the Unbounded Claims of the African Traders and British American Slaveholders. With a Copious Appendix: Containing, an Answer to the Rev. Mr. Thompson's Tract in Favour of the African Slave Trade. Letters Concerning the Lineal Descent of the Negroes from the Sons of Ham. The Spanish Regulations for the Gradual Enfranchisement of Slaves. A Proposal on the Same Principles for the Gradual Enfranchisement of Slaves in America. Reports of Determinations in the Several Courts of Law Against Slavery, Etc. London, B. White and E. and C. Dilly, 1776. 67 + 107 p.

Sharp, Granville. The Law of Liberty; or, Royal Law,

by Which All Mankind Will Certainly Be Judged! Earnestly Recommended to the Serious Consideration of All Slaveholders and Slave Dealers. London, B. White and E. and C. Dilly, 1776. 55 p.

Sharp, Granville. The Law of Passive Obedience, or Christian Submission to Personal Injuries; Wherein Is Shown, That the Several Texts of Scripture, Which Command the Entire Submission of Servants or Slaves to Their Masters Cannot Authorize the Latter to Exact an Involuntary Servitude, nor, in the Least Degree, Justify the Claims of Modern Slaveholders. London, B. White and E. and C. Dilly, 1776. 102 p.

Sharp, Granville. Letter from Granville Sharp, Esq. of London, to the Maryland Society for Promoting the Abolition of Slavery, and the Relief of Free Negroes and Others, Unlawfully Held in Bondage. Baltimore, D. Graham, L. Yundt, and W. Patton, 1793. 11 p.

Sharp, Granville. The Law of Retribution; or, A Serious Warning to Great Britain and Her Colonies, Founded on Unquestionable Examples of God's Temporal Vengeance Against Tyrants, Slave-Holders and Oppressors. London, W. Richardson, 1776. 357 p.

Sheldon, Luther Harris. The Moral Responsibility of the Citizen and Nation in Respect to the Fugitive Slave Bill. A Discourse Delivered April 10, 1851, on Occasion of the Public Fast, in the Orthodox Congregational Church, Townsend, Mass., by Rev. L. H. Sheldon. Andover, J. D. Flagg, 1851. 30 p.

Sherman, John. Lecompton Constitution. John Sherman, of Ohio, in the House of Representatives, Jan. 28, 1858, on the Admission of Kansas as a State under the Lecompton Constitution. [Washington, D. C.] Congressional Globe Office [1858]. 8 p.

Sherman, John. The Republican Party—Its History and Policy. Speech of John Sherman of Ohio at Cooper's Institute in the City of New York, April 13, 1860. 8 p.

Sherwood, Mary Martha. Dazee, or the Recaptured Negro. Newburyport, W. & J. Gilman, 1822. 48 p.

Shipherd, Jacob R. History of the Oberlin-Wellington Rescue. Comp. by Jacob R. Shipherd. With an Introduction by Prof. Henry E. Peck and Hon. Ralph Plumb. Boston, J. P. Jewett and Company; New York, Sheldon and Company [Etc., Etc.], 1859. 280 p.

Sidney, Joseph. An Oration, Commemorative of the Abolition of the Slave Trade in the United States; Delivered Before the Wilberforce Philanthropic Association, in the City of New York, on the Second of January, 1809. By Joseph Sidney. New York, J. Seymour, 1809. 20 p.

Signal of Liberty. Weekly. Ann Arbor, Mich. April 26, 1841 to February 5, 1848. Edited by Guy Beckley and Theodore Foster. Organ of the Michigan Anti-Slavery Society. Followed by Michigan Liberty Press, Published in Battle Creek, Mich.

Simpson, J. McC. The Emancipation Car, Being an Original Composition of Anti-Slavery Ballads, Composed Exclusively for the Under Ground Rail Road. Zanesville, O., Sullivan & Brown, 1874. 152 p. [Simpson was a Negro, elder in charge of the Zion Baptist Church, Zanesville, Ohio. The book is a collection of poems and songs written by him while a student at Oberlin, but not published until after the War.]

Sims, Thomas. Trial of Thomas Sims on an Issue of Personal Liberty, on the Claim of James Potter, of Georgia, Against Him, as an Alleged Fugitive from Service. Arguments of Robert Rantoul, Jr. and Charles G. Loring, with the Decision of George T. Curtis, Boston, April 7–11, 1851. Phonographic Report by Dr. James W. Stone. Boston, Wm. S. Damrell & Co., 1851. 47 p.

Sipkins, Henry. An Oration on the Abolition of the Slave Trade; Delivered in the African Church, in the City of New York, January 2, 1809. By Henry Sipkins, a Descendant of Africa. New York, J. C. Totten, 1809. 21 p.

Slade, William. Speech of Mr. Slade, of Vermont, on the Abolition of Slavery and the Slave Trade in the District of Columbia. Delivered in the House of Representatives, December 20, 1837. To Which Is Added the Intended Conclusion of the Speech, Suppressed by Resolution of the House. [Washington, D. C., 1837.] 24 p.

Slade, William. Speech of Mr. Slade, of Vermont, on the Right of Petition; the Power of Congress to Abolish Slavery and the Slave Trade in the District of Columbia; the Implied Faith of the North and South to Each Other in Forming the Constitution; and the Principles, Purposes, and Prospects of Abolition. Delivered in the House of Representatives, on the 18th and 20th of Jan., 1840. Washington [D. C.], Gales & Seaton, 1840. 45 p.

Slade, William. Speech of Mr. Slade, of Vermont, on the Subject of the Abolition of Slavery and the Slave Trade Within the District of Columbia. Delivered in the House of Representatives, December 23, 1835. [Washington] National Intelligencer Office, 1836. 11 p.

Slave Market of America. New York, American Anti-Slavery Society, 1836. Broadside, with 9 woodcuts and text.

The Slave Trade Not Declared Piracy by the Act of 1820. United States vs. Wm. C. Corrie. Presentment for Piracy. Opinion of the Hon. A. G. Magrath, District Judge in the Circuit Court of the United States for the District of South Carolina, upon a Motion for Leave to Enter a Nol.

Pros. in the Case. Charleston, S. C., S. G. Courtenay & Co., 1860. 31 p.

Slavery in America. Report of the Meeting of the Birmingham Auxiliary to the Baptist Missionary Society. From the Birmingham Philanthropist of July 19, 1836. Birmingham, B. Hudson, 1836. 24 p.

The *Slavery* of Poverty, with a Plan for Its Abolition. New York, Printed and Sold for the New York Society for the Abolition of All Slavery by John Windt, 1842. 16 p.

The Slave's Friend. Monthly. New York, N. Y. 1836–1839. Published by the American Anti-Slavery Society, for children.

Slicer, Henry. Speech of Rev. Henry Slicer, Delivered in the General Conference at Indianapolis, 28th May, 1856, on the Subject of the Proposed Change in the Methodist Discipline, Making Non-Slave Holding a Test or Condition of Membership in Said Church. [Washington, D. C., H. Polkinhorn, 1857.] 8 p.

Smith, Caleb Blood. Slavery in the Territories. Speech of Caleb B. Smith, of Indiana, on the Extension of Slavery in the Territories of the United States: Delivered in the House of Representatives of the United States, July 31, 1848. Washington, D. C., Printed by J. & G. S. Gideon, 1848. 16 p.

Smith, E. An Inquiry into Scriptural and Ancient Servitude, in Which It Is Shown That Neither Was Chattel Slavery; with the Remedy for American Slavery. Mansfield, Ohio, Published by Author at Western Branch Book Concern of the Wesleyan Methodist Connection of America, 1852. 244 p. Same. Second Thousand. Mansfield, Western Branch Book Concern of the Wesleyan Methodist Connection of America, 1852. 251 p.

Smith, E. Uncle Tom's Kindred; or, The Wrongs of the Lowly, Exhibited in a Series of Sketches and Narratives in Ten Volumes. 10 vols. Mansfield, O., 1853. E. Smith, for Wesleyan Methodist Connection of America.

Smith, Elihu Hubbard. A Discourse, Delivered April 11, 1798, at the Request of and Before the New York Society for Promoting the Manumission of Slaves, and Protecting Such of Them as Have Been or May Be Liberated. New York, T. and J. Swords, 1798. 30 p.

Smith, Gerrit. Abstract of the Argument, in the Public Discussion of the Question: "Are the Christians of a Given Community the Church of Such Community?" Made by Gerrit Smith in Hamilton, N. Y., April 12th, 13th, 14th, 1847. Albany, S. W. Green, 1847. 38 p.

Smith, Gerrit. Abstract of the Argument on the Fugitive Slave Law, Made by Gerrit Smith, in Syracuse, June, 1852, on the Trial of Henry W. Allen, U. S. Deputy Marshal, for Kidnapping. Syracuse, The Daily Journal Office [1852]. 32 p.

Smith, Gerrit. Address Reported by Gerrit Smith to the Jerry Rescue Convention, Held in Syracuse, October 1, 1857. Broadside, 3 p. 20 × 30 cm.

Smith, Gerrit. An Address to the Three Thousand Colored Citizens of New York Who Are the Owners of One Hundred Twenty Thousand Acres of Land in the State of New York, Given to Them by Gerrit Smith, Esq., of Peterboro, September 1, 1846. New York, 1846. 20 p.

Smith, Gerrit. Anti-Fugitive Slave Law Meeting, N. Y., Jan. 9, 1851, Presided Over by Frederick Douglass. Resolutions and Address.

Smith, Gerrit. Anti-Sectarian Convention, Presbyterian Church, Peterboro, October 10, 11, 1849. Resolutions, Address, and Letter of Gerrit Smith.

Smith, Gerrit. Gerrit Smith's Reply to Colored Citizens of Albany. Peterboro, March 13, 1846.

Smith, Gerrit. Letter of Gerrit Smith to Hon. Gulian C. Verplanck. Whitesboro, Press of *The Friend of Man,* 1837. 18 p.

Smith, Gerrit. Letter of Gerrit Smith to Hon. Henry Clay. New York, American Anti-Slavery Society, 1839. 54 p.

Smith, Gerrit. Letter of Gerrit Smith to S. P. Chase, on the Unconstitutionality of Every Part of American Slavery. Albany, S. W. Green, Patriot Office, 1847. 12 p.

Smith, Gerrit. No Slavery in Nebraska: No Slavery in the Nation: Slavery an Outlaw. Speech of Gerrit Smith, on the Nebraska Bill. In Congress, April 6, 1854. [Washington, 1854]. 24 p.

Smith, Gerrit. Sermons and Speeches of Gerrit Smith. New York, Ross & Tousey, 1861. 198 p.

Smith, Gerrit. Speech of Gerrit Smith, in Congress, on the Reference of the President's Message. December 20, 1853. Washington, D. C., Buell & Blanchard, 1853. 15 p.

Smith, Gerrit. Speech of Gerrit Smith, Made in the National Convention of the Liberty Party, at Buffalo, October 21, 1847, on the Character, Scope, and Duties of the Liberty Party. Albany, S. W. Green, Patriot Office, 1847. 8 p.

Smith, Gerrit. Speech of Gerrit Smith, on the Country, Delivered at the Cooper Institute, New York, December 21, 1862. New York, Baker & Godwin, 1862. 8 p.

Smith, Gerrit. Speeches of Gerrit Smith in Congress, 1853–1854. New York, Mason Brothers, 1855. 423 p.

Smith, Gerrit. Substance of the Speech Made by Gerrit Smith, in the Capitol of the State of New York, March 11th and 12th, 1850. (Constitutional Argument). Second Ed.—Enlarged, Syracuse, V. W. Smith & Co.. 1850. 38 p.

Smith, Goldwin. Does the Bible Sanction American Slavery? Cambridge, Sever & Francis, 1863. 107 p. Same. Oxford and London, J. Henry and J. Parker, 1863. 128 p.

Smith, James McCune. The Destiny of the People of Color, A Lecture Delivered Before the Philomathean Society and Hamilton Lyceum, in January, 1841. New York, Published by Request, 1843. 16 p.

Smith, James McCune. A Lecture on the Haytien Revolutions; with a Sketch of the Character of Toussaint L'Ouverture, Delivered at the Stuyvesant Institute (for the Benefit of the Colored Orphan Asylum), February 26, 1841. New York, Daniel Fanshaw, 1841. 28 p.

Snethen, Worthington G. The Black Code of the District of Columbia, in Force September 1st, 1848. New York, for the American and Foreign Anti-Slavery Society, 1848. 61 p.

Society of Congregational Friends. Proceedings of the Yearly Meeting of Congregational Friends, Held at Waterloo, N. Y., from the 4th to the 6th of Sixth Month, Inclusive, 1849. With an Appendix. Auburn, Oliphant's Press, 1849. 45 p.

Society for the Mitigation and Gradual Abolition of Slavery Throughout the British Dominions. Address to the People of Great Britain and Ireland, Unanimously Adopted at the General Meeting of the London Anti-Slavery Society, Held April 23, 1831. London, S. Bagster, 1831. 3 p.

Society for the Mitigation and Gradual Abolition of Slavery Throughout the British Dominions. The Injurious Effects of Slave Labour: An Impartial Appeal to the Reason, Justice, and Patriotism of the People of Illinois on the Injurious Effects of Slave Labour. Philadelphia & London, Ellerton and Henderson, 1824. [A reprint of Morris Birkbeck's pamphlet.]

Some Particulars of the Late Boston Anti-Slavery Bazaar; with a Sketch of the Anti-Slavery Movement in the United States. Dublin, Webb and Chapman, 1842. 24 p.

[Sommersett Case]. An Argument in the Case of James Sommerset, a Negro, Lately Determined by the Court of King's Bench: Wherein It Is Attempted to Demonstrate the Present Unlawfulness of Domestic Slavery in England. To Which Is Prefixed a State of the Case. By Mr. Hargrave, One of the Counsel for the Negro. London, Printed for the Author, 1772. 82 p.

The South Bend Fugitive Slave Case, Involving the Right to a Writ of Habeas Corpus. New York, Anti-Slavery Office, 1851. 24 p.

South Middlesex Conference of Churches. The Political Duties of Christians. A Report Adopted at the Spring Meeting of the South Middlesex Conference of Churches, April 18, 1848. Boston, Andrews & Prentiss, 1848. 40 p.

[Southard, Nathaniel]. The "Negro Pew": Being an Inquiry Concerning the Propriety of Distinctions in the House of God, on Account of Color. Boston, Isaac Knapp, 1837. 108 p.

Southard, Nathaniel. Why Work for the Slave? Addressed to the Treasurers and Collectors in the Anti-Slavery Cent-A-Week Societies by Nath'l Southard. New York, American Anti-Slavery Society, 1838. 12 p.

Southern and Western Liberty Convention. The Address of the Southern and Western Liberty Convention Held at Cincinnati, June 11 & 12, 1845, to the People of the United States, with Notes by a Citizen of Pennsylvania (C. D. Cleveland). New York, William Harned, 1845. 15 p. Same. [Philadelphia, Office of the American Citizen, 1845.] 15 p.

Southern and Western Liberty Convention, Cincinnati, 1845. Principles and Measures of True Democracy. The Address of the Southern and Western Liberty Convention, Held at Cincinnati, June 11, 1845, to the People of the United States; Also, the Letter of Elihu Burritt to the Convention. Cincinnati, Gazette Office, 1845. 15 p.

Southern and Western Liberty Convention, Cincinnati, 1845. The Address of the Southern and Western Liberty Convention, to the People of the United States; the Proceedings and Resolutions of the Convention; the Letters of Elihu Burritt, Wm. H. Seward, William Jay, Cassius M. Clay, William Goodell, Thomas Earle and Others. Cincinnati, Gazette Office, 1845. 24 p.

Spencer, Icabod Smith. Fugitive Slave Law. The Religious Duty of Obedience to Law; A Sermon Preached in the Second Presbyterian Church in Brooklyn, November 24, 1850. New York, M. W. Dodd, 1850. 31 p.

Spirit of Liberty. Weekly. Pittsburgh, Penn. 1841–1843. Edited by Reese C. Fleeson. Published by the Western Pennsylvania Anti-Slavery Society.

[Spofford, Ainsworth Rand]. The Higher Law Tried by Reason and Authority. New York, S. W. Benedict, 1851. 54 p.

Spooner, Lysander. A Defence for Fugitive Slaves, against the Acts of Congress of February 12, 1793, and Sept. 18, 1850. Boston, Bela Marsh, 1850. 4, 72 p.

Spooner, Lysander. An Essay on the Trial by Jury. Boston, Bela Marsh, 1852. 224 p.

Spooner, Lysander. The Unconstitutionality of Slavery. Boston, Bela Marsh, 1845. 156 p. Same: Boston, Bela Marsh, 1847. 132 p. Same: Boston, Bela Marsh, 1853. 298 p. Appendix A. Fugitive Slaves.

Appendix B. Suggestions to Abolitionists. Same: Boston, Bela Marsh, 1860. 289 p.

[Stacy, George W.]. Anti-Slavery Hymns, Designed to Aid the Cause of Human Rights. Containing Original Hymns Written by Abby H. Price, and Others of Hopedale Community, with a Choice Selection from Other Authors. Hopedale, Mass., Community Press, 1844. 36 p.

Stanfield, James Field. The Guinea Voyage. A Poem, in Three Books. London, James Phillips, 1789. 37 p.

Stanton, Benjamin. Negro Equality—The Right of One Man to Hold Property in Another—The Democratic Party a Disunion Party—The Success of the Republican Party the Only Salvation for the Country. Speech of Hon. Benjamin Stanton, of Ohio. Delivered in the U. S. House of Representatives, May 3, 1860. [Washington, D. C., Republican Congressional Committee, 1860.] 8 p.

Stanton, Benjamin. Speech of Hon. Benjamin Stanton, of Ohio, in the House of Representatives, April 23, 1856, on the Power of Congress to Exclude Slavery from the Territories. [Washington, D. C., Buell & Blanchard, 1856.] 8 p.

Stanton, Elizabeth *Cady*. The Slave's Appeal. Albany, Weed, Parsons and Company, 1860. 7 p.

Stanton, Henry B[rewster]. Debate at the Lane Seminary, Cincinnati. Speech of James A. Thome, of Kentucky, Delivered at the Annual Meeting of the American Anti-Slavery Society, May 6, 1834. Letter of the Rev. Dr. Samuel H. Cox, Against the American Colonization Society. Boston, Garrison & Knapp, 1834. 16 p.

Stanton, Henry Brewster. Remarks of Henry Brewster Stanton in the Representatives Hall, on the 23rd and 24th of February, 1837 Before the Committee of the House of Representatives, of Massachusetts, to Whom Was Referred Sundry Memorials on the Subject of Slavery. Boston, I. Knapp, 1837. 84 p.
Same. Fifth Edition. Boston, 90 p.

Star of Emancipation [Poetry & Prose]. Boston, for the Fair of the Massachusetts Female Emancipation Society, 1841. 108 p. [The only one issued; none for other fairs.]

Starkborough and Lincoln Anti-Slavery Society [Vermont]. Address of the Starkborough and Lincoln Anti-Slavery Society, to the Public. Presented 11th Month, 8th, 1834. Middlebury, Knapp & Jewett, 1835. 36 p.

Starr, Frederick, Jr. What Shall Be Done with the People of Color in the United States? A Discourse Delivered in the First Presbyterian Church of Penn Yan, New York, November 2d, 1862. Albany, Weed, Parsons and Company, 1862. 30 p.

Stearns, Charles. Facts in the Life of General Taylor; the Cuban Blood-Hound Importer, the Extensive Slave-Holder and the Hero of the Mexican War. Boston, the Author, 1848. 35 p.

Stearns, Charles. The "Fugitive Slave Law" of the United States, Shown to Be Unconstitutional, Impolitic, Inhuman, and Diabolical. Boston, Bela Marsh, 1851. 36 p.

Stearns, Charles. The Way to Abolish Slavery. Boston, the Author, 1849. 36 p.

Stearns, Isaac. Right and Wrong, in Mansfield, Mass. Or, an Account of the Pro-Slavery Mob of October 10th, 1836: When an Anti-Slavery Lecturer [Charles C. Burleigh] Was Silenced by the Beat of Drums, &c., with Some Reasoning in Favor of Emancipation. By Isaac Stearns. Appendix, Containing a List of Officers and Members of the Mansfield Anti-Slavery Society. Pawtucket, Mass., R. Sherman, 1837. 61 p.

Stearns, Oliver. The Gospel Applied to the Fugitive Slave Law: A Sermon Preached to the Third Congregational Society of Hingham, on Sunday, March 2, 1851. Boston, Wm. Crosby and H. P. Nichols, 1851. 28 p.

Stearns, William Augustus. Slavery, in Its Present Aspects and Relations. A Sermon Preached on Fast Day, April 6, 1854, at Cambridge, Mass. Boston, James Munroe & Co., 1854. 47 p.

Stebbins, Giles Badger. Facts and Opinions Touching the Real Origin, Character, and Influence of the American Colonization Society: Views of Wilberforce, Clarkson, and Others, and Opinions of the Free People of Color of the United States. Preface by Hon. William Jay. Boston, J. P. Jewett and Company [Etc.], 1853. 224 p.
Same: Cleveland, O., Jewett, Proctor, and Worthington, 1853, 224 p

Steele, J. The Substance of an Address Delivered by Rev. J. Steele in the Associate Reformed Synod of the West at Their Meeting in Steubenville, on the Evening of October 16th, 1829, on the Question of Making the Holding of Slaves a Term of Communion in the Church. Washington, Guernsey Co., Ohio, Hamilton Robb, 1830. 43 p.

Steele, Joshua. Mitigation of Slavery, in Two Parts. Part 1: Letters and Papers of the Late Hon. Joshua Steele. Part 2: Letters to Thomas Clarkson, by William Dickson, LL.D. London, R. and A. Taylor, 1814. 528 p.

Stevens, Abel. An Appeal to the Methodist Episcopal Church, Concerning What Its Next General Conference Should Do on the Question of Slavery. New York, Trow, 1859. 48 p.

Stevens, Charles Emery. Anthony Burns, A History. Boston, John P. Jewett & Co., 1856. 295 p.

Stevens, Thaddeus. Speech of Mr. Thaddeus Stevens, of Pennsylvania, in the House of Representatives, on the Reference of the President's Annual Message. Made in Committee of the Whole, February 20, 1850. [Washington, D. C.] Buell & Blanchard [1850]. 8 p.

Stevens, Thaddeus. Speech of Hon. Thaddeus Stevens, of Pennsylvania. In the U. S. House of Representatives, Wednesday, Feb. 20, 1850, in the Committee of the Whole on the State of the Union, on the Reference of the President's Annual Message. Philadelphia, Anti-Slavery Office, 1850. 12 p.

Stevens, Thaddeus. Speech of Hon. T. Stevens, in Reply to the Attack on Gen. Hunter's Letter. [n.p., 1862.] 15 p.

Steward, Austin. Twenty-Two Years a Slave, and Forty Years a Freeman; Embracing a Correspondence of Several Years, While President of Wilberforce Colony, London, Canada West, by Austin Steward. Rochester, N. Y., William Alling, 1857. 360 p.
Same. Third Edition: Rochester, N. Y., Allings & Cory, 1861. 360 p.

Stewart, Alvan. Slavery in New Jersey; Legal Argument Before the Supreme Court of the State of New Jersey, at the May Term, 1845, at Trenton, for the Deliverance of Four Thousand Persons from Bondage. New York, Finch & Weed, 1845. 52 p.

Stewart, Alvan. Writings and Speeches of Alvan Stewart, on Slavery. Edited by Luther Rawson March. New York, A. B. Burdick, 1860. 426 p.

Stewart, Moses. Conscience and the Constitution, with Remarks on the Recent Speech by the Hon. Daniel Webster in the Senate of the United States on the Subject of Slavery. Boston, Crocker & Brewster, 1850. 119 p.

Stockton, Lucius Horatio. Argument on the Question of Slavery, Delivered Before the Hunterdon County Meeting, at the State House in Trenton, N. J. by Lucius Horatio Stockton, Esq., January 12, 1820. [Trenton, 1820.] 22 p.

Stone, Thomas Treadwell. An Address Before the Salem Female Anti-Slavery Society, at Its Annual Meeting, December 7, 1851. Salem, Wm. Ives & Co., 1852. 27 p.

Stone, Thomas Treadwell. The Martyr of Freedom. A Discourse Delivered at East Machias, November 30, and at Machias, December 7, 1837. By Thomas T. Stone, Pastor of a Church in East Machias, Me. Boston, Isaac Knapp, 1836. 156 p.
Same: Second Edition. Boston, Isaac Knapp, 1838. 31 p.

Storrs, George. Mob, under Pretense of Law, or, The Arrest and Trial of Rev. George Storrs at Northfield, N. H., with the Circumstances Connected with That Affair and Remarks Thereon. Concord, E. G. Chase, 1835. 22 p.

Story, Joseph. A Charge Delivered to the Grand Jury of the Circuit Court of the United States, at Its First Session in Portland, for the Judicial District of Maine, May 8, 1820, and Published at the Unanimous Request of the Grand Jury and of the Bar. Portland, A. Shirley, 1820. 21 p.

Story, Joseph. A Charge Delivered to the Grand Juries of the Circuit Court, at October Term, 1819, in Boston, and at November Term, 1819, in Providence, and Published at Their Unanimous Request. [Boston? 1819.] 8 p.

Stowe, Harriet Beecher. Facts for the People. A Key to Uncle Tom's Cabin Presenting the Original Facts and Documents upon Which the Story Is Founded. Together with Corroborative Statements Verifying the Truth of the Work. Boston, John P. Jewett & Co., 1853. 262 p.

Stowe, Harriet Beecher. Uncle Tom's Cabin; or, Life among the Lowly. 2 Vols. Boston, John P. Jewett & Co., 1852. [First published in National Era, June, 1851–April, 1852.]

Stowell, Sir William Scott. The Judgment of the Right Hon. Lord Stowell Respecting the Slavery of the Mongrel Woman, Grace, on an Appeal from the Vice-Admiralty Court of Antigua. Michaelmas Term, 1827. By John Haggard. London, W. Benning, 1827. 49 p.

[Stratton, Samuel], (Defendant). Report of the Holden Slave Case, Tried at January Term of Court of Common Pleas, County of Worcester, A.D. 1839. Published by the Board of Directors of the Holden Anti-Slavery Society. Worcester, Colton & Howland, 1839. 32 p.

Streeter, S. W. American Slavery, Essentially Sinful. A Sermon. Oberlin, Ohio, J. M. Fitch, 1845. 23 p.

Stroud, George M. A Sketch of the Laws Relating to Slavery in the Several States of the United States of America. Philadelphia, Kimber and Sharpless, 1827. 180 p.
Same: Second Edition, with Some Alterations and Considerable Additions. Philadelphia [H. Longstreth], 1856. 125 p.

Stuart, Charles. A Letter on the American Colonization Society, Addressed to the Editor of the "Herald of Peace." December 1st, 1831. By Captain C. Stuart. Birmingham, B. Hudson, 1832. 14 p.

Stuart, Charles. A Letter to Thomas Clarkson, by James Cropper. And Prejudice Vincible; or the Practicability of Conquering Prejudice by Better Means Than by Slavery and Exile; in Relation to the American Colonization Society. Liverpool, Egerton Smith and Co., 1832. 24 p.

Stuart, Charles. A Memoir of Granville Sharp, to Which Is Added Sharp's "Law of Passive Obedience" and an Extract from His "Law of Retribution." New York, American Anti-Slavery Society, 1836. 156 p.

Stuart, Charles. The American Colonization Scheme Further Unravelled. Bath, J. and J. Keene. 30 p.

Stuart, Charles. Is Slavery Defensible from Scripture? To the Rev. Dr. Hincks, Killileagh. [Belfast, News-Letter Office, 1831.] 15 p.

Stuart, Charles. Remarks on the Colony of Liberia and the American Colonization Society. With Some Account of the Settlement of Coloured People at Wilberforce, Upper Canada. London, Printed by J. Messeder, 1832. 16 p.

Stuart, Charles. The West India Question. Immediate Emancipation Would Be Safe for the Masters;—Profitable for the Masters;—Happy for the Slaves;—Right in the Government;—Advantageous to the Nation;—Would Interfere with No Feelings but Such as Are Disgraceful and Destructive; Cannot Be Postponed Without Continually Increasing Danger. An Outline for Immediate Emancipation; and Remarks on Compensation. London, Simpkin and Marshall, 1832. 44 p.

Same. Reprinted from the [English] Quarterly Magazine and Review of April, 1832. New Haven, Hezekiah Howe & Co., 1833. 43 p.

Same. Second American Edition. Newburyport, Charles Whipple, 1835. 35 p. [With Stuart's name spelled Stewart.]

Same. Newburyport, Charles Whipple, 1838. 35 p.

Sturge, Joseph. A Visit to the United States in 1841; by Joseph Sturge, the British Abolitionist. London, Hamilton, Adams & Co., 1842. 192 p.

Sturge, Joseph, and Harvey, Thomas. The West Indies in 1837; Being the Journal of a Visit to Antigua, Montserrat, Dominica, St. Lucia, Barbadoes, and Jamaica, Undertaken for the Purpose of Ascertaining the Actual Condition of the Negro Population of Those Islands. By Joseph Sturge and Thomas Harvey. London, Hamilton, Adams, & Co., 1838.

Sumner, Charles. The Anti-Slavery Enterprise; Its Necessity, Practicability, and Dignity, with Glimpses at the Special Duties of the North. An Address Before the People of New York, at the Metropolitan Theatre, May 9, 1855. Boston, Ticknor and Fields, 1855. 36 p.

Sumner, Charles. Argument of Charles Sumner, Esq. Against the Constitutionality of Separate Colored Schools, in the Case of Sarah C. Roberts vs. the City of Boston, Before the Supreme Court of Massachusetts, Dec. 4, 1849. Boston, B. F. Roberts, 1849. 32 p.

Sumner, Charles. The Barbarism of Slavery. Speech of Hon. Charles Sumner, on the Bill for the Admission of Kansas as a Free State in the United States Senate, June 4, 1860. Washington, D. C., Buell & Blanchard, 1860. 32 p.

Same: Boston, Thayer & Eldridge, 1860. 118 p.

Same: Albany, Weed, Parsons & Co., 1860. 28 p.

Same: New York, The Young Men's Republican Union, 1863. 80 p.

Sumner, Charles. The Crime Against Kansas; the Apologies for the Crime; the True Remedy. Speech by Charles Sumner of Massachusetts, in the Senate of the United States, May 19, 20, 1856. Boston, J. P. Jewett & Co., 1856. 95 p.

Same: Washington, D. C., Buell & Blanchard, 1856. 32 p.

Same: New York, New York Tribune, 1856. 31 p.

Sumner, Charles. Defense of Massachusetts. Speech of Hon. Charles Sumner of Massachusetts on the Boston Memorial for the Repeal of the Fugitive Slave Bill, and in Reply to Messrs. Jones of Tennessee; Butler of South Carolina, and Mason of Virginia, Delivered in the Senate of the United States, June 26, 28, 1854. Washington [D. C.], Buell & Blanchard, 1854. 16 p.

Sumner, Charles. The Demands of Freedom. Speech of Hon. Charles Sumner, in the Senate of the United States, on His Motion to Repeal the Fugitive Slave Bill. February 23, 1855, Washington, D. C., Buell & Blanchard, 1855. 8 p.

Sumner, Charles. Duties of Massachusetts at This Crisis. A Speech of Hon. Charles Sumner, Delivered at the Republican Convention at Worcester, Sept. 7, 1854. [n.p., 1854.] 8 p.

Sumner, Charles. Emancipation! Its Policy and Necessity as a War Measure for the Suppression of the Rebellion. Speech of Hon. Charles Sumner, at Faneuil Hall, Oct. 6, 1862. [Boston, 1862.] 23 p.

Sumner, Charles. Final Protest for Himself and the Clergy of New England Against Slavery in Kansas and Nebraska Speech of Hon. Charles Sumner of Massachusetts on the Night of the Passage of the Kansas and Nebraska Bills, in the Senate of the U. S., May 25, 1854. Washington, D. C., Buell & Blanchard, 1854. 8 p.

Sumner, Charles. Freedom National; Slavery Sectional. Speech of Hon. Charles Sumner, of Massachusetts, on His Motion to Repeal the Fugitive Slave Bill, in the Senate of the United States, August 26, 1852. Washington, D. C., Buell & Blanchard, 1852. 31 p.

Same: Boston, Ticknor, Reed & Fields, 1852. 78 p.

Same: Tenth Edition. Washington, Buell & Blanchard, 1853. 31 p.

Sumner, Charles. Immediate Emancipation a War Measure! Speech of Hon. Charles Sumner, of Massachusetts, on the Bill Providing for Emancipation in Missouri. In the Senate of the United States, February 12th, 1863. [Washington, D. C., H. Polkinhorn, 1863.] 3 p.

Sumner, Charles. Indemnity for the Past and Security for the Future. Speech of Charles Sumner of Massachusetts on the Bill for the Confiscation of Property and the Liberation of Slaves Belonging to Rebels, in the Senate of the United States, May 19, 1862. Washington [D. C.], 1862. 16 p.

Sumner, Charles. The Kansas Question. Speech by Charles Sumner of Massachusetts, Reviewing the Action of the Federal Administration upon the Subject of Slavery in Kansas, Delivered in the Senate of the United States, May 17th and 20th, 1856. Cincinnati, George C. Blanchard, 1856. 32 p.

Sumner, Charles. The Landmark of Freedom. Speech of Hon. Charles Sumner, Against the Repeal of the Missouri Prohibition of Slavery North of 36°30′. In the Senate, February 21, 1854. [Washington, D. C., Buell & Blanchard, Printers, 1854.] 23 p.
Same: [Washington, D. C., Congressional Globe Office, 1854.] 16 p.

Sumner, Charles. Last Three Speeches on Kansas and Freedom. Feb. 7th, March 6th, and May 19th and 20th, 1856. By Charles Sumner. Boston, Higgins and Bradley, 1856. 134 p.

Sumner, Charles. Ransom of Slaves at the National Capital. Speech of Hon. Charles Sumner, of Massachusetts, on the Bill for the Abolition of Slavery in the District of Columbia, in the Senate of the United States, March 31, 1862. Washington [D. C.], Congressional Globe Office, 1862. 13 p.

Sumner, Charles. The Rebellion: Its Origin and Mainspring. An Oration Delivered by Hon. Charles Sumner, under the Auspices of the Young Men's Republican Union of New York, November 27, 1861. New York, Young Men's Republican Union, 1861. 16 p.

Sumner, Charles. The Republican Party; Its Origin, Necessity and Permanence. Speech of Hon. Charles Sumner, Before the Young Men's Republican Union of New York, July 11th, 1860. New York, J. A. H. Hasbrouck & Co., 1860. 16 p.

Sumner, Charles. The Slave Oligarchy and Its Usurpations. Speech of Hon. Charles Sumner, November 2, 1855, in Faneuil Hall, Boston. [Washington, D. C., Buell & Blanchard, 1855.] 16 p.

Sumner, Charles. Union and Peace! How They Shall Be Restored. A Speech of the Hon. Charles Sumner of Massachusetts, Delivered Before the Republican State Convention at Worcester, Oct. 1, 1861. Boston, Wright & Potter, 1861. 8 p.

Sumner, Charles. Universal Emancipation Without Compensation. Speech of Hon. Charles Sumner, on the Proposed Amendment of the Constitution Abolishing Slavery Through the United States, in the Senate of the United States, April 8, 1864. Washington, D. C., H. Polkinhorn, 1864. 16 p.

Sumner, Charles. War Powers of Congress. Speech of Hon. Charles Sumner, of Massachusetts, on the

House Bills for the Confiscation of Property and the Liberation of Slaves Belonging to Rebels, Delivered in Senate of the United States, June 27, 1862. Washington, D. C., Scammell & Co., 1862. 7 p.

Sunderland, LaRoy. Anti-Slavery Manual, Containing a Collection of Facts and Arguments on American Slavery. New York, Piercy & Reed, 1837. 162 p.
Same: Second Edition. New York, S. W. Benedict, 1837. 142 p.
Same: Third Edition, Improved. New York, S. W. Benedict, 1839. 155 p.

Sunderland, LaRoy. The Testimony of God Against Slavery, or A Collection of Passages from the Bible, Which Show the Sin of Holding Property in Man. With Notes. Boston, Webster & Southard, 1835. 104 p.

Sunderland, LaRoy. The Testimony of God Against Slavery: A Collection of Passages from the Bible, Which Show the Sin of Holding and Treating the Human Species as Property. With Notes. To Which Is Added the Testimony of the Civilized World Against Slavery. Second Edition. Boston, I. Knapp, 1836. 177 p.
Same: New York, R. G. Williams, 1836. 177 p.

Swan, James. A Dissuasion to Great Britain and the Colonies from the Slave Trade to Africa. Shewing the Injustice Thereof, Etc. Revised and Abridged. Boston, Printed by J. Greenleaf, 1773. x, 11, 41 p.

Swift, Zephaniah. An Oration on Domestic Slavery. Delivered at the North Meeting-House in Hartford, on the 12th Day of May, A.D. 1791. At the Meeting of the Connecticut Society for the Promotion of Freedom, and the Relief of Persons Unlawfully Holden in Bondage. Hartford, Hudson & Goodwin, 1791. 23 p.

Talbot, Thomas Hammond. The Constitutional Provision Respecting Fugitives from Service or Labor, and the Act of Congress, of September 18, 1850. Boston, B. Marsh, 1852. 128 p.

Tallmadge, James. Speech of the Hon. James Tallmadge, of Duchess County, New York, in the House of Representatives of the United States, on Slavery. Boston, Ticknor & Company, 1849. 24 p.

Tappan, Benjamin. Remarks of Mr. Tappan, of Ohio, on Abolition Petitions, Delivered in Senate, February 4, 1840. 4 p.

[Tappan, Lewis]. Address to the Non-Slaveholders of the South, on the Social and Political Evils of Slavery. New York, American and Foreign Anti-Slavery Society [1843]. 58 p.

[Tappan, Lewis]. The African Captives. Trial of the Prisoners of the Amistad on the Writ of Habeas

Corpus, Before the Circuit Court of the United States, for the District of Connecticut, at Hartford; Judges Thompson and Judson, September Term, 1839. New York, 143 Nassau Street, 1839. 47 p.

Tappan, Lewis. The Fugitive Slave Bill: Its History and Unconstitutionality; with an Account of the Seizure and Enslavement of James Hamlet, and His Subsequent Restoration to Liberty. New York, American and Foreign Anti-Slavery Society, 1850. 36 p.

Same: Third Edition. New York, William Harned, 1850. 36 p.

Tappan, Lewis. Immediate Emancipation the Only Wise and Safe Mode. [New York, 1861]. 16 p.

Tappan, Lewis. Important Intelligence from Liberia [Letter from Louis Sheridan]. New York, 1838. 3 p.

[Tappan, Lewis]. Letters Respecting a Book "Dropped from the Catalogue" of the American Sunday School Union in Compliance with the Dictation of the Slave Power. New York, American and Foreign Anti-Slavery Society, 1848. 36 p.

Tappan, Lewis. Proceedings of the Session of Broadway Tabernacle [New York City], Against Lewis Tappan, with the Action of the Presbytery and General Assembly. New York, 1839. 64 p.

Tappan, Lewis. Reply to Charges Brought Against the American and Foreign Anti-Slavery Society, Etc. With an Introduction by John Scoble. London, Richard Barrett, 1852. 24 p.

Taunton (Mass.) Union, for the Relief and Improvement of the Colored Race. Report of the Proceedings and Views of the Taunton Union, for the Relief and Improvement of the Colored Race; Together with the Constitution of the Society, and a List of Officers, Chosen, May, 1835. Published by the Board of Managers. Taunton, Bradford & Amsbury, 1835. 14 p.

Thacher, George. No Fellowship with Slavery. A Sermon Delivered June 29, 1856, in the First Congregational Church, Meriden, Conn. Meriden, L. R. Webb, 1856. 20 p.

Thatcher, Benjamin Bussey. Memoir of Phillis Wheatley, a Native African and a Slave. Second Edition. Boston, Geo. W. Light, 1834. 36 p.

[Thatcher, Benjamin Bussey]. Remarks on the American Colonization Society. From the Christian Examiner and General Review [Nov., 1832]. Providence, M. Robinson, 1833. 36 p.

Thayer, Eli. Speech of Hon. Eli Thayer, Delivered in Mechanics Hall, Worcester, August 10, 1860, in Defense of Free Labor, and the Rights of American Citizens. [n.p., n.d.]

Thayer, Eli. The Suicide of Slavery. Speech of Hon. Eli Thayer of Mass. Delivered in the House of Representatives, March 25, 1858. Washington, Buell & Blanchard, 1858. 8 p.

Thayer, Eli. The Territorial Policy. Speech of Eli Thayer of Mass., in Reply to Hon. Mr. Curtis and Hon. Mr. Gooch. Delivered in the U. S. House of Representatives, May 11, 1860. [Washington, D. C., 1860]. 8 p.

Thomas, E. A Concise View of the Slavery of the People of Colour in the United States; Exhibiting Some of the Most Affecting Cases of Cruel and Barbarous Treatment of the Slaves by Their Most Inhuman and Brutal Masters; Not Heretofore Published: And Also Showing the Absolute Necessity for the Most Speedy Abolition of Slavery, with an Endeavor to Point Out the Best Means of Effecting It. To Which Is Added, a Short Address to the Free People of Colour. With a Selection of Hymns, &c. &c. Philadelphia, E. Thomas, 1834. 178 p.

[Thomas, William] Defensor, pseud. The Enemies of the Constitution Discovered, or an Inquiry into the Origin and Tendency of Popular Violence. Containing a Complete and Circumstantial Account of the Unlawful Proceedings at the City of Utica, October 21st, 1835; the Dispersion of the State Anti-Slavery Convention by the Agitators, the Destruction of a Democratic Press, and of the Causes Which Led Thereto. Together with a Concise Treatise on the Practice of the Court of His Honor Judge Lynch . . . Accompanied with Numerous Highly Interesting and Important Documents. New York, Leavitt, Lord & Co., 1835. 183 p.

Thome, James Armstrong, and Kimball, J. Horace. Emancipation in the West Indies. A Six Months' Tour in Antigua, Barbadoes and Jamaica, in the Year 1837. New York, Published by the American Anti-Slavery Society, 1838. 489 p.

Same: Second Edition, New York, American Anti-Slavery Society, 1839. 412 p.

Thompson, George [of Oberlin]. The Prison Bard; or, Poems on Various Subjects by George Thompson, for Four Years and Eleven Months a Prisoner in Missouri for Attempting to Aid Some Slaves to Liberty. Written in Prison. Hartford, William H. Burleigh, 1848. 215 p.

Thompson, George [of Oberlin]. Prison Life and Reflections; or, A Narrative of the Arrest, Trial, Conviction, Imprisonment, Treatment, Observations, Reflections, and Deliverance of Work, Burr, and Thompson, Who Suffered an Unjust and Cruel Imprisonment in Missouri Penitentiary, for Attempting to Aid Some Slaves to Liberty. Three Parts in One Volume. By George Thompson, One of the Prisoners. Oberlin, James M. Fitch, 1847. 417 p. Third Edition. Hartford, A. Work, 1849. 377 p.

Same: Hartford, A. Work, 1851. 377 p.

Same: Fifteenth Thousand. Dayton, Published by the Author, United Brethren Printing Establishment, 1860. 377 p.

Thompson, George [of Liverpool]. An Address to the Ladies of Glasgow and Its Vicinity upon the Present Aspect of the Great Question of Negro Emancipation. Delivered in Mr. Anderson's Chapel, John St., Glasgow, on Tuesday, March 5, 1833, by George Thompson. Also, Some Account of the Formation of the Glasgow Ladies' Anti-Slavery Association. Glasgow, David Robertson [etc., etc.], 1833. 42 p.

Thompson, George. An Appeal to the Abolitionists of Great Britain, in Behalf of the Cause of Universal Emancipation. Edinburgh, William Oliphant and Son, 1837. 32 p.

Thompson, George. Discussion on American Slavery, Between George Thompson, Esq., Agent of the British and Foreign Society for the Abolition of Slavery Throughout the World, and Rev. Robert J. Breckinridge, Delegate from the General Assembly of the Presbyterian Church in the United States, to the Congregational Union of England and Wales, Holden in the Rev. Dr. Wardlaw's Chapel, Glasgow, Scotland on the Evenings of the 13th, 14th, 15th, 16th, 17th of June, 1836. Boston, Isaac Knapp, 1836. 187 p.

Same: Second American Edition, with Notes, by Mr. Garrison. Boston, Isaac Knapp, 1836. 80, 23 p.

Thompson, George. Lectures of George Thompson, with a Full Report of the Discussion Between Mr. Thompson and Mr. Barthwick, the Pro-Slavery Agent, Held at the Royal Amphitheatre, Liverpool, (Eng.) and Which Continued for Six Evenings with Unabated Interest. Compiled from Various English Editions—Also, a Brief History of His Connection with the Anti-Slavery Cause in England, by William Lloyd Garrison. Boston, Isaac Knapp, 1836. 190 p.

Thompson, George. Letters and Addresses, by George Thompson, During His Mission in the United States, from Oct. 1, 1834, to Nov. 27, 1835. Boston, I. Knapp, 1837. 126 p.

Thompson, George, ed. Slavery in America. A Reprint of an Appeal to the Christian Women of America by Angelina E. Grimké of Charleston, South Carolina, with Introduction, Notes, and Appendix by George Thompson. Edinburgh, William Oliphant and Son, 1837. 56 p.

Thompson, George. Speech of George Thompson, Esq., on the Divisions among American Abolitionists, Delivered at the Annual Meeting of the Glasgow Emancipation Society, 2d August, 1841.

Reprinted, with Corrections from the Glasgow Argus. 8 p.

Thompson, George. The Substance of Mr. Thompson's Lecture on Slavery, Delivered in the Wesleyan Chapel, Irwell Street, Salford, Manchester, (Eng.). Manchester, Printed by S. Wheeler and Son; Boston, Re-printed by I. Knapp, 1836. 24 p.

Thompson, George, and Wright, Henry Clarke. The Free Church of Scotland and American Slavery. Substance of Speeches Delivered in the Music Hall, Edinburgh, During May and June 1846, by George Thompson, Esq. and the Rev. Henry C. Wright. With an Appendix, Containing the Deliverances of the Free Church on the Subject of Slavery, 1844, 1845, and 1846, and Other Valuable Documents. Edinburgh, Scottish Anti-Slavery Society, 1846. 104 p.

Thompson, George, and Wright, Henry C. The Free Church and Her Accusers: The Question at Issue. A Letter from G. Thompson, Esq., to Henry C. Wright; and One from Henry C. Wright to Ministers and Members of the Free Church of Scotland. Glasgow, George Gallie, 1846. 12 p.

Thompson, Joseph Parrish. The Duties of the Christian Citizen. A Discourse, by Joseph P. Thompson, Pastor of the Broadway Tabernacle Church. New York, S. W. Benedict, 1848. 24 p.

Thompson, Joseph Parrish. The Fugitive Slave Law; Tried by the Old and New Testaments. New York, William Harned, 1850. 35 p.

Thompson, Joseph Parrish. No Slavery in Nebraska. The Voice of God Against National Crime. New York, Ivison & Phinney, 1854. 30 p.

Thompson, Joseph Parrish. Teachings of the New Testament on Slavery. New York, J. H. Ladd, 1856. 52 p.

[Thomson, Mortimer]. Great Auction Sale of Slaves, at Savannah, Georgia, March 2d and 3d, 1859. Reported for the Tribune. New York, American Anti-Slavery Society [1859]. 28 p.

Thornton, William. Political Economy; Founded in Justice and Humanity. In a Letter to a Friend. By W. T., Washington. City of Washington, [D. C.], S. H. Smith, 1804. 24 p.

Tiffany, Joel. A Treatise on the Unconstitutionality of American Slavery; Together with the Powers and Duties of the Federal Government, in Relation to That Subject. Cleveland, O., J. Calyer, [1849]. 144 p.

Titus, Frances W. Narrative of Sojourner Truth. Boston, [Yerrington], 1850. 144 p.

Torrey, Jesse. American Slave Trade; or, An Account of the Manner in Which the Slave Dealers Take Free People from Some of the United States of America, and Carry Them Away, and Sell Them as Slaves in Other of the States; and of the Horrible Cruelties Practised in the Carrying on of This Most Infamous Traffic: With Reflections on the Project for Forming a Colony of American Blacks in Africa, and Certain Documents Respecting That Project. By Jesse Torrey, Jun. Physician, London: Repr. by C. Clement, and Published by J. M. Cobbett, 1822. 119 p. First Published in Philadelphia in 1817, as a Portraiture of Domestic Slavery.

Torrey, Jesse. A Portraiture of Domestic Slavery in the United States; with Reflections on the Practicability of Restoring the Moral Rights of the Slave, Without Impairing the Legal Privileges of the Possessor; and a Project of a Colonial Asylum for Free Persons of Colour; Including Memoirs of Facts on the Interior Traffic in Slaves, and on Kidnapping. Philadelphia, Published by the Author, John Bioren, Printer, 1817. 94 p.
  Same. Second Edition: Ballston Spa, Published by the Author, 1818. 108 p.

Toulmin, J. R. Slavery. An Ode. Lexington, [Ky.] May 7, 1803. Broadside. 1 p. 20 × 32 cm. [Antislavery poem, inscribed by Author:] "From the Author; in Testimony of Respect for Him Who Occupies the Presidential Office [Thomas Jefferson]: to Whose Candid Consideration the Following Subject Is Respectfully Submitted."

Tower, Philo. Slavery Unmasked: Being a Truthful Narrative of a Three Year's Residence and Journeying in Eleven Southern States; To Which Is Added the Invasion of Kansas, Including the Last Chapter of Her Wrongs. Rochester, E. Darrow & Brother, 1856. 432 p.

The Tract Society and Slavery. Speeches of Chief Justice Williams, Judge Parsons, and Ex-Governor Ellsworth: Delivered in the Center Church, Hartford, Conn. at the Anniversary of the Hartford Branch of the American Tract Society, January 9th, 1859. Hartford, Elihu Geer, 1859. 26 p.

Tracy, Joseph. Colonization and Missions. A Historical Examination of the State of Society in Western Africa, as Formed by Paganism and Mohammedanism, Slavery, the Slave Trade and Piracy, and of the Remedial Influence of Colonization and Missions. Boston, T. R. Marvin, 1845. 40 p.
  Same. Fifth Edition. Revised and Enlarged. Boston, T. R. Marvin, 1846. 40 p.

Treadwell, Seymour Boughton. American Liberties and American Slavery. Morally and Politically Illustrated. New York, John S. Taylor, [etc.] 1838. 466 p. [Treadwell became editor of the *Michigan Freeman* in 1839.]

Trew, J. M. An Appeal to the Christian Philanthropy of the People of Great Britain and Ireland, in Behalf of the Religious Instruction and Conversion of Three Hundred Thousand Negro Slaves. London, J. M. Richardson, 1826. 48 p.

Trial of Thomas Sims, on an Issue of Personal Liberty, on the Claim of James Potter of Georgia, Against Him, as an Alleged Fugitive from Service. Arguments of Robert Rantoul, Jr., and Charles G. Loring, with the Decision of George T. Curtis. Boston, Wm. S. Damrell & Co., 1851. 47 p.

Triumph of Equal School Rights in Boston. Proceedings of the Presentation Meeting, Held in Boston, Dec. 17, 1855; Including Addresses by John T. Hilton, Wm. C. Nell, Charles W. Slack, Wendell Phillips, Wm. Lloyd Garrison, Charles Lenox Remond. Boston, R. F. Wallcut, 1856. 24 p. [A meeting of colored citizens for the purpose of presenting a testimonial to W. C. Nell for his efforts in opening the public schools to colored children.]

True American. Lexington, Ky. June 3, 1845–October 21, 1846. Edited by Cassius M. Clay.

Trumbull, Lyman. Affairs in Kansas Territory. Speech of Hon. Lyman Trumbull, of Illinois, Delivered in the Senate of the United States, March 14, 1856, on Motion to Print 31,000 Extra Copies of the Reports of the Majority and Minority of the Committee on Territories, in Reference to Affairs in Kansas. Washington [D. C.], Buell & Blanchard, 1856. 16 p.

Trumbull, Lyman. Remarks of Lyman Trumbull on Seizure of the Arsenal at Harper's Ferry, Va., and Liberty, Mo., and in Vindication of the Republican Party and Its Creed in Response to Senators Chesnut, Yulee, Saulsbury, Clay and Pugh. Delivered in the United States Senate, Dec. 6–8, 1859. Washington, D. C., Buell & Blanchard, 1859. 16 p.

Trumbull, Lyman. Speech of Hon. Lyman Trumbull, of Illinois, on Introducing a Bill to Confiscate the Property of Rebels and Free Their Slaves; Delivered in the Senate of the United States, December 5, 1861. Washington, [D. C.], Congressional Globe Office, 1861. 7 p.

Tucker, St. George. A Dissertation on Slavery, with a Proposal for the Gradual Abolition of It, in the State of Virginia. Philadelphia, Printed for Mathew Carey, 1796. 106 p.
  Same. Philadelphia, Printed for Mathew Carey, 1796. New York, Reprinted, 1861. 104 p.

Tucker, St. George. Letter to a Member of the General Assembly of Virginia, on the Late Conspiracy of the Slaves; with a Proposal for Their Colonization. Baltimore, Bonsal & Niles, 1801. 23 p.

Tufts, Samuel N. Slavery, and the Death of John

Brown. A Sermon Preached in Auburn Hall, Auburn, Sabbath Afternoon, Dec. 11th, 1859. By Rev. Samuel N. Tufts, Pastor of the Auburn Free Baptist Church. Lewiston [Me.], Printed at the Journal Office, 1859. 20 p.

Tyler, Edward Royall. Slaveholding a Malum in Se, or Invariably Sinful. Hartford, Case, Tiffany & Co., 1839. 48 p.
Same: Hartford, S. S. Cowles, 1839. 48 p.

The *Uncle Tom's Cabin* Almanack; or, Abolitionist Memento. For 1853. London, J. Cassell [1852]. 70 p.

Underwood, Almon. A Discourse on the Death of the Late Rev. C. T. Torrey, a Martyr to Human Rights, Delivered in Newark, N. J., June 7, 1846. Newark, Small & Ackerman, 1846. 16 p. [Torrey died in the Maryland state penitentiary while serving a six-year term at hard labor for aiding fugitives.]

Union College Anti-Slavery Society. First Annual Report of the Union College Anti-Slavery Society, with an Address to Students and an Appendix. Schenectady, S. S. Riggs, 1836. 16 p.

Union, Pennsylvania, Anti-Slavery Society. Address of the Union Anti-Slavery Society Auxiliary, No. 2, to the Congregation of the Western Presbyterian Church. Read and Adopted December 24, 1838. Philadelphia, Published by Order of the Society, 1838. 25 p.

The Unionist. Weekly. Brooklyn, Conn. August 1, 1833—Edited by William H. Burleigh and Charles C. Burleigh. [Established to help Prudence Crandall.]

Unitarian Church, England. American Slavery. Report of a Meeting of Members of the Unitarian Body, Held at the Freemason's Tavern, June 13th, 1851, to Deliberate on the Duty of English Unitarians in Reference to Slavery in the United States. London, E. T. Whitfield, 1851. 23 p.

Van Buren, Martin. Opinions of Martin Van Buren, Vice President of the United States, upon the Powers and Duties of Congress, in Reference to the Abolition of Slavery Either in the Slave-Holding States or in the District of Columbia. To Which Are Added Sundry Documents Showing His Sentiments upon Other Subjects. Washington, Blair & Rives, 1836. 32 p.

Vassa, Gustavus. The Interesting Narrative of the Life of Gustavus Vassa, the African. Seventh Edition, Enlarged. London, Printed for the Author, 1793. 360 p.

Vassa, Gustavus. The Life of Olaudah Equiano, or Gustavus Vassa, the African. Written by Himself.

Two Volumes in One. Boston, Isaac Knapp, 1837. 294 p.

Vassa, Gustavus. The Life and Adventures of Olaudah Equiano; or Gustavus Vassa, the African. From an Account Written by Himself. Abridged by A. Mott. Added, Remarks on the Slave Trade. New York, Wood, 1829. 36 p.

[Vaux, Roberts]. An Impartial Appeal to the Reason, Interest, and Patriotism of the People of Illinois, on the Injurious Effects of Slave Labour. [Philadelphia, 1823.] 16 p.

Vaux, Roberts. Memoirs of the Lives of Benjamin Lay and Ralph Sandiford; Two of the Earliest Public Advocates for the Emancipation of the Enslaved Africans. Philadelphia, Solomon W. Conrad, 1815. 73 p.

Vaux, Roberts. Memoirs of the Life of Anthony Benezet. Philadelphia, Printed; York, Reprinted for W. Alexander, 1817. 152 p.

Vermont Anti-Slavery Society. First Annual Report of the Vermont Anti-Slavery Society, Presented at Middlebury, February 18, 1835. Montpelier, Knapp and Jewett, 1835. 24 p. [Titles of subsequent annual reports do not vary.]

Vermont Telegraph. Weekly. Brandon, Vt. September 30, 1828–1843. Edited by Ephriam Maxham, 1828–1834. Founded as Organ of Baptists. Purchased by Orson S. Murray, 1834, and Continued as an Anti-Slavery Journal, the First Such Paper in Vermont. Removed to Ohio about 1842.

Vincent, Rev. James. American Slavery Defeated in Its Attempts Through the American Board of Commissioners for Foreign Missions to Find a Shelter in the British Churches. Being a Correspondence with the Congregational Union of England and Wales, on the "American Board of Missions and Slavery," with the Discussion Which Followed at the Autumnal Meetings of the Union at Newcastle, in October, 1854. London, T. Tweedie, 1854. 48 p.

Vinton, Samuel Finley. Substance of an Argument of Samuel F. Vinton, for the Defendants in the Case of the Commonwealth of Virginia vs. Peter M. Garner and Others, for an Alleged Abduction of Certain Slaves. Delivered before the General Court of Virginia, at Its December Term, 1846. Marietta, O., Intelligencer Office, 1846. 32 p.

Virginia. Governor Thomas W. Gilmer. Message of the Governor of Virginia, Communicating a Correspondence Between the Governors of Virginia and New York, in Relation to Certain Fugitives from Justice. Printed by Order of the House of Delegates of Virginia. Richmond, Samuel Shepherd, 1840. 58 p.

The Voice of the Fugitive. Semi-weekly. Windsor, Canada. January 1, 1851–1853. Edited by Henry Bibb. Title varies. Imprint: Sandwich and Windsor.

A *Voice* to the United States of America, from the Metropolis of Scotland; Being an Account of Various Meetings Held in Edinburgh on the Subject of American Slavery, upon the Return of Mr. George Thompson, from His Mission to That Country. Edinburgh, William Oliphant and Son, 1830. 51 p.

Wade, Benjamin Franklin. Plain Truths for the People. Speech of Senator Wade, of Ohio. Delivered in the Senate of the United States, March 13 and 15, 1858. Washington, [D. C.] Buell & Blanchard [1858]. 16 p.

Wade, Benjamin F. Property in the Territories. Speech of Hon. Benjamin F. Wade, of Ohio. Delivered in the Senate of the United States, March 7, 1860. Washington, D. C., Buell & Blanchard, 1860. 14 p.

Wade, Benjamin Franklin. They "Stoop to Conquer"; or, The English Swindle. Speech of Senator Wade, of Ohio. Delivered in the United States Senate, April 27, 1858. Washington, D. C., Buell & Blanchard, 1858. 7 p.

Wade, Edward. Slavery Question. Speech of Hon. Edward Wade, of Ohio, in the House of Representatives, August 2, 1856. Washington, D. C., Buell & Blanchard, 1856. 14 p.

Waldron, Henry. Modern Democracy against the Union, the Constitution, the Policy of Our Fathers, and the Rights of Free Labor. Speech of Hon. Henry Waldron, of Michigan. Delivered in the House of Representatives April 26, 1860. [Washington, D. C., Republican Executive Congressional Committee, 1860.] 7 p.

Walker, David. Walker's Appeal, in Four Articles; Together with a Preamble to the Colored Citizens of the World, but in Particular, and Very Expressly to Those of the United States of America. Written in Boston, in the State of Massachusetts, Sept. 28, 1829. Second Edition, with Corrections, &c. Boston, D. Walker, 1830. 80 p.
Same. Third and Last Edition. Boston, David Walker, 1830. 88 p.

Walker, David. Appeal, in Four Articles, with a Preamble, to the Colored Citizens of the World, but in Particular to Those of the U. S. Written in Boston, Mass. Sept. 28th, 1829. Boston, 1829. 76 p.
See also Henry Highland Garnet.

Walker, James Barr. The Slaves. A Poem Written by Appointment of the Faculty of the Western Reserve College, for the Commencement in 1831. Hudson, Ohio, Office of the Ohio Observer, 1835. 8 p.

Walker, Jonathan. The Branded Hand. Trial and Imprisonment of Jonathan Walker, at Pensacola, Florida, for Aiding Slaves to Escape from Bondage. With an Appendix, Containing a Sketch of His Life. Boston, Pub. at the Anti-Slavery Office, 1845. 119 p.
Same. Boston, The Anti-Slavery Office, 1846. 126 p.
Same. Boston, The Anti-Slavery Office, 1850. 126 p.

Walker, Jonathan. A Brief View of American Chattelized Humanity, and Its Supports. By Jonathan Walker, Late of Florida, Where He Was Put in the Pillory, Fined, Branded with Hot Irons, Imprisoned Eleven Months, &c. &c., by the Government of the United States, for an Attempted Act of Humanity. Boston, the Author, 1846. 36 p.

[Walker, Jonathan]. A Picture of Slavery, for Youth. By the Author of "The Branded Hand" and "Chattelized Humanity." Boston, J. Walker and W. R. Bliss [184–?]. 36 p.

Walker, Robert James. Argument of Robert J. Walker, Esq. Before the Supreme Court of the United States, on the Mississippi Slave Question, at January Term, 1841. Involving the Power of Congress and of the States to Prohibit the Inter-State Slave Trade. Philadelphia, J. C. Clark, 1841. 88 p.

Wallace, C. W. A Sermon on the Duty of Ministers to Oppose the Extension of American Slavery, Preached in Manchester, N. H., Fast Day, April 3, 1857. Manchester, N. H., Fisk & Gage, 1857. 30 p.

Walsh, Robert. An Appeal from the Judgments of Great Britain Respecting the United States of America. Part First, Containing an Historical Outline of Their Merits and Wrongs as Colonies; and Strictures upon the Calumnies of the British Writers. Second Edition. Philadelphia, Mitchell, Ames and White, 1819.

[Walsh, Robert] a Philadelphian, pseud. Free Remarks on the Spirit of the Federal Constitution, the Practice of the Federal Government, and the Obligations of the Union, Respecting the Exclusion of Slavery from the Territories and the New States. Philadelphia, A. Finley, 1819. 116 p.

Ward, James Wilson. Slavery a Sin That Concerns Non-Slaveholding States. A Sermon Delivered on the Day of the Annual Fast in Massachusetts, March 28, 1839. Boston, I. Knapp, 1839. 32 p.

Ward, Jonathan. American Slavery, and the Means of Its Abolition. Boston, Perkins & Marvin, 1840. 26 p.

Ward, Jonathan. Father Ward's Letter to Professor Stuart, Brentwood, N. H., August, 1837. [Newburyport, Charles Whipple, 1837.] 10 p.

Ward, Samuel Ringgold. Autobiography of a Fugitive Negro: His Anti-Slavery Labours in the United States, Canada, & England. London, J. Snow, 1855. 412 p.

Wardlaw, Ralph. The Jubilee: A Sermon Preached in West George Street Chapel, Glasgow, on Friday, August 1st, 1834, the Memorable Day of Negro Emancipation in the British Colonies. Glasgow, A. Fullarton & Co., 1834. 37 p.

[Warner, Samuel]. Authentic and Impartial Narrative of the Tragical Scene Which Was Witnessed in Southampton County (Virginia) on Monday the 22nd Day of August Last, When Fifty-Five of Its Inhabitants (Mostly Women and Children) Were Inhumanely Massacred by the Blacks! Communicated by Those Who Were Eye Witnesses of the Bloody Scene, and Confirmed by the Confession of Several of the Blacks While under Sentences of Death. New York, Warner & West, 1831. 38 p.

[Warren, H., and Eastman, Zebina]. Slave Code of the State of Illinois; Being an Abstract of Those Laws Now in Force in This State, Which Affect the Rights of Coloured People, as Such, Both Bond and Free. With Notes. Genius of Liberty—Extra. [First published by the executive committee of Will County Anti-Slavery Society.]

Watkins, James. Narrative of the Life of James Watkins, Formerly a "Chattel" in Maryland, U. S.; Containing an Account of His Escape from Slavery, Together with an Appeal on Behalf of Three Millions of Such "Pieces of Property," Still Held under the Standard of the Eagle. Bolton, Kenyon and Abbatt, 1852. 48 p.

Watkins, William J. Our Rights as Men; An Address Delivered in Boston, before the Legislative Committee on the Militia, February 24, 1853, in Behalf of Sixty-Five Colored Petitioners, Praying for a Charter to Form an Independent Military Company. Boston, Benjamin F. Roberts, 1853. 21 p.

Watson, Henry. Narrative of Henry Watson, a Fugitive Slave. Boston, Bela Marsh, 1848. 48 p.
Same. Second Edition. Boston, Bela Marsh, 1849. 48 p.
Same. Third Edition. Boston, Bela Marsh, 1850. 48 p.

Webb, Richard Davis. The National Anti-Slavery Societies in England and the United States; or, Strictures on "A Reply to Certain Charges Brought Against the American and Foreign Antislavery Society, Etc., Etc.; by Lewis Tappan of New York, United States; With an Introduction, by John Scoble." Dublin, C. Hedgelong, 1852. 56 p.

Webb, Samuel. Speech of Samuel Webb, in the National Anti-Slavery Convention Held at Albany, N. Y., on the First Day of August, 1839. Philadelphia, Merrihew and Thompson, 1840. 20 p.

Webster, Daniel. Letter from Citizens of Newburyport, Mass., to Mr. Webster, in Relation to His Speech Delivered in the Senate of the United States on the 7th March, 1850, and Mr. Webster's Reply. Washington, Gideon and Co., 1850. 20 p.
Same: Washington, Gideon and Co., 1850. 16 p.

Webster, Daniel.
Today Massachusetts Erects the Statue of Daniel Webster. Freemen and Christians, Read His Counsel to the Commonwealth!

Daniel Webster on the Fugitive Slave Law: "My public speeches show my opinion to have been decidedly in favor of a proper, efficient, and well-guarded law for the recovery of fugitive slaves. In my judgment, the present law is constitutional; and all good citizens are bound to respect and obey it; just as freely and readily as if they had voted for it themselves. I think agitation on the subject ought to cease."

"I hold the Fugitive Slave Law to be a law entirely constitutional, highly proper, and absolutely essential to the peace of the country."

"I put it to the sober and sound minds at the North, as a question of morals and a question of conscience. What right have they, in their legislative capacity, or any other capacity, to endeavor to get round this constitution, or to embarrass the free exercise of the rights secured by the Constitution to the persons whose slaves escape from them? None at all, none at all: Neither in the forum of conscience, nor before the face of the Constitution, are they, in my opinion, justified in such an attempt. Here is a well-founded ground of complaint against the North, Which Ought to Be Removed; which calls for the enactment of proper laws, authorising the judicature of this government, in the several states, to do all that is necessary for the recapture of Fugitive Slaves, and for their restoration to those who claim them. Wherever I go, and wherever I speak on the subject, and when I speak here, I desire to speak to the whole north, I say that the South has been injured in this respect, and has a right to complain."

"I notice that, in one of the meetings holden lately in the very heart of New England, and Said to Have Been Very Numerously Attended, the Members Unanimously Resolved "That, as God is Our Helper, We will not suffer any person charged with being a fugitive from labor to be taken from among us; and to this resolve we pledge our lives, our fortunes, and our sacred honor! These persons do not seem to have been aware that the purpose thus avowed by them is distinctly treasonable!"

"Depend upon it, the law will be executed in its spirit and letter. It will be executed in all the great Cities—here in Syracuse—in the midst of the next Anti-Slavery Convention, if the occasion shall arise.

Then we shall see what becomes of their lives and their sacred honor."

"We call upon Massachusetts to discharge that duty (the catching of fugitive slaves) as an affair of high morals and high principles. The question now is, whether she will conquer her prejudices! Any man can perform an agreeable duty—it is not every man who can perform a disagreeable duty."

"I will say again in the City of Boston, If I am spared to have an opportunity, that you of the South have as much right to recover your fugitive slaves, as the North has to any of its rights and privileges of navigation and commerce."

"The excitement in Boston caused by the Fugitive Slave Law is fast subsiding, and it is thought that there is now no probability of any resistance, if a fugitive should be arrested." Boston, September 17, 1859.

Webster, Delia A. Kentucky Jurisprudence. A History of the Trial of Miss Delia A. Webster of Lexington, Kentucky, Dec'r 17–21, 1844, Before the Hon. Richard Buckner. On the Charge of Aiding Slaves to Escape from That Commonwealth—With Miscellaneous Remarks Including Her Views on American Slavery, Written by Herself. Vergennes, N. W. Blaisdell, 1846. 84 p.

Webster, Noah. Effects of Slavery, on Morals and Industry. By Noah Webster, Jun., Esq., Counsellor at Law and Member of the Connecticut Society for the Promotion of Freedom. Hartford, Hudson and Goodwin, 1791. 56 p.

Same. Hartford, Hudson and Goodwin, 1793. 50 p.

The Weekly Advocate, Established for and Devoted to the Moral, Mental and Political Improvement of the People of Color. Vol. 1, Nos. 1–8. January 7–February 25, 1837. New York, 1837. Continued as the Colored American.

[Weld, Theodore Dwight]. Slavery and the Internal Slave Trade in the United States of North America; Being Replies to Questions Transmitted by the Committee of the British and Foreign Anti-Slavery Society, for the Abolition of Slavery and the Slave Trade Throughout the World. Presented to the General Anti-Slavery Convention, Held in London, June, 1840. By the Executive Committee of the American Anti-Slavery Society. London, Thomas Ward and Co., 1841. 280 p.

Weld, Theodore Dwight. See Anti-Slavery Examiner.

Wesley, John. Thoughts upon Slavery. London, R. Hawes, 1774. 53 p.

Same. London Printed; Reprinted in Philadelphia, Joseph Crukshank, 1774. 83 p.

Same. Fourth Edition. Dublin, W. Whitestone, 1775. 28 p.

Same. New York, Wesleyan Anti-Slavery Society, 1834. 24 p.

West Brookfield Anti-Slavery Society. Correspondence of the W. Brookfield Anti-Slavery Society, and Rev. Moses Chase. [Boston, 1842.] 31 p.

West Brookfield Anti-Slavery Society. An Exposition of Difficulties in West Brookfield, Connected with Anti-Slavery Operations, Together with a Reply to Some Statements in a Pamphlet Put Forth by "Moses Chase, Pastor of the Church," Purporting to Be a "Statement of Facts in the Case of Deacon Henshaw." By the Board of Managers of the W. B. Anti-Slavery Society. West Brookfield, Mass., The Anti-Slavery Society, 1844. 59 p.

Western Citizen. Weekly. Chicago, Ill. July 1, 1842–October, 1853. Edited by Zebina Eastman (protégé of Benjamin Lundy).

West Randolph, Vt., Anti-Slavery Convention, 1858. Proceedings of the Anti-Slavery Convention Held at West Randolph, Vermont, August 24th and 25th, 1858. New York, American Anti-Slavery Society, 1858. 24 p.

Weston, George Melville. The Poor Whites of the South. Washington, D. C., Published by the Republican Association, 1856. 7 p.

Weston, George Melville. The Progress of Slavery in the United States. Washington, D. C., Buell & Blanchard, 1857. 301 p.

Same: Washington, D. C., the Author, 1858. 80 p.

Weston, George Melville. Southern Slavery Reduces Northern Wages. An Address by George M. Weston, of Maine, Delivered in Washington, D. C., March 25, 1856. [Washington, D. C., 1856.] 8 p.

"What Is Life or Rest to Me! So Long as I Hold a Commission Direct from God Almighty to Act Against Slavery." John Brown. Broadside.

What of the Night? or the Recent History, Present Condition, and Future Prospects of the Great Anti-Slavery Struggle in the Methodist Episcopal Church. Second Edition, New York, Anti-Slavery Union of the Black River Conference, 1860. 24 p.

Wheatley, Phillis. Poems on Various Subjects, Religious and Moral. By Phillis Wheatley, Negro Servant to Mr. John Wheatley, of Boston, in New England. London, Printed for A. Bell, Bookseller, Aldgate; and Sold by Messrs. Cox and Berry, King Street, Boston, 1773. 124 p.

Same. Albany, Reprinted from the London Edition, Barber & Southwick, 1793. 89 p.

Wheaton, Josephus. The Equality of Mankind and the Evils of Slavery, Illustrated: A Sermon, Delivered on the Day of the Annual Fast, April 6, 1820. Boston, Crocker & Brewster, 1820. 24 p.

Wheaton, N. S. A Discourse on St. Paul's Epistle to Philemon; Exhibiting the Duty of Citizens of the Northern States in Regard to the Institution of Slavery; Delivered in Christ Church, Hartford;

Dec. 22, 1850. Hartford, Case, Tiffany and Company, 1851. 31 p.

Wheeler, Jacob D. A Practical Treatise on the Law of Slavery. Being a Compilation of All the Decisions Made on the Subject, in the Several Courts of the United States, and the State Courts. With Copious Notes and References to the Statutes and Other Authorities, Systematically Arranged. New York, Allen Pollock, Jr.; New Orleans, B. Levy, 1837. 476 p.

Whipper, William. Eulogy on William Wilberforce, Esq., Delivered at the Request of the People of Colour of the City of Philadelphia. In the Second African Presbyterian Church, on the Sixth Day of December, 1833. By William Whipper. Philadelphia, William P. Gibbons [1834]. 35 p.

Whipple, Charles K. The Family Relation as Affected by Slavery. Cincinnati, American Reform Tract and Book Society, 1858. 24 p. [Known as Rejected Tract, having received prize of $200 and afterward being rejected by publishing committees.]

Whipple, Charles King. The Methodist Church and Slavery. By Charles K. Whipple. New York, American Anti-Slavery Society. Boston, 1859. 31 p.

Whipple, Charles King. The Non-Resistance Principle: With Particular Application to the Help of Slaves by Abolitionists. Boston, R. F. Wallcut, 1860. 24 p.

[Whipple, Charles King]. Slavery and the American Board of Commissioners for Foreign Missions. New York, American Anti-Slavery Society, 1859. 24 p.

Whipple, Charles King. The Powers That Be Are Ordained of God. Boston, Dow & Jackson, 1841. 8 p.

Whitefield, George. Three Letters from the Reverend Mr. G. Whitefield: Viz. Letter I. To a Friend in London, Concerning Archbishop Tillotston. Letter II. To the Same, on the Same Subject. Letter III. To the Inhabitants of Maryland, Virginia, North and South Carolina, Concerning Their Negroes. Philadelphia, B. Franklin, 1740. 16 p.

Whiteley, Henry. Excessive Cruelty to Slaves. Three Months in Jamaica, in 1832: Comprising a Residence of Seven Weeks on a Sugar Plantation. London, 1832. 16 p.

Whitestown (N. Y.) Anti-Slavery Society. Circular of the Executive Committee of the Whitestown and Oneida Institute Anti-Slavery Societies. Utica, William's Press [n.d.]. 7 p.

Whitney, L. A Parallel Between the Traitor Judas Iscariot, and the Authors and Supporters of the Fugitive Slave Bill. Ontario Messenger, Extra.

Whittier, John Greenleaf. Justice and Expediency; or, Slavery Considered with a View to Its Rightful and Effectual Remedy, Abolition. New York,

American Anti-Slavery Society, 1833. [Anti-Slavery Reporter, I, No. 4, pages 49–63].

[Whittier, John Greenleaf] ed. The North Star: The Poetry of Freedom, by Her Friends. Philadelphia, Merrihew and Thompson, 1840. 117 p.

Whittier, John Greenleaf. Our Countrymen in Chains! [verse]. New York, American Anti-Slavery Society, 1835. Broadside.

Whittier, John Greenleaf. Poems Written During the Progress of the Abolition Question in the United States, Between the Years 1830 and 1838. Boston, I. Knapp, 1837. 103 p.

Whittier, John Greenleaf. Voices of Freedom, by John G. Whittier. Fourth Edition. Philadelphia, T. S. Cavender [etc.], 1846. 192 p.

Whittier, John Greenleaf. A Sabbath Scene. Boston, John P. Jewett and Company, 1854. 29 p.

Wilberforce, William. An Appeal to the Religion, Justice, and Humanity of the Inhabitants of the British Empire, in Behalf of the Negro Slaves in the West Indies. London, J. Hatchard and Son, 1823. 77 p.

Wilkerson, James. Wilkerson's History of His Travels and Labors, in the United States, as a Missionary, in Particular, That of the Union Seminary, Located in Franklin Co., Ohio, Since He Purchased His Liberty in New Orleans, La., Etc. Columbus, O., 1861. 43 p.

[Williams, Isaac]. Aunt Sally; or, The Cross the Way of Freedom. A Narrative of the Slave-Life and Purchase of the Mother of Rev. Isaac Williams, of Detroit, Michigan. Detroit, 1858.

Williams, James [Apprenticed Laborer in Jamaica]. A Narrative of Events Since the 1st of August, 1834, by James Williams. Together with the Evidence Taken under a Commission Appointed by the Colonial Office to Ascertain the Truth of the Narrative, and the Report of the Commissioners Thereon: The Whole Exhibiting a Correct Picture of a Large Proportion of West Indian Society and the Atrocious Cruelties Perpetrated under the Apprenticeship System. London, Central Emancipation Committee, 1838. 64 p.

Williams, Peter. A Discourse Delivered on the Death of Capt. Paul Cuffe, Before the New York African Institution, in the African Methodist Episcopal Zion Church, October 21, 1817. New York, B. Young and Co., 1817. 16 p.

Williams, Peter. An Oration on the Abolition of the Slave Trade. Delivered in the African Church, in the City of New York, January 1, 1808, by Peter Williams Jun., a Descendant of Africa. New York, Samuel Wood, 1808. 26 p.

Williamson, Passmore, Respondent. Case of Passmore Williamson. Report of the Proceedings on the Writ of Habeas Corpus, Issued by the Hon. John K.

Kane, Judge of the District Court of the United States for the Eastern District of Pennsylvania, in the Case of the United States of America ex rel John H. Wheeler vs. Passmore Williamson, Including the Several Opinions Delivered; and the Arguments of Counsel, Reported by Arthur Cannon, Esq. Philadelphia, U. Hunt & Son, 1856. 191 p.

Willson, Edmund Burke. The Bad Friday: A Sermon Preached in the First Church, West Roxbury, June 4, 1854; It Being the Sunday after the Return of Anthony Burns to Slavery. Boston, John Wilson & Son, 1834. 16 p.

Willson, James Renwick. Tokens of the Divine Displeasure, in the Late Conflagrations in New-York, & Other Judgments, Illustrated. Newburgh [N. Y.], C. U. Cushman, 1836. 46 p.

Willson, S. W., Sunderland, LaRoy, George Storrs, and Others. An Appeal on the Subject of Slavery; Addressed to the Members of the New England and New Hampshire Conferences of the Methodist Episcopal Church. Together with a Defence of Said Appeal, in Which Is Shown the Sin of Holding Property in Man. Boston, David H. Ela, 1835. 48 p.

Wilmot, David. Slavery in the Territories. Speech of Hon. D. Wilmot, of Pennsylvania, in the House of Representatives, May 3, 1850, in Committee of the Whole on the State of the Union, on the President's Message Transmitting the Constitution of California. [Washington, D. C., Congressional Globe Office, 1850.] 8 p.

Wilson, Henry. Aggressions of the Slave Power. Speech of Hon. Henry Wilson, of Massachusetts, in Reply to Jefferson Davis, Delivered in the Senate, Jan. 26, 1860. Washington [D. C.], Buell & Blanchard [1860].

Wilson, Henry. Are Workingmen "Slaves"? Speech of Hon. Henry Wilson, of Massachusetts, in Reply to Hon. J. H. Hammond, of S. C., in the Senate, March 20, 1858, on the Bill to Admit Kansas under the Lecompton Constitution. [Washington, D. C., Buell & Blanchard, 1858.] 16 p.

Wilson, Henry. The Crittenden Compromise—A Surrender. Speech of Henry Wilson, of Mass., Delivered in the Senate, February 21st, 1861, on the Resolutions of Mr. Crittenden Proposing Amendments to the Constitution of the United States. [Washington, D. C., 1861.] 16 p.

Wilson, Henry. Personalities and Aggressions of Mr. Butler. Speech of Hon. Henry Wilson, of Massachusetts, in the Senate of the United States, June 13, 1856. Washington, D. C., Buell & Blanchard [1856]. 8 p.

Wilson, Henry. Speech of Hon. Henry Wilson, of Mass., in the Senate, March 27th, 1862, on the Bill to Abolish Slavery in the District of Columbia, Introduced by Him December 16th, 1861, Referred to the District Committee, and Reported Back with Amendments by Mr. Morrill. Washington, D. C., Scammell & Co., 1862. 8 p.

Wilson, Henry. Speech of Hon. Henry Wilson, of Massachusetts, on the President's Message on the Lecompton Constitution. Delivered in the Senate, February 3d and 4th, 1858. Washington, D. C., Buell & Blanchard, 1858. 16 p.

Wilson, Henry. The State of Affairs in Kansas. Speech of Hon. Henry Wilson, of Mass. In the Senate, February 18, 1856. Washington, D. C., Republican Association of the District of Columbia, 1856. 15 p.

Wilson, Henry. The Suppression of the Slave Trade. Speech of Hon. Henry Wilson, of Mass. Delivered in the Senate of the United States, May 21, 1860. Washington, D. C., Buell & Blanchard, 1860. 8 p.

Wilson, Henry. Territorial Slave Code. Speech of Hon. Henry Wilson, of Massachusetts, Delivered in the Senate of the United States, January 25, 1860. Washington, D. C., Buell & Blanchard, 1860. 24 p.

Wilson, James. The Slavery Question. Speech of Hon. James Wilson, of Indiana. Delivered in the House of Representatives, May 1, 1860. Washington, F. H. Sage [1860]. 16 p.

Wilson, James. Speech of Mr. Jas. Wilson, of N. Hampshire, on the Political Influence of Slavery, and the Expediency of Permitting Slavery in the Territories Recently Acquired from Mexico. Delivered in the House of Representatives of the United States, Feb. 16, 1849. Washington, J. & G. S. Gideon, 1849.

Wilson, William. The Great American Question, Democracy vs. Doulocracy! or, Free Soil, Free Labor, Free Men, & Free Speech, against the Extension and Domination of the Slaveholding Interest. A Letter Addressed to Each Freeman of the United States, with Special Reference to His Duty at the Approaching Election. Cincinnati, E. Shepard's Steam Press, 1848. 88 p.

Wilson, William Dexter. A Discourse on Slavery: Delivered Before the Anti-Slavery Society in Littleton, N. H., February 22, 1839, Being the Anniversary of the Birth of Washington. Concord, Asa McFarland, 1839. 51 p.

Winchester, Elhanan. The Reigning Abominations, Especially the Slave Trade, Considered as Causes of Lamentations; Being the Substance of a Discourse Delivered in Fairfax County, Virginia, December 30, 1774. And Now Published with Several Additions. London, H. Trapp, 1788. 32 p. Same. Boston, Christian Freeman Office, 1841.

Winthrop, R. C. Admission of California. Speech of the Hon. R. C. Winthrop, of Mass., on the President's Message, Transmitting the Constitution of California. Delivered in the Committee of the Whole in the House of Representatives of the United States, May 8, 1850. Washington [D.C.], Gideon & Co., 1850. 28 p.

Winthrop, R. C. Speech of Mr. Winthrop, of Massachusetts, on the Right of Petition, Delivered in the House of Representatives of the United States, January 23d and 24th, 1844. Washington [D. C.], Gales and Seaton, 1844. 19 p.

Wisconsin Legislature. Resolutions of the Wisconsin Legislature, on the Subject of Slavery; with the Speech of Samuel D. Hastings in the Assembly, Madison, Jan. 27, 1849. New York, Wm. Harned, 1849. 31 p.

Wisconsin. Supreme Court. Unconstitutionality of the Fugitive Slave Act. Decisions of the Supreme Court of Wisconsin in the Cases of Booth and Rycraft. Milwaukee, R. King & Co., 1855. 218 p.

Wolcott, Samuel. Report on Fellowship with Slavery Republished from the Minutes of the Evangelical Consociation, Rhode Island, June 14, 1854. [n.p., n.d.]

Wolcott, Samuel. Separation from Slavery. Being a Consideration of the Inquiry, "How Shall Christians and Christian Churches Best Absolve Themselves from All Responsible Connection with Slavery?" Boston, American Tract Society [n.d.]. 46 p. [$100 prize essay by Church Anti-Slavery Society.]

[Woods, Joseph]. Thoughts on the Slavery of the Negroes. London, James Phillips, 1784. 32 p.

Woolman, John. Considerations on Keeping Negroes; Recommended to the Professors of Christianity of Every Denomination. Part Second. Philadelphia, B. Franklin and D. Hall, 1762. 52 p.

Woolman, John. Considerations on Slavery, Addressed to the Professors of Christianity of Every Denomination, and Affectionately Recommended to Their Sober, Unprejudiced Attention. Baltimore, Thomas Maund, 1821. 35 p.

Woolman, John. Extracts on the Subject of Slavery, from the Journal and Writings of John Woolman, of Mount Holly, New Jersey, a Minister of the Society of Friends, Who Died at York, England, A.D. 1772. Published for an Association of Individual Members of the Society of Friends, in the City of New York. New York, M. Day & Co., 1840. 24 p.

Woolman, John. A Journal of the Life, Gospel Labours, and Christian Experiences of That Faithful Minister of Jesus Christ, John Woolman, Late of Mount-Holly, in the Province of New Jersey, North America. To Which Are Added, His Works, Containing His Last Epistle and Other Writings. Dublin, R. M. Jackson, 1794. 464 p.

Woolman, John. Some Considerations on the Keeping of Negroes. Recommended to the Professors of Christianity of Every Denomination. Philadelphia, James Chattin, 1754. 24 p.

Woolman, John. The Works of John Woolman. In Two Parts. Philadelphia, Joseph Crukshank, 1774. 436 p.
   Same. Third Edition. Philadelphia, Benjamin & Jacob Johnson, 1800.

Worcester, Leonard. A Discourse on the Alton Outrage, Delivered at Peacham, Vermont, December 17, 1837. Published by Request of the Caledonia Association. Concord, N. H., Asa McFarland, 1838. 16 p.

Worcester (Mass.) Convention of Ministers. Proceedings of the Convention of Ministers of Worcester County, on the Subject of Slavery; Held at Worcester, December 5 & 6, 1837, and January 16, 1838. Worcester, Massachusetts Spy Office, 1838. 22 p.

Worcester [Mass.] Anti-Slavery Society. Fourth Annual Course of Lectures, 1855–[185]6 [Schedule]. Worcester, Henry J. Howland, 1855. 3 p.
   Nov. 9. John P. Hale
   Nov. 16. Joshua R. Giddings
   Nov. 23. Horace Mann
   Nov. 30. Henry Wilson
   Dec. 7. Mary E. Webb
   Dec. 14. Edmund Quincy
   Dec. 21. Jane E. Jones
   Dec. 28. E. D. Culver
   Jan. 4. Theodore Parker
   Jan. 11. William Lloyd Garrison
   Jan. 18. Charles L. Remond
   Jan. 25. Ralph Waldo Emerson

[Worcester, Samuel Melancthon]. Essays on Slavery: Re-Published from the Boston Recorder & Telegraph, for 1825. By Vigornius, and Others. Amherst, Mass., M. H. Newman, 1826. 83 p. [Of these Essays six numbers are by Vigornius, one by a Carolinian, one by Philo, and nine by Hieronymus.]

Words for Working-Men. [1853.]
   First Series. Slavery and the Bible. 8 p.
   Second Series. Origin of Slavery, and Its Relations to Constitutional Law. 8 p.
   Third Series. Encroachments of Slavery on the North. 8 p.
   Fourth Series. Wesley's Thoughts on Slavery. 8 p.
   Fifth Series. Popular Objections to the Anti-Slavery Movement Considered. 8 p.

Wright, Elizur, Jr. The Sin of Slavery, and Its Remedy; Containing Some Reflections on the Moral Influence of African Colonization. New York, Printed for the Author, 1833. 48 p.
   Same: New York, Printed for the Author, 1833. 52 p.

Wright, Henry Clarke. American Slavery: Two Letters from Henry C. Wright to the Liverpool Mercury, Respecting the Rev. Drs. Cox and Olin, and American Man-Stealers. Dublin, Webb and Chapman, 1846. 4 p.

Wright, Henry Clarke. American Slavery; Proved to Be Theft and Robbery, Which No Circumstances Can Justify or Palliate, with Remarks on the Speeches of Rev. Doctors Cunningham and Candlish before the Free Presbytery of Edinburgh. Edinburgh, Quintin Dalrymple, 1845. 24 p.

Wright, Henry Clarke. Anthropology; or, The Science of Man: In Its Bearing on War and Slavery, and on Arguments from the Bible, Marriage, God, Death, Retribution, Atonement and Government in Support of These and Other Social Wrongs. In a Series of Letters to a Friend in England. Cincinnati, E. Shepard, 1850. 96 p.

Wright, Henry Clarke. Ballot Box and Battle Field. To Voters under the United States Government. Boston, Dow & Jackson's Press, 1842. 20 p.

Wright, Henry Clarke. Christian Church; Anti-Slavery and Non-Resistance Applied to Church Organizations. Boston, Anti-Slavery Office, 1841. 17 p.

Wright, Henry C. The Dissolution of the American Union, Demanded by Justice and Humanity as the Incurable Enemy of Liberty. With a Letter to Rev. Drs. Chalmers, Cunningham and Candlish, on Christian Fellowship with Slaveholders: And a Letter to the Members of the Free Church, Recommending Them to Send Back the Money Obtained from Slaveholders, to Build Their Churches and Pay Their Ministers. Addressed to the Abolitionists of Great Britain and Ireland. London, Chapman, Brothers, & Co., 1846. 46 p.

Wright, Henry C. Free Church Alliance with Man-stealers. Send Back the Money. Great Anti-Slavery Meeting in the City Hall, Glasgow, Containing Speeches Delivered by Messrs. Wright, Douglass, and Buffum, from America, and by George Thompson, Esq., of London, with a Summary Account of a Series of Meetings Held in Edinburgh by the Above Named Gentlemen. Glasgow, E. Gallie [etc.], 1846. 58 p.

Wright, Henry Clarke. Manstealers: Will the Free Church of Scotland Hold Christian Fellowship with Them? An Address, by Henry C. Wright. Glasgow, the Glasgow Emancipation Society, 1845. 16 p.

Wright, Henry Clarke. The Natick Resolution; or, Resistance to Slaveholders the Right and Duty of Southern Slaves and Northern Freemen. Boston, Printed for the Author, 1859. 36 p.

Wright, Henry Clarke. No Rights, No Duties; or Slaveholders, as Such, Have No Rights; Slaves, as Such, Owe No Duties. An Answer to a Letter from Hon. Henry Wilson, Touching Resistance to Slaveholders Being the Right and Duty of the Slaves, and of the People and States of the North. Boston, Printed for the Author, 1860. 36 p.

Yates, William. Rights of Colored Men to Suffrage, Citizenship, and Trial by Jury; Being a Book of Facts, Arguments and Authorities, Historical Notices and Sketches of Debates, with Notes. Philadelphia, Merrihew and Gunn, 1838. 104 p.

Young, Joshua. God Greater Than Man. A Sermon Preached June 11, after the Rendition of Anthony Burns. Burlington, Vt., Samuel B. Nichols, 1854. 26 p.

Young, Joshua. Man Better Than a Sheep. A Sermon Preached Thanksgiving Day, Nov. 24, 1859. Burlington [Vt.], E. A. Fuller, 1859. 22 p.

Young Men's Fremont and Dayton Central Union. The New "Democratic" Doctrine. Slavery Not to Be Confined to the Negro Race, but to Be Made the Universal Condition of the Laboring Classes of Society. New York [n.d.]. 4 p.

Young Men's Liberty Association. Proceedings of the Young Men's Liberty Convention Held in Jackson, Michigan, October 1st, 1845; and Constitution and Address of the Young Men's Liberty Association. Jackson, Hitchcock and Myrick, 1845. 16 p.

The Youth's Cabinet, Devoted to Liberty, Peace, Temperance, Purity, Truth. Weekly. Boston, Mass. April 28, 1837–1841. Edited by Nathaniel Southard.

Zion's Watchman. Weekly. New York, N. Y. 1836–April 9, 1842. Edited by LaRoy Sunderland. Published as New York Watchman in 1841 and 1842.

No 5		
Negroes	Berry	1000
	Berry	900
	Ishmael	800
Little Harriet & Son		1050
	Amanda	650
	Georgia Ann	650
Little	Waity	500
	Oliver	400
	Mose	325
	Betsy	125
Sandy & Matilda		10
Mules	Hager	175
"	Dick	5
"	Pete	100
Hors	Frank	75
Oack	Ass	25
Ploughs & gear		5
Carpenters Tools		5
Narrow tread Waggon		15
Household & Kitchen fur		50
Stock	Hogs	35
	Cattle	12
	Sheep	45	6947

No 6		
Negroes	Billy	1000
	Albert	900
	Phill	800
Big Harriet & Sandy		1050
	Eliza	800
	Warren	600
Old Anthony		400
	Scipio	600
	Peggy	300
Mules	Sal	150
"	Kit	100
Mare	Dan	135
Ploughs & gear		5
Carpenters Tools		5
Shot gun		15
Household & Kitchen furniture		50
Stock Hogs		35
Cattle		12
Sheep		45
		6990